AMONG THE DEAD CITIES

OTHER BOOKS BY THE SAME AUTHOR

AMONG THE DEAD CITIES

*Is the Targeting of Civilians
in War Ever Justified?*

A. C. Grayling

BLOOMSBURY

First published in Great Britain 2006
This paperback edition published 2007

The right of A. C. Grayling to be identified as author
of this work has been asserted by him in accordance with
the Copyright, Designs and Patents Act 1988

Maps by Reginald Piggot

Bloomsbury Publishing Plc, 36 Soho Square, London W1D 3QY

A CIP catalogue record for this book
is available from the British Library

ISBN 9780747586036

10 9 8 7 6 5 4 3 2 1

Typeset by Hewer Text UK Ltd, Edinburgh
Printed in Great Britain by Clays, St Ives plc

All papers used by Bloomsbury Publishing are natural,
recyclable products made from wood grown in well-managed
forests. The manufacturing processes conform to the
environmental regulations of the country of origin

www.bloomsbury.com/acgrayling

'The term "war crimes" . . . includes . . . murder, extermination, enslavement, deportation and other inhuman acts committed against any civilian population before or during the war.'

US State Department to the British Ambassador in Washington, 18 October 1945

CONTENTS

Acknowledgements

My warm thanks go to Naomi Goulder, Bill Swainson, George Gibson, Jo Foster and Catherine Clarke for various but always invaluable help in the preparation of this book. It could not have been written without the existence of the British Library, the London Library, the Imperial War Museum Duxford, and the Royal Air Force Museum Hendon, and certainly not without the many fine historians of the Second World War, and particularly the historians of its air war aspects, to all of whom my indebtedness is gratefully manifested in the notes and bibliography.

Picture Credits

B24 Liberators on a bombing run. (*Dpa Bilderdienste, Frankfurt/M*)

Air Marshall Sir Arthur Harris. (*Hulton Archive/Getty Images*)
Air Marshall Sir Charles Portal. (*Time & Life/Getty Images*)
Crew of a Lancaster bomber. (*Fox Photos/Getty Images*)

An Allied bomber above its target. (*Imperial War Museum*)
B-17 Flying Fortresses in 'box' formation. (*Bildarchiv Preussicher Kulturbesitz*)

Aachen in 1900. (*Ullstein Bild*)
Würzburg in 1938. (*Ullstein Bild*)
The rooftops of old Hamburg. (*Ullstein Bild*)
Lübeck before 1900. (*Ullstein Bild*)

Berlin under attack in July 1944. (*Bildarchiv Preussicher Kulturbesitz*)
Hamburg burning during Operation Gomorrah, July 1943. (*Chronos-Media*)
The Hamburg University bookshop after Operation Gomorrah. (*Denkmalschutzamt Hamburg Bildarchiv*)

Nuremberg, 1945. (*Bildarchiv Preussicher Kulturbesitz*)
Hannover, 1945. (*Stadtarchiv Hannover*)

Berlin, 1944. (*Bildarchiv Preussicher Kulturbesitz*)
Cologne, 1945. (*Bettman/Corbis*)

Victims of the Dresden bombing, 14 February 1945. (*Hulton Archive/Getty Images*)
Victims of the firebombing of Hamburg, Operation Gomorrah, July 1943. (*Archiv Michael Födrowitz*)

Survivors of Operation Gomorrah, Hamburg, July 1943. (*Ullstein Bild*)

General Curtis Le May, 3 August 1945. (*Bettman/Corbis*)

A B-29 'bombing up', 24 November 1944. (*Hulton Archive/Getty Images*)

A B-29 on a bombing run over Osaka, Japan. (*Imperial War Museum*)
Osaka under attack by 500 B-29 Superfortresses on 1 June 1945. (*Imperial War Museum*)
Osaka as it looked to aerial reconnaissance on 9 June 1945. (*Imperial War Museum*)

Tokyo's Ginza Street before being bombed in 1945. (*Imperial War Museum*)
Bombs falling on Kobe, 4 June 1945. (*Imperial War Museum*)
Kamamatsu destroyed by bombing, 9 June 1945. (*Imperial War Museum*)

The atom bomb exploding over Nagasaki. (*Corbis*)

Hiroshima after the explosion of the atom bomb, 1945. (*Corbis*)
Survivor, Nagasaki. (*Corbis*)

Maps

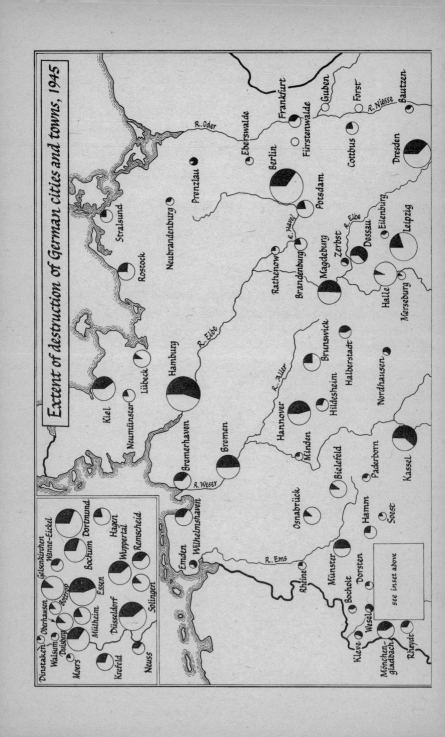

Extent of destruction of German cities and towns, 1945

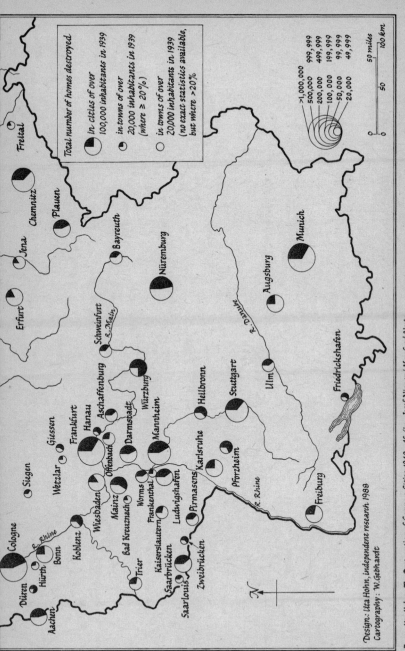

Total number of homes destroyed

in cities of over 100,000 inhabitants in 1939

in towns of over 20,000 inhabitants in 1939 (where ≥ 20%)

in towns of over 20,000 inhabitants in 1939 (no exact statistics available, but where >20%)

>1,000,000
500,000   999,999
200,000   499,999
100,000   199,999
50,000   99,999
20,000   49,999

50 miles
100 km.

Freital
Chemnitz
Plauen
Jena
Erfurt
Bayreuth
Nürnberg
Munich
Augsburg
Schweinfurt
R. Main
Aschaffenburg
Hanau
Frankfurt
Giessen
Wetzlar
Siegen
Offenbach
Darmstadt
Würzburg
Mannheim
Heilbronn
Stuttgart
Ulm
Friedrichshafen
R. Danube
Wiesbaden
Mainz
Bad Kreuznach
Worms
Frankenthal
Ludwigshafen
Karlsruhe
Pforzheim
Pirmasens
Freiburg
R. Rhine
Koblenz
Bonn
Hürth
Cologne
R. Rhine
Aachen
Düren
Trier
Kaiserslautern
Saarbrücken
Saarlouis
Zweibrücken

Design: Utta Hohn, independent research 1988
Cartography: W. Gebhardt

From: Utta Hohn, *The Destruction of German Cities 1940–45* (in: Josef Nipper / Manfred Nutz (Eds), *Wartime Destruction and Rebuilding of German Cities*, Cologne 1993, pp. 3–23)

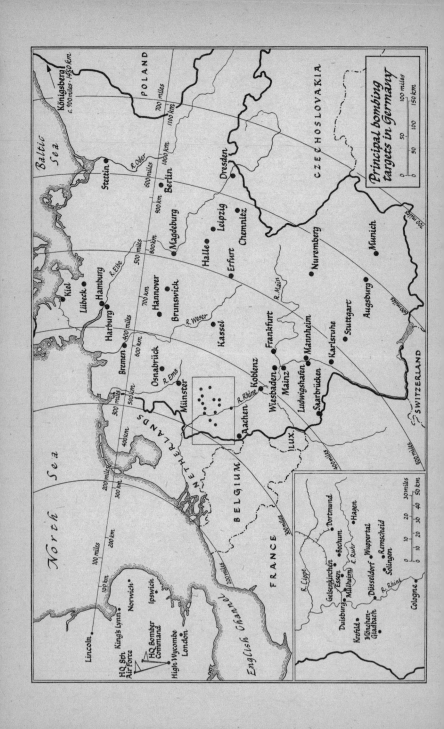

Principal bombing targets in Germany

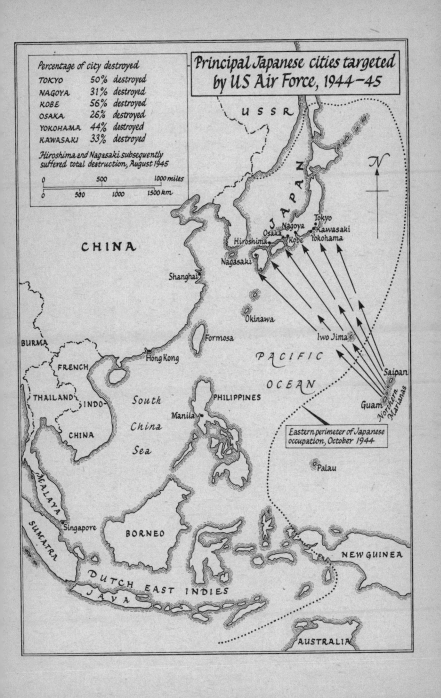

Principal Japanese cities targeted by US Air Force, 1944-45

Percentage of city destroyed

TOKYO	50%	destroyed
NAGOYA	31%	destroyed
KOBE	56%	destroyed
OSAKA	26%	destroyed
YOKOHAMA	44%	destroyed
KAWASAKI	33%	destroyed

Hiroshima and Nagasaki subsequently suffered total destruction, August 1945

0   500   1000 miles

0   500   1000   1500 km

U.S.S.R.

N

J A P A N

CHINA

Tokyo
Nagoya   Kawasaki
Osaka   Yokohama
Hiroshima   Kobe

Nagasaki

Shanghai

Okinawa

BURMA

Formosa

Iwo Jima

P A C I F I C

Hong Kong

Saipan

FRENCH

O C E A N

THAILAND

INDO-

South

PHILIPPINES

Guam

Northern Marianas

CHINA

China

Manila

Sea

Eastern perimeter of Japanese occupation, October 1944

Palau

MALAYA

Singapore

BORNEO

NEW GUINEA

SUMATRA

D U T C H   E A S T   I N D I E S

J A V A

AUSTRALIA

For
Madeleine Grayling,
Luke Owen Edmunds,
Sebastian, Thomas, Nicholas and Benjamin Hickman
and Flora Zeman
who are our future
and need us to do justice in all things.

Preface to the Paperback Edition

Because of the lively debate occasioned by this book on its publication in hardback, I have included in this paperback edition a Postscript discussing the main points raised by reviewers and correspondents. I extend my thanks both to the new friends I made through that debate and to the critics for all their contributions. I was especially impressed by the courtesy and knowledge displayed by those I met during a recent book tour in the United States, and by the care taken by American reviewers to read the book thoroughly and engage with its arguments.

Few books escape having a glitch here or there, typically in the form of typographical errors or editorial oversights. In this case, the most egregious was a mismatch between the cover illustration and copy relating to it. The hardback cover consisted of a striking photograph of B-24 Liberators on a daylight bombing run. The picture was taken by Bill Washburn, whose extraordinary skill in capturing aircraft at war is wonderfully on display in that photograph. The cover copy wrongly described the aircraft in the picture as Lancasters. One official attribution (by the US Air Force Museum) says that the action depicted took place near Tours in France on 16 June 1944, but the World War II maven Tom Philo gives what seem incontestable grounds for saying that the picture was taken over Bremen in Germany in January 1945.

The happy side of the mistaken attribution, whatever the right one, was some new email friendships with people who really know their aircraft and their history. I appreciate all those who have sent me further information and points of view about the matters discussed in this book; the Postscript profits from their contributions.

London, October 2006

1

Introduction: Was it a Crime?

IN THE COURSE of the Second World War the air forces of Britain and the United States of America carried out a massive bombing offensive against the cities of Germany and Japan, ending with the destruction of Dresden and Tokyo, Hiroshima and Nagasaki. Was this bombing offensive a crime against humanity? Or was it justified by the necessities of war?

These questions mark one of the great remaining controversies of the Second World War. It is a controversy which has grown during the decades since the war ended, as the benefit of hindsight has prompted fresh examination of the 'area bombing' strategy – the strategy of treating whole cities and their civilian populations as targets for attack by high explosive and incendiary bombs, and in the end by atom bombs.

Part of the reason why the area-bombing controversy continues to grow is that in today's Germany and Japan people are beginning to speak about what their parents and grandparents endured in the bomber attack, and to see them as victims too, to be counted among the many who suffered during that immense global conflict. What should we, the descendants of the Allies who won the victory in the Second World War, reply to the moral challenge of the descendants of those whose cities were targeted by Allied bombers?

This fact – that the descendants of the bombed have begun to raise their voices and ask questions about the experience of their parents and grandparents – provides one powerful reason why it matters today to try to reach a definitive settlement of the controversy.

Another and connected reason is that history has to be got right before it distorts into legend and diminishes into over-simplification, which is what always happens when events slip into a too-distant past. At time of writing there are still survivors of those bombing campaigns, both among those who flew the bombers and those who were bombed by them. Historians of the future will in part be guided by judgements we make now. With our proximity to the war, its survivors still in our midst or close to our personal memories, but with the hindsight of a generation's length from the events, what we say will help shape the future's understanding of this aspect of the Second World War.

A third and even more contemporary reason for revisiting Allied area bombing is to get a proper understanding of its implications for how peoples and states can and should behave in times of conflict. We live in an age of tensions and moral confusion, of terrorism and deeply bitter rivalries, of violence and atrocity. What are the moral lessons for today that we can learn from the vast example of how, when bombing brought civilians into the front line of the conflict in the Second World War, the Allies acted?

In the decades after 1945 these implications were obscured by the fact that a much larger and more important moral matter occupied the mental horizon of the post-war world, and quite rightly so – the Holocaust. This egregious crime against humanity was a central fact of Nazi aggression and the racist ideology driving it, and in comparison to it other controversies seemed minor. Other controversies do not fade through lack of attention, but grow unnoticed, until – as we have seen in recent years with neo-Nazi efforts to exploit the victimhood of the bombed for their own political purposes – they become a worse problem than if they were addressed with clarity, frankness and fairness.

In all these ways a new urgency attaches to the question: did the

Allies commit a moral crime in their area bombing of German and Japanese cities? This is the question I seek to answer definitively in this book.

To explain my personal motivation for trying to answer this question, I need only describe what I can see from where I sit writing these words. There is a small park across the road from my house in south London, completely grassed over, with a scattering of chestnut and linden trees standing in it. The trees have been growing there for half a century, and are close to maturity. As always, the chestnuts are first to break into leaf in spring; in the height of summer the lindens' tassels of yellow flowers make a fine show against the dark green of their heart-shaped leaves. It is easy to judge the age of these trees, because the open space in which they stand became a park just a little over fifty years ago, so the trees and their park began life together. Before then, for a few years, that open space was filled with ruins, a bare scar of bricks and rubble cleared to ground level. Before then again it was a row of houses; a dozen of them, three-storeyed semi-detached Victorian villas identical to the others still standing near by – one of them being the house where I live, and from whose windows I look out.

The green and tranquil appearance of this little London park belies the reason for its existence. It is in fact a Second World War bombsite. The houses that stood there were blown up in the Blitz of 1940–1. It is possible to follow the line of bombs that destroyed them as they fell in this street, to be succeeded by more falling in the next street – there is a little park there too, also with fifty-year-old linden trees – and on to the very big park just beyond. Until 29 December 1940 this big park was not an open stretch of grass and playing fields, but a tangle of crowded built-up streets on either side of the Surrey Canal. It is now, as a result of one of the worst nights of the Blitz on London, an expanse of 120 acres containing football and cricket pitches, a lake, cycling paths, shrubberies, and avenues of trees. Here and there stubborn protuberances of broken brick and concrete remain, half buried beneath ivy, with some ruined adjoining walls standing beside them. One street is left intact in the park, with houses along one side and a stoutly constructed Victorian school on the other, still alive with children each day in term time (my youngest child began her education there).

The street and its school protrude into the park's open spaces as a reminder of what had been a densely crowded urban scene, and therefore as a memorial to the nights when bombs rained down on London, killing and destroying. Contemplating the street where I live and the surrounding area, I am daily reminded of the horrors of that time, and the memory drives home a point too often forgotten once wars end and memories dim: that in discussions of war and its effects on humanity, there is an argument that says that deliberately mounting military attacks on civilian populations, in order to cause terror and indiscriminate death among them, is a moral crime.

Is this assertion – 'deliberately mounting military attacks on civilian populations is a moral crime' – an unqualified truth? If it is, people in today's Western democracies must revisit the recent past of their countries to ask some hard questions about their behaviour in the great wars of the twentieth century, so that the historical record can be put straight. Attacks on civilian populations have often happened in wars throughout history, but this fact does not amount to a justification of the practice. If ever such a practice could be justified or at least excused, it will be because the following questions have received satisfactory answers. Are there ever circumstances in which killing civilians in wartime is morally acceptable? Are there ever circumstances – desperate ones, necessities, circumstances of danger to which such actions are taken as a defensive measure – that would justify or at least exonerate turning civilians into military targets? Can there be mitigating factors that would compel us to withhold the harshest judgement from those who planned and ordered such attacks? If one committed a crime in preventing or responding to a worse crime, would that mitigate or – more – even excuse the former?

We need to know the answers to these questions, because they are crucial to resolving the controversy about Allied area bombing in the Second World War. It cannot be right to hold that the mere fact of being a victor in a conflict sanitises one's actions; if questions arise about the morality of what one's own side did in winning a war, they should be squarely addressed and honestly answered.

Because moral questions about Allied area bombing (otherwise called 'carpet bombing', 'saturation bombing', 'obliteration bombing' and 'mass bombing') are deeply controversial, they arouse strong feelings. In discussion of these questions – discussion that began during the war itself – there have been outright defences of the Allied bombing campaigns (on various grounds but mainly that of military necessity) and outright condemnations, the former by far in the majority. Alternatively writers have said, 'this question is too difficult, and must be left to philosophers to debate'. This last is the challenge taken up here.

Two things must be made emphatically clear at the outset. First, it is unquestionably true that if Allied bombing in the Second World War was in whole or part morally wrong, it is nowhere near equivalent in scale of moral atrocity to the Holocaust of European Jewry, or the death and destruction all over the world for which Nazi and Japanese aggression was collectively responsible: a total of some twenty-five million dead, according to responsible estimates. Allied bombing in which German and Japanese civilian populations were deliberately targeted claimed the lives of about 800,000 civilian women, children and men. The bombing of the aggressor Axis states was aimed at weakening their ability and will to make war; the murder of six million Jews was an act of racist genocide. There are very big differences here.

But if the Allied bombing campaigns did in fact involve the commission of wrongs, then even if these wrongs do not compare in scale with the wrongs committed by the Axis powers, they do not thereby cease to be wrongs. The figure of 800,000 civilians killed by Allied bombing, almost all of them in the course of deliberately indiscriminate attacks on urban areas, is staggeringly high in its own right, and even so says nothing about the injured, traumatised and homeless, who in many respects suffered worse.

The debate about the question has often been clouded by comparing what the Allies did with what the Axis did in the way of immoral actions, always (and rightly) to the credit of the Allies – only to leave the matter there, as if drawing the comparison by itself resolves matters. It does not; which is the reason for revisiting the question and trying to settle it.

But nothing in this book should be taken as any form of revisionist apology for Nazism and its frightful atrocities, or Japanese militarism and its aggressions, even if the conclusion is that German and Japanese civilians suffered wrongs. A mature perspective on the Second World War should by now enable us to distinguish between these two quite different points. Revisionist excuses for Nazism are unacceptable, and it has to be acknowledged that large numbers of people in Germany in the Nazi era, quite possibly the majority of them, supported Hitler in much of what he did. This has made many think that the civilian populations of the Axis countries deserved what they got, and that therefore it is a waste of time wringing one's hands over the question whether the Allies committed wrongs. But – again – such an attitude will not do. An SS trooper who machine-gunned unarmed Jews in an open pit might merit a death sentence for the crime; but a civilian who had given Hitler a stiff-arm salute and approved of his policies, and who otherwise worked as (say) an accountant, scarcely merits being executed (by bombing) for doing so. And whereas an SS trooper would be identified and prosecuted before punishment, the Nazi-supporting accountant might die in a civilian bomb shelter alongside someone who disliked Hitler and did not support the Nazis' war. Thus even if the first person's death were merited by the mere fact of his Nazism – which it is not – his companion's death would be too high a price for it.

In any case, these thoughts do not address the main point, which remains that if the Allies countered great Axis wrongs with lesser wrongs, the latter remain wrongs.

Still – and here the need for nuance enters – justice requires that one ask, Was it the case that these wrongs – if such they were – committed in countering greater wrongs, were unavoidable or necessary? Is there a plea of justification or mitigation that can be entered in their behalf, if they need either? For one must remember this: killing a man is wrong; but if one man kills another in self-defence, or in defending his family from murderous attack, the wrong in question at least becomes subject to qualification. So this too has to be taken into account, once the full picture has been considered.

The second thing that must be emphatically clear is that this examination of the moral status of Allied area bombing is not intended to impugn the courage and sacrifice of the men who flew RAF and USAAF bombing missions over Nazi-dominated Europe. Criticism – or even merely discussion – of the morality of the Allied bombing campaigns has often been read as tantamount to impugning the contributions made by those aircrews, and as devaluing their sacrifices in fighting what was after all a just war, and a necessary one, against wicked and dangerous aggressors.

Nothing in this book should be taken as detracting from the bravery of those men. It does not take much to imagine what it was like to fly into hostile skies, to face attacks by fighters and anti-aircraft guns, to see burning aeroplanes falling from the sky with one's comrades in them, and to know that the odds are against surviving the dozens of missions over enemy territory that one's duty made obligatory.

Nevertheless, if the actions that required such courage amounted to the commission of wrongs, the courage with which they were carried out does not alter the fact that they were wrongs. This has been an argument often implicitly offered, as when historians of the bombing war in 1939–45 refuse to address the moral question by saying that to do so is unjust to the pilots and gunners, navigators and bomb-aimers who risked their lives to carry the war to those who had started it and who threatened the world with oppression.

This defence is often given the support of an added justification. In the circumstances of the time, the number of those who thought that bombing civilians was wrong was not large. Many, and almost certainly a majority, of the civilian populations of Britain and America were in favour of it, regarding it as both revenge and punishment well deserved by the Axis powers. In doing what they did, Allied aircrews therefore had popular support as well as their explicit orders from government and high command. In 1945, as concentration camps were liberated inside Germany (the British and American people first saw shocking newsreel footage from Belsen and Buchenwald in the spring of 1945; Auschwitz had been reached by Russian troops some months earlier but it was empty, having already been evacuated) popular anger against Germans waxed even greater. In consequence, accompanying newsreels showing devastated cities had the effect of making the Allied home populations think that Germany's punishment – as the country which had inflicted war on the rest of the world, and whose people had behaved with appalling inhumanity – was fitting.

All this means that the airmen who clambered aboard their bombers and flew into the dangerous skies of Nazi-controlled Europe, were buoyed by the belief that they were fighting a just war – which was true – and doing so acceptably to their own, which was also true. To be told after the war, and moreover by people who never had to face the dangers they faced, that they had been party to the commission of a moral crime, and in the retrospective light of subsequent international law a legal crime also, must understandably feel like a bitter insult.

No such insult is here intended to the men who flew into peril over Europe in the Second World War.

To explain just how far from this is the intention in what follows, a fragment of autobiography might help. When I was a small boy in the decade after the war's end, one of my fantasies was of being a Spitfire pilot in the Battle of Britain. I spread my arms and rushed about the garden making machine-gun noises as I swooped on imaginary Dorniers and Heinkels, Ju-88s and Messerschmitts. But my interest in the history of the 1940s air war was not limited to fighter battles. I read everything I could about all the air war's aspects, and built scale models of most types of aircraft flown in it, from the biplane Gloucester Gladiators still in service when the war began, to the ME 262 jet fighters in service with the Luftwaffe when the war ended – including not only minority types like Lysanders and Swordfish and modified versions like clipped-wing Spitfires for desert warfare, but every one of the bomber types from Whitleys and Hampdens to the magnificent Avro Lancaster.

The RAF was of course the home team, but I was keen to know about the other air forces and their equipment, and to read about the experience of their flyers. And I took what opportunities offered to attend air shows and museums of flight. In the Imperial War Museum, not far from my home in London, one can peer into the cockpit of a Lancaster, and muse on what it was like to see the searchlights and the bursts of flak rising about one, seeking one's death. The only time I ever suffered chilblains was on a spring day at Duxford in Cambridgeshire, where a score of Spitfires had been assembled to perform fly-pasts, the sound of their Merlin Rolls-Royce engines – that amazingly beautiful and utterly distinctive sound – flowing as music to the ears of the watching crowds. The chilblains came because I could not let go of the railing all day long as I watched those famous aircraft fly with exquisite grace, and land and take off like eagles.

This absorbing passion led me to take some flying instruction, and to welcome any opportunity (quite a few offered while I was living in central Africa) to take the controls of a Piper Cub, a twin-engined Cessna, or a war-remaindered DC-3 Dakota, for part of a flight among the thermals above the African savannah. This interest and its practical expression fed into the vivid curiosity I felt about the air war of the 1940s. And part of it was – and remains – the profoundest respect for anyone who went to war in the air in those fraught times.

This included the bombing war; for to sit at the controls of an aeroplane that requires attention to keep straight and level on a steady compass setting – as was the case with the old crab-walking DC-3, perhaps not greatly dissimilar to a Wellington or Halifax bomber in handling qualities – is to learn to wonder at how those brave men could repeatedly venture into the violent nights over the Ruhr or Berlin.

But although I have the greatest admiration for these individuals and their courage in fighting a just war, they are not the subject of this enquiry. Their story has been often and stirringly told, as befits those who as young men saw themselves as serving their country, and the cause of right, to their best ability. Nothing I say here is intended to reduce by one iota what is owed to them and especially to the 55,000 of their comrades who died in RAF Bomber Command, and the 40,000 who died in the USAAF bomber forces in Europe and the Pacific, during World War II.

My aim in this book lies quite elsewhere. It is the specific one of examining the Allied bombing of Germany and Japan in order to settle the question whether it was in whole or in part immoral. The task is in effect a judicial one – a passing of judgement – and to do that one has to take fully into account the circumstances of the time, the intentions and the state of knowledge of the principal decision-makers, and the effects of the practical application of their decisions.

Earlier in this chapter I reported the assertion that 'deliberately mounting military attacks on civilian populations, in order to cause terror and indiscriminate death among them, is a moral crime'. I then asked: Are there ever circumstances in which killing civilians in wartime is not a moral crime? Are there ever circumstances – desperate ones, circumstances of danger to which such actions constitute a defence – that would justify or at least exonerate them?' I take the assertion and these questions as my terms of reference.

I begin by telling the story of the bomber war as conducted by the Allies (chapter 2), and describing its effects on Germany and Japan (chapter 3). This provides the factual background to the investigations in the chapters that follow. It is hard not to mention, as this story unfolds, the many difficult questions it raises, but in general I leave discussion of them to appropriate places in the later chapters.

I then discuss the sources of Allied thinking about bombing, what intentions the Allied leaders formed on this basis, and how those intentions translated into strategy (chapter 4). Key questions arise here, because if there is culpability in the case, it is going to lie with the intentions formed, and the decisions deliberately taken and implemented, by the Allied leaders.

Then I look at the arguments put forward during the war against the strategy of area bombing, and the efforts made to stop it (chapter 5). This is important as showing that the campaigns were not uncontroversial even as they took place, and that everyone involved was acutely aware of the questions that could be asked about them, and the moral dilemmas they posed.

At the war's end the Allies put Nazi and Japanese leaders on trial as war criminals. I look at the principles used in the trial of the Nazi leaders – the Nuremberg Principles – to see how the Allied conduct of the air war would stand up in the light of those same principles if the roles at Nuremberg had been reversed. Relevant aspects of subsequent international law took account of what happened on all sides in the Second World War as its empirical basis; it is significant to see what this post-war judgement implies for the Allied bombing campaigns (chapter 6). And I look at the defences offered – often eloquent, and containing important points and arguments that must be taken seriously – of the area-bombing strategies of the Allies; defences that include, among other things, the military justification for, or even the military necessity of, the bombing strategies pursued (chapter 7).

With all these considerations to hand, I then and finally offer a judgement about the morality of the Allied bombing campaigns in the Second World War, and the reasons for my judgement (chapter 8). Among these latter are, I believe, some points that have not previously figured in discussion of the Allies' air attack on Germany and Japan, and they might be particularly significant ones.

It is important to note that although surveying the history of area bombing in the Second World War is necessary for deciding the moral question asked by this book, I do not attempt a history of the bombing war as a whole. Area bombing was only part of the bombing war, though a very large part for Britain's RAF Bomber Command in Europe, and a very large part for the United States Army Air Force in the Pacific theatre. In Europe the USAAF did not, as a matter of chosen policy, engage in area bombing, although in a dramatic change of tactics it did so over Japan in the last months of the war. Because the USAAF became fully engaged in the bombing war in Europe only in late 1943, and because it devoted its endeavours there to precision bombing of specific industrial and military targets rather than 'saturation' bombing of civilian populations, if figures most prominently in the following pages when the air attacks on Japan become central to the story.

As a final preliminary, I must mention a coincidence of mainly personal interest. The phrase adopted as the title of this book, *Among the Dead Cities*, occurs in a report prepared by an Allied group assigned to find a suitable venue for holding criminal trials of Nazi leaders at the war's end. Nuremberg was chosen not only because it had been the scene of spectacular Nazi rallies before the war, but also because it had been 90 per cent destroyed by bombing, and seemed therefore to be an object lesson in itself, graphically illustrating the punishment brought upon Germany by the Nazis' criminal liability for instigating world war and committing unspeakable atrocities during its course. The report, in allusion to Nuremberg's ruin by bombing, described it as being 'among the dead cities of Germany'.

Imagine my surprise when, late in the process of writing this book, I came across the code-name for the last bombing raid carried out against Nuremberg by the RAF, on the night of 16–17 March 1945. The code-name was my own name – 'Grayling'. The city had already been heavily damaged by numerous earlier raids, and the *Altstadt*, Nuremberg's historic centre, by then existed only as rubble. But the 277 Lancasters and 16 Mosquitoes of 'Grayling' pounded its rubble even further into dust, leaving 529 people dead and among other things burning down the Steinbuhl district, almost the only part of the city then still standing.

It was a costly raid from Bomber Command's point of view. Luftwaffe night-fighters shot down 24 Lancasters, 8.7 per cent of the night's force, nearly double what Bomber Command regarded as an 'acceptable' loss rate during the height of the bombing war; and this despite the fact that by March 1945 the Luftwaffe had been almost entirely swept from the skies. It was effectively the last gasp of the Luftwaffe air defence; in the remaining month of Bomber Command operations, which ended on 25 April 1945, losses were nothing like so high, and almost always light.

The coincidence of the raid's name – for that is all it is – extends to the fact that this final bombing of Nuremberg should so painfully illustrate the cost to both sides in the titanic struggle whose morality is here under discussion. Nuremberg also reminds us that as the cases for and against the bombing war's moral status are put, there looms in the background a decision already taken: one that concerns the moral status of Nazism and its crimes, which the menacingly triumphalist rallies of Nuremberg prefigured, and which the ruin of Nuremberg and the Third Reich unequivocally proves was unacceptable to the rest of mankind.

2

The Bomber War

O N THE NIGHT of 24 July 1943, in the hour before midnight, a fleet of 791 heavily laden Royal Air Force bombers took off from bases in the flat and relatively unpopulated counties of eastern England, and aimed their noses across the North Sea. In their bases at Wangerooge and Heligoland the Luftwaffe's radar operators could see the stream of aircraft beginning to approach, and they put their night-fighter and anti-aircraft defences on alert. The stream moved steadily eastwards above latitude 54 degrees, and the watching Germans judged that if it turned south before the coast of Schleswig-Holstein, its likely target would be Bremen; but if it crossed the neck of the Danish peninsula before turning south, it would most likely be aiming for Berlin.

At fifteen minutes after midnight, just as the Luftwaffe ground controllers were beginning to plot interception points for their night-fighters, the orderly cluster of traces on their radar screens suddenly and startlingly dissolved into a snowstorm of writhing streaks and dashes. It looked as if the bomber stream, already large, had suddenly multiplied hundreds of times over, and begun to move in all directions at once. The Luftwaffe night-fighter pilots were equally thrown into confusion, for their airborne radar – mounted cumbersomely on their aircraft's noses like old-fashioned television aerials – had likewise gone haywire.

The cause was a simple technical innovation employed for the first time by RAF Bomber Command: a device called 'Window', consisting of strips of tinfoil cut to correspond to the wavelength of German radar frequencies. Dropped in clusters from the bombers at one-minute intervals, 'Window' disrupted the defenders' radar, effectively blinding its operators and the crews of the night-fighters patrolling above them.

Still, the night-fighter pilots had their eyes, and observers on the ground their ears. The former saw yellow marker flares appear in the sky over the mouth of the Elbe river, and then the latter heard the sound of many aircraft swinging south above them, like the distant humming of a huge swarm of bees. At last it was clear that the night's target was neither Bremen nor Berlin, but Hamburg.

What no one could guess, either among the Luftwaffe defenders or Hamburg's citizens as they heard the air-raid warnings begin, was that the assault about to be unleashed on the city – a series of bombing raids lasting a week and a half – would be something new and terrible even by the standards of industrialised violence so far experienced in the Second World War. This was Operation Gomorrah, mounted by RAF Bomber Command with the aim of wiping Hamburg from the map of Europe.

The choice of name for the operation was apt. The Book of Genesis tells how the 'cities of the plain', Sodom and Gomorrah – the latter means 'submersion' – were destroyed by a rain of fire and sulphur from the sky. When Abraham (not Lot, who had been forbidden to look) rose from sleep the morning after the event, and stood on a peak in his mountain fastness, he 'looked toward Sodom and Gomorrah, and toward all the land of the plain, and beheld, and lo, the smoke of the country went up as the smoke of a furnace'; the cities were no more.

Operation Gomorrah consisted of five major and several minor attacks on Hamburg on the nights of 24–5, 27–8, 29–30 July and 2–3 August, and in the daylight hours of 25 and 26 July. Small forces of Mosquitoes followed on days subsequent to the main raids to cause

annoyance and take photographs. The two daylight raids were carried
out by the United States Eighth Army Air Force, which sent fleets of
230 bombers on each occasion to attack Hamburg's shipyards and
engineering plants. The American raids did not much affect the
citizens of Hamburg in their residential areas and city centre, whereas
the raids by the RAF most certainly did; these latter had as their
aiming point Hamburg's most central point, the *Altstadt* – the old
city. But it was the Americans who suffered most among the attackers,
because angry German fighters were waiting for them in force on each
of their daylight raids, and gave the American formations a severe
mauling. Nineteen B-17 Flying Fortresses were shot down over
Hamburg on 25 July alone.

On the first night of bombing the RAF's Lancasters, Halifaxes,
Stirlings and Wellingtons dropped 2,396 tons of bombs on the city,
the majority of them incendiaries. These latter were small bombs
filled with highly flammable chemicals, among them magnesium,
phosphorus and petroleum jelly. The phosphorus could not be
doused with water, and it clung to whatever it splashed over, burning
fiercely. Large clusters of incendiaries were dropped to scatter fires
across the target area, simultaneously broken apart by high explosive
(HE) bombs and thereby made readier for combustion. A proportion
of the HE bombs were time-delayed, armed to go off in the hours and
sometimes days after the beginning of a raid in order to disrupt efforts
by emergency workers to put out fires, rescue the injured, mend water
and gas pipes, and shore up unstable buildings.

Bomber Command had quickly grasped the value of incendiaries.
During the Blitz on London and other British cities in 1940–1, civil-
defence authorities issued warnings about the Luftwaffe's 2-lb.
thermite and magnesium incendiaries. Cigarette cards bore the
legend,

The 2lb magnesium bomb does not explode, its only object being
to start a fire. It will probably penetrate no further than an attic or
an upper floor, setting light to anything within a few feet. Vast

numbers of these light bombs can be carried by a single aeroplane, and many more fires started than could be dealt with by fire brigades.

The Blitz lesson had been well learned in retaliation. On the second major attack by the RAF during Operation Gomorrah, during the night of 27–8 July, Hamburg's fire-fighters were overwhelmed by the torrents of incendiaries that fell on to the city, so many and in such concentration that they initiated a terrifying phenomenon: a fire-storm. Fires in different streets progressively joined together, forming into vast pyres of flame that grew rapidly hotter and eventually roared upwards to a height of 7,000 feet, sucking in air from the outlying suburbs at over a hundred miles an hour to fuel their oxygen hunger, creating artificial hurricanes 'resonating like mighty organs' as W. G. Sebald put it, which intensified the fires further.[1] It was the first ever firestorm created by bombing, and it caused terrible destruction and loss of life. Its greatest intensity lasted for three hours, snatching up roofs, trees and burning human bodies and sending them whirling into the air. The fires leaped up behind collapsing façades of buildings, roared through the streets, and rolled across squares and open areas 'in strange rhythms like rolling cylinders'.[2] The glass windows of tramcars melted, bags of sugar boiled, people trying to flee the oven-like heat of air-raid shelters sank, petrified into gro-tesque gestures, into the boiling asphalt of the streets.

The bomber crews reported that they could feel the heat of the city's fires in their aircraft as they made their bombing runs. The next day smoke from the destroyed city rose 25,000 feet into the sky. Little bluish flames still flickered around some of the disfigured corpses. The victims of the first attack were either blown up, suffocated in their air-raid shelters from which the air had been sucked away, or cremated instantly in the raging fires outside. Many bodies were found so shrivelled by the heat that adult corpses had shrunk to the size of infants.[3]

On this second night raid, 787 bombers had crossed the Denmark peninsula as if intent on Berlin, only to swing back and attack Hamburg from the north-east. This attack was much more accurate than the first, and its high degree of concentration was one of the principal factors in the creation of the devastating firestorm. Some commentators cite also the hot dry July weather as a contributory factor, and the fact that bomb and fire damage from the earlier raids, and strain on the city's emergency services, made the city more vulnerable.

By the third night attack on 29–30 July the effectiveness of 'Window' had diminished because the German defences had worked out ways to take countermeasures, and as a result RAF losses were higher and the bombing less accurate. More night-fighters were allocated to Hamburg's defence, and with them day-fighters whose pilots adapted themselves to their nocturnal task by taking advantage of the raging fires in the city, flying very high and watching for the bombers underneath them to become silhouettes against the glow.

The fourth and final night raid, on 2–3 August, was the least effective of all because Hamburg lay under thickly piled clouds, the rain from which helped the fire-fighters on the ground while obscuring the target from attackers in the air. Only half the bomber stream could locate the city despite the fact that it was still burning, and none of the marker flares could be seen in the murk. Nevertheless the series of attacks had already done their worst. In over 3,000 sorties above the city in four separate raids, the RAF had dropped more than 9,000 tons of bombs, the majority of them incendiaries. Only eighty-six of its bombers had been lost, a remarkably low rate for which the novelty of Window takes the credit. Bomber Command felt that it had scored an outstanding success; its official historians wrote, 'the victory was complete. In the earlier months and years of the war it was without precedent, and in those that were still to come it was never excelled'.[4] This was a sentiment shared at the time by the bomber crews themselves; one said,

The first two raids on Hamburg were so *obviously* successful to those of us who took part in them. And this was, in itself, unusual. Forgetting the standard line-shooting, one returned from most trips in what I would call a neutral frame of mind. Relief to be back and glad that one more was under your belt – and that was about all. But, with those two to Hamburg, there was an added exhilaration which came from the absolute conviction – actually on the night – that we had pulled off something special.[5]

In Hamburg itself, sentiment was of course very different. No one knows exactly how many died, but at least 45,000 corpses lay among the smoking ruins, with many more injured and traumatised. Half the city had been reduced to rubble – a total of 30,480 buildings according to official contemporary German figures. The shock of the devastating attack was felt across Germany. A tidal wave of one and a quarter million refugees from the city flowed to the very borders of the country during the following months, carrying with them first-hand news of the city's sufferings.[6]

The Official History remark just quoted – 'the victory was complete' – implies that Operation Gomorrah was a high point in RAF Bomber Command's endeavours in the Second World War. In one sense it was, because the ratio of damage inflicted to losses incurred was so favourable to the bombers. But it was not a high point in terms of tonnages of bombs dropped or devastation caused. Rather, it marked a beginning; the real beginning of the kind of bombing campaign that the British government and its Air Force commanders in the bomber force had been planning since early in the war, but had until then only been able to deliver occasionally and with great effort – as in the first 1,000-bomber raids on Cologne, Essen and Bremen on 30 May, 1 June and 25 June 1942 respectively. That month of effort had effectively been a one-off; such raids could not be repeated for some time afterwards, for the numbers involved had been plumped up considerably by aircraft and crews borrowed from Training Command and (less hazardously) Coastal Command, and as a result losses were unacceptably high – in the Bremen raid forty-nine bombers were lost. It was only in 1943, the fourth year of the war, that the RAF began to have the resources and equipment to bomb on a scale and in a manner required by the philosophy of 'area bombing', the official term for attacks aimed at civilian populations.

Those resources continued to mount as the war progressed, and alongside them, from 1943 onwards, the United States Army Air Force likewise grew in strength, contributing greatly to winning control of the European skies. The USAAF did this not by area bombing after the manner of the RAF, but by tactical bombing of key industrial resources for Germany's defence against air attack, and by fighting the Luftwaffe out of the sky partly by means of its formidably many-gunned Flying Fortress bombers, but more especially its Lightning and Mustang long-range fighter escorts. It was constant policy that, in the European theatre of war the USAAF did not follow the RAF's example of deliberate targeting of civilians, but concentrated almost wholly on military and industrial targets. In the Japanese theatre matters were otherwise; there the USAAF adopted exactly the RAF technique of incendiary area attacks upon cities.

Allied domination of the European skies was at last so complete that in the final months of bombing, from the autumn of 1944 to the official stand-down of the bombing campaign in April 1945, the Allies were able to fly over enemy territory in greater safety. The same was true in the Pacific theatre; as the US forces came close enough to Japan to mount bombing raids from captured islands, the air defence of the Japanese homeland was almost non-existent. This is a key fact in explaining how it is that the greatest percentage of bombs dropped in the entire war, and therefore the greatest destruction of German and Japanese cities, occurred in the war's final months – when the war, in the opinion of most qualified commentators, was already won.[7]

This controversial point plays a significant part in the moral assessment of the Allied bombing campaigns, for in addition to the main question about whether deliberate targeting of civilian populations was morally acceptable, the remorseless and continued destruction of German and Japanese cities when victory was near forces one to raise the further question: was there a half-spoken intent on the part of the Allies, and most particularly among those closely associated with the planning and prosecution of the bombing campaigns, to effect what might be called 'culturecide' upon the two main Axis powers? Destroying cities meant – in addition to killing and traumatising many tens of thousands of people – destroying monuments, libraries, schools and universities, art galleries, architectural heritage, the cultural precipitate and the organs of corporate life that make an identifiable society.

In 1942 a decision was taken by the War Cabinet and the Air Staff to destroy all of Germany's cities with populations over 100,000, and among the plans made for post-war Germany – a plan partially implemented by events – was one that saw a territorially divided and diminished Germany turned into a solely agricultural region, with neither the industries nor the economic structure (including the educational and cultural institutions required to service it) to permit the resurrection, as had happened after the First World War, of another powerful and warlike Germany intent upon a European imperium. In the event, Cold War realities – whose imminence was already apparent before the war's official end in Europe in May 1945 – would have made the victorious Allies anyway quick to abandon this notion, and to see the point of helping Germany to rebuild as an industrial power. But even if the punitive conception of making Germany a farm inhabited by bucolics was one only among a number of suggestions being canvassed on the subject of what to do with post-war Germany, it cannot be allowed the comfortable status of 'just one of those ideas'. It is diffusely linked with the massive obliterating endeavour of the Allied bombers, and therefore is an idea that must not be left to slip into the shadows of history without an examination of its implications for the great moral question that the Allied bombing raises.[8] Apart from anything else, ignoring such matters only hands them on a platter to neo-Nazis and right-wing extremists who use them for unsavoury political ends, not for frank inspection of the past and the precepts it offers.

No understanding of questions about the morality of Allied area bombing in the Second World War can be attempted without having before us the following three matters: what actually happened in the bombing war; what was known, thought, intended and hoped by those who carried it out; and what effect it had. These last two points are dealt with in subsequent chapters. Here I now turn, as a necessary preliminary, to give a brief history of the bomber war, as the background of fact for those discussions.

On 3 September 1939, only minutes after Prime Minister Neville Chamberlain announced the British government's declaration of war on Germany, air-raid sirens sounded over London. Sixty thousand beds had been prepared in the capital's hospitals for what was expected to be immediate massive air attack, and the apprehensive citizenry might have feared, when they heard that first siren, that 60,000 extra beds would not be sufficient. In the event, it transpired that the air-raid warning was the result of a lone French aviator's forgetfulness about filing a flight plan.

The assumption behind the provision of thousands of extra hospital beds in London was that Germany would bomb civilian areas indiscriminately, as it had done in the First World War, and as all theorists of air war since 1918 had predicted would be an inevitable feature of future wars. By contrast, RAF Bomber Command was under strict instructions not to attack targets on the mainland of Europe, in order to avoid the risk of civilian casualties. One of the chief reasons for this was that Chamberlain did not want to provoke retaliatory attacks on British cities. And at first both Germany and Britain were restrained towards each other in the matter of bombing, which on the British side anyway started immediately: on 3 September itself, within hours of Chamberlain's declaration of war on Germany, a group of Hampden and Whitley bombers attempted to find and attack a fleet of German warships reportedly at sea near Wilhelmshaven.[9] They failed; but even as they returned unblooded from the hunt, a flight of ten Whitley bombers was setting course for the Ruhr – to drop not bombs but leaflets on the civilian population, inviting them to surrender.

Chamberlain's reluctance to allow bombing that might harm civilians had as its ostensible reason an assurance he had given, two days before the outbreak of war, that Britain would not bomb civilians. The assurance came in response to an appeal by President Roosevelt of the United States that the European nations would not permit 'bombardment from the air of civilian populations or un-fortified cities'. Another – more pragmatic – reason was that Britain was weaker than Germany in the air, and needed time to build strength.

This self-denying ordinance lasted until May 1940; but RAF's Bomber Command was not fully in a position to deliver major attacks on Germany until 1942, and even then it was 1943 before its campaign was able to reach levels – still not fully sustainable – of the kind desired by its planners and prosecutors. It was only in 1944 that the numbers of bomber crews, bomber aircraft and bombs began to reach those levels.

The weakness of Bomber Command at the beginning of the war was the result of several co-operating causes. At the close of hostilities in 1918 Britain possessed the mightiest air force in the world, but within two years its strength had been reduced by a massive nine-tenths. The reasons were a combination of peacetime expenditure savings, a general revulsion against the idea of war, and the opposition of the Army and Navy to the existence of a separate air force. The nascent air force might have vanished altogether had it not been for the redoubtable independence struggle fought by the RAF's chief, Sir Hugh Trenchard, and the sudden revival of military anxieties in 1923, induced by France's occupation of the Ruhr over Germany's default on reparations. By then the RAF was down to a mere three squadrons from the 382 squadrons of 1918.[10] The Ruhr crisis prompted Parliament to vote a substantial increase in RAF funding, aimed at building within five years a 'Home Defence Air Force' of 52 squadrons, two-thirds of them bombers.[11]

In the event, when Hitler came to power in 1933 the Home Defence Air Force had risen only to 42 squadrons. The Nazi aim of rapidly building an air force was limited by none of the dithering and penny-pinching of British and French attitudes. Germany had a strong civil-aviation sector, dozens of amateur flying clubs, a growing aircraft-manufacturing industry, and secret cadres of pilots trained during the Weimar years. And because the Luftwaffe was starting from scratch it could arm itself with the latest metal monoplanes with retractable undercarriage, very different from the wooden fixed-wheel biplanes still being flown by the British and French air forces.

The RAF had a secret weapon of its own, however: excellent training. This was the legacy of Air Marshal Sir Hugh Trenchard, forged during his time as Chief of the Air Staff from 1919 to 1929. Despite the paucity of resources available to his command, Trenchard built an infrastructure that outstripped anything elsewhere in the world: the cadet college for officer pilots at Cranwell, the Staff College for senior personnel at Andover, and a number of other research and training establishments for all aspects of the force's work. The system of short-service commissions – four years full-time service followed by five years in the reserve – ensured a pool of highly trained pilots who could instantly be called upon in an emergency. When war broke out in September 1939 the RAF could summon more than 700 pilots from among former members of the Oxford University Air Squadron alone.[12]

The destabilising presence of the Nazi regime on the world stage from 1933 onwards, together with the increasingly dangerous situation in the Far East following Japan's invasion of Manchuria and China, prompted the British government to reconsider its defence policies. In 1934 it announced an enlargement of the RAF to 75 squadrons by 1939. In March 1935 Hermann Goering officially announced the birth of the Luftwaffe, and shortly afterwards Hitler told the British ambassador in Berlin that his new air force was already as large as the RAF. Whether the information was correct or not did not matter; it galvanished London into boosting RAF targets yet again, to 112 squadrons – and not by 1939 but 1937. The aim was to ensure equality of strength with the Luftwaffe by that date, but German rearmament was proceeding much more quickly than London realised, so even with its revamped target RAF strength still lagged behind.

These plans were premised on the old concept of the 'balance of power'. In October 1935 Italy invaded Abyssinia. This was the last straw for the balance-of-power argument, which rested on arrangements invented long beforehand, at the Congress of Vienna in 1815. By the 1930s that structure was fragmenting fast, and the international situation appeared more menacing by the month. By the end of 1935 British policy-makers had at last accepted that war was a greater likelihood than peace, and they began to address themselves seriously to the task of preparing for it. The game of squadron numbers did not meet the situation by itself; new types of aircraft, manufacturing capacity to produce them, and an adequate depth of reserves were all required. The result was a plan called 'Scheme F', the first of a series of detailed arrangements to meet all aspects of air-defence needs.[13]

An immediate consequence of Scheme F was that designs of heavy bombers began to appear on drawing-boards. In some of the successor plans, notably Scheme J, priority was given to fighter-aircraft design and production because the need for defence of British air space was recognised as more urgent.[14] In fact it was already the case – luckily, from the point of view of Britain's solitary survival in the face of German aggression in 1940 – that matters were well advanced in the design of new fighters. Chief among them was the elegant and highly effective Supermarine Spitfire, evolved from the design of a beautiful seaplane which had won the Schneider Trophy (an air-speed prize), and the Hawker Hurricane, the robust gun-platform that so ably played its part in defending the English skies in the fateful summer of 1940.[15] Britain also, and every bit as importantly, had the life-saving technological advantage of radar, without which the Battle of Britain might well have been lost.

Because of Scheme J the heavy bomber designs were left in a much less advanced state, and what RAF Bomber Command had available when war began was nowhere near suited to the task it faced.[16] It consisted of 53 front-line squadrons, each notionally – but only notionally – of 16 aircraft. There was no reserve, which meant that a third of these squadrons had to be withdrawn into non-operational status for training and reinforcement purposes. And the aircraft available – Blenheims, Whitleys, Hampdens, Wellingtons and Battles – were in their different ways too slow, light, under-armed and outdated for the war that broke upon them.[17]

To understand how the concept of 'area bombing' – targeting civilian populations in urban areas – evolved out of Britain's clear initial policy of avoiding harm to civilians, one has to know something of how the bomber war itself evolved. This is because in the perilous years 1940–2 Britain had only one resource for carrying the war to Germany, and that was Bomber Command; but, as just remarked, Bomber Command was a largely ineffective instrument while it had only Whitleys, Hampdens and the others at its disposal. The policy of area bombing was a response to a set of problems and a need: problems of navigation and bomb-aiming which made the task of finding and hitting precise targets exceedingly difficult, and the need for a forceful way of delivering blows at Nazi Germany which would hurt it and therefore its will and capacity to make war.

These facts were made plain very early in the war, in the intermittent series of attacks mounted by Bomber Command against German warships in Wilhelmshaven, the Schillig Roads, and the Heligoland Bight, and in reconnaissance flights over northern Germany. Bad weather made these efforts sporadic in the autumn of 1939 and the winter of 1939–40, but they were enough to teach some bitter lessons about the inadequacies of the types of aircraft at Bomber Command's disposal.

At very first, though, the auguries seemed good; a daylight raid on elements of the German fleet in the Heligoland Bight on 3 December 1939 saw all twenty-four of the attacking Wellingtons survive flak and assaults by ME 109 and 110 fighters. One of the German planes was damaged by return fire from a Wellington, adding to the sense that a tight formation of bombers could defend itself well, given that each Wellington had four machine guns in its rear turret.

But the optimism was premature. Ten days later a Royal Navy submarine damaged two German cruisers in torpedo attacks, and as the cruisers struggled back into the Jade Estuary leading to Wilhelmshaven, a dozen Wellingtons were sent to deliver the *coup de grâce*. Low clouds covered the sky over the target area, forcing the bombers to fly beneath them, at less than 600 feet. Anti-aircraft fire from warships and armed merchantmen in the estuary did the Wellingtons much damage, but then the barrage suddenly stopped, signifying the arrival of a flock of Messerschmitt 109s. Within minutes five Wellingtons had been shot down, and a sixth was so badly damaged that it crashed on landing when, with great difficulty, it managed to reach its home base in eastern England.

Four days later, on 18 December 1939, twelve out of twenty-four Wellingtons were shot down, again over Wilhelmshaven. It was another daylight attack, this time conducted in brilliant sunshine under a clear blue sky. Indeed the weather was so good that operators of the Luftwaffe's experimental Freya radar stations at Heligoland and Wangerooge could not believe how suicidally the RAF offered itself to the Messerschmitts stationed near by.

The attrition rate of 50 per cent on this and the earlier raid was disastrous, not least because Bomber Command was under orders to conserve its forces while reserves were built up and new crews trained. The reasons for the heavy losses were quickly identified. One was that the Wellingtons had fuel tanks in their port wings which were neither self-sealing nor protected by armour plating. Enemy fire directed there either set the Wellington ablaze, or at best drained it of fuel. The Wellington was a rather inflammable aircraft anyway, and hits anywhere could be disastrous. Another reason was that although the Wellington had four rear-mounted machine guns, it was vulnerable to beam attack, a weakness made worse – and this is a third reason – by its low air speed relative to the Messerschmitt fighters, which could easily catch and overtake it, then swing round and mount another assault, with no hope of the Wellington outrunning its attacker.

The Air Officer Commanding No. 3 Group in Bomber Command from which this mauled squadron came, Air Vice-Marshal John Baldwin, was convinced that bombers would be safe if they stayed in tight formation, using their combined fire-power to fend off attackers. It was a doctrine that, later, the United States Army Air Force vigorously adhered to, but with an aeroplane much more likely to make it work: the Flying Fortress B-17, bristling with guns at every angle. Baldwin was sure that inexperience had led his men to break formation during the 18 December débâcle, thus making themselves vulnerable. But Lieutenant-Colonel Carl Schumacher of the Luftwaffe, who had led the attacking Messerschmitts that day, later wrote that although the damage inflicted on some of his fighters was the result of the 'tight formation and excellent rear-gunners of the Wellington bombers', it was their discipline that had actually been their undoing; 'their maintenance of formation and rigid adherence to course,' Schumacher said, 'made them easy targets to follow.'[18]

The disaster of 18 December showed the Air Staff that they needed to change their thinking, not least about the wisdom of daylight raids. But even as they debated how best to use their limited forces – and their limitations were becoming daily more obvious in every sense – the pace of war forced them up an even steeper learning curve. In April 1940 Germany invaded Norway, and the British and French responded by landing an expeditionary force. The venture was a failure; the Allied force was driven back into the sea within two weeks of arriving. Sorties by Wellingtons and Hampdens against German ships crossing the Skagerrak were brutally repulsed; on 12 April eight out of twelve Hampdens were shot down trying to find the famous

German warships *Scharnhorst* and *Gneisenau*. The method of their destruction spoke volumes about their capacity as machines of war. ME 110s simply flew up and took a position parallel to them and a little ahead, a mere hundred or so yards away, thus sitting comfortably out of the Hampdens' limited line of fire; and then the German rear gunners aimed at the Hampden pilots in their cockpits, and killed them.[19] Following the 12 April débâcle Hampdens were reserved to night operations only.

On the night of 16–17 April a solitary Whitely was despatched to Oslo to bomb the airfield there in the hope of denying it to German squadrons. Only Whitleys among the aircraft at Bomber Command's disposal had the range to fly that far. The crew had a hard time; navigation was made difficult by cloud cover obscuring vital landmarks, and although the city itself was found under a gap in the cover, its outlying airport was still obscured, and moreover under fog. The crew could see nothing. At that point in the war standing orders were that bombing was to occur only on definite visual identification of a target, to avoid accidental harm to civilians; so the Whitley had to turn for home without attacking.

Although Oslo's airport was bombed in the next few days by small formations of Whitleys, the range limitation and the navigational difficulties involved were ominous signs. How could deep-penetration attacks on Germany itself be contemplated in the light of these problems? The month of operations over Norway between 9 April and 10 May had seen thirty-three bombers lost, with scarcely anything to show by way of return in damage to the enemy.

But the worst section of the learning curve had yet to be climbed.

During the 'phoney war' – the period between September 1939 and May 1940 during which there was no actual ground fighting in western Europe – the squadrons sent to France as part of the British Expeditionary Force provided the Air Staff at home with greatly more matter to ponder. The aircraft in question were all Fairey Battles, classed as 'light bombers' or 'fighter-bombers' to distinguish them from the Wellingtons, Whitleys and Hampdens which then counted as 'heavy bombers'. The Battle squadrons formed what was called the Advanced Air Striking Force. Events proved that they were, by a considerable margin, the least effective elements in Britain's air fleet. On 30 September 1939 five of them flying an 'armed reconnaissance' over the Siegfried Line were attacked by ME 109s, and only one got home. Thereafter they flew almost always at night only, and even then kept as much as possible out of harm's way. Their most adventurous endeavour of the 'phoney war' was to drop leaflets over the Rhineland in February 1940. Efforts were vigorously made to replace the Battles with Blenheim light bombers, but by the time the 'phoney war' became suddenly real on 10 May 1940 – the day on which the German blitzkrieg in the west began – only two of the Battle squadrons had been replaced by Blenheims.

It was the ferocious defensive fighting between 10 May and the end of the Dunkirk evacuation of the British army on 3 June 1940 that revealed the inadequacies of the Battles, for all that they were flown with extraordinary courage. In the very first day of serious fighting, thirty-two Battles were sent against the German advance through Luxembourg, and thirteen were shot down by anti-aircraft fire. All the rest were damaged. Three hours later a second attack, also of thirty-two Battles, was launched against this dangerous target, and this time Messerschmitts appeared and helped the anti-aircraft batteries to shoot down ten more of them. These were completely unsustainable rates of loss, and yet what the Battles were achieving in return was practically nothing. The image of Polish cavalry galloping at German Panzers comes to mind. The next day, as a result of a Luftwaffe attack, one of the two new Blenheim squadrons was destroyed in its entirety as it stood on the grass of the Vaux airfield near Soissons, its crews drinking tea while they waited for flying orders. That afternoon eight Battles returned to the fray over Luxembourg; only one came back.

A significant consequence of the Wehrmacht thrust into the Low Countries was that on 10 May 1940 Neville Chamberlain resigned, and Winston Churchill took his place in Downing Street. The change-over immediately led to a more assertive use of British air resources. Bomber Command's first large attack on German soil occurred on the night of 11–12 May, when thirty-six Whitleys and Hampdens set off to bomb the transport links around Mönchengladbach. About half reached the target; of these, three were shot down.

Efforts to halt the German advance necessitated bombing the bridges over the Albert Canal at Maastricht, and repeated and costly efforts were made both by French and British bombers to do so. On 11 May four out of twelve Blenheims, flying from bases in England, were shot down and all the rest damaged, with no effect on the bridges. The next day seven out of nine Blenheims were destroyed in a repeat attack, still without success.

And so the attrition went on, proving beyond any doubt the drastic inadequacies of Britain's bomber force. The effective end of the Advanced Air Striking Force came on 14 May, the day a major German attack in the Sedan sector surprised the French 2nd Army and rendered the entire circumstance of the war critical for the Allies. In a desperate effort to gain time, the French high command asked for every available French and British bomber to be thrown at the German advance. By the end of that day the French air force had ceased to exist, and Britain's Advanced Air Striking Force was in tatters, having lost twenty-six out of forty-two aircraft committed to the fray.

The French implored the new British government to send ten more Hurricane squadrons to France, but Air Marshal Sir Hugh Dowding, C-in-C Fighter Command, bluntly told the War Cabinet that Britain could not be saved from invasion unless every available fighter were kept back to maintain air superiority over the Channel. Losses among fighter planes in France had been very high; between the beginning of the invasion on 10 May and the last day of the Dunkirk withdrawal, seventy-one Hurricanes and Gladiators had been lost. But even as early as 14 May Dowding felt that the situation in France was irrecoverable, and was thinking grimly ahead. Churchill, however, had to do something to help not only the French but his own reeling forces; and all he had available was Bomber Command. He ordered it to do what it could from its bases in England.

Bomber Command had already begun to make night attacks on the transport links in the rear of the German advance, in an effort to slow it down and disrupt its supplies. The embargo on attacking other targets near civilian centres still held. But then an event occurred that shocked everyone, and began to loosen the no-civilian-attacks ethos prevailing in most of London's political and military minds. This crucial event was the Luftwaffe's bombing of Rotterdam on the same fateful 14 May 1940.

In the days since 10 May the Dutch had been giving their German attackers a difficult time, though outnumbered and outgunned. German landings on the beaches north of The Hague were almost annihilated by extraordinarily courageous Dutch pilots flying out-moded Fokker biplanes. It took three days for the Panzers under General Rudolf Schmidt's command to arrive at the outskirts of Rotterdam, where exhausted advance units of German paratroops had been pinned down since their initial attack.

Schmidt sent a message to the commander of the Dutch defenders of Rotterdam, Colonel Pieter Willem Scharroo, saying that if the Dutch did not surrender he would summon the Luftwaffe to mount a devastating attack on the city. The German high command was pressing Schmidt urgently to take Rotterdam so that the forces being delayed there could press on towards France through Belgium, thus pre-empting the British landing that was imminently expected on the Dutch coast. Time was of the essence for blitzkrieg, and the Dutch were making the Wehrmacht lose too much of it.

Scharroo had to relay the surrender demand to his government in The Hague, whose ministers replied that they would send a delega-tion to Rotterdam. The clock was ticking ominously, but Schmidt was prepared to wait; at last he was told that the Dutch delegation would reach the city at 2 p.m. At 1.30 p.m. he sent a signal to

Luftflotte 2, one hundred of whose Heinkel 111 bombers had been waiting on standby, to cancel their attack. Alas, five minutes before his message reached Luftflotte 2 HQ the last of those Heinkels had already taken off from their bases near Bremen. By the time Schmidt's signal was relayed from HQ to the bombers' controllers at the bases, the bombers were over Dutch territory, and had entered radio silence preparatory to their attack.

Frantic efforts to contact the bombers were repeatedly made by the base controllers, but unavailingly. Schmidt was told of the problem, and alerted his troops to fire red flares the moment they saw the bombers, to make them abort the mission. When the first wave of Heinkels appeared over the city from the south the flares duly went up, but the Heinkel pilots did not notice them; they were too busy searching for their aiming-point in the centre of the old city through the hazy glare of the afternoon sun and the smoke from flak bursts, and too distracted by concentrating on the line of the shining Maas river which was directing them to their target. Fifty-seven aircraft dropped their loads of 250-lb and 500-lb bombs into the city centre, shattering it and setting it on fire; then they climbed away towards the south-east and home.

The leader of the second wave, approaching from the south-west after a long detour, was also concentrating hard on the target area, now marked by fires and pillars of smoke; but perhaps because of the different angle of approach and the better play of light, out of the corner of his eye he saw a red flare, and instantly swung away, radioing 'Abort! Abort!' to the following aircraft. He was the only pilot to see a flare, and until his group of Heinkels had returned to base the other crews were astonished by the abrupt cancellation of their attack.

It was, however, too late. The first wave of attackers had dropped one hundred tons of explosives and incendiaries on Rotterdam, killing 900 civilians and reducing the heart of the old city to rubble. Two hours later Rotterdam's defenders surrendered. In London the next morning, and indeed in every city in the world outside the Axis countries, newspapers blazoned the horror of the attack, claiming 30,000 dead and characterising the German demolition of the old city as an act of unmitigated barbarism.[20]

As far as the British War Cabinet was concerned, the fact that the Luftwaffe had mounted an area-bombing attack on a city changed the stakes. It was irrelevant that the city was garrisoned and defended; it was crowded with civilians, and the early high casualty estimates made it appear to be an atrocity. Everyone had learned to fear just such an atrocity as a result of bombings in earlier wars, chief among them the Zeppelin and Gotha raids on Britain in the First World War, and the attack on Guernica in the Spanish Civil War.[21] And it was irrelevant that the bombing of Rotterdam had in one sense been a terrible mistake; the Germans had contemplated, then planned, then actually put into execution, the deliberate and indiscriminate bombing of a city, and the efforts made to abort its execution could not change that.

In fact, German aircraft had already bombed civilian targets in the war. Warsaw in September 1939 was the notable example, but the alchemy of distance made it a different case. In those days the world was a much larger place, and distances were felt to be so great – not just in spatial and temporal terms, but more importantly in psychological ones – that the significance of events was almost always inversely related to them. For that reason the bombing of Warsaw, far away in the east of Europe, did not have the same impact on British sensibilities as the bombing of Rotterdam just across the Channel. As a result of the Rotterdam bombing, indeed on the very day after it – 15 May 1940 – Churchill's War Cabinet authorised bombing raids east of the Rhine for the first time. That same night ninety-nine bombers took off for the Ruhr, their official targets the oil plants, steel foundries and transport links in the region. There was a tacit understanding that there could be no guarantee of avoiding civilian casualties, but still the Air Staff insisted in their directive to Bomber Command that targets should be identified positively before they were attacked, and added, 'In no circumstances should night bombing be allowed to degenerate into mere indiscriminate action, which is contrary to the policy of His Majesty's Government.' Rotterdam had brought Germany's home territory under the bomb-sights of the Royal Air Force, but despite it the British still maintained the official appearance of restraint so far as the explicit targeting of civilians was concerned.[22]

The limited and largely ineffectual nature of Britain's bombing efforts in the early stages of the war not only lasted until early 1942, but in fact got worse. The exception was Bomber Command's work in attacking the ships and barges being gathered for Operation Sealion, Germany's projected invasion of Britain in the summer of 1940. Here something of a victory could be claimed. The Command's bombers repeatedly attacked assemblages of German shipping in the Atlantic ports of occupied Europe, and achieved significant results in the process, making a vital contribution to the failure of Hitler's invasion plans.

Operation Sealion was scheduled to begin on 15 September; on 12 September Germany's Navy Group West HQ signalled to Berlin: 'Interruptions caused by the enemy's air forces, long-range artillery and light naval forces have become a major problem. The harbours of Ostend, Dunkirk, Calais and Boulogne cannot be used as night anchorages because of the danger of English bombing and shelling.' The next line of text doubtless warned Hitler that his invasion plans were very seriously at risk, for it underlined Goering's failure to conquer the English skies – 'Units of the British Fleet are now able to operate almost unmolested in the Channel' – and this was the achievement of RAF Fighter Command in the Battle of Britain. But the contribution of the bombers was clear. 'Owing to these difficulties,' Navy Group West HQ continued, 'further delays are expected in the assembly of the invasion fleet.' The clear implication was that an invasion could not take place until October at the earliest; by which time the tides and weather would be against it.

Hitler postponed the invasion to 17 September. On the morning of the preceding day Navy Group West HQ sent another signal about the effects of RAF bombing: 'Considerable casualties have been inflicted on transports in Antwerp. Five transport steamers have been badly damaged, one barge sunk, two cranes destroyed, and an ammunition train blown up. Several sheds are still burning.' That night bombers sank a flotilla of invasion barges and two transport ships at sea off Boulogne, while all the ports along the coast between Antwerp and Le Havre were subjected to heavy attacks. On the day scheduled for the invasion Navy Group West HQ again signalled Berlin, 'The very severe bombing together with naval bombardment from across the Channel makes it necessary to disperse the naval and transport vessels already concentrated in the Channel, and to stop further movement of shipping to the invasion ports.'

Hitler had urged Goering to a last all-out endeavour to capture the skies over the Channel and southern England, and the hardest and most famous efforts of RAF Fighter Command's 'Few' followed during the course of that week. When it was at last clear that the Luftwaffe had failed, Hitler ordered the invasion fleet to be dismantled and dispersed, well away from Bomber Command's attentions.

As this shows, although most glory rightly belongs to the RAF's hard-pressed fighter pilots – it does not put matters too high to say that for a few critical weeks in the summer of 1940, world history rested in the hands of a few hundred young Britons – nevertheless the bomber crews also played an important role in combating the invasion menace. It was perhaps one of the best moments of the RAF's bomber war, though it has never been characterised as such.

But Bomber Command's efforts to hurt Germany by disrupting its communications and industry were greatly less successful. Attacks on canals (which transported a third of German production) and railway marshalling yards were persistent, costly and mainly ineffective. The huge marshalling yards at Hamm, the nerve centre of the German railway system, were attacked eighty-five times in the year June 1940 to June 1941 – that is an average of three times a fortnight – with scarcely any impact on movement of trains.[23] A scheme to drop incendiary bombs on German forests and crops was also tried, but soon abandoned; the surplus numbers of incendiaries manufactured for this endeavour were kept in stock, and later dropped on cities when 'area bombing' began in earnest.

The next step towards the all-out war of area bombing occurred on the night of 24–5 August 1940. On that night a group of Luftwaffe bombers accidentally dropped their loads on London. They had been aiming for the Short aircraft factory at Rochester and the nearby oil-storage tanks on the banks of the Thames, but they were off course. The next morning a furious signal from Goering to the headquarters of the luckless bomber group announced that the aircrews responsible were to be transferred to infantry duties straight away.

In London, however, no one knew that the bombing was a mistake. The War Cabinet ordered an immediate retaliation in the interests of boosting home morale, overriding the protests of Bomber Command, which did not feel that it had enough time to prepare. A force of eighty-one bombers was mustered and sent to Berlin the very next night, 25–6 August. Only a third of them claimed to have got there and dropped their bombs on the designated targets; a further third said that they had found Berlin but in the difficult weather could not see well enough to identify their targets; and the rest – save for three aircraft that were lost – either bombed alternative targets or aborted and returned home early.

The material effect of the raid was that a few bombs fell on the outskirts of Berlin, doing scarcely any harm to anything other than Goering's reputation, for he had been adamant beforehand that the RAF would never be able to bomb the city. Its residents were shocked by the attack, and more so by others that followed in the ensuing weeks. Morale plummeted, a fact reported to London by independent observers. (Later, when Berlin became the subject of a major area-bombing campaign, morale did the exact opposite, rising not falling; proving the paradoxical nature of civilian responses to crisis conditions.) News of the effect on morale encouraged the Air Staff in

London to continue attacking Berlin whenever weather and other circumstances permitted, with its electricity and gas supplies as the official targets. 'The primary aim of these attacks,' said the relevant Air Staff Directive to Sir Charles Portal, then chief of Bomber Command, 'will be to cause the greatest possible disturbance and dislocation both to the industrial activities and to the civil population generally in the area.' Among Bomber Command's other duties, which during late 1940 and the whole of 1941 involved attempts to bomb the German navy and its dockyards, Berlin was therefore a recurrent target, and with it other industrial and transportation targets in Germany.

The restriction to visually identified targets remained, and with it the official avoidance of deliberate bombing of civilians, though the words 'the greatest possible disturbance and dislocation . . . to the civil population' suggest that thought on the matter was evolving. And indeed, as events proved, the days of both restrictions were numbered, because the most significant event in the bombing war during this early period now happened: the promotion on 25 October 1940 of Sir Charles Portal to the position of Chief of the Air Staff, his place as head of Bomber Command being taken by Sir Richard Peirse. With hindsight one can see that Portal's appointment was a crucial factor in the changes soon to come in Bomber Command strategy; for it was he who, more than anyone else – though enthusiastically supported by Sir Arthur Harris, who succeeded Peirse in early 1942 – led the way to deliberate targeting of civilian populations in Germany's cities.

The first indication of Portal's influence in this respect came five days after his appointment as Chief. On that day he sent Peirse his first directive. The directive told Peirse that Bomber Command's priorities were to be Germany's oil supplies and its aluminium and component factories. But it also ominously said that regular large-scale attacks were to be carried out on major urban areas and industrial centres, 'with the primary aim of causing very heavy material destruction which will demonstrate to the enemy the power and severity of air bombardment and the hardship and dislocation which will result from it'.

When Portal's first directive was issued, no one could have guessed what its words would soon come to mean in real terms; but they had cast a die.

Thus was Portal's presence announced, less than a week into his new responsibilities. By itself it was not intended to herald a change towards an area-bombing strategy, and it did not amount to a repudiation of the hitherto official policy of eschewing indiscriminate bombing of targets where civilian casualties were likely. This was to come some months later, on 9 July 1941. But between Portal's first directive and the July 1941 directive, RAF bomber crews gradually became less observant of the restrictions that had hitherto hampered it. Its efforts to bomb industrial and port targets in Germany increasingly, and without censure, caused 'collateral damage' to housing and civilian facilities near the factories, marshalling yards, oil installations and harbour-works that it attacked.

The thoughts forming in Portal's mind were much influenced by the London Blitz, which was already in full swing, having started on 7 September with a large-scale raid on the Docklands area of the city.[24] According to one version of events, the Luftwaffe's switch from bombing Fighter Command airfields to bombing London – thereby easing the pressure on Fighter Command, no small factor in its ability to hold on to English skies, and hence a fatal error by Germany – was part of the tit-for-tat begun by the accidental Luftwaffe bombing of London on 24–5 August, and the RAF's retaliatory bombing of Berlin on the next and subsequent nights. Hitler had been at his retreat at the Berghof during August, but when Berlin was bombed he returned to the city and summoned to his office Field Marshal Erhard Milch, Inspector-General of the Luftwaffe and Goering's deputy. Hitler ordered Milch to increase the manufacture of heavy bombs, evidently with a change of bombing tactics in mind. A few days later Hitler addressed a mass rally at the Sportpalast in Berlin, in the course of which he spoke about the RAF bombing raids, saying that since he had driven the British into the channel he had deliberately not responded to the provocation of their bombing raids, but that now, lest they take this as a sign of weakness, he was going to teach them a lesson. In his familiar and carefully rehearsed mounting style of rhetoric, he said to wild acclaim,

> If the British air force drops two thousand or three thousand or four thousand kilograms of bombs, then we shall drop a hundred and fifty thousand, two hundred and thirty thousand, three hundred thousand, four hundred thousand, one million kilograms . . . When they say that they will attack our cities, then we will wipe out their cities . . . The hour will come when one of us will break, but it will not be National Socialist Germany![25]

No doubt this is part of the explanation for the change of Luftwaffe tactics, but there were other factors too. According to Paul Deichmann, a former Luftwaffe general and author of a post-war study of the Luftwaffe, military reasons were chief among them.[26] These were that Luftwaffe intelligence had overestimated the losses of RAF fighters in 11 Group, based to the south and south-east of London, and now wished to draw the fighter reserves of 12 Group into the fray from north of London. Attacking the capital would be the perfect way to do this. Deichmann claimed that he had been personally told as much by Field Marshal Albert von Kesselring, who with his other commanders had been assessing the balance of forces preparatory to launching Operation Sealion.

But the reliability of this account is thrown into doubt by the fact that when the Luftwaffe switched its attack to London, it did so primarily at night, when not only its own fighter escorts were unable to fly, but the RAF fighters found it difficult to fly also. The night-bombing tactic was therefore irrelevant to the object of defeating the British fighter force in the sky, and since it involved no attacks on 12 Group airfields, neither would it destroy it on the ground.

The switch to night bombing is in fact much more plausibly explained by the Luftwaffe's high losses during the Battle of Britain. In the six weeks between 15 July and 31 August 1940 the Luftwaffe had 621 bombers destroyed, with 344 damaged, a casualty rate of 69 per cent. Add this to the 724 lost or damaged aircraft in the period between 10 May and mid-July – that is, between the invasion of the Low Countries and the beginning of the Battle of Britain – and it becomes evident that the Luftwaffe's attrition rate was too high to be sustainable. Speaking in 1945, the commander of the German fighters in Luftflotte III, which fought in the Battle of Britain, said that he had urged a change to night attacks early in the battle because of the Luftwaffe's high losses; he described the battle as 'a sort of air-Verdun, in which the Germans were at a disadvantage'.[27]

It is clear enough that the new aim premised by the change to bombing London and other cities – for London was not alone in receiving the visitations of the Luftwaffe from September 1940 onwards – was the hope that it would disrupt British war production and affect 'morale'. General Jodl had said as early as 30 June 1940 that 'occasional terror raids announced as "reprisals", and the depletion of Britain's food stocks, will paralyse the people's will to resist, and eventually break it altogether, forcing their government to surrender'.[28] Hitler made it clear that he alone would decide if and when bombing should explicitly target civilians, though it was obviously a live option for him; 'if eight million go mad, it would be a catastrophe; after that even a little invasion would go a long way,' he remarked.[29] But the ostensible target of Luftwaffe bombing was the economic and industrial capacity of Britain, and its governmental institutions. Thus the full force of German bombing was felt by London's docks, the City, Whitehall, and the dense residential districts of the East End and south London where the capital's factories were mainly located. When British civilian casualties mounted, Berlin could claim both that they were (to use more recent terminology) 'collateral damage', and also revenge for RAF bombing of German civilians.

The Luftwaffe's effort to disrupt Britain's economy and pound its population into submission lasted from 7 September 1940 until the German invasion of Russia in May 1941. The result was considerable destruction – one raid alone, on 29 December 1940, almost obliterated the City of London – and by the end of that period there were 30,000 British dead and 50,000 injured. But civilian morale did not break, and the British economy did not falter; war production increased quickly and steadily throughout the period, and continued to do so for the rest of the war.

But no one in Britain took these facts to be any indication of the inadequacy of bombing to bring about the submission of an enemy. As both the British and the Germans knew, the Luftwaffe lacked the means to do worse, because it had no true heavy bomber. One was planned – the Heinkel 177 – and if it had come into existence in large numbers and had been used to assault Britain, the result might have been more like the devastation caused to Germany by the genuinely big heavy bombers that entered Allied service as the war progressed.

Even so, the Blitz was a horrific event, which did much to make the idea of severe retaliation against German cities more acceptable – even, indeed, welcome – to many in the British (and later, when the United States entered the war in December 1941, the American) public at large – though not, as we shall see, to all.

If any one event in the Blitz was especially significant in preparing the ground for the strategy hinted by Portal in his first directive, it was not any of the raids on London, but the devastating attack on Coventry on the night of 14–15 November 1940. The psychological effect of this attack, the largest and most intense air raid of the war to that point, was enormous; but not in shaking British will: rather the contrary. And it turned American and world opinion against Germany even more.

It has been claimed that the War Cabinet knew there was going to be a massive attack on Coventry, but took no action in order to protect its intelligence sources.[30] Whether or not this claim is true, the fact is that Bomber Command attempted pre-emptive attacks on Luftwaffe bomber airfields in France and Belgium that night, having at least been told that a major raid was expected on an unnamed British city.[31] German propaganda after the Coventry attack said that it was a retaliation for RAF bombing of Munich. The Bomber Command War Diaries record a number of raids on unspecified German cities in the preceding two months, and one of them might well have been Munich, but the city is not mentioned by name. When one sets the cultural and (to the Nazis) political importance of Munich alongside the severity of the Coventry raid, the claim comes to have a ring of truth.

The raid on Coventry lasted ten hours, starting at twenty minutes past seven in the evening of 14 November 1940, and ending at a quarter past six the following morning. The German communiqué which described the raid as a retaliation for Munich went on to say that the bombing was targeted at the many military-related engineering works in the city, but contemporary British reports pointed out that because of the heavy anti-aircraft fire that greeted them, the Luftwaffe aircraft had to maintain very high altitudes from which accurate bombing was impossible. The result was that HE and incendiary bombs fell everywhere on the city indiscriminately. Night-fighting skills and technical capacities were still very rudimentary in RAF Fighter Command, which was therefore unable to do much to mitigate the attack.

The German communiqué went on to claim that the raid was the heaviest of the war, with over 500 bombers involved. The damage they did to Coventry was extensive: its fourteenth-century cathedral was destroyed, its tram system smashed, its gas and water supplies put out of action, four and a half thousand of its houses demolished, three-quarters of its factories damaged, and 600 of its citizens killed, with over 800 more injured.

This was not the first attack on Coventry – there had been several minor ones in preceding weeks – and it was not the last; the city was bombed forty-one more times in the course of the war, and had to put up with hundreds of air-raid alarms when Luftwaffe bombers were on their way to other cities. But this was the biggest attack Coventry suffered, and the psychological effect on the nation and its government was profound.

Given that London had been suffering under a nightly blitz since September, the special significance attached to the attack on Coventry in the moonlit middle of November 1940 might seem odd. But as the Official Narrative observes, the Coventry bombing was 'an occasion of singular importance in the history of air warfare', because for the first time in history, air power 'was massively applied against a city of small proportions with the object of ensuring its obliteration'.[32]

In the winter of 1940–1 Bomber Command was no bigger than it had been a year before in numbers of front-line aircraft, but it was nevertheless gaining strength as a consequence of the inflow of newly trained aircrews, many of them from the Dominions and colonies (together with several squadrons of French and Polish fliers who had escaped to Britain), and the gearing-up of aircraft and munitions production. The first new heavy four-engined bombers did not begin to arrive in service until later in 1941, bringing teething-troubles with them, but the existing bombers were by now somewhat improved, with self-sealing fuel tanks and armour-plating fitted over vulnerable points.

During this winter and the following spring and summer of 1941, Peirse's bombers made fitful efforts to find and bomb oil plants, and made many sorties against industrial cities and ports, among them Essen, Cologne, Dusseldorf, Duisberg, Kiel, Hamburg and Bremen. Berlin remained a target whenever opportunity offered, and frequently Bomber Command had to take a part in the vital Battle of the Atlantic, a war of tonnages between German U-boats and merchant convoys crossing from America with vital supplies. So far as results were concerned, Bomber Command's main thrust against industrial and port targets remained largely ineffectual, and sometimes quite nugatory, as when photographs taken during an air raid supposedly on the giant Krupp armament works in Essen showed that the bombers had flattened a forest instead.

As this incident showed, the worst problems affecting Bomber Command related to navigation and bombing accuracy. Aircrews were wont to claim that they had reached targets and bombed them, though some of them realised that their endeavours were often extremely approximate. In the summer of 1941 Lord Cherwell, Churchill's scientific adviser, persuaded the latter to have bombing efficiency investigated by a member of the War Cabinet Secretariat, Daniel M. Butt. Butt studied hundreds of photographs taken during and after bombing operations, and compared them with aircrew reports and target orders. His devastating conclusions were published in August 1941. They were that many bomber aircraft never found their targets at all; even in good weather on moonlit nights, only two-fifths of bombers found their targets, but in hazy or rainy weather only one in ten did so. On moonless nights the proportion fell to a hopeless one in fifteen. In all circumstances, of those that reached their designated target only a third of them placed their bombs within five miles of it.[33]

On these results, the bombing campaign was a massively wasteful and futile effort. In September 1941 Portal sent Churchill a plan for 'Coventry-style' attacks on Germany's forty-five largest cities, claiming that if a force of 4,000 bombers could be built up and unleashed in this fashion, the war would come to an end in six months. But Churchill, still fuming in response to the Butt Report, replied, 'It is very debatable whether bombing by itself will be a decisive factor in the present war . . . the most we can say is that it will be a heavy and I trust seriously increasing annoyance.'[34] The reasons he gave were that Luftwaffe defences would quite likely overwhelm the bomber attack, that only a quarter of bombs were falling anywhere near their targets, and that anyway the British population had shown that being bombed merely 'stimulated and strengthened' civilian resistance.

Portal knew that despite the Butt Report and Churchill's irritation, Bomber Command was all that Britain had in the way of an offensive arm, so he responded quietly by reminding Churchill that new navigation and bomb-aiming technologies were being devised, and that new heavy bombers were being built to benefit from them. He received in reply a less cantankerous letter assuring him that Bomber Command would continue to receive full support from the War Cabinet for its role.

And by this time its role had come 180 degrees round from the one to which it had been restricted in the war's opening months. For on 9 July 1941 Portal's Air Staff – with the sanction of course of the War Cabinet – had issued a new directive to Bomber Command, switching its primary attention from oil and naval targets to 'dislocating the German transportation system' and '*destroying the morale of the civil population as a whole and of the industrial workers in particular*'.[35] With these fateful words the area bombing campaign became explicit and deliberate policy.[36]

There was one final step before the area-bombing policy began to take major effect. Sir Richard Peirse was still in charge of Bomber Command, and his Command was still doing its best with inadequate aircraft and navigation aids all through 1941, until a disastrous raid on Berlin on the night of 7–8 November ended his career, and caused a temporary retrenchment in the bombing campaign.

Portal's second-in-command on the Air Staff, Wilfrid Freeman, had throughout 1941 been urging Portal to discontinue raids on Berlin on the grounds that they were futile and costly, a view that he felt inclined to apply to much of the Command's efforts, as indeed the Butt Report confirmed. But Portal's response was to say that taking a few tens of tons of bombs away from other targets to 'get four million people out of bed and into the shelters' in Berlin was worth it. In fact the cost was not merely one of tonnages: loss rates of 16 per cent of aircraft sent to bomb Berlin were experienced in the summer months of 1941, with very little damage to show in return, for on every occasion less than half of the bombers sent found the city.

But on the night of 7–8 November things got even worse. It has been supposed that Peirse wished to rebut Butt by mounting an impressive attack on the German capital, and for that reason mustered the biggest force of the war so far – 392 aircraft, 169 of them detailed to bomb Berlin, the rest to attack a variety of targets between the Atlantic coast and the Ruhr. In the event the weather was worse than expected, and less than half the Berlin force reached the city. Because it was at the extreme end of the range for Wellingtons and Whitleys, and because the poor weather made them suffer heavy icing which caused their straining engines to use up more fuel, most had virtually empty tanks on reaching home. But 12.5 per cent of them did not reach home. Given that the upper limit for a bearable loss rate was 5 per cent this represented not just a failure but a major disaster for Bomber Command.

Portal investigated the failure thoroughly, and in early January 1942 concluded that Peirse had displayed poor judgement in authorising the attacks to go ahead when the weather reports showed that they should be aborted. Within days of Portal's discussing his findings with Churchill, Peirse was sent to command the nascent air forces in the Far East, and a man of quite different character and talents was summoned to take his place: Sir Arthur Harris.

When Harris took up his post at Bomber Command HQ in High Wycombe on 22 February 1942 he was forty-nine years of age, and looked like a portly and not very friendly bank manager of the old-fashioned type. His appearance completely belied his colourful past. He had left school at the age of seventeen to go to Rhodesia, with the aim of learning how to farm. By the age of twenty-one he was a farm manager, but in the interim had also engaged in gold-mining, cattle-ranching, game-hunting, and driving teams of oxen. At the outbreak of the 1914–18 war he joined the Royal Rhodesian Regiment and walked hundreds of miles through the veld of South-West Africa, hunting Germans. Determined henceforth to 'go to war sitting down' he returned to England, mastered the rudiments of flying in a half-hour lesson at Brooklands airfield, and was commissioned into the

Royal Flying Corps. He had experience both as a night-fighter shooting down Zeppelins over England, and as a squadron commander on the Western Front. Daily from his cockpit he saw the miles of trenches and mud and struggling men central to that epic struggle, and the sight engendered in him an emphatic belief: that wars should be won from the air. That opinion was unchanged when he took the helm of Bomber Command twenty-five years later.

During the 1920s Harris commanded squadrons in the Middle East and India, and developed techniques of night-bombing with the already obsolescent aircraft then in service, among them the Vickers Virginia two-engined 'heavy bomber' biplane. He made the standard ascent of all senior officers through staff college, and served in the Air Ministry and in procurement in the United States, from which he wrote acerbic memoranda about the taste displayed by American military personnel for hot dogs (Harris was a gourmet – indeed perhaps, as his figure suggests, a gourmand). But in between he was Air Officer Commanding Bomber Command's No. 5 Group, then equipped with the difficult and inadequate Hampdens. His handling of this command, evidenced by his lower than average loss rate despite at the same time showing an appetite for attack, had demonstrated his qualities to Portal before the latter asked him to serve as his deputy on the Air Staff. It was here, evidently, when the two men were in daily contact, that Portal saw in Harris the man he wanted for Bomber Command HQ at High Wycombe, for it cannot be doubted that their thinking about bombing strategy was very close, that Portal's belief in area bombing as the way to win the war exactly chimed with Harris's view, and that the policies which issued from the Air Staff under Portal's leadership indubitably had input from Harris. One night during the Blitz – the night of 29 December 1940 – Harris and Portal went up on the Air Ministry roof to watch the City of London burning under Luftwaffe attack, and saw the dome of St Paul's 'standing out in the midst of an ocean of fire'.[37] After watching in silence for a time, Harris said to Portal, 'Well, they are sowing the wind.'[38]

*   *   *

The bombing force that Harris took over was still weak, but beginning to grow in strength and capability. It had recently been equipped with a new navigational device called GEE, and with increasing numbers of the new four-engined heavy bombers that first appeared on drawing-boards in 1936. Chief among them was the Avro Lancaster, a remarkably successful aircraft which became the mainstay of the bomber force, and which flew its first operational sorties in March 1942 within weeks of Harris taking office.

Much more pertinent, though, was a new directive from the Air Staff, which had been issued on 14 February 1942 in preparation for Harris's assumption of command at High Wycombe. It stated in unequivocal terms, 'The *primary object* of your operations should now be focused on *the morale of the enemy civil population*, and in particular on the industrial workers.'[39] In the summer of that year a pamphlet was dropped on Germany, purporting to be the text of a broadcast given (in German) by Harris, warning its population of the dire threat it faced:

> We are bombing Germany, city by city, and ever more terribly, in order to make it impossible for you to go on with the war. That is our object. We shall pursue it remorselessly. City by city; Lubeck, Rostock, Cologne, Emden, Bremen, Wilhelmshaven, Duisberg, Hamburg – and the list will grow longer and longer. Let the Nazis drag you down to disaster with them if you will. That is for you to decide . . . We are coming by day and by night. No part of the Reich is safe . . . people who work in [factories] live close to them. Therefore we hit your houses, and you.[40]

In fact Harris himself made no such broadcast; it was a propaganda exercise by 'enthusiastic amateurs', as Harris called them, in the Political Warfare Department, seeking to profit from the alarm in Germany caused by the first series of raids organised by Harris. The sanguinary tones of the supposed broadcast attracted criticism from those opposed to the idea of 'saturation' or 'carpet' bombing (terms more accurately descriptive than 'area bombing'), which annoyed Harris, who took himself to be doing his best to win the war. As it happens, Harris had agreed to the use of his name on the pamphlet without reading it; but nothing in his views would have led him to disagree with its contents anyway.[41]

Because Bomber Command's primary focus was now the 'enemy civil population', the Air Staff was eager to experiment with a bombing technique using a high proportion of incendiaries. For this purpose the old Hanseatic city of Lubeck on the Baltic coast was chosen, because it contained many timbered buildings dating from medieval times. As justification for the attack it is always said that Lubeck was the main port for iron ore entering Germany from neutral Sweden, and moreover was home to a U-boat training station. But the timbered medieval buildings were a temptation for incendiary experiments, and therefore on the night of 28–9 March 1942 a force of 234 RAF bombers took off, of which 191 claimed to reach the target. 'The result,' writes Denis Richards, 'was devastation on a scale never before inflicted by Bomber Command; the later raiders could see the conflagration a hundred miles ahead.'[42] Harris himself wrote, 'On the night of 28–9 March, the first German city went up in flames.' A thousand people died in Lubeck; within a month another of the wooden Hanseatic cities was in ashes, this time Rostock, 70 per cent destroyed in three raids between 23 and 26 April. Here the ostensible justification was a persuasive one – there was a Heinkel factory in the city's southern suburbs.

The outrage in the German leadership at the destruction of these medieval towns inspired the retaliatory 'Baedeker' raids on Norwich, Bath, Exeter, York and (later, as a reprisal for the massive Cologne attack of 30–1 May) Canterbury. In fact the Baedeker raids began even before the Rostock bombing; Exeter was attacked on 23 April as a reprisal for the attack on Lubeck, but the fact that Rostock was attacked on the same night angered the Germans more. On 24 April Baron Gustav Braun von Sturm said, 'We shall go out and bomb every building in Britain marked with three stars in the Baedeker Guide', thus giving the series of raids their name. The Luftwaffe's reprisals killed 1,637 people, injured 1,760, and destroyed 50,000 buildings, including York's ancient Guildhall and Bath's beautiful Assembly Rooms.[43] At this stage of the war it might have seemed as if it was not only the Luftwaffe that was sowing the wind; but the balance of power was altering inexorably against Germany in the bombing war, as Harris's ambitions very soon showed. For Lubeck and Rostock had whetted his appetite for an even greater spectacular: a 1,000-bomber raid to wipe out a city and prove his contention that bombing can win a war by terrifying and pounding a population into surrender. It was also part of his and Portal's motivation to erase the impression of ineffectiveness left by Peirse on the minds of the War Cabinet. Thus was 'Operation Millennium' – the 1,000-bomber raid on Cologne – set in motion.

The effective front-line force that Harris inherited when he first stepped through the doors at Bomber Command HQ in High Wycombe was 600 aircraft. To launch 1,000 aircraft into the sky all at the same time meant that he had to get the support of Training Command, Coastal Command, and Army Co-operation Command. He wrote to their respective chiefs to say that he, with the backing of Portal and the Air Staff, 'proposed at about the full moon to put over the maximum force of bombers on a single and extremely important town in Germany, with a view to wiping it out in one night, or at least two'.[44] The city chosen was Hamburg, with Cologne as second choice. Preparations involved ground crews working long hours to make all the aircraft ready, among other things fitting a number of them with GEE equipment, necessitating special training for the navigators who were to use them.

The idea was that by massing 1,000 bombers over a city in the space of an hour and a half, the defences of the city – its fire-fighters and medical services as well as its anti-aircraft batteries – would be overwhelmed, and the concentration of explosive and incendiary power would lay it waste. The fear of collisions among so many aircraft was abated by organising the fleet into three separate bomber streams issued with careful timing instructions; the bombing was to be carried out from 8,000 feet, and the aircraft were loaded with a maximum capacity of incendiaries, among them a seeding of delayed-fuse 4-lb. 'X' bombs designed to kill or scare away fire-fighters after they had arrived at the scene of a blaze.

Despite the last-minute withdrawal of Coastal Command aircraft because of Admiralty fears about the effect of their absence on the Atlantic battle, and despite several days of delays occasioned by adverse weather, Harris at last made his choice of which target to attack. It was Cologne. At 9 p.m. on the evening of 30 May his mighty air fleet took off, carrying with it Harris's hope of persuading his political masters to continue building the air armada he believed could win the war. Interestingly, at this point the available armada was still technically far below what Harris knew would be required for the devastation of Germany by bombs; his first 1,000-bomber fleet contained over 600 Wellingtons, and only seventy-three Lancasters.

Nevertheless the 900 bombers that reached the target between them dropped 915 tons of incendiaries and 840 tons of high explosives. More damage was done to the city on this one night than all previous air raids on it put together. Over 600 acres of the city were flattened, and its gas, water, electricity and transport amenities badly disrupted. Some 13,000 buildings were destroyed, making 45,000 people homeless; but amazingly for an attack of such magnitude, only 469 people were killed – a mark of the level of preparedness of German cities, whose air-raid precautions and shelters were extremely well organised.

British public morale was greatly boosted by the raid, and Harris's gamble – he had committed his entire front line and all his reserves in one throw of the dice – was vindicated. He had wanted to show what a really big air raid could do, and it was from his point of view an unqualified success. In his memoirs he wrote, 'My own opinion is that we should never have had a real bomber offensive if it had not been for the 1000 bomber attack on Cologne, an irrefutable demonstration of the power of what was to all intents and purposes a new and untried weapon.'[45]

But what also convinced Churchill and the War Cabinet to continue building Bomber Command's strength was the fact Harris did not have the resources to repeat such a large attack more than two more times that summer. The second 1,000-bomber attack was against Essen, and was largely unsuccessful because the bomber streams became spread out in time and space, and scattered their loads to little real effect over a wide area of the Ruhr. The third, against Bremen, was less successful still, proving expensive in lost aircraft because the weather was adverse and the inexperienced crews sent to make up numbers suffered badly at the German defenders' hands.

Harris was experimenting against the day when he had the right bombers in the right numbers to prove his theory that very big bomber formations would overwhelm defences by delivering their loads in a concentrated manner over a short period of time, the aim being to cause destruction, shock and casualties on a scale that would bring about logistical paralysis and the failure of the German will to fight. But in the summer of 1942 his Command was still in the process of re-equipping with the new big bombers, and although the pace of production and training was rising all the time, it had not yet reached the levels he and Portal required. And of course problems remained. The need for better navigation and bomb-aiming was only fitfully being met, with GEE sometimes proving effective and sometimes not, and bomb-sights and aiming effectiveness still far from satisfactory. The War Diaries suggest that between half and three-quarters of bombs dropped in this period were still well off target.[46] Moreover the German defences were improving all the time; Bomber Command's average loss rate in the first half of 1942 was 4.3 per cent of sorties, and the percentage kept rising over the rest of the year.

Nevertheless there could be no remission of the bombing war; one of the chief factors in necessitating its continuation at the highest possible intensity was that Russia was in desperate straits, and needed its Western allies to do everything they could to distract as much of Germany's attention from the Eastern Front as they could.[47]

The first task was to make Bomber Command's efforts count for more by addressing the deficiencies in navigation. Against Harris's initial resistance the Air Staff formed a special group, the Pathfinder Force, to achieve excellence in navigation and to lead bombing raids to their targets, there to mark them with flares and to drop incendiaries so that following bombers could use the resulting fires as aiming-points.[48]

The Pathfinders had a sticky start, the first raids they led going badly astray. Indeed on the very first of them the force they led ended by bombing a village in Denmark instead of their proper target, which was a submarine yard in Flensburg on the Baltic coast. To make matters worse, German scientists had now worked out how to jam GEE. Even when the Pathfinders began to find their targets with a higher degree of accuracy, as in the attack on Nuremberg on the night of 28–9 August 1942, ill luck still seemed to dog Bomber Command's efforts; 14 per cent of the bombers on this raid were lost, a disastrous number. The main victims were the now-ageing Wellingtons, still forming one-third of the bomber force, but failing badly in their contest with German air defences. Their replacements – the Halifaxes, Lancasters and Stirlings (these latter, with their inability to make good altitude, a rather unsuccessful aircraft) – were still feeling their way into service.

Bomber Command might have welcomed some relief in this transitional period, as new aircraft and techniques were coming on stream, but events in the wider war would not permit them to have it. The fighting in North Africa was intensifying, and the Command had to include Italy in its work. Genoa, Milan, Turin and other targets took up the bulk of its efforts in the autumn months of 1942; 1,646 sorties were flown against Italy, with a loss rate of only 3.7 per cent. The Italian raids were understandably popular with aircrews, who found the defences they encountered there much weaker than German ones.

By the end of 1942 keen-eyed spectators could see that the tide was turning in the war in almost all its aspects, and Bomber Command was not excepted. In Russia the Germans were suffering major setbacks, prefiguring the terrible nemesis of Hitler's aggressions. While Allied arms were beginning to enjoy success in North Africa – Montgomery's offensive at El Alamein began on 23 October, and the Anglo-American landings in French North Africa took place in November – Bomber Command was beginning to feel the effect of new technologies designed to solve its navigation and bomb-aiming problems. These were OBOE, a long-distance wireless navigational aid directing aircraft to their targets, and H2S, a radar system for recognising what lay below an aircraft, so that it could locate its target from above and aim more accurately. OBOE could only direct a few aircraft at a time, but with the Pathfinder Force finding its feet this was not too great a restriction. H2S promised greater effectiveness all round, but especially in bad weather. Gadgets were becoming available for countering German defence technology too, among them a means of jamming German radar.

These advances came not a moment too soon. Bomber Command's loss rate had crept up to 6.7 per cent by the autumn of 1942 (recall that the maximum acceptable rate was 5 percent, and even that was too high: it meant lives as well as aircraft lost), and most of the increase was owed to the growing effectiveness of the Luftwaffe's night-fighters. But things were changing. What Harris in his memoirs called 'the preliminary phase' was over; he could now contemplate mounting a proper offensive. The new heavy bombers were entering Bomber Command's squadrons in real force as 1943 dawned. During the preceding year, leaving aside the artificially concocted 1,000-bomber raids, the average maximum force that could be sent against a target was 250 aircraft, with a large admixture of the increasingly obsolescent types. In the first months of 1943 the average was 450 aircraft, almost all of the new large four-engined type.[49] Two-thirds of the squadrons in Bomber Command were equipped with Lancasters and Halifaxes by the spring of 1943, and by that year's end there were sixty-five operational bomber squadrons, four of them equipped with the fast, high-flying wooden Mosquitoes, which were superbly adapted for the tasks of reconnaissance, pathfinding, target marking, and photography after the event. This was a major boost in offensive power; the new heavy aircraft carried more than double the bomb load of the old – two and a half tons as against one ton. Accompanied by improved Pathfinder performance and the new technological aids, this increase in striking capability represented a sea-change.[50]

And this was just part of a continuing increase in strength; the curve was reaching upwards on an ever steeper slope. By March 1944 an average of 1,000 aircraft was available each day to Harris, by then all of the heavy type.[51]

In all, Portal and Harris could hope for a much more effective year in 1943. Harris was especially keen to prove his theory, long since abandoned by Churchill and the War Cabinet, and by now perhaps only half held by Portal, that intense bombing could win the war by itself. Although Churchill no longer agreed with Harris on this point, he nevertheless remained convinced that bombing was an important element of the war effort. At the Casablanca Conference held at the beginning of that year (14–23 January 1943), he and President Roosevelt of the United States decided that round-the-clock bombing of Germany was an important adjunct of their aim to invade Europe, first through Sicily in 1943, and then through France in 1944.

As this last point shows, a highly important added factor was by then in the picture. This was that the United States Army Air Force had entered the bombing war against Germany too, its contributions increasing during 1943. Its efforts were tentative at first, and attended by heavy losses because its aircraft bombed by day and did not yet have long-range fighter-plane protection. But by the beginning of 1944 the American bomber force was having a powerful effect.

In fact, units of the US Eighth Army Air Force had first arrived in Britain in 1942 under the command of General Ira Eaker, but they needed time to prepare, and their first bombing raid was not carried out until 17 August 1942, a modest affair comprising eighteen B-17s under Spitfire escort, which bombed a factory near Rouen in France. By the end of the air war in April 1945 the presence of the USAAF was a decisive factor; the 'Mighty Eighth', as its England-based bomber force came to be called, was then deploying 200,000 personnel in the European theatre, and could put 2,000 aircraft into the air at any one time, its raids defended by the exceptionally effective Mustang and Lightning long-range fighters. But all this was yet to come.

Harris could not embark on an all-out bombing war on Germany straight away, though, because his Command was called upon to help in the Battle of the Atlantic by attacking Germany's submarine bases. Harris believed in advance that these attacks would be a futile distraction – and so indeed they proved; the submarine pens lay under impenetrable masses of concrete, and were unaffected by bombing, though the French coastal towns and populations around them were not. Harris fumed, eager to use his new resources to pound Germany itself.

At last, in March, he was able to return his attention to this task. Between 5 March and the end of July 1943 Harris waged what he called 'the Battle of the Ruhr', aimed at causing maximum damage and disruption to the industrial cities of the Ruhr valley, and the workers who lived in them. It began with an attack on Essen, where the huge Krupps armament factories were situated, and continued with repeated visits to Essen, Duisberg and Bochum. In the longer nights of the early part of the battle, Harris sent his bombers elsewhere in Germany also – to Berlin, Kiel, Frankfurt, Stuttgart and Mannheim among other targets – but as the days shortened, making the longer flights into Germany more hazardous, he concentrated more intensively on the Ruhr, and caused great material damage to its towns: Dortmund and Mulheim were devastated, as were Wuppertal and Elbefeld, and Bochum and Oberhausen were not much less severely handled. In the attack on Elbefeld on 24–5 June, in which 630 bombers took part, more than 1,800 people were killed.

If anything showed the increasing power of Bomber Command's attacks, it was the fact that when 600 of its aircraft bombed Cologne on the night of 3–4 July, they did more damage than the previous year's 1,000-bomber raid, in the process killing 4,400 people. A repeat attack five nights later added greatly to the process of 'dehousing' the city's population; the two raids destroyed the homes of 350,000 people in all. One of the express aims of the campaign was to create paralysing logistical difficulties for the Nazi authorities in having to deal with so many people dead, injured, bereft of homes and domestic resources – and of course to reduce the effectiveness of the survivors in their factory work.[52]

It seems impossible to believe that these attacks could not have had an effect on industrial output and therefore the German capacity to wage war. Yet – in ways and for reasons to be discussed later – whatever the disruption and inconvenience, until close to the end of the war German industrial production continued to rise. Bomb damage to factories was repaired within days or at most weeks, and output resumed.

Even the most spectacular of the bombing achievements of 1943 – the Dam Buster raid – did not have the desired effect of crippling German industrial activity. The raid was an amazing feat of technology coupled with great flying skill and courage. Its heroes were Barnes Wallis, the eccentric genius who invented many unusual and sometimes effective devices of war, in this instance the celebrated 'bouncing bomb', and Guy Gibson – who won the VC for the feat – and his crews, who had to fly very low into the teeth of anti-aircraft fire to drop their bouncing bombs accurately. Eight of the nineteen aircraft that carried out the attack were lost; 52 out of their 133 aircrew were killed, and three captured.

In the event, the breaches in the Mohne and Eder dams (the Soper dam could not be breached) did not shut off the electricity supply to the Ruhr industries, and although 1,294 people died in the rush of water from the breached dams, the figure is tiny in comparison to the hope that many towns would be drowned by flooding. The Official History states that 'the total effect was small'; its chief result was to raise morale mightily at home among the war-benighted British.[53]

If the Dam Buster raid was spectacular, the already described Hamburg attacks known as 'Operation Gomorrah' were equally so from Bomber Command's point of view. What placed their measure of destructiveness and death above that of such badly hit Ruhr towns as Wuppertal and Elbefeld was the firestorm caused by the intense concentration of bombs dropped. The Hamburg experience reinforced Harris's conviction that bombing was *par excellence* the war-winning weapon, and he was determined to continue his efforts to prove it.

But events elsewhere in the war prevented Harris from mounting any more 'Hamburgs' for the time being. The situation in Italy was poised on a knife-edge, and the War Cabinet wanted Bomber Command to turn its attention to Milan, Turin and Genoa. This was no hardship to Bomber Command's crews; they greatly preferred north Italy to Germany. The loss rate on raids there was very low, in large part because when bombing started the defenders' searchlights became stationary and the anti-aircraft guns stopped firing, suggesting that their crews knew where the better part of valour lay. Fighter defences in the Italian skies, likewise, were effectively non-existent.

Harris claimed that Bomber Command's activities in Italy were the reason for Mussolini's fall. Doubtless they were part of the reason; but there were many factors at play, and it is not clear that bombing in north Italy was individually more significant than any of those others. Allied air forces were operating over southern and central Italy with great intensity, and British and American troops were fighting their way up the peninsula. Moreover, the Italian population at large did not have, and perhaps throughout the war had never had, an appetite for Mussolini's war. Most of the fighting done in their country was by Germans.

But when the effects of Bomber Command's work over Milan and the other cities were surveyed soon afterwards, the extent of the damage it had caused was painfully clear. In Milan the factories of Alfa Romeo, Pirelli, Breda and Isotto-Fraschini among others had all been badly damaged; so had the city itself, and within it some of its treasures. La Scala opera house was damaged, and at the church of Santa Maria della Grazie just one wall remained standing – the wall bearing Leonardo's mural of the Last Supper.[54]

The Ruhr attacks, 'Operation Gomorrah', and the success of endeavours in Italy to which Bomber Command had contributed, led Churchill to write to Harris on 11 October, 'The War Cabinet have asked me to convey to you their compliments on the recent successes of Bomber Command . . . Your Command, with the day-bomber formations of the 8th Air Force fighting alongside it, is playing a foremost part in the converging attack on Germany now being conducted by the forces of the United Nations on a prodigious scale.' Churchill also had in mind the fact that Harris's bombers had also achieved success in a precision-bombing raid on Peenemunde, where Hitler's secret weapons were being developed, and had continued to inflict damage on German cities, among them Nuremberg, several times attacked and badly damaged during 1943. Harris circulated Churchill's letter to the whole of Bomber Command, together with his reply, in which he said, 'It is an unfailing sense of strength to us to realise that every bomb which leaves the racks makes smoother the path of the armies of the United Nations as they close in to the kill.'[55]

Heartened by this exchange, Harris decided that the time had come to put his theory about the war-winning capacity of bombing to a yet fuller test. The obvious target for a 'Hamburg' was Berlin, which until then had not been as hard hit as the cities of western and northern Germany because of its great distance from the bomber airfields of eastern England – it was nearly twice as far away as the cities of the Ruhr. Distance meant opportunity for the German defences, especially its night-fighters, and of course it also posed greater difficulties of navigation and greater strain on the nerves of RAF crews. But as the longer nights of the autumn of 1943 approached, Harris made his plans for an assault on Berlin, and on the night of 18–19 November he launched it, calling it 'the Battle of Berlin'. By this time he had a regular daily average of 800 bombers at his disposal, and the navigational technologies that had become available at the beginning of the year were now operating with efficiency and effectiveness. He felt that he had a real chance to show what a powerful bomber force could do. He wrote in optimistic and excited vein to Churchill saying, 'We can wreck Berlin from end to end . . . It will cost us between 400–500 aircraft. It will cost Germany the war.'

In the four months November 1943–March 1944 repeated heavy attacks were made on Germany's capital. Much damage was done, and in just two nights of raids early on – those of 22–3 and 23–4 November – 9,000 Berliners were killed or injured. Increasing use of H2S meant that the bomber stream did not have to fly along a corridor of marker flares to their target, thus showing Luftwaffe night-fighters where to find them. And Harris's increased resources meant that he could send decoy raids of several hundred aircraft against other cities, and also use a special force of fighters on 'Intruder' missions to distract the Luftwaffe night-fighters, and to jam its radar with a variety of electronic countermeasure devices which the RAF's scientists were at constant pains to invent.

Enthused by the early promise of the Berlin campaign, Harris wrote to the Air Staff, iterating his claim that his bombers could win the war by themselves provided that Lancaster production and maintenance was given the highest priority, that the successful navigational aids now available were produced more rapidly so that all – or as many as possible – of his bombers could individually have them; and that he be allowed so to organise missions that the rate of loss be kept below 5 per cent. In effect the letter was a repeat of Harris's consistently held view that if Bomber Command's needs were given priority, and if he were given operational latitude, there would be no need for a land invasion of the European continent, which meant a bloody infantry war to conquer Germany. Bombing would, he insisted, do it by itself.

Churchill's War Cabinet, and the Chiefs of Staff committee which advised it, did not stint Harris, but equally its members – Churchill included – still did not believe that bombing alone would win the war. The most they thought it would do would be to weaken Germany. And despite all the advantages accruing to Harris in aircraft numbers and technical advances, the Berlin campaign was nowhere near the success he had hoped. One reason was that Bomber Command could not even then manage to 'wreck Berlin' by itself. The words Harris had actually written to Churchill before the campaign were, 'We can wreck Berlin from end to end if the USAAF will come in on it.' This was unrealistic. One problem was that the USAAF was still not in a position to manage so deep a penetration of Germany. This, remember, was November 1943, and the long-range fighter planes needed by the American bombers for protection during their daylight attacks were only just becoming available in operational terms. At that point the Flying Fortress echelons, for all their formidable armament, were still finding their war a too costly one. Moreover, American bombers attacked by day because US policy in the European theatre remained strictly focused on precision attacks upon vital military and industrial targets, so General Ira Eaker would anyway not have been permitted to join Harris's attempt to obliterate Berlin.

All these factors meant in practical terms that the periods elapsing between each of Harris's attacks, even when they took place on successive nights, gave Berlin's population time to recover, despite the great material damage to the city's fabric. To add to the problems for Bomber Command, weather conditions were consistently against its Berlin forays, and after the promising early attacks there were a number that became diffused over target, with a rising percentage of bombs falling harmlessly in the Brandenburg countryside. On the raid of 16–17 December a disaster overtook the bombers when they returned to their bases, finding the weather there so bad that twenty-nine Lancasters crashed. Some of the crews parachuted to safety, but 140 crewmen died.

Harris's big campaign against Berlin lasted until March 1944, and took place amidst continued heavy bombing of many other cities in

Germany. It did not destroy German morale or bring the Nazi regime to its knees. Its cost to Bomber Command was high in numbers of aircraft and air crews lost; and as a result most commentators, and the Official History, conclude that 'the Battle of Berlin' was a failure. 'The Luftwaffe hurt Bomber Command more than Bomber Command hurt Berlin' was how one commentator summarised matters,[56] and the Official History's judgement was painfully brusque in going further: 'The Battle of Berlin was more than a failure, it was a defeat'.[57] One of the primary reasons was that the Luftwaffe's night-fighter and ground-defence forces had proved too effective. If circumstances elsewhere were not changing, the outcome of the 'Battle of Berlin' would have been major grounds for rethinking by everyone involved in the RAF's bomber campaign.[58]

By February 1944 the USAAF was ready to contribute greatly more to the bomber war over Germany than had hitherto been possible. In 1943 it had made a courageous and hazardous start on its daylight mission, suffering terrible casualties during its ill-fated attacks on a crucial industrial bottle-neck in the German war economy, the ball-bearing factory in Schweinfurt. The attacks took place on 17 August and 14 October 1943, and the Eighth Army Air Force lost 120 bombers in the process. The October débâcle in effect amounted to a great victory for the Luftwaffe, which by this means forced the Eighth to suspend its daylight operations over Germany. During the course of 1943 the Eighth's bombers increasingly received protection from P-38 Lightning and P-47 Thunderbolt fighters, fine aircraft but still not able to accompany the bombers far enough into Germany to make daylight raids less than potentially suicidal. But in the first months of 1944 the Eighth began to have at its disposal the out-standing Mustang fighter, powered by Rolls-Royce Merlin engines and capable of flying with the bombers all the way to Berlin and back. This meant that it could start making a really major contribution.

With this resource the picture changed. At the Casablanca Conference a year before, in January 1943, the Allied leaders had called for round-the-clock bombing of Germany. Harris had without success asked for it in his Berlin campaign; now at last it was going to be possible, and in a co-ordinated and cohesive way known as the 'Combined Bomber Offensive'. Between February 1944 and the stand-down of the air campaign in April 1945 – with the important exception of the summer of 1944, when the American and British bomber forces switched to tactical (that is, battlefield) bombing in the weeks before D-Day and the summer months following it – their joint forces could together pound the German homeland, and they did so with constantly increasing ferocity.

One main target of the co-ordinated assault was the Luftwaffe, by means of attacks on the factories that produced its aircraft and spare parts. The first manifestation of the new arrangement was 'Big Week', commencing 19 February 1944 with an 800-aircraft night raid by RAF Bomber Command on Leipzig, home to four Messerschmitt factories and a ball-bearing plant. The Americans followed next day with 200 aircraft, a further 800 of its bombers raiding a variety of other cities at the same time. The RAF bombed the city, the USAAF bombed the factories. The pattern thus set continued for the remainder of the week, with hundreds of aircraft from Bomber Command attacking at night, and hundreds of aircraft from the Eighth Army Air Force attacking by day, unleashing an almost incessant rain of bombs on Germany. Stuttgart, Brunswick, Halber-stadt, Regensburg, Schweinfurt and Augsburg were just some among the aiming-points of major raids. Augsburg's ancient city centre – to take just one example of the effects – was obliterated in the Bomber Command attack of 25–6 February 1944.

'Big Week' was just the start. The combined offensive might as well be called 'big year', given that it continued, on either side of the D-Day period of tactical bombing, as it started – only more so. In fact when the period of tactical bombing ended and the attacks on the German homeland resumed in full force in the autumn of 1944, the effect was massively greater, because by then the Allied air forces had virtual control of the skies, and their aircraft and munitions factories had kept on producing *matériel* in ever greater quantities. What had happened at Augsburg at the end of February, and what happened to Frankfurt at the beginning of March – 'a blow,' as Frankfurt's own municipal report put it, 'which simply ended the existence of the Frankfurt which had been built up since the Middle Ages'[59] – was to be the fate of many German towns, bombed and so far unbombed, before the order came to stop the bombing in April 1945.

Harris did not want to switch from the area bombing of cities to tactical bombing in support of 'Operation Overlord', the Allied invasion of Normandy. He had consistently believed and argued that bombing would make a land invasion unnecessary; but even when, in January 1944, he recognised that Overlord was an inevitability, he protested in writing that his force was not adapted to tactical bombing and must be allowed to continue to weaken the German heartland. 'It can be stated without fear of contradiction that the heavy bomber is a first-class strategic weapon and one of the least effective tactical weapons,' he said in a lecture as late as 15 May 1944, given to the headquarters of 21 Army Group at which Field Marshal Sir Bernard Montgomery was present.[60]

Portal in the end had to order Harris to collaborate with the planning for Operation Overlord. At a meeting on 25 March attended by the RAF's highest command and the scientific adviser Professor Zuckermann, a plan was drawn up for presentation to Churchill, based on the idea of bombing key rail centres in France and Belgium. The advantage was that it promised paralysis of German battlefield logistics; the disadvantage was that it risked French and Belgian civilian casualties. Portal estimated that the acceptable upper limit of such casualties would be 10,000 people. Legend has it that one of those present – Air Chief Marshal Sir Trafford Leigh-Mallory – remarked that he did not want to go down to posterity as a man who had killed thousands of Frenchman, to which Harris growled in reply, 'What makes you think you're going down to posterity?'[61]

Harris reserved his greatest scorn for what he called 'panacea' plans

– plans premised on the idea that a single factor would win the war: attacks on oil facilities, attacks on ball-bearing factories, and – as in this plan – attacks on railway communications. He wrote to a personal friend,

> Our worst headache has been a panacea plan devised by a civilian professor whose peacetime forte is the study of the sexual aberrations of the higher apes. Starting from this sound military basis he devised a scheme to employ almost the entire British and US bomber forces for three months or more in the destruction of targets mainly in France and Belgium.[62]

But Harris was a military man, and once he had been given an order and had lost the argument against it, he obeyed it to his best ability. His bombers went to war on the railway network of France and Belgium on 18 April 1944, mounting sixty such attacks between then and D-Day, and earning Portal's plaudits and Churchill's gratitude that 'care had been taken to avoid heavy civilian casualties'. This showed that RAF Bomber Command could conduct precision attacks avoiding civilian deaths as much as possible: a point much to be borne in mind.

In fact the tactical work of the two bomber forces was a major success overall, and in its way greatly more effective as a contribution to winning the war than the years of urban area bombing beforehand. In addition to railway centres, the bombers attacked airfields, munitions dumps and military encampments. Harris was still able to mount area attacks against a variety of German cities on moonless nights, arguing (plausibly enough) that it stopped the Germans from sending anti-aircraft defences to France. But the main thrust of the air attack was tailored to the needs of the impending invasion, including – in the immediate run-up to it – bombing of coastal batteries and defences. On the night of 4–5 June, Bomber Command dropped its greatest load of the war to date, battering the coastal defences – over 5,000 tons of bombs. The navy was shelling the same target at the same time, and between the two forces nine out of the Germans' ten Normandy batteries were rendered incapable of sustained fire.[63]

In the weeks after D-Day, Bomber Command flew over 3,500 sorties to interdict German communications, scoring notable successes – just one example of which, early in the invasion, was its delaying a shipment of Panzers travelling to the front by train, by precision bombing of a railway tunnel. All this work was undertaken at a very low loss rate. It included close tactical support of troops on the ground, and attacks on German naval units attempting to disrupt supplies across the Channel. Rather like its successes against the German invasion fleet of 1940, Bomber Command's part in the invasion of 1944 might be one of its chief glories of the war.

At the time, though, Harris was itching to resume area bombing, and another panacea – a return to the idea of hurting German oil supplies – served only to irritate him. But it too was an order, and Bomber Command duly joined the Eighth in attempting to limit the flow of fuel to Germany's tanks and aircraft. Losses were brutally high on these raids – on one of them, to Wesseling, nearly a third of the attacking aircraft were lost – and it was almost a relief to both air forces that the needs of the tactical situation recalled them from oil targets deep in Germany to military and transport targets in France.

The success of Allied air power in this period was in part a matter of sheer numbers. Between them the two air forces mustered 14,000 aircraft of all types, and the Luftwaffe faced them with 1,000. In a telling remark on this disparity in strength, Denis Richards in his history of the bombing war says, 'So overwhelming was the air superiority of the Allies . . . that once substantial ground forces and their supplies had been successfully landed and positioned for battle, the issue could hardly be in doubt.'[64] The circumstances, remember, were that Soviet forces were making headway in the east too. The Germans were capable – and proved it – of prolonging the battle by means of their formidable abilities and determination, especially in the east where fighting to the death seemed vastly preferable to submitting to a vengeful and brutal enemy.

But the inevitability of an Allied victory was by this time – the autumn of 1944 – plain to all who could count and add. For even though at this stage of the war German military production was still increasing, it had no chance of competing with the overwhelming productive power of the Allies, chief among them the United States; nor did it have the manpower reserves to last much longer, whereas the manpower of America and the British Empire, then still just intact, was far from being exhausted. So the war was effectively won by the end of summer 1944; no one on the Allied side believed anything other than that victory was a matter of time. The Allied determination to have nothing but unconditional surrender was one factor in ensuring that seven more months of bitter fighting remained; demanding unconditional surrender leaves defenders with a sense of nothing to lose, though in fact the loss Germany thereby incurred was tremendous. It was in this period that Bomber Command dropped more than a third of the total tonnage of bombs it unleashed on Germany in the entire war; and it was in this period that it turned its attention to towns and cities until then unscathed, in search of targets where enough was still standing to make it worth while to knock them down.

In mid-September 1944, Bomber Command returned to the control of the Air Staff in its new combined Allied guise, having been under General Dwight D. Eisenhower's orders for the main period of the invasion. The nights were beginning to draw in; long nights meant safer conditions for flying into Germany to bomb. Harris wrote to Churchill to say that because of the tactical support given to the ground war following D-Day, Germany itself had been given a 'considerable breather' and must now be attacked again, using the Allies' vast air superiority to 'knock Germany finally flat'. Churchill replied that although he continued to disagree that bombing could do it all alone, he liked Harris's spirit, and encouraged him in his intent: 'I am all for cracking everything in now on to Germany that can be spared from the battlefields.'[65]

These words were music to Harris's ears, and gave him what he needed to ignore the thrust of a new directive issued to him on 25 September, expressly requiring him to regard oil installations and communications as his *primary* objective, and only *secondarily* the 'general industrial capacity' of Germany, which in effect meant cities. These latter raids were meant to be carried out whenever weather or other conditions made attacks on the primary oil targets difficult. In the light of Churchill's encouragement, however, Harris took his 'secondary' target orders to be in effect a *carte blanche* to resume area attacks. It was operationally up to him to decide whether conditions were right for precision bombing of oil installations, or whether it would be better to attack cities. He now had a mighty force; it gave him, on an average day, 1,400 bombers almost all of the best type: Lancasters and Halifaxes, supported by Mosquitoes. (By April 1945 this figure rose to 1,600 operational bombers per day.) Technology had continued to develop too, making navigation and bombing accuracy ever better. And the Luftwaffe had been defeated during the invasion months, and was now a rump of its former self.

This all meant that, from Harris's point of view, conditions were perfect for the demolition of Germany's cities. He did not hesitate to take advantage of them. Nothing better reveals his intentions than the fact that only 6 per cent of the bombs his Command dropped in the war's final months were on oil targets. Harris's superiors kept pressing him to attack oil, and he kept attacking cities: already devastated Cologne was visited by 733 bombers in the daylight hours of 28 October, by 905 bombers on 30–1 October, and by 493 bombers on 31 October–1 November. This was a bombing of rubble into powder. Losses to the attacking force were 0.4 per cent; the cities were all but defenceless.

Portal's efforts to keep Harris's mind on oil targets resulted in a strengthened restatement of the oil directive, issued on 1 November. Intelligence assessments then, and evaluation after the war aided by Albert Speer's own accounts of the situation in Germany, showed that oil was absolutely the crucial consideration. Yet Harris could not be budged from his disdain for 'panaceas'. After receiving Portal's reissued directive he replied that weather and circumstances were the decisive factors in choosing targets, so that when weather was against precision raids on refineries and the like, 'bombing anything in Germany was better than bombing nothing'. Moreover, he continued, although he disagreed with the 'panacea merchants' he was doing his best to attack oil – though there were fifteen major German cities not yet attacked, and he was convinced that completing the 'city programme' would be a greater factor in hastening the war's end than anything the Allied ground forces could do. The fifteen unscathed major German cities on his destruction list included Dresden.[66]

Portal replied, 'I have at times wondered whether the magnetism of the remaining German cities has not in the past tended as much to deflect our bombers from their primary objectives as the tactical and weather difficulties you describe.' Evidently Portal, from his more senior position, had learned to see a wider war. In response Harris had a trump card, apart from Churchill's support; it was the claim that in the interests of his crews' safety, he had to keep the German defences guessing about where the next attack would be; if they were all on oil installations, the defence could be concentrated, and Bomber Command losses – now very low – would rise dramatically. Portal attempted yet again to get Harris to focus on oil, and the quarrel between them escalated – until Harris forced Portal's hand by hinting that Portal should dismiss him if he, Portal, disagreed with the way he, Harris, was running his war. Portal replied soothingly, saying that he could of course continue to 'flatten some at least of the cities Harris had been naming'[67] but (rather forlornly) trusting that Harris would do his best on oil.

Thus the cities scheduled for demolition on Harris's list met their fate. Attacks on oil did indeed increase in January 1945, but an intervention by no less than Churchill boosted Harris's city-demolition plan. The Prime Minister wanted Bomber Command to do something to interfere with the German retreat from Breslau in the face of the Soviet advance. Portal sought the agreement of the Allied Chiefs of Staff for a big attack on Berlin, Dresden, Leipzig and Chemnitz, where 'a severe blitz will not only cause confusion in the evacuation from the East but also hamper the movement of troops from the West'.[68] On 3 February the US Eighth Air Force attacked Berlin as part of this endeavour, mounting one of their biggest raids: 1,000 bombers, with railway and administrative sites as their primary targets. The devastation was enormous and the German authorities said that 25,000 Berliners were killed. After ten days of bad weather the next major effort took place – this time against Dresden.

Eight hundred RAF bombers attacked on the night of 13–14 February 1944; and the next day and the day after, the Americans followed with 300 and 200 aircraft respectively. The Americans aimed at the railway marshalling yards, but the RAF night attack of the 13–14 used a stadium in the city centre as its aiming-point. The majority of bombs dropped in Bomber Command's night attack were incendiaries, 650,000 of them. The firestorm that resulted wiped out the Baroque city, and killed somewhere in the region of 25,000 people.[69]

The destruction of Dresden was an epochal moment. Suddenly and markedly, attitudes to the whole strategy of area bombing changed among those who had supported or at least tolerated it throughout its employment. An outcry went up in Germany of course, but the first effect was the shock felt in the United States when the words of an RAF intelligence officer were quoted by an American war correspondent covering Allied HQ. The RAF officer told a press briefing that the Allied Air Chiefs were employing a strategy of 'deliberate terror-bombing of German population centres as a ruthless expedient of hastening Hitler's doom'.[70] The words reached front pages in the United States, but were censored in England.

But the risk that public concern over the destruction of Dresden would escalate into a major problem for the Allied governments was defused by something even more horrifying: the news of what was found when Belsen, Buchenwald and other camps were liberated by Allied troops. Newsreel footage from the concentration camps hugely revived anger and hostility towards Germany. For many in this mood, the area bombing in general and the destruction of Dresden in particular seemed no more than just punishment.

Churchill, however, had for some time been pondering the possibility that Germany and its army might be needed in a forthcoming struggle against the Soviet Union, and news of the destruction of Dresden gave him disturbing second thoughts. In the weeks that followed Dresden, other historical cities found themselves subjected to seemingly arbitrary attack, their residents bemusedly convinced that they were bombed for the simple reason that they had not already been bombed, and that the huge number of RAF bombers needed something to do (the USAAF bombers were still mainly attacking oil and transport targets – and helping to win the war thereby). Such cities as Worms, Mainz, Würzburg, Hildesheim, Gladbeck, Hanau and Dulmen were among them.[71] These facts seemed cumulatively to weigh on Churchill's mind. No doubt too Sir Anthony Eden, his Foreign Secretary, and others had been making him think more carefully about the post-war world, and about the problems of reconstruction and social order in post-war Germany in particular. At last he wrote to Portal and the other Chiefs of Staff on 28 March, in a minute quoted by the Official Historians: 'It seems to me that the moment has come when the question of bombing German cities for the sake of increasing the terror, though under other pretexts, should be reviewed. Otherwise we shall come into control of an utterly ruined land. The destruction of Dresden remains a serious query against the conduct of Allied bombing.'[72]

The effect of this minute has been a source of controversy ever since, and will be discussed again in the course of these chapters. But area bombing virtually ceased after Churchill sent it, and the last raid by RAF heavy bombers took place just over three weeks later, on 25–6 April.

As soon as Bomber Command's war was over, it began the much more agreeable humanitarian task of ferrying relief supplies to the devastated regions of Europe, and bringing prisoners of war back home to Britain.

The main thrust of this story has so far been about RAF Bomber Command for the good reason that until early 1944 it carried the bulk of the air war to Germany. In 1943, but especially from early 1944, the US Eighth Air Force joined it as a major player, and to the American intervention is owed the destruction of the Luftwaffe in the air by combat, and its disablement on the ground by choking its fuel supplies.

As noted already, the attitudes and strategies of the Eighth Army Air Force differed both officially and in practice from that of Bomber Command. Where most of the latter's campaign consisted of area bombing of population centres, the Americans attempted more precise targeting, flying by day so that they could see the marshalling yards, bridges, oil plants and factories they were aiming to hit. They did not eschew area bombing entirely in the European theatre of war, but officially it was not their way.

When elements of the US Army Air Force began arriving in Britain in 1942 the USAAF overall commander, Lieutenant-General 'Hap' Arnold, the commander of its forces in Britain, Major-General Carl 'Tooey' Spaatz, and the commander of the bomber groups in those forces, Brigadier-General Ira Eaker, were all of one mind, both with each other and with Portal and Harris, about the war-winning potential of bombing. But the Americans differed greatly from their British counterparts in their view of how that was to be done. For them the right way was the destruction of key aspects of the enemy's industrial capacity. For the British, after the failures of the early years of the war, it was by attacking enemy 'morale'.

The American strategy of bombing in daylight was justified by their belief that the massive firepower of their aircraft, flying in tight 'boxed' formations, would keep enemy fighters away. The Flying

Fortresses carried heavier-calibre guns than did British aircraft – .5 as opposed to .33 – and more of them, providing overlapping fields of fire from the tail, the upper, lower and beam waist positions, and the nose. The power of the .5 machine gun was formidable, and much respected by Luftwaffe fighter pilots. But the latter quickly got the measure of the way American bomber formations sought to defend themselves, and the Americans as quickly therefore learned the shortcomings of their tactics. This was the main reason why the Eighth's attack on Germany itself, apart from the catastrophic Schweinfurt raids of 1943, had in effect to wait until Mustang escorts were available to protect their raids from January 1944 onwards.

Because their greater protective plating and armament added weight and reduced space, the American aircraft carried at most only half the bombing load of the RAF's heavies. This was true when the mainstay of Bomber Command was the Wellington, when the Eighth Air Force was arriving and making its tentative start in 1942; and the disparity was greater still when Bomber Command's superlative Lancasters were the mainstay of the British attack, with the Eighth continuing to operate B-17 and B-24 Fortresses. (American air forces in Europe and North Africa did not receive the B-29 'Superfortress', which operated only in the Pacific theatre.) But great bomb weight was not necessarily a decisive factor in precision bombing, and nor was exceptionally large numbers of aircraft. Because of the demands on the USAAF in North Africa and the Pacific, its concentration of aircraft in the European theatre did not reach high levels until 1944.

For all these reasons, therefore, it was RAF Bomber Command that did the main work in pounding Germany for most of the war, and that is why histories tend to devote more pages to its activities. But in doing so, they overlook the crucial role of the US Eighth Army Air Force in defeating the Luftwaffe. It is worth repeating that the Eighth did this by attacking the factories that produced it, by fighting it out of the air, and – crucially – by bombing the sources of the fuel it needed to fly, which was the single most significant factor in grounding the Luftwaffe in the closing phase of the war.

But they also overlook the astonishing contrast between the strategy of the American bombing campaign in Europe and the strategy of the American bombing campaign over Japan. Hereby hangs a tale. For whereas American bombers in Europe concentrated on precision attacks, over Japan they resorted to wholly indiscriminate area raids.

A bombing campaign over the home islands of Japan was not an option for US forces until the Mariana Islands were in their possession. From the autumn of 1943 efforts were made to attack Japanese factories in Manchuria and Kyushu from bases in China, but the effort was a limited one, partly because the B-29s had to compete with Chinese forces for supplies of fuel and bombs being brought laboriously from India. That meant they could only mount a couple of strikes each month, and the overall effect of these efforts was minor. When in November 1944 long-range attacks could be launched against the Japanese islands from Tinian, Saipan and Guam, the China-based B-29s were transferred to join the campaign.

But it was in March 1945 that the main thrust of sustained American heavy air attacks against Japan really began. They were seen as subserving both the primary objective of forcing Japan to surrender without an invasion, and reducing the Japanese 'will to resist' as a preliminary to invasion should one prove necessary. The remit given to the USAAF was 'disruption of railroad and transportation system by daylight attacks, coupled with destruction of cities by night and bad-weather attacks'[73] In the event, the city attacks came first; the 'urban area attacks were initiated in force in March 1945, the railroad attack was just getting under way when the war ended [in August 1945]'.[74]

The reason for the delay between November 1944, when the airfields on the captured Marianas became operational, and March 1945, when the area bombing of Japanese cities began, was one of logistics: at first the bombers available in the Marianas were few, and the Japanese fighter resistance was still significant enough to limit their activities. The small forces of bombers dropped their loads in daylight from very high altitudes – 30,000 feet – in an effort to disrupt Japanese aircraft production, but at best they managed to get only 10 per cent of their bombs near their targets.

In March 1945 the strategy changed. The remit described above was issued, and more aircraft had become available for its realisation. It was also by now recognised that Japanese fighters were far less effective at night; so the area-bombing campaign started with night-time incendiary attacks on the four principal Japanese cities of Tokyo, Nagoya, Osaka, and Kobe, all of them made of wood. The bombers flew in at low altitude – 7,000 feet – which allowed them to carry heavier loads of incendiaries, and to bomb more accurately. The commander of XXI Bomber Command was General Curtis E. LeMay, to whom the credit is given for devising the strategy of low-level night attacks. He ordered his B-29 Superfortresses to be stripped of some of their guns so that they could carry even more incendiaries.

The first attack took place on the night of 9–10 March 1945. It was against Tokyo, which received 1,667 tons of incendiary bombs on fifteen square miles of its most densely populated districts. They were burned to the ground in a ferocious firestorm that killed more than 85,000 people.[75] The death and destruction here was greater than that caused by either of the atom bombs dropped in August that year on Hiroshima and Nagasaki. It was the most destructive of the area attacks apart from the atom bombings, but the others that followed – in which over 9,000 tons of incendiaries fell on the remaining three principal cities, destroying thirty-one square miles of them – were devastating enough.

Over the next five months General LeMay extended the area-bombing campaign across Japan. In all, according to the US Strategic Bombing Survey for the Pacific theatre, nearly half of the built-up areas of sixty-six Japanese cities was destroyed. Adding the casualties from the atom-bomb attacks, a total of 330,000 people were killed and a further 460,000 injured. 'The principal cause of civilian deaths,' says the US Survey, 'was burns.'[76]

The consummation of the area bombing of Japan was of course the dropping, on 6 and 9 August 1945 respectively, of single atom bombs on each of Hiroshima and Nagasaki. Between them the two atomic blasts killed 100,000 people and destroyed half the buildings in each city. The US Strategic Bombing Survey paid particular attention to the effects of these attacks, given the immense curiosity of the US government about the capacities of its new weapon – a curiosity for which there were significant reasons, some obvious and some controversial. The Survey Report descends to detailed scrutiny of such things as the effect (for example) of the difference made to radiation burns by whether the victim was wearing clothes or not. Authorities in Washington were especially interested in the Survey's conclusion that 'the damage and casualties caused at Hiroshima by the one atomic bomb dropped from a single plane would have required 220 B-29s carrying 1,200 tons of incendiary bombs, 400 tons of high explosives, and 500 tons of anti-personnel fragmentation bombs, if conventional weapons, rather than an atomic bomb, had been used'.[77]

The atom-bomb attacks cause grave concern for many about the morality of United States area bombing over Japan, just as the firebombing of Dresden does for RAF Bomber Command and the US Eight Air Force, which accompanied it. These attacks stand out because of special circumstances – the beauty and cultural importance of Dresden; the first use of the stupendous power of the atom as a weapon. But they do not differ in principle from the firebombings of Tokyo and Hamburg, or any other area-bomb attacks on German and Japanese cities. Except, perhaps in one respect: that if area bombing is a moral crime, then the bombings in the last six months of the war in both the European and Japanese theatres of war have what lawyers call an aggravated character – an intensified moral questionability, partly because victory was no longer genuinely doubtful, and partly because the motives for dropping the atom bombs might have been additional to realisation of the Allied war aims regarding Japan.[78]

Such is the story of the bombing war. The next task is to see what effect it had on those beneath the bombers and their bombs in Germany and Japan.

3

The Experience of the Bombed

O N THE EVENING of 27 July 1943 the western districts of Hamburg were still dotted with fires from the first RAF attack three nights earlier. Stocks of coal and coke heaped in the open air were smouldering fiercely, and at night made a vivid glow that could be seen for scores of miles in every direction. This posed an air-raid danger, so the authorities ordered a maximum effort to extinguish the fires. When the bombers returned for the great firestorm attack of 27–8 July, their bombs fell chiefly in the east of the city; the municipal fire-fighting appliances were still struggling with the coal fires in the western districts.

Most of the civilians 'dehoused' in the first attack had been evacuated, and although many others had also been trying to leave they were discouraged by the authorities because of strain on transport facilities. Reinforcements were arriving in the city in the form of extra flak batteries, and in the warm summer nights their crews slept on the ground next to their guns.

Many of the city's residents did likewise, finding patches of grass outside the public air-raid shelters and resting their heads on their bundles, ready to hurry into the shelters as soon as bombing started. When the air-raid warning sounded on 27 July everyone readied themselves to take shelter, but for more than an hour nothing happened: no bombing, no bombers, no flak; so they hesitated at the entrances of the shelters, and after a time returned to their patches of grass. The citizens of Hamburg did not know it, but the bomber stream was passing to the north of the city, ready to swing round and attack from the east. Bomber Command planners hoped that an approach from this unexpected quarter of the sky would disorganise the defences. And so it did. The attackers' bombs fell on the most densely populated districts east of the Elbe – Billwarder Ausschlag, crammed with eight-storey workers' apartment blocks, St Georg, Barmbek, Wandsbek, and the three areas of Hamm – Hamm-Nord, Hamm-Süd and Hammerbrook.

Gunners manning flak batteries could not take shelter as others could, and for that reason had a perilous grandstand view of what happened as the bombers arrived over their target. Leutnant Hermann Bock – who had been born in Hamburg, and was now commander of a flak battery which had been sent hastily from Mönchengladbach to strengthen the defences of his native city – wrote:

> Hamburg's night sky became in minutes, even seconds, a sky so absolutely hellish that it is impossible even to try to describe it in words. There were aeroplanes held in the probing arms of the searchlights, fires breaking out, billowing smoke everywhere, loud, roaring waves of explosions, all broken up by great cathedrals of light as the blast bombs exploded, cascades of marker bombs slowly drifting down, stick incendiary bombs coming down with a rushing noise. No noise heard by humans – no outcry – could be heard. It was like the end of the world. One could think, feel, see and speak of nothing more.[1]

Hamburg's citizens had to take turns as fire wardens in their places of work. They had uniforms and steel helmets, some rudimentary training, and instructions to watch for fires and put them out as quickly as possible. In some cases the 'fire wardens' were, despite the appearance of authority and expertise bestowed by the uniforms, just young teenagers (as also were the gunners on flak batteries). One, a sixteen-year-old girl, described how she cowered in a cellar as the walls around her shook and cracked, while she and her companions prayed silently. One of their number, another young girl, became hysterical – as if presciently so: the girl's mother and grandmother were killed at her home that night.[2] Another fire warden, older and more experienced, described trying to remain on watch on the steps of his shelter, ready with his comrades to hasten out at the first sign of flames, when the firestorm struck without warning:

> Suddenly there came a rain of fire from heaven. We tried to get out to pump but it was impossible. The air was actually filled with fire. It would have meant certain death to leave the shelter . . . Smoke seeped into the shelter through every crack. Every time you opened the steel doors you could see fire all around . . . Then a storm started, a shrill howling in the street. It grew into a hurricane . . . The whole yard, the canal, in fact as far as we could see, was just a whole, great, massive sea of fire.

Another survivor described the howling of the firestorm as 'the devil laughing'.[3]

The firestorm started in Hammerbrook at about 1.20 a.m., the ferocious heat of the inferno sucking in air at hurricane speeds and reaching temperatures of 800 degrees centigrade or more. The bombing was still in progress, and lasted for another half an hour, spreading the area of the firestorm beyond its original core to the outer suburbs and into the city centre. In all, an area of about four square miles (ten square kilometres) was effectively incinerated.[4] The firestorm raged until 3.30 a.m., more than an hour after the last bombs had been dropped.

During the firestorm its victims were confronted with a terrible choice: to stay in their cellars, where the temperatures were rising to impossible heights, the air was filling thickly with smoke, and the buildings above them were crashing down; or risk running outside where the air itself seemed to be aflame. Survivors from the margins of the firestorm – few people within its perimeters survived – described the scene in apocalyptic terms.

> They spoke of the tremendous force of hot, dry winds against which even strong men were unable to struggle, and which forced open doors of houses and broke the glass in their windows. Anything light was immediately whipped away, bursting into flames as it went . . . what appeared to be 'bundles of flames' or 'towers or walls of fire' sometimes shot out of a burning building and along a street. There were 'fiery whirlwinds' which could snatch people in the street and immediately turn them into human torches while other people, only a few yards away, were untouched. The wind was always accompanied by clouds of sparks which looked like 'a blizzard of red snowflakes' and all survivors remember the shrieking, howling of the storm as it raced through the streets.[5]

In the 'pan of a gigantic oven' that Hamburg had become, the searing winds changed direction violently and unpredictably, sweeping the walls of fire along with them. Women found their light summer frocks bursting into flame, and tore them off to run naked from the inferno.[6] In the cellars, otherwise unscathed people suffocated to death. Police reports and eyewitness accounts later confirmed many of the horror stories told 'of demented Hamburgers carrying bodies of deceased relatives in their suitcases – a man with the corpse of his wife and daughter, a woman with the mummified body of her daughter, or other women with the heads of their dead children'[7]. One of these shocking details is to be found in an account, quoted by W. G. Sebald, given by someone who saw refugees from Hamburg trying to board a train in Bavaria, in the struggle dropping a suitcase which 'falls on the platform, bursts open and spills its contents. Toys, a manicure case, singed underwear. And last of all, the roasted corpse of a child, shrunk like a mummy, which its half-deranged mother has been carrying about with her, the relic of a past that was still intact a few days ago'.[8]

Some families survived together: 'Mother wrapped me in wet sheets, kissed me, and said, Run!' reported Traute Koch, aged fifteen at the time of the attack, and living in Hamm.

> I hesitated at the door. In front of me I could see only fire – everything red like the door of a furnace. An intense heat struck me. A burning beam fell in front of my feet. I shied back, but then when I was ready to jump over it, it was whipped away by a ghostly hand. I reached . . . the building in front of which we had arranged to meet again . . . Someone came out, grabbed me in their arms, and pulled me into the doorway. I screamed for my mother and somebody gave me a drink – wine or schnapps – I still screamed and then my mother and my little sister were there. About twenty people had gathered in the cellar. We sat, holding tightly to each other and waited. My mother wept bitterly and I was terrified.[9]

Others were not so lucky. Rolf Witt, who lived in Borgfelde, close to the epicentre of the firestorm, made a dash for freedom from the chokingly smoke-filled cellar where he was sheltering with his parents and others. He thought his parents were following close behind, but when he looked back they were not there, and he saw that their apartment block had collapsed. 'I never found my parents and it was never sure where or how they died. I have always felt guilty that I abandoned them. Later, when their shelter was cleared, they found fifty-five bodies – at least they found fifty-five skulls . . . I never met another survivor from my home or the houses at the back.'[10]

A greengrocer who lived near the canal in the Loschplatz told the compiler of a police report following the raid:

> Many people started burning and jumping into the canal. Horrible scenes took place at the quay. People burned to death with horrible suffering; some became insane. Many dead bodies were all around

us and I became convinced that we too would perish here. I crouched with my family behind a large stack of roofing material. Here we lost our daughter. Later on, it transpired that she had jumped into the canal and almost drowned but was saved by an army officer and she returned to us early next morning. Please spare me from having to describe further details.[11]

When the firestorm was over, a stream of refugees began to leave the city, first in a trickle, then in a mighty flood. Traute Koch and her mother and sister at first went home, only to find the house a pile of rubble. They could not stand staring at it for long because the ground beneath their feet was too hot.

We came to the junction of the Hammer Landstrasse and Louisen-weg. I carried my little sister and also helped my mother climb over the ruins. Suddenly, I saw tailors' dummies lying around. I said, 'Mum-my, no tailors lived here and, yet, so many dummies lying around.' My mother grabbed my arm and said, 'Go on. Don't look too closely. On. On. We have to get out of here. Those are dead bodies.'[12]

A fireman searched for his war-disabled brother.

I only got to the Heidenkampsweg. In the entrance to the Maizena Haus [a large office building] I saw a lot of dead, naked people on the steps. I thought that they had been killed by a blast bomb and been blown out of the basement air raid shelter. What surprised me was that the people were all lying face downwards. Only later did we find out that these people had died there through lack of oxygen. I climbed over the ruins further into the damaged area. There were no people alive at all. The houses were all destroyed and still burning. In the Süderstrasse I saw a burnt out tramcar in which naked bodies were lying on top of each other. The glass of the windows had melted. Probably these people had sought refuge from the storm in the tram. I eventually reached my brother's home on the Grevenweg; it was just a heap of smoking bricks. I helped to clear their shelter five weeks later. There was only charred bones and ash. I found a few objects that belonged to my relatives – their house keys and some coins that my nephew was always playing with.[13]

A woman who hurried to Hamburg the day after the firestorm to find her parents, had to fight with sentries posted to keep people from entering the worst-affected areas. Anne-Lies Schmidt said,

My uncle and I went on foot into this terror. No one was allowed into the devastated district but I believe that one's stubbornness becomes stronger at the sight of such sacrifice. We fought bodily with the sentries on duty and we got in. My uncle was arrested.

Four-storey-high blocks of flats were like glowing mounds of stone right down to the basement. Everything seemed to have melted . . . Women and children were so charred as to be unrecognisable; those that had died through lack of oxygen were half charred and recognisable. Their brains tumbled from their burst temples and their insides from the soft parts under the ribs. How terribly must these people have died. The smallest children lay like fried eels on the pavement. Even in death they showed signs of how they must have suffered – their hands and arms stretched out as if to protect themselves from that pitiless heat.

I found the bodies of my parents but it was forbidden to take them because of the danger of epidemic. Nothing to remember them by. No photographs. Nothing! All their precious little possessions they had taken to the basement were stolen. I had no tears. The eyes became bigger but the mouth remained closed tight.[14]

When the bombers left Hamburg that night they could see it burning from 120 miles away. Two nights later they were back; and they were back yet again a further three nights after that.

*   *   *

The distinguished Australian statesman Richard Casey, later Lord Casey of Berwick, kept a diary while serving in Churchill's War Cabinet. He recorded watching with Churchill a film showing RAF bombers in action over the Ruhr. 'All of a sudden Churchill gives a start,' Casey wrote, 'and he says to me "Are we animals? Are we taking this too far?" I tell him it wasn't us who had started all this and that this was what it was about: us or them.'[15] Casey's robust reply forms part of the standard justification given for the bomber war, but the Prime Ministerial pang of conscience thus recorded was by far not the only one Churchill had – though at other times, especially earlier in the war, he made uncompromising pronouncements about the necessity of unleashing an 'exterminating attack' on the Nazi home-land[16] – nor does it represent more than a hint of the reason why he had it. This was that Churchill knew what relatively few others did: exactly what was being dropped from the bombers as they passed high over the flashes of explosions and the pulsing regions of fire below them.

To say that the bomb loads consisted of a mixture high explosive and incendiary weapons does little to convey what that meant in practice. Those sheltering in cellars during a Bomber Command raid felt the mighty thud and tremor of high explosives falling about them, and the accompanying alternation of suction–pressure–suction–pressure they caused.[17] They learned to distinguish by sound the different kinds of incendiaries that showered down among the big bombs. A rustle like a flock of birds suddenly taking off represented a stick of incendiaries breaking apart as it neared the ground, sending indivi-dual incendiaries in all directions. An explosion like a sudden crack was a 12-kilogram fire bomb, shooting out flames to a distance of eighty metres. A big splash was a 14-kilogram fire bomb, which spread liquid rubber and benzene over a radius of fifty metres. The sound of a wet sack flopping heavily down was a canister containing twenty litres of benzol. A sharp explosion heralded a 106-kilogram bomb that hurled out rags soaked in benzene or heavy oil, or it was a 112-kilogram bomb that ejected a thousand patties of benzol and rubber over the surrounding area.[18] Phosphorus, magnesium and thickened or gelled petroleum (the best example of which is 'napalm', invented at Harvard University in 1942 and used by the USAAF in Japan later in the war) were almost impossible to extinguish, splashing viscously and adhesively over buildings and people like lava, and burning at ferocious temperatures. People who leaped into canals when splashed with burning phosphorus found to their horror that it would spontaneously reignite when they got out of the water.

Among the incendiaries were scattered 2-kilogram 'X' bombs with a delayed fuse, designed to explode later when fire-fighters and other emergency workers had arrived on the scene.

The firestorm of Hamburg on the night of 27–8 July 1943, heralded as one of RAF Bomber Command's greatest successes in its area-bombing campaign, does not have the historical status of the fire-bombing of Dresden on the night of 13–14 February 1945, nor of the firebombing of Tokyo on 9–10 March 1945, nor of the atom bomb attacks on Hiroshima and Nagasaki on 6 and 9 August 1945 respectively. The reasons are obvious ones. Dresden was a city of great beauty, one of the cultural treasures of Europe, and its immolation occurred at a time and in circumstances which many have found hard to justify. (I return to the Dresden bombing later.) The firebombing of Tokyo caused even greater immediate loss of life than the devastation of Hiroshima. The atom-bomb attacks were different again; they were *sui generis*, involving the use of a new weapon of unprecedented destructive power, the manner of whose effects on the cities and the people – especially, as regards the latter, the lingering effects of radiation sickness, and the still longer-term effects of illness and trauma – had no parallel even in the worst episodes of bombing in that or any other war. (I return to the Japanese bombings later, too.)

But there are other questions about Dresden, Tokyo, Hiroshima and Nagasaki. They fall into a category made special not just by their character but by their timing. The bombing of Hamburg in Operation Gomorrah took place at the height of the war, when the outcome of the struggle was not yet certain, even though the Allied powers knew that they had industrial and manpower advantages that so far outstripped those of the Axis states that the balance of likelihood already lay well on their side.[19] These other, later, bombings occurred when almost everyone involved could see that the war's end was approaching. One can seriously ask for their justification even if one is already persuaded that such area attacks as Operation Gomorrah, conducted at the height of the war, were necessary or at least warranted by the circumstances at the time.

This is not intended to beg a question about any part of the Allies' area-bombing campaigns. If Operation Gomorrah cannot be justified on moral grounds, then the massive deposit of explosive and incendiary power unleashed by the Allies between September 1944 and August 1945 has less chance of being so. Of this, more later.

In any case, the experience of those subjected to bombing in Hamburg can serve as an example of what it was like for those subjected to bombing anywhere, whether in Coventry early in the war or Tokyo close to its end. For each individual who experienced the terrifying ordeal of being on the receiving end of tons of high explosives and incendiaries, there can be no fine distinctions between occasions. There is scarcely need for a competition in ghastliness here. In recalling details of the aftermath of the firebombing of Dresden, the writer Kurt Vonnegut – a prisoner of war in Dresden at the time – described how the asphyxiated but otherwise unscathed bodies of victims in cellars were cremated by flame-throwers directed down the cellar stairs from the street.[20] In recounting the experiences of individuals in Hiroshima, John Hersey described how a Jesuit priest found a group of about twenty soldiers who had been looking up at the *Enola Gay* as it flew above them high over the city, and whose eyes had in consequence been liquefied by the flash of the bomb, so that the jellies ran down their cheeks like tears.[21]

In the latter case the frisson of dread created by the thought of what atomic weaponry can do affects those who contemplate it more than those who actually suffer from it; for whether it is an atom bomb rather than tons of high explosives and incendiaries that does the damage, not a jot of suffering is added to its victims that the burned and buried, the dismembered and blinded, the dying and bereaved of Dresden or Hamburg did not feel.

This remark applies to the immediate trauma, of course: the real difference came afterwards, for to their blast deaths and injuries the atom bombs added years of illness and later premature deaths from cancer and other diseases. But from the point of view of those who dropped the bombs, these latter longer-term consequences were at best matters of speculation. What they knew when they planned to drop the atom bombs is what they knew when they planned to drop tons of high explosive and incendiaries on urban areas: that they would kill many, among them the elderly and children, and would destroy much in the way of buildings, facilities, schools, clinics, shops, houses, libraries, bus stations, vehicles, and an uncountable number of valuable things, even if only sentimentally so. That was the certainty on which the attacks were premised. And that is what they made happen. This is a bare statement of fact, on which all can agree, whether or not area bombing was right or wrong, necessary or otherwise.

Even before the war in Europe was over, the US authorities instituted a survey of the effects of strategic bombing on Nazi Germany. The resulting Summary Report of the United States Strategic Bombing Survey (European War) was published on 30 September 1945. One of its principal aims was to provide information for use by the high command in the Pacific theatre as it pondered the application of air power to the war against Japan.

After the surrender of Japan a Strategic Bombing Survey was instituted for the Pacific theatre too. It resulted in a much longer Summary Report, which was published on 1 July 1946. The reason for the greater length of the Pacific report was its detailed focus on the results of the atom-bomb attacks, and the fact that the survey team had longer to collect and digest its data.

Both reports are models of their kind, and make absorbing and instructive reading for anyone wishing to understand the reasons for, and the value of, the strategic bombing carried out in the Second World War, and the difference made by the advent of atomic weapons.

As one would expect, to a great extent the effects of the bombing campaigns depended upon how well prepared Germany and Japan respectively were for aerial attack, and how their populations responded to it. In the Pacific report the US survey team stated that 'Japan's will and capacity for reconstruction, dispersal, and passive defence were less than Germany's'.[22] This might have been a function of the fact that whereas Germany sustained five years of bombing attacks – in three of these years very heavy attacks – Japan experienced nine months of bombing, and in that time suffered nearly the same number of civilian casualties as did Germany. The survey gives the figures as follows:

Total civilian casualties in Japan, as a result of 9 months of air attack, including those from the atomic bombs, were approximately 806,000. Of these, approximately 330,000 were fatalities. These casualties probably exceeded Japan's combat casualties [that is, soldiers, sailors and airmen] which the Japanese estimate as having totalled approximately 780,000 during the entire war. The principal cause of civilian death or injury was burns. Of the total casualties approximately 185,000 were suffered in the initial attack on Tokyo of 9 March 1945. Casualties in many extremely destructive attacks were comparatively low. Yokahoma, a city of 900,000 population, was 47 percent destroyed in a single attack lasting less than an hour. The fatalities suffered were less than 5000.[23]

One reason for the high casualty rate in Tokyo was the relative unpreparedness of the population, and the firestorm that raged through the wooden city. As a result of the Tokyo bombing, other cities made fire breaks by tearing down whole streets of buildings. In some cities the fear of an attack grew proportionally with the length of time that the city remained unscathed. 'The day before the bomb was dropped on Hiroshima,' writes John Hersey, 'the city, in fear of incendiary raids, had put hundreds of schoolgirls to work helping to tear down houses and clear fire lanes. They were out in the open when the bomb exploded. Few survived.'[24]

This, though, was five months after the Tokyo attack, which suggests that organisation of defence against air attack was not optimal. The main precaution taken by Japanese civilians was to flee the towns; an estimated eight and a half million urban dwellers sought shelter in rural districts. Everywhere in Japan civilians could see American aircraft flying overhead, on their way to or from bombing raids, unchallenged because the Japanese air force had ceased to resist. The demoralising effect of this was as great as that caused by actually being a victim of an air raid.

A striking aspect of the air attack was the pervasiveness with which its impact on morale blanketed Japan. Roughly one-quarter of all people in cities fled or were evacuated, and these evacuees, who themselves were of singularly low morale, helped spread discouragement and disaffection for the war throughout the islands. This mass migration from the cities included an estimated 8,500,000 persons. Throughout the Japanese islands, whose people had always thought themselves remote from attack, United States planes criss-crossed the skies with no effective Japanese air or anti-aircraft opposition. That this was an indication of impending defeat became as obvious to the rural as to the urban population.[25]

Matters were considerably different in Germany. Its Nazi rulers – the Party and the State were one and the same – anticipated war because they knew they were going to start one, and as early as 1935 had begin to plan air-raid alarm systems and shelters, first-aid services, and methods for dealing with gas attacks. Large underground shelters and massive above-ground shelters were built, and the entire programme of defence against bombing was intensified in 1940 when an emergency decree from the Führer's office nominated eighty-two cities as key sites for special air-raid defence.

One of them was Cologne. By the time of the 1,000-bomber raid on 30–1 May 1942 the city had public shelters for 75,000 people, with twenty-five special deep bunkers for a further 7,500 (and twenty-nine additional such bunkers in process of being built). A total of 42,000 small air-raid shelters had been provided under or next to houses and apartment buildings for residents. Fourteen auxiliary hospitals had been constructed, giving an extra 1,760 emergency beds. The total cost of air-raid defences in Cologne prior to the 1,000-bomber raid was thirty-nine million marks. It was money well spent. The 1,000 bombers dropped 2,500 tons of high explosives and incendiaries, and destroyed centuries of history; the German dead numbered 469.[26]

Very soon after the drone of bombers had receded westwards in the early hours of 31 May 1943, the roads to Cologne started to fill with lorries bringing relief supplies – 34,000 items of clothing for adults, 50,000 items of clothing for children, 61,000 sheets, 90,000 boxes of soap powder, 100,000 metres of curtain material, 700,000 cakes of soap, 10,000,000 cigarettes. Bonn and Dusseldorf sent clerks to help local officials in Cologne deal with claims for war damage, and within a month 140,000 claims had been processed. When all claims had been processed (370,000 of them) a total of 126 million marks was paid out in damages to citizens. A small army of helpers arrived to assist the 5,200 workmen in Cologne detailed to clean up the city: 2,500 soldiers, 3,400 glaziers, and 10,000 building workers.[27]

The pattern was repeated whenever and wherever severe bombing occurred, at least up until the later part of 1944. When Frankfurt was repeatedly bombed in February and March 1944, losing the whole of its old city centre and large tracts of its suburbs, relief trains arrived after the raids bringing kettles of noodle soup with meat, bread and butter, and sausages.[28]

The efficiency and energy of the German people comes as no surprise, and prompts two immediate and contrary questions. The first is: how could Bomber Command hope to defeat a people capable of such swift and robust responses to what it could drop on them in the way of bomb loads? And the second is: what would Germany have been capable of as a military power, if it had not had to repair homes and water supplies, and supply sheets and soap to bombed cities?

Hamburg is an example of Bomber Command's efforts to answer the first question. If a German city could bounce back so quickly from a massive bombing attack, as Cologne had done after the 1,000-bomber raid of the previous year, then the bombing attack needed to be even more massive. The target needed to be attacked again and again, both before recovery could start, and afterwards to hamper its efforts. The weight and frequency of attack was the crucial factor; early in the war Bomber Command could not mount anything like the scale of assault required to demoralise Germany's populace and paralyse it logistically. In mid-1943 it was able to manage an Operation Gomorrah. By the last year of the war, and certainly in its last six months, Bomber Command and the Eighth Air Force between them were close to the required scale, and their effect on the urban landscape of Germany was clear for all to see.

The answer to the second question is one that plays a significant part in defences of the Allied bombing campaign. It is related to a larger fact about the effects of bombing on Germany: which is that it did not halt the growth of productivity in German industry, whose output grew throughout the war until its last months, and was at a markedly higher level at the end of 1944 than it had been in 1940. The question: what might Germany have done if it had not been bombed almost daily for all those years? takes on extra weight in the light of this consideration.

The facts and figures of Germany's war production are themselves a matter of record, but controversy surrounds their significance. Until 1942 the Germany economy was far from being on a 'total war' footing, partly because the Nazi leadership believed that its wars would be quick and successful, and partly because it wished to keep economic activity as normal as possible in order not to burden the populace, wishing to avoid a repeat of the situation that followed the First World War when economic dislocation stirred popular unrest. This is not to say that Germany's economy was functioning exactly as normal; to pay for their military adventures in the war's opening years the Nazi government increased taxes sharply between 1938 and 1941, and limits on consumer activity raised levels of saving fivefold in the same period.

But when by the beginning of 1942 Germany found itself facing a longer and more demanding struggle than it had anticipated – by then it was fighting on several fronts simultaneously and suffering serious reverses on two of them (Russia and North Africa) – it accepted the need to move the economy on to a more dedicated war footing. On 8 February 1942 Hitler appointed Albert Speer as Minister of Armaments and Munitions, a post made vacant that same day by the death of Fritz Todt in a somewhat mysterious air crash. Todt was convinced that the difficulties being experienced on the Eastern Front portended the defeat of the Reich, and he ill-advisedly told Hitler so. A few hours later he was dead, and a few hours after that, Speer was given his job. Speer had until then been Hitler's architect, and because architecture and grandiose schemes for magnificent Thousand-Year Reich cities stood high among Hitler's hobbies, Speer was a favourite. He had designed and in a remarkably short time built Hitler's splendid new Chancellery in Berlin, and had even designed the furniture for the Führer's office in it. Hitler thought him the man for the job; and he was abundantly proved right.

Speer's standing with Hitler meant that it was easy for him to take responsibility for war production away from Hermann Goering's Reichswerke and Four-Year Plan, and from the Wehrmacht's Armament Office, which had made itself unpopular with industry because of its continual interfering. By centralising and streamlining the organisation of procurement, thereby improving the co-ordination of industrial efforts to meet both military and domestic demand, Speer rapidly increased output. This was not achieved by converting more German industry to military production – a fuller war mobilisation of the economy came later, after Speer had with great difficulty per-suaded Hitler to allow him to do it – but by making better use of what was already being done.[29] The US Strategic Bombing Survey for Europe points out that the German economy's ability to keep increasing production year on year to the end of 1944 showed that it was very under-utilised in the war's early years. 'Germany's early commitment to the doctrine of the short war was a continuing handicap,' the Survey team wrote:

> Neither plans nor state of mind were adjusted to the idea of a long war. Nearly all German sources agree that the hope for a quick victory lasted long after the short war became a long one . . . The increase [in production] cannot be considered a testament to the efficiency of dictatorship. Rather it suggests the degree of industrial under-mobilisation in the earlier years. An excellent case can be made that throughout the war top government management in Germany was not efficient.[30]

However inefficient government management was, the result of Speer's appointment was that between 1942 and the autumn of 1944 the production of rifles doubled, the production of hand grenades trebled, and the production of artillery pieces increased sevenfold. Three times as many aircraft were built in 1944 as in 1941. At the war's end Nazi Germany had ten million men between the ages of 18 and 38 in uniform (this ignores the additional numbers, effectively useless, of the 'Volkssturm' home guard, in which boys from the age of 16 and men up to the age of 60 served). Despite the stories of bootless troops wearing summer uniforms on the Russian front in winter, which happened not because of production failures but because of military failures, the soldiers fighting in the streets of

Berlin in May 1945 still had boots, rifles, artillery pieces, ammunition and hand grenades.[31]

How did the German economy sustain this prodigious effort? One factor was that Germany had conquered almost all of Europe, and had its resources to use at will. The industrial and agricultural capacity of occupied and client states was available for the Reich's purposes, for example the bread-basket of the Ukraine, the coal and iron reserves of Silesia, the Romanian oil fields of Ploesti, and the sophisticated automotive, aircraft, electronics and armament factories of France, Czechoslovakia and Holland.[32]

Another factor is the immense labour resource that fell into Germany's hands by the same means. Contract labour from conquered and client states, slave labour and prisoners of war, added vastly to Germany's productive capacity. By the end of 1941 there were 3.5 million foreign labourers in Germany, including prisoners of war; a year later there were 4.6 million, most of the new influx from the Soviet Union; and by the autumn of 1944 there were 7.65 million, of whom 1.9 million were prisoners of war. These foreign workers accounted for more than a quarter of all those employed in the German economy. They made up half of the agricultural labour force, and a third each of the mining and construction industries. The largest contingents consisted of Russians and Poles, numbering respectively 2.12 million and 1.68 million. When not actually prisoners – who were paid nothing, and were effectively worked to death if they were Jewish or from the East – the foreign workers were paid relatively little, and not very well fed.[33]

It is no exaggeration to say that prisoners in the SS concentration camps were worked to death. One of the most notorious of the work camps was Mittelbau-Dora, which existed to serve armaments production – most notoriously, of the V2 'wonder weapon' – in a vast network of underground tunnels near Nordhausen. The eleven-mile tunnel system had been built before the war to store Germany's strategic oil reserves. In the damp chilly air where the prisoners both lived and, for long arduous hours, worked, fed on minuscule rations, the death rate was very high. Not many lasted more than a matter of weeks even if they arrived in good health.[34]

The presence of foreign labourers, under whatever guise, meant that although the Wehrmacht made heavy demands on home-grown German manpower, the supply of labour was always sufficient for large numbers to be diverted to repair bomb damage in cities, factories and railway marshalling yards, to clear rubble, and to collect and cremate the dead, without compromising industrial and agricultural production.

A third factor is that Germany plundered a vast amount of wealth from the conquered territories, and from its own and conquered Jewish populations. Jewish banks were taken over by German ones, shops and factories, homes and their contents, indeed fixed and liquid assets of all kinds, together amounting to the wealth of an advanced country, were taken costlessly into German hands; and supplemented yet further the Nazi state's productive capacity.

With these advantages it is not surprising that German production quickly recovered from any industrial damage that occurred as a result of bombing attacks, even those as devastating as Operation Gomorrah. Of the 574 large factories in Hamburg, 186 were completely destroyed in Operation Gomorrah, and with them 4,118 of the 9,068 small factories. Half the workers in war-related industrial production in Hamburg were laid off for up to two months.[35] The precision daylight bombing of the harbour and submarine works by Flying Fortresses of the US Eighth Army Air Force sank or damaged 180,000 tons of shipping and, according to post-war calculations, diminished total wartime U-boat production by 26 or 27 vessels. But the net loss of production in Hamburg's big factories amounted to a mere 1.8 months' output only; 'Patriotism, the German character and the SS were enough to ensure that in the absence for many months of further heavy raids, Hamburg made a remarkable recovery.'[36]

Speer was very anxious when he first received news of the damage caused by Operation Gomorrah. He said that another half-dozen such raids would cripple Germany's war production and force it to surrender. When he saw how quickly Hamburg recovered, however, he revised his opinion. Moreover, the expense of effort by Bomber Command was such that it could not mount any more Operation Gomorrahs for a while, not least because the cities Speer was worried about – Berlin, Munich, Stuttgart, Frankfurt, Leipzig and Augsburg – required such long flights over enemy territory that to attack them would invite high losses. Indeed, the 'Battle of Berlin' waged by Harris in the winter of 1943–4 in his effort to prove that bombing alone could win the war, proved this very point. The 'Battle of Berlin' was a costly defeat for Bomber Command, and it was not until Germany was on its knees in the winter of 1944–5 that Bomber Command could begin to 'knock Germany flat' as Harris phrased it: which in effect meant that Harris could achieve his aim only when Germany was already all but defeated.[37]

The second question, What would German industry have succeeded in doing if there had been no area-bombing campaign? has in fact received quantified answers. According to the US Strategic Bombing Survey for Europe, German industry lost 9 per cent of production in 1943 and 17 per cent in 1944 because of area bombing. The figures were based on a small sample, so the British figures might be more indicative, though they are even less flattering: they have it that in the second half of 1943 German industrial production was down 8.2 per cent, in the second half of 1944 it was down 7.2 per cent, and in the first four months of 1945 it was down 9.7 per cent. The figures for specific areas of war production are the significant ones: the British survey estimated that armament output was down by about 3 per cent in 1943 and less than 1 per cent overall for 1944. 'Considering that urban bombing had taken up about 45% of Bomber Command's efforts in terms of tonnage dropped,' writes Denis Richards, 'these estimates seemed to show that the area offensive had profoundly disappointing results.'[38]

The principal target of Bomber Command's area-bombing endeavours, remember, was 'morale' – the 'will of the people' of Germany to continue making war. On this point the man responsible for keeping up German morale was, to begin with, even more worried than Speer about the ability of Germany to survive, although in this case the anxiety concerned the psychological survival of its people. The man in question was Joseph Goebbels, Minister of Propaganda.

After Lübeck was bombed on 28–9 March 1942 as an experiment in incendiary attack, Goebbels wrote in his diary, 'The damage is really enormous. I have been shown a newsreel of the destruction. It is horrible. One can well imagine how such a bombardment affects the population.'[39] During the Battle of the Ruhr in the following spring and summer he visited some of the target cities, in Dortmund exclaiming that the raid of 23–4 May 1943 had 'virtually totally destroyed' the city.[40] He was, however, surprised and pleased when, going on a walkabout in Berlin during the 1943–4 winter blitz of the city, crowds cheered him and patted him on the back: the Berliners were angered by the bombing, and welcomed the speeches in which he spoke of revenge.[41] This was so despite the ferocity of the attacks. 'The picture that greeted my eye in the Wilhelmplatz was one of utter desolation,' he wrote in his diary. 'Hell itself seems to have broken loose over us.'[42] And he had no illusions about the extent or importance of the damage that was being done. After the bombing of Leipzig on 2–3 December 1943 he wrote, 'The centre of the city was especially hard hit. Almost all public buildings, theatres, the University, the Supreme Court, the Exhibition Halls etc have been completely destroyed or seriously damaged. About 150,000–200,000 people are without shelter.' (He did not mention that the Exhibition Halls had been commandeered for the production of Junkers aircraft.)[43]

But until the closing months of the war, morale did not break. Even those actively opposed to Nazism were made grimly determined by the bombing, if only to weather the storm: 'We repair because we must repair,' wrote Ruth Andreas-Friederich, an anti-Nazi activist, because we couldn't live another day longer if one forbade us the repairing. If they destroy our living room, we move into the kitchen. If they knock the kitchen apart, we move over into the hallway. If only we can stay 'at home'. The smallest corner of 'at home' is better than any palace in some strange place. For this reason all who have been driven out of the city by the bombs return home someday. They work with shovel and broom, with hammer, pliers and pick-axes. Until one day over the bombed-out foundations a new 'at home' exists. A Robinson-Crusoe lodge perhaps. But it is still 'at home'. The last thing one saves from a burning house is a pillow because it is the last piece of 'at home'.[44]

Goebbels sought to counter the morale challenge of bombing with an incessant stream of speeches and articles. He was still doing so even in the last devastating weeks of the war, with an article entitled 'Life Goes On' in *Das Reich* for 16 April 1944. In it, in a vein by then far too falsely optimistic, he spoke of the spirit with which the German people had survived under bombing – helping each other, pooling their resources, rebuilding their homes and factories, getting to work even if they had to walk miles over rubble-strewn streets, bearing hardships patiently and with humour. This picture was true of Germany at least into the autumn of 1944. Survivors of Operation Gomorrah reminisced that bombed-out families lived communally together in cellars, sharing everything and encouraging one another.[45] The *Berlin Diaries* of Marie Vassiltchikov describe the mutual help that was commonplace during the winter of the Berlin blitz.[46] It was even possible to say that the frequency of the bombing raids 'began to convert the experience of living under the bombs almost into a routine'.[47]

But as the bombing and the ground fighting intensified hugely in the final months of the war, turning Germany into a horrendous killing-ground and displacing millions of its people, the spirit cracked; Goebbels' 'Life Goes On' was published as the exact opposite was happening.

But the collapse of German morale at the very end of the war was not the result of bombing alone, nor was it even largely because of it. What finally unnerved a population that had borne so much during the final three years of the war, were two things. One was the newly severe hardships of the last months under the inexorable and palpable inevitability of defeat. The other was panic fear of the Russians – a fear exacerbated by the Nazi leadership's years of hysterical anti-Soviet propaganda, which proved self-fulfillingly true as a result of the cruel treatment to which the Germans had subjected the Russians, who now in their own turn, as the Red Army fought its way to Berlin, unleashed a season of terror on their defeated enemies, in the form of a revenge orgy of brutality and rape.[48]

But until those final months the effect of years of bombing on German civilian morale was very limited, even indeed counter-productive. So also – and this might well be part of the reason why – was the effect on the material conditions of German civilian life, despite the huge amount of attrition to the country's housing stock, 20 per cent of which was destroyed or damaged (485,000 dwellings were totally destroyed, and 415,000 heavily damaged).[49] The US Strategic Bombing Survey for Europe is unequivocal on this score:

A word should perhaps be added on the effect of the air war on the German civilian and on the civilian economy. Germany began the war after several years of full employment and after the civilian standard of living had reached its highest level in German history. In the early years of the war – the soft war period for Germany – civilian consumption remained high. Germans continued to try for guns and butter. The German people entered the period of the air war well stocked with clothing and other consumer goods. Although most consumer goods became increasingly difficult to obtain, Survey studies show that fairly adequate supplies of clothing were available for those who had been bombed out until the last stages of disorganisation. Food, though strictly rationed, was in nutritionally adequate supply throughout the war. The Germans' diet had about the same calories as the British.[50]

What, then, did the bombing achieve in quantifiable terms? In the war as a whole, according to the US Strategic Bombing Survey, bombs killed 305,000 German civilians and injured 780,000. Other estimates give an upper limit on the number of German bombing dead as close to 500,000. Some of these deaths were caused by the Eighth Army Air Force, but by far the greater part was the result of RAF area bombing.

In return for this number of civilian deaths in Germany, Bomber Command suffered the deaths of 55,000 of its own members. Taking the highest figure for German civilian deaths, this makes a ratio of one Bomber Command airman killed for every 9 German civilians killed. Taking the lower estimate, it is a ratio of one British airman for every 5.5 German civilians.

In 1940 Bomber Command dropped 5,000 tons of bombs on Germany. In 1941 it dropped 23,000 tons. In 1942 it dropped 37,000 tons. In 1943 it dropped 180,000 tons. In 1944 it dropped 474,000 tons. And in the four months January–April 1945 inclusive, when the war was already palpably won, it dropped a mammoth 181,000 tons (an annual rate of 724,000, just for comparison). This last figure is nearly one fifth of the total for the whole war put together, and it represents a bombing inundation. These totals exclude US Eighth Army Air Force tonnages.

At a rough estimate, these figures suggest that it took 2.25 tons of bombs to kill one German civilian. It also means that it took one ton of bombs to destroy or damage one German flat or house. The number of Bomber Command aircraft lost in the process was 7,700.

Just in material terms, therefore, Bomber Command's war on Germany represents a very expensive campaign indeed.

The fact that it took so many tons of bombs to kill people and destroy buildings is partly a function of the fact that a high proportion of the bombs were dropped well away from their intended targets, many of them in open fields, because of problems with navigation and bomb-aiming. This was diminishingly so as the war went on, but optimal conditions for bombing – in clear daylight without inter- ference from defences – were only achieved very late in the war in Germany, and in the nine months of the US bombing of Japan. In fact, the 'good bombing conditions' of the USAAF campaign over Japan explain why the casualty and destruction figures in Japan exceed those of Germany, despite the fact that the latter was bombed continuously for five years and the former for less than one year.

What the figures just given for Germany do not yet show is the military cost to Germany of defending against air attack – specifically, in terms of the number of anti-aircraft guns and fighter planes required for home defence, therefore keeping them away from the Eastern and later Western front lines. Justifiers of the RAF area- bombing campaign keenly strees this point. Historians of the air war point out that some 10,000 of the Germans' excellent 88-mm. artillery pieces had to be deployed as anti-aircraft guns in the homeland when they could have been used in their other chief role on the Eastern Front as anti-tank guns. They also point out that the necessities of air defence meant that aircraft production had to be focused on fighters rather than bombers, which further weakened German capacity to wage war effectively. (They have in mind the tactical use of bombers over battlefields.) Moreover, of the bombers Germany produced, none were heavy bombers, and its light bombers were in no position to compete with the tonnages that the RAF's Lancasters and Halifaxes could carry.

And finally, the historians point out that a million men were required to man the homeland defences, and a further million to serve as emergency workers in the cities, representing a significant drain on manpower resources – all directly attributable to the bombing campaign.[51]

These are good points, though not quite as good as they look. Those who manned the anti-aircraft guns were not suitable as front-line troops, and had much more the character of 'Volkssturm' recruits than fully trained soldiers. They included boys as young as sixteen and men over thirty-eight years of age. The majority of the men and women who manned emergency services were not additional to factory and business workers, but the self-same people detailed to take their turn on air-raid precaution and fire-watch duties. The lack of bombers, heavy or light, was not regarded as a problem by the German leadership because throughout the war they were busy devising missiles to take the place of bombers – the V1 and V2 rockets were merely the beginnings of what was planned to be an arsenal of such. It is true that Hitler personally delayed the ME 262 jet fighter's appearance in the war because he mistakenly demanded that it should be converted into a bomber for tactical use, suggesting a belated awareness of a deficit in this aspect of Germany's air capabilities. But it is likely that he thought of this as a stop-gap while the missile programme was under development.

Taken all in all, the argument that the bombing campaign diverted a slice of Germany's war effort to home defence is correct, but as these remarks show, the diversion was not as significant as an unqualified statement of it suggests.

Almost every authority on the subject of Bomber Command's area-bombing campaign agrees that it was a failure – a failure in military terms, that is; answers to the question of its ethics come later. It sought to undermine the morale and weaken the will of the German people, and it signally failed to do either. It has been pointed out that it represented the war's single longest continuous battle, in which its front line was engaged with the enemy on most days of the war. This extraordinary fact is a testament to the fortitude and endurance of air crews and ground crews, the energy of the force's high command, the dedication of factory workers who produced the bombers and the bombs, and the ingenuity of scientists who waged a war of ideas against an equally clever and inventive enemy. But for the mighty endeavour thus represented, the result of its effort to break the enemy's heart was not just null but actually contrary to hopes.

The question whether the area-bombing effort to some extent slowed the pace of increase of German war production remains open. It certainly did not halt it, or prevent it from growing. And when, close to the end of the war, German production did at last falter and finally halt, other and more compelling factors had became operative in causing that to happen – among them precision bombing of the kind to which most of the US Eighth Army Air Force's effort had been dedicated.

This last point leads to something else that almost every authority is in agreement about, namely what the successes of the bombing campaigns in Europe actually were. There were two. One was the precision bombing carried out throughout their presence in the European theatre by the US Eighth Army Air Force and later the Fifteenth Army Air Force operating from Italy, and (with a few honourable exceptions such as the Dam Busters raid) late in the war by Bomber Command too. The other was the contribution made by tactical bombing to the success of the invasion on and after D-Day in 1944.

An examination of the details of this latter show that in post-D-Day operations in the invasion area, ground-attack fighters and fighter-bombers were the major air factor in assisting the Allied struggle.[52] Nevertheless before the invasion, and in the two months immediately following it, bombing forces of the RAF and the US Eighth Army Air Force played a major role in reducing defences on the invasion coasts, and disrupting communications behind the German lines. The bombers were far from perfect tactical weapons – a point on which Sir Arthur Harris always vigorously insisted – but they proved much more effective in the role than he expected or, presumably, wanted.[53] They attacked harbours, fuel and ammunition dumps, and at times enemy forces in strongholds preventing the advance of the Allied ground forces. One such was Caen, which (with great loss of French civilian life) Bomber Command reduced to rubble on 7 July 1944 after Montgomery had requested that it be softened up before an infantry advance upon it. As it happened, this speciality of Bomber Command was not quite what the troops on the ground needed, for the rubble blocked their way, and if it did not make capture of Caen more difficult, it certainly introduced new difficulties in place of the old.[54]

Harris laid on a spectacular 1,000-bomber raid to clear the way for the Canadian First Army in its advance towards Falaise on 7–8 August 1944. A War Office observer was deeply impressed by the sight, as were the Canadian troops themselves: the noise, flame and smoke were tremendous. A week later in the same combat zone some of Harris's bombers strayed off target and killed sixty-five Canadians in a 'friendly fire' incident that took the shine off the previous week's efforts. But when in September 1944 Bomber Command was released from its obligations to the ground war, Harris received fulsome thanks from Eisenhower for what the Command had done, and Harris himself was awarded the US Order of Merit by President Roosevelt.

Much more important still, however, was the success of what many, and especially the American bomber leaders, regarded as the true strategic value of the bomber: the attack on crucial sectors of Germany's war production, and, most crucially of all, its oil supplies. If there is a single thing that bombing can be said to have contributed to Allied victory over Nazi Germany, it is precisely this: its success in severely limiting the fuel supplies needed by the Wehrmacht and Luftwaffe. Harris, it will be remembered, was strongly against the 'panacea' of singling out oil or anything else – ball-bearings, or railway marshalling yards – that the economic warfare experts had identified at their desks as a bottle-neck in German production, and which, if pinched, would strangle the German war effort. But Harris was wrong, and the experts and the Americans were right.

Repeated bombing attacks on the oil fields of Romania and Hungary, on synthetic oil plants in Germany, and on oil refineries near Vienna, Bleckhammer and Odenthal, in the end proved fatal to

Germany. The oil campaign started in earnest in the spring of 1944 when attacks were mounted – and sustained – on the synthetic oil plants at Leuna, Brux, Bohlen, Zeitz, Lutzendorf, Magdeburg and a number of other sites. Speer sought an emergency meeting with Hitler to press him to take emergency measures in response. As a result, Hitler appointed Edmund Geilenberg to the post of Reich commissioner with special responsibility for oil supplies, and gave him priority to requisition 350,000 workers for repair of oil plants and for the task of moving production to new underground sites. But the effort had come too late; as fuel supplies dwindled during the rest of 1944 and into the final months of the war, aircraft were grounded, tanks halted, training for replacement pilots could not be maintained, and most of the new and highly effective Messerschmitt 262 jet-fighter aircraft, of which over 1,200 had been produced by the end of 1944 and which might have considerably prolonged the war, had neither fuel to fly nor trained pilots to fly them.[55] The ME 262s were anyway extremely fuel-hungry aircraft, and those that went into action had to be towed to the end of their runways to conserve fuel – by cows, so Adolf Galland reports, to further save the fuel of tractors and lorries.[56]

Speer's acute anxieties over fuel were fully justified. Before bombing attacks on the oil infrastructure began in May 1944, Germany was producing an average of 316,000 tons a month. Bombing caused production to fall to 107,000 tons in June 1944, and 17,000 tons in the following September. Aviation fuel from the synthetic-oil plants fell from 175,000 tons in April 1944 to 30,000 in June and then to 5,000 tons in September. In his letter to Hitler of 30 June 1944 Speer wrote, 'The enemy has succeeded in increasing our losses of aviation gasoline up to 90 percent by 22 June. Only through speedy recovery of damaged plants has it been possible to regain partly some of the terrible losses.'[57]

Despite his wholly misplaced scepticism about the oil 'panacea', Harris came to recognise the value of the attack on oil – after the war's end. In his memoirs he wrote,

In the weeks before the end of the war all the German armed forces were immobilised by lack of fuel. The amount of oil produced by the synthetic oil plants and other factories was so little that it would not have paid the enemy to use up fuel in conveying it to the armed forces. The triumph of the offensive against oil was complete and indisputable.[58]

One cannot help feeling that Harris, now wise after the event, was exploiting what turned out to be one of the few unequivocal successes that could be claimed for bombing. He had not been merely sceptical, he had been scathing about the oil 'panacea', and – worse – had bitterly resisted the efforts of Portal and the Air Staff to make him concentrate upon it. As an officer he had of course eventually obeyed, grudgingly and a little belatedly, and during the course of the four combat months of 1945 Bomber Command carried out seventy-four operations against oil targets, half of them by day and half by night, dropping 43,636 tons of bombs in the process. The RAF effort against oil was however far less than that of the USAAF; between them the lion's share of the work was done by the US Eighth Army Air Force from its bases in England and the US Fifteenth Army Air Force from its bases in Italy, profiting from their greater experience of accurate daylight bombing.

An example of the effort made is the series of attacks on Leuna, the Germans' largest synthetic-oil plant. It was strongly defended by effective smoke-screen machines and a massive anti-aircraft-gun concentration. It was one of the least popular assignments for air crews in the war, because it was one of the most dangerous. Leuna was attacked twenty-two times between May and December 1944, twenty times by the US Eighth Army Air Force and twice by the RAF. Every time it was attacked it was repaired, but always at a lower level of output, averaging a mere 9 per cent of full capacity over the period.[59] The US Strategic Bombing Survey reported:

Consumption of oil exceeded production from May 1944 on. Accumulated stocks were rapidly used up, and in six months were practically exhausted. The loss of oil production was felt acutely by the armed forces. In August the final run-in time for aircraft engines was cut from two hours to one-half hour. For lack of fuel, pilot training, previously cut down, was further curtailed. Through the summer, the movement of German Panzer Divisions in the field was hampered . . . By December, according to Speer, the fuel shortage had reached catastrophic proportions. When the Germans launched their counter-offensive on December 16, 1944 [the Ardennes offensive], their reserves of fuel were insufficient to support the operation. They counted on capturing Allied stocks . . . In February and March of 1945 the Germans massed 1200 tanks on the Baranov bridgehead at the Vistula to check the Russians. They were immobilised for lack of fuel, and overrun.[60]

It is right to add that although attacks on oil plants proved far more than the 'panacea' Harris believed it to be, major war production declined in almost all sectors from the autumn of 1944. On 27 January 1945, in a letter to General Heinz Guderian, Speer reported that coal and steel output were sharply down, as was aircraft production. Speer had planned to manufacture 12,000 fighter planes in the last three months of 1944, but only 8,600 were actually built. (One might, in the circumstances, write 'only'.)[61] The fact that output was at these levels so late in the war is itself a function of the bombing campaign, which had caused aircraft factories to be dispersed and hidden.

It is also right to add that the historians disagree among themselves as to whether the laurel should be given to attacks on oil supplies or on transportation in the final year of the war. The US Strategic Bombing Survey for Europe was definite in its opinion that oil mattered most, whereas others focus on the disruption of railway links within the Reich. In a detailed study of the German war economy Alfred Mierjewski concluded that the transportation crisis caused by bombing of railways in the autumn of 1944 meant that coal supplies from the Ruhr and Silesia to factories everywhere in Germany were interrupted, and were responsible for their downturn in output. Speer organised a rapid transfer of labour to railway-repair work, and supplies moved again; but when the transport links were attacked again in the first months of 1945, the progress of Allied ground forces from both east and west meant that the problem had become irremediable.[62]

But now a new question has to be asked, suggested by the contrast between the bombing of Germany and the bombing of Japan. In the case of Japan, a relatively short and catastrophic air attack was quickly followed by Japanese surrender. It is too easy to conclude a causal connection between the facts here; 'this follows that so that caused this' is a logical fallacy. At the same time it seems highly relevant to ask whether there is a causal connection, especially given that the devastating bombing campaign was concluded by the atom bomb attacks, followed within mere days by the unprecedented appearance of Emperor Hirohito on national radio to announce his country's surrender.

If it turns out that American bombing of Japan is the key factor in ending the Pacific war, then it has to be concluded that Sir Arthur Harris and all the theoreticians of bomber power (see the next chapter) were right in holding that a sufficient weight of aerial attack will bring an enemy to his knees and thus end a war. And then the explanation of why this did not happen in the case of Germany would be that, until the closing stages of the war, the Allies simply did not have enough bomb weight – as for example would have been provided by the atom bomb – with which to achieve this effect.

One can imagine someone arguing that too little weight of attack would indeed have effects contrary to the desired one; the effects, that is, of strengthening an enemy's morale, and – worse – the enemy's capacity to survive and resist bombing. For if a bombing attack was incremental from a low starting level, as happened with Bomber Command's activities from 1940 onwards, enemy defences and preparedness would increasingly learn how to deal with it, so that even as the weight of attack increased, its effect would be negated by the equally increasing capacity of the enemy to absorb it.

But if enough – so this argument continues – in the way of aircraft and bombs had been available to deliver a massive and sustained assault right from the beginning, the war would have ended in months rather than years, as happened when at last Japan came under just such bombing.

Are these arguments right? It all turns on whether there are factors other than bombing involved in Japan's surrender, and on their relative degree of significance. The answer to this in turn depends upon whether the reason for Japan's surrender was civilian or military. If civilian vulnerability was what impelled surrender, then bombing probably played a large part in it. Civilian vulnerability could be a function of hunger or other privations, but in the circumstances it would be plausible to see it as arising either from the shock of bombing, or fear of further devastation of the kind wrought by atomic bombs, or both.

If, however, the reason for Japan's surrender was military – that is, based on a realisation that the war could not be won – then bombing was not the decisive factor, even if it was a contributory one. In this latter case, Sir Arthur Harris and the theoreticians of bombing as a war-winning strategy could not appeal to the Japanese example as a vindication.

The question of why Japan surrendered in August 1945 is a complex one, and this is not the place for a full analysis of it. The conclusion reached by Robert Pape in his detailed and masterly dissection of the matter is however unequivocal:

The principal cause of Japan's surrender was the ability of the United States to increase the military vulnerability of the home islands sufficiently to persuade Japanese leaders that their defence was highly unlikely to succeed. The key military factor causing this effect was the sea blockade, which crippled Japan's ability to produce and equip forces necessary to execute its strategy. The most important factor accounting for the timing of the surrender was the Soviet attack against Manchuria [9 August 1945, the same day as the Nagasaki bomb], largely because it convinced recalcitrant Army leaders that the homeland could not be defended.

Contrary to the assertion of the Strategic Bombing Survey that bombing was so effective that even if there had been no atomic bomb, Soviet attack, or planned American invasion, surrender would have occurred at exactly the same time, in actuality the naval blockade, invasion threat, and Soviet attack ensured that surrender would have occurred at *precisely* the same time even if there had been no strategic bombing campaign.[63]

Pape's view is based on an examination of Japan's military and civilian leadership decisions in the final year of the Pacific war. As he states, he expressly dissents from the conclusion of the US Strategic Bombing Survey for the Pacific war, which was that even without the atom bombs the strategic-bombing effort was the decisive factor. This conclusion might appear odd to some, for whom the atom-bomb attacks appear to be precisely what adds the final weight of force that the area-bombing campaign over Germany lacked. If anything could be supposed to render the USAAF campaign against Japan decisive, therefore, the atom bombs would be it. Yet the Survey concluded that they were inessential to the outcome.

That surprising view, and the fact that Pape's analysis, careful and convincing though it is, no doubt remains controversial among some historians of the Pacific war, can be left as open matters here, for the present concern is tangential to them. The present concern requires only that we note that the claim that area-bombing was a *major* factor in victory is hotly disputed for Japan and denied for Germany. This matters because defenders of the campaigns draw heavily on their supposed military efficacy or even necessity.

More important still is how these considerations bear on the question of the morality of area bombing. If area bombing was unavoidable as a means of defeating the Axis powers – especially given the moral status of the Axis powers themselves – a claim of justification, or at very least mitigation, must be entertained. If area bombing was not an essential component in the defeat of the Axis powers, the degree of their exposure to moral questioning rises. To this matter, of course, I return in detail later.

The longer-term effects of area bombing on Germany and Japan – not just on the physical fabric of their countries, but more importantly on the psychological fabric of their societies – constitutes an entirely different story, and a very complex one. It figures as part of the much larger story of post-war German and Japanese attitudes to the war as a whole, and it takes contrastingly different forms in the two nations. (An excellent place to begin exploring these matters is Ian Buruma's *The Wages of Guilt*[64]). The guilt felt about the Holocaust by most individual Germans of the immediate post-war generations, and by German society as a required collective stance, for long made it impossible for them to see the catastrophe they experienced in 1945 as anything other than deserved punishment. Japanese attitudes to the war as a whole lie behind a characteristically equivocal mask of demurral; but when one talks to individuals about the atom bombings of Nagasaki and Hiroshima, one learns that Japan sees them as war crimes.[65]

This makes some Japanese intellectuals angry with their own. Buruma reports an occasion on which the writer Kenzaburo Oe castigated his country as racist and as never having faced up to its crimes in the Second World War.[66] Oe was in conversation with Günter Grass at a book fair just at the time that the separated parts of Germany were reuniting, an event that Grass deprecated: 'Auschwitz should have made reunification impossible; a unified Germany was a danger to itself and the world,' he said.[67] Whereas Grass's assertion was characteristic of a standard German attitude, Oe's was uncharacteristic of Japanese attitudes. But as Buruma points out, even though Japan had to answer for atrocities in China and against prisoners of war, the sexual slavery of Korean women, the notorious

'Unit 731' in Manchuria, where appalling medical experiments were conducted on live human guinea pigs referred to by the Japanese staff as 'logs', and the acts of aggression in precipitating war first against China and then against the United States, it nevertheless had no Holocaust to answer for, and Nazi Germany had all these things or their equivalents to answer for *and* the Holocaust.[68]

The Holocaust throws such a deep and jagged shadow over the Second World War that the sum total of harm done by all other non-Holocaust-related means is diminished by it; which is one reason why there has been so little said about culpabilities on the Allied side of the struggle – culpabilities which pale in comparison to Nazi atrocity, and which the victor nations have therefore allowed themselves to neglect. Dresden makes periodic appearances on public consciousness, but very few people (apart from apologists for ultra-right-wing interests; but they are not interested in truth or historical proportion; they have other fish to fry) see that the Allied area bombing campaigns over Germany and Japan merit inspection and evaluation. For if they constitute a wrong, even though it is dwarfed by the Holocaust and other Axis-committed aggressions and atrocities, they would still be a wrong. And that, to repeat, is what is being examined here.

4

The Mind of the Bomber

A FTER THE OPERATION Gomorrah attacks on Hamburg, Bomber Command's chief, Air Marshal Sir Arthur Harris, said 'I had always wanted to have a real dead set at Hamburg. It was the second biggest city in Germany and I wanted to make a tremendous show.'[1] Hamburg's size was one reason why it was chosen for a major display of bombing power. A big city could be hurt even if bombing was not especially accurate. Another reason was that it is relatively easy to find, because it lies on the River Elbe near a coast with a shape easily recognisable from high in the air even at night. A third reason was that it is relatively easy to get to, not involving too long a trip for the bomber stream, which meant less time exposed to Luftwaffe night-fighters; and moreover much of the trip there and back could be carried out over the North Sea, empty of flak, searchlights and Luftwaffe airfields.

Harris's remark is interesting as giving a glimpse into the mind of a man who, on an almost daily basis, planned bombing raids – 'area bombing', 'carpet bombing', indiscriminate raids – upon densely inhabited cities, and sent hundreds of aircraft, carrying tons of explosives and incendiaries, to carry them out. The remark has an impersonal air, which does not quite represent the man who made it; for it is false to say that Harris was merely a callous and unimaginative man for whom mass killing by bombing was a matter of indifference.

He was indefatigably concerned with the welfare of his Bomber Command personnel, he was fully conscious that he was sending young men in his charge to their deaths almost every day – and having lived in London during the Blitz, and watched the City burning around St Paul's Cathedral, he had a clear idea of what he was unleashing on German civilians.[2] He was not a man of culture, and he was certainly capable of the kind of toughness required to carry out a policy of mass killings on a regular basis; but balance requires that one remember that (in the phrase much then employed) 'there was a war on', and he took himself to be in command of a campaign that would not only defend his own country from a dangerous aggressor, but would win the war to boot, and thereby destroy the regime which had plunged the world into catastrophe.[3] And like other proponents of area bombing as a war-winning strategy, he could claim to believe that it would shorten the war and therefore save lives overall – especially on his own side, by rescuing tens of thousands of young soldiers from the hazards of invasion. This, certainly, is what Americans claimed after the war in defence of their bombing of Japan, and especially the atom-bomb attacks.

Some might say, regarding the point about Harris's personal experience of watching London burn after the Luftwaffe's big fire raid of 29 December 1940, that his knowledge of what he was inflicting on Germany was not only clear but vengefully so. An anecdote is often repeated to illustrate this. Harris, driving himself at high speed back to his HQ in High Wycombe after an Air Ministry meeting in London, was stopped by two police motor-cyclists. One of them said, 'Sir, you are travelling much too fast; you might kill someone.' Harris replied, 'I'm on important business. Now that you mention it, it is my business to kill people: Germans.' Allegedly the policeman replied, 'Are you Air Marshal Harris, sir?' and when Harris confirmed that he was, the policeman said, 'That's different, sir; sorry I stopped you. Follow us,' and the two acted as outriders to speed Harris home. Harris told an aide afterwards, 'It was the quickest trip I ever made – they must have liked me.'[4]

Harris's assertion about the nature of his business was not merely flippant. In a discussion with the Air Ministry about the types of bombs to be used in attacks on German cities, Harris maintained that the proportions should be two-thirds incendiaries to one-third high explosives. This was in response to the Air Ministry's view that the blitz on Britain, and the RAF's experimental incendiary bombing of the wooden city of Lübeck, suggested that bomb loads should consist wholly of incendiaries. 'I am always being pressed to concentrate entirely on incendiaries,' he wrote to the Ministry,

> but I do not agree with this policy. The moral [that is, psychological] effect of HE is vast. People can escape from fires, and the casualties on a solely fire-raising raid would be as nothing. What we want to do in addition to the horrors of fire is to bring the masonry crashing down on top of the Boche, to kill Boche, and to terrify Boche; hence the proportion of HE.'[5]

Had Harris known of the horrific effects of firestorms rather than just City of London-type fires, he might have been as sanguine and sanguinary about incendiaries as high explosives. At any rate, his attitude to the purpose of area bombing was unequivocal, and thus on record: 'we want . . . to bring the masonry crashing down on top of the Boche, to kill Boche, and to terrify Boche.'

Nor did he think that this purpose should be disguised. In November 1943, effectively announcing the launching of his 'Battle of Berlin', he stated publicly that Berlin, the heart of Nazi Germany, would be attacked repeatedly 'until it ceased to beat'. Lord Salisbury, a vocal critic of the area-bombing policy, wrote to the Minister for Air, Sir Archibald Sinclair, complaining that Harris's statement was contrary to official government policy, which was that bombs were aimed only at industrial and military targets, not at civilian areas. Since the government was loath to acknowledge the area-bombing policy publicly, Sinclair gave a prevaricating reply. Harris was annoyed by this on two counts. First, he thought that his air crews would not get proper recognition for their endeavours if the endeavours themselves were not officially recognised. And second and relatedly, since area bombing at night was a largely inaccurate proceeding, any suggestion that Bomber Command was trying to hit precise targets would inevitably invite criticism, because by that criterion Bomber Command would always appear to fail.[6]

Harris's attitudes to area bombing, which he said required that people with 'sensitive minds' should not seek leadership positions in the bombing force,[7] rested on his unshakeable belief that war was to be won by attacking the morale of an enemy population until its will to resist was broken. He had seen the trenches of the First World War from his biplane, and he thought that the pain and expense of ground fighting could be made unnecessary by the right application of enough power from the air. This fixed belief governed his thinking to such an extent that, as noted in the preceding chapter, he could not accept the logic of precision bombing – in the case of his virtual insubordination to the Air Staff, of oil targets – except as a minor ancillary to the main task.

But in thinking this way, Harris was merely following the precepts of earlier theorists of air power, and they in turn had extrapolated their views from the experience of bombing in the first three decades of flight (that is, from 1910 to 1939) in the First World War, colonial wars, and the Spanish Civil War. Understanding the development of this thinking explains the beliefs and intentions in the minds of those responsible for bombing policy in both the British and American militaries (and as we have already seen, British and American thinking about bombing diverged significantly for a time). This is crucial, for in seeking to judge the morality of the Allied bombing campaign, one has to have a clear picture of what was known, what was believed, and what was hoped by those who carried it out.

One also has to know the circumstances that influenced their thinking in carrying it out – specifically, the state of the war at the time they committed themselves to one or another policy. This chapter concerns the first of these two crucial matters; the second I defer to chapter 7 where arguments in defence of area bombing are considered.

In 1899 an international peace conference was held at The Hague. It had been suggested by an adviser to Russia's Czar Nicholas II, the outstanding Russian international-law theorist Fedor Fedorovich Martens, as an appropriate sequel to a series of conferences held in The Hague earlier in the 1890s, all aimed at building a regime of international law.

Queen Wilhelmina of the Netherlands served as the 1899 conference's host, so that with its two royal sponsors it had the highest official sanction. Its purpose was not to settle a current war (though one was just then beginning in South Africa between the British and the Afrikaaners of the Boer Republics, and a short but highly consequential one had just ended between the United States and Spain, extending American influence from the Caribbean to the Pacific). The conference's aim, rather, was to frame the conditions for lasting international peace. The principal behind it is summarised in the celebrated 'Martens clause', named for the conference's prime mover, which gave preliminary encapsulation to the idea of a legal framework governing conflict between nations:

> Until a more complete code of the laws of war is issued, the High Contracting Parties think it right to declare that in cases not included in the Regulations adopted by them, populations and belligerents remain under the protection and empire of the principles of international law, as they result from the usages established between civilised nations, from the laws of humanity and the requirements of the public conscience.[8]

The eloquence of the last thirty-seven words of this passage well suits the ideal they express: *populations and belligerents remain under the protection and empire of the principles of international law, as they result from the usages established between civilised nations, from the laws of humanity and the requirements of the public conscience.*

With remarkable prescience the conference gave consideration to the matter of aerial bombing, in the form of 'projectiles or explosives' launched from balloons (heavier-than-air manned flight was still four years away). The preamble to the Declaration accordingly drawn up, known as Hague IV, quoted the St Petersburg Declaration of 1868, in which an International Military Commission hosted by Russia's Imperial Cabinet agreed to forbid the use of specified projectiles, among them exploding or incendiary bullets. The St Petersburg Declaration reads:

On the proposition of the Imperial Cabinet of Russia, an International Military Commission having assembled at St. Petersburg in order to examine the expediency of forbidding the use of certain projectiles in time of war between civilised nations, and that Commission having by common agreement fixed the technical limits at which the necessities of war ought to yield to the requirements of humanity, the Undersigned are authorised by the orders of their Governments to declare as follows:

Considering:

That the progress of civilisation should have the effect of alleviating as much as possible the calamities of war;

That the only legitimate object which States should endeavour to accomplish during war is to weaken the military forces of the enemy;

That for this purpose it is sufficient to disable the greatest possible number of men;

That this object would be exceeded by the employment of arms which uselessly aggravate the sufferings of disabled men, or render their death inevitable;

That the employment of such arms would, therefore, be contrary to the laws of humanity;

The Contracting Parties engage mutually to renounce, in case of war among themselves, the employment by their military or naval troops of any projectile of a weight below 400 grams, which is either explosive or charged with fulminating or inflammable substances . . .

The Contracting or Acceding Parties reserve to themselves to come hereafter to an understanding whenever a precise proposition shall be drawn up in view of future improvements which science may effect in the armament of troops, in order to maintain the principles which they have established, and to conciliate the necessities of war with the laws of humanity.

Were we discussing these matters *viva voce*, it might be appropriate to pause for a minute's silence to ponder the good sense and humanitarian impulse animating these words, written down now so long ago, in their effort to restrain the murderous uses to which misapplications of burgeoning science were even then tending. The men gathered in St Petersburg could not see what science would produce by 1945, as proved on two August mornings in Japan that year; but they felt the onrush of dangers, and were men of good faith. The key words are unequivocal: 'The Contracting or Acceding Parties reserve to themselves to come hereafter to an understanding whenever a precise proposition shall be drawn up *in view of future improvements which science may effect in the armament of troops*, in order *to maintain the principles which they have established, and to conciliate the necessities of war with the laws of humanity.*'

Inspired by this example, and looking ahead, those gathered at The Hague in 1899 agreed to 'prohibit, for a term of five years, the launching of projectiles and explosives from balloons, or by other new methods of a similar nature'. As the time restriction to five years implies, the Declaration was meant to be a stop-gap until a formal Law of War could be agreed by the international community. The absence of agreement on a Law of War – wars, such as the Boer War and the Sino-Japanese war, among other things, put talk of such a thing far on to the back burner – made it necessary for the stop-gap to remain in force, so Hague IV was renewed by another Hague conference in 1907, and in the same terms. By this time the phrase or by 'new methods of a similar nature' had taken on added meaning; the air was already filling with aeroplanes. This gave the irony that attends human endeavours full play, for it meant that the declaration was still in force when – inevitably, and in defiance of Hague IV – the first bombs were dropped from the air on 1 November 1911, by a pilot in the Italian forces fighting the Ottoman Turks in Libya.

As we know too well, agreements and declarations, however full of good sense and humanity, have no hold on mankind when fighting starts; but they provide a benchmark for thinking about the rights and wrongs of what happens once it does; and they seldom leave much room for excuses. The principles, and even more the spirit, of both the St Petersburg Declaration of 1868 and the Hague IV Declaration of 1899 and 1907, are crystal clear; and the first act of bombing in the Libyan desert blew a hole right through them both.

That first bombing was carried out by Lieutenant Giulio Gavotti, an artillery spotter in the Italian army. Entirely on his own initiative he took four grenades with him on a flight over the Ottoman army encampment at Ain Zara, and threw them from his Taube mono-plane on to the angry Turks below. No one was hurt. News of the escapade was greeted with disgust and disdain by civilised opinion, which chiefly thought it unsporting. But military men thought otherwise, and immediately began to research ways of making it an effective resource of war.

All the major nations of Europe designed and produced bomber aircraft during the First World War, and some of them began before the war started. Both France and Germany did so, the former developing its Voisin bomber and the latter adapting the Zeppelin dirigible for the purpose. Appropriately therefore, one of the earliest air actions of the First World War was the bombing of the Zeppelin base at Metz-Frascaty by Voisin aircraft on 14 August 1914. The Voisin was a durable steel-framed pusher biplane which, as the war went on, was equipped with increasingly more powerful engines, in the end allowing it to carry 300 kilograms of bombs (660 lb.). France had a force of about 600 Voisins which it used to attack the German lines of the Western Front. It did not have the range to penetrate Germany itself, and the French were loath to use it against occupied areas where French citizens lived; so its use remained purely tactical. The Zeppelin, as we shall see, was by contrast the first truly strategic bomber, being used in raids against towns in England.

Russia and Italy were not far behind France in acquiring bomber aircraft. The Imperial Russian Air Service provided itself with the giant 'Ilya Mourometz' designed by Igor Sikorsky, the first-ever four-engined aeroplane. It was a prodigy for its time; able to stay in the air for over five hours at a stretch, with a speed of 85 miles an hour and a 'ceiling' of 9,000 feet, it bristled with machine guns and was capable of carrying a maximum bomb load of 700 kilograms (1,540 lb). The Imperial Russian Air Service trained its bomb-aimers well, and the Ilya Mourometz had an excellent record for bombing accuracy. Under the command of Major-General M. V. Shidlovski the Russian bomber fleet was one of the successes of that country's generally unsuccessful endeavours on the Eastern Front.

Italy entered the war relatively late, in May 1915, and although otherwise ill-prepared for taking part in a major conflict, it by that time had a force of three-engined Caproni bombers in service. The Caproni was capable of crossing the Alps at 95 miles per hour, carrying 540 kilograms of bombs (1,190 lb), and accordingly did so, seeking targets in Austro-Hungarian territory.

The United States was neither a major producer of aircraft nor a major air power in the First World War. It had the Curtiss 'Jenny' biplane on which its pilots trained (and which after the war became the staple of the 'barnstormer' fliers), but when US army aviators entered the war in the spring of 1918 they were equipped with the French-made Nieuport and Spad fighter planes, and took no part in bombing activities.

In August 1914 Britain had no bomber aircraft, though soon after hostilities began, the Royal Navy indented for some, offering a design specification for an aircraft of modest capacity compared to those in service elsewhere among the belligerents: a twin-engined two-seater which could fly at 75 miles per hour and carry 50 kilograms of bombs (110 lb). The result was the Handley Page 0/100, which entered service in November 1916. Although at first reserved to navy-related operations, it soon saw service on the Western Front and as a night bomber.

It was the Germans who proved the most adventurous bombers in the Great War, beginning with Zeppelins and later the feared Gotha C-V bomber, whose enormous 24-metre wingspan made it a terrifying sight when it swept over civilian targets, dropping explosives. Between them, Zeppelins and Gothas mounted 103 raids over Great Britain, ostensibly attacking industrial and military targets but in fact bombing towns and cities. Between January 1915 and November 1916 Zeppelins conducted 208 sorties, and from May 1917 to May 1918 Gothas conducted 435 sorties, between them dropping approximately 300 tons of bombs on Britain in what was a curtain-raiser for the practice of area bombing. In the process they killed 1,400 Britons and injured 3,400 more, and did about three million pounds' worth of damage to property at 1914 values.

But most of all the Zeppelins and Gothas created great panic, and gave rise to the belief – the false belief, as it too late proved – that bombing civilian populations is a weapon of peculiar psychological potency. For by one of the more terrible of history's ironies, hindsight shows that a little bombing or even the mere sight of bombers swooping overhead, terrifies populations that are not used to them; but a bit more bombing than Britain received in the First World War has a rebound effect on morale, as witnessed in both Britain and Germany in the Second World War. If Germany had mounted a more sustained and weighty area-bombing attack on British towns and cities in 1916–18, intelligent observers would have seen that it was in fact counter-productive – and therefore, although murderous and destructive, uselessly so.

Indeed, intelligent observers might have recognised this truth anyway. At first there was great panic in towns struck by Gothas.

Their first attack fell on Folkestone in May 1917, killing 95 people and injuring 195, the largest single blow of any bombing raid to that date. A wave of horror ran through the country. But it quickly subsided; no mass hysteria followed, nor any uprisings against the government, making popular demands to end the war. Instead the Gotha raids provoked a strong military reaction. A home-defence fighter group came into existence (Arthur Harris among its pilots) to defend against bomber raids, which it did with such success that, first, Zeppelins had to be withdrawn from the attack, and then Gothas had to switch to night bombing. Moreover a ring of barrage balloons went up to protect London, tethered so high that Gothas had difficulty overflying them; and searchlights and anti-aircraft guns entered service. These formidable defences proved effective. Between September 1917 and May 1918, sixty-one Gothas were shot down over the British Isles, an attrition rate too great for the Germans to sustain. After May 1918 the bombers were limited to attacking along the Western Front; they had been seen off.[9]

But although the Gotha bombings did not cause a collapse in civilian morale, it was understandable enough why observers concluded the contrary. They played the game of extrapolation. The citizens of Folkestone were shocked by the Gotha raid. In other towns workers had to quit their benches to take shelter when an attack occurred, or if the attack came at night they were tired the next day as a result of the sleeplessness caused. Imagine – so the observers told themselves and one another – bomber fleets tenfold, a hundredfold, larger, coming over every day and dropping many more bombs. Of course it was easy for them to conclude that the result would be devastating to civilian ability to function. Here was the seed of subsequent theory about bombing.

In the first years of manned heavier-than-air flight it was noted that biplanes flew better than monoplanes. It was predicted that the aeroplanes of the future would therefore have twelve wings. This is an example of the game of extrapolation and its too frequent result. The game of bombing extrapolation followed this pattern. However, it did so only for the natural extension of Gotha and Ilya Mourometz bombers to Lancasters. With their heavy bomb loads the Lancasters multiplied the quantum of death and destruction in area bombing, but this not only diminished the effect on morale, it reversed it.

But what if the extrapolation were carried on, beyond the bombing capacity of a thousand Lancasters, all the way to the nuclear weapons of the post-Second World War period? Perhaps here at last the doctrine about morale comes into its own; for the very thought of the area-bombing effect of nuclear weapons has, at time of writing, been enough to stop anyone actually using them, and has kept wars 'local' (not that this is any consolation to those involved in them). To stop a war starting has to be the desirable logical limit of a bombing policy which sees bombs as a way of stopping wars once started. Does this mean that the strategic-bombing theory is, after all, right – provided that the bombing capacity is such that a single attack could wipe out entire cities in a blow, killing millions rather than 'merely' tens of thousands?

One thought in response might be to say that the aptly named 'MAD' thesis applied to nuclear weapons – 'mutually assured destruction' – is such that if it advanced beyond its deterrent purpose and a major nuclear exchange occurred between two or more nations, the area bombing thus carried out would end the war not because of effect on morale (although such an effect would certainly exist) but because the combatant nations would be physically incapable of continuing after the first assaults. To have a war-winning effect on morale, nuclear weapons would best be deployed by one country against another which could not retaliate in kind.

But this, again, would quite likely be self-defeating in another way, for the victor country would not be able to exploit any advantages over the defeated country, tracts of which would be uninhabitable as a result of radioactive fall-out, and the citizens of which would likely be in a highly dependent state, placing great and costly long-term demands on medical services and other aid, which the putative victor would have to provide.

These considerations suggest that if the theory of the effect on morale of area bombing is thought to come into its own at last in the nuclear age, it continues to do so self-defeatingly. Were Sir Arthur Harris still alive, he would see that even the 'right' weight of bombing power would still not be much use as a war-winning weapon, even if, as in this last scenario, it indeed won a war – with the hollowest of victories.

The rapid evolution of aircraft and their impact on warfare had an electric effect in the years 1914–18. In Britain the air forces of the British army and navy – respectively, the Royal Flying Corps and the Royal Naval Air Service – were reorganised jointly into the Royal Air Force, and in 1918 a dedicated bomber command was set up within it, led by the redoubtable Sir Hugh Trenchard. Remarkably, the British air force had leaped from practically nothing in 1914 to a force of 300,000 men by the war's end, and in that same four-year period Britain manufactured 50,000 aircraft of all military types. These prodigious facts in part explain why it is that in the decade and more after the war, even though air forces in most countries (and not least the United Kingdom) were rapidly reduced in size, military theoreticians should dwell on the possibilities of air warfare, and why some diplomatic initiatives among the major powers should try – futilely as it proved – to bring about international agreement on limiting or even banning the military use of aircraft, especially for bombing.

The theoreticians were quickly off the mark. In fact the first of them, in order both of time and significance for the area-bombing theory, had arrived at his views well before the outbreak of the First World War, after he had seen just three aircraft and before he had himself flown in one. This was Giulio Douhet, an extraordinary individual from the Savoy region of north Italy, who wrote books about military theory (and plays and poems besides) before enlisting in the Italian military in 1909. He was put in command of the fleet of nine aircraft sent to Libya for the war there with the Turks, and was therefore in charge when three aerial firsts were scored: the first aeroplane reconnaissance in combat conditions, which occurred on 23 October 1911, the first bombing (see p. 124) on 1 November 1911, and the first aircraft shot down (by Turkish rifle fire).

As a result of his Libyan activities Douhet was given command of the Italian army's newly formed aviation battalion. He had ideas about how an Italian air capacity should evolve, and lobbied tirelessly but fruitlessly for purpose-built bombers for his force. In the end he commissioned a bomber aircraft on his own initiative from the aero designer Gianni Caproni, who as a result produced the eponymous three-engined bomber described above. But since Douhet had done this without official sanction he was stripped of his aviation command and sent to an infantry regiment instead. His military career came to an end when he was court-martialled and imprisoned for a year after writing an article predicting disaster for the Italian army on account of its many deficiencies. (He was all too soon proved right; the disaster duly occurred at Caparetto in 1917 where, in their worst-ever defeat, Italy's forces suffered over half a million casualties.[10])

Released from military duties and obligations, Douhet devoted himself to writing about the future of war. He produced a book that has become a classic of its kind: *The Command of the Air*, published in 1921. In it is set out the theory adopted, in all fundamentals, by RAF Bomber Command in the Second World War.[11] It was also highly influential on American air-power thinking, as we shall see.

The nub of Douhet's thesis is by now familiar, since it is exactly the thesis premised by Bomber Command from February 1942 onwards, and constituted Sir Arthur Harris's article of faith. It is that bombing should be targeted at the civilian population of an enemy state in order to break its morale and make it force its government to sue for peace. Terror, material destruction and privation caused by shortages of food and other necessities are the key elements.

Take the centre of a large city and imagine what would happen among the civilian population during a single attack by a single bombing unit [Douhet wrote]. I have no doubt that its impact on the people would be terrible . . . What civil or military authority could keep order, public services functioning, and production going under such a threat? . . . A complete breakdown of the social structure cannot but take place in a country subjected to this kind of merciless pounding from the air. The time would soon come when, to put an end to horror and suffering, the people themselves, driven by the instinct for self-preservation, would rise up and demand an end to the war.[12]

This thesis might as well be called the Douhet–Trenchard thesis, for when Sir Hugh Trenchard was placed in charge of the newly formed RAF's bombers in 1918, he set about building a force that would put exactly this view into effect. The British members of a group set up in 1917 to co-ordinate British, French and American air policy, the Inter-Allied Aviation Committee, expressed Trenchard's view in words that might have directly inspired Douhet: '[the effect of bombing civilian targets] would be that the German government would be forced to face very considerable and constantly increasing civil pressure which might result in political disintegration.'[13] The war ended before Trenchard could carry out the policy to any great extent, but he adhered vigorously to it in thinking about how to prosecute a war against Britain's natural enemy – the French: 'I feel that although there would be an outcry,' he wrote in 1925 after asserting that the French population should be bombed if hostilities resumed between the neighbours, 'the French in a bombing duel would probably squeal before we did.'[14] Believing that wars would be very short if civilian bombing were central to them, Trenchard argued that there would be no point in attacking industrial targets. Like Douhet his entire focus was on the 'moral [i.e. morale] effect': 'The nation that would stand being bombed longest would win in the end . . . The end of war is usually attained when one nation has been able to bring such pressure to bear on another that public opinion obliges the government to sue for peace.'[15] This has the further implication that it is vital to get in the earliest blows, before the enemy can mount an attack on the morale of one's own civilians.

For reasons that no one has been able to fathom, and on no known empirical basis, Trenchard asserted that the ratio of moral to material effect created by bombing is 20:1. But together with his general view it gave rise to the belief that what would win a war consisting of a bombing duel is national character; and naturally Trenchard and most of his fellow officers felt that this gave the British a long head start over possible Continental adversaries, especially the French.[16] Pape quotes one senior British officer remarking that during the First World War 'casualties affected the French more than they did the British. That would have to be taken into consideration too, but the policy of hitting the French nation and making them squeal before we did is a vital one – more vital than anything else'. The underlying assumption here appears to be, to put it bluntly, racist. It was, for example, claimed by J. F. C. Fuller that the people who most had panicked during Gotha raids on London in 1917 were 'East End Jews'. In the 1920s, British forces used bombing to keep order among Iraqi and Afghanistani tribesmen, and the ease with which bombing pacified them was taken as confirmation not only of the general efficacy of bombing but its peculiar efficacy in cases where people 'lacked moral fibre' – a failing universally attributed by British colonisers to those they colonised. Not coincidentally, Arthur Harris served in the Middle East in command of a bomber force at that time, and doubtless his Douhet–Trenchard outlook was much boosted by the experience.[17]

As mentioned in chapter 2, during the 1920s the RAF was fighting for its separate existence against the encroachments of the Royal Navy and the Army, and Trenchard, now chief of the RAF, needed arguments to persuade the government to keep in being what had become a rump force. The bombing arguments played a crucial part. It was not only Trenchard who advanced them; he had compelling support from the distinguished military historian Basil Liddell Hart, who in a book published in 1925 made an eloquent case for the idea that bombing would make wars shorter and cheaper, and would save lives overall.[18] 'When it is realised that [strategic bombing would inflict] a total of injury far less than when [a war is] spread over a number of years, the common sense of mankind will show that the ethical objection to this form of war is at least not greater than to the cannon-fodder wars of the past.'[19] He went so far as to add that the war would end even more quickly and cheaply (in lives lost) if gas were used: 'gas may well prove the salvation of civilisation from the otherwise inevitable collapse in the case of another world war.'[20] An implication of Liddell Hart's view was that the deterrent effect of gas attacks from the air might prevent war altogether – an argument standardly deployed by those in favour of nuclear weapons.

Trenchard was so taken with these views that he had copies of Liddell Hart's book sent to his senior colleagues and to the new RAF staff college at Andover. He was not to know then that Liddell Hart would later dramatically change his mind; in 1942, when the true effects of area bombing were plain to see, Liddell Hart wrote, 'It will be ironical if the defenders of civilisation depend for victory upon the most barbaric, and unskilled, way of winning a war that the modern world has seen . . . We are now counting for victory on success in the way of degrading war to a new level – as represented by indiscriminate (night) bombing and indiscriminate starvation.'[21]

By 1928 Trenchard found it necessary to qualify the expression of his views, if not the views themselves, no doubt because the nagging voice of moral conscience was intruding from directions outside RAF staff-college seminars. In a memo to other service chiefs in the Army and Navy – the source of these doubts – he now conceded that it is 'contrary to the dictates of humanity [to carry out] the indiscriminate bombing of a city for the sole purpose of terrorising the civilian population'. But he maintained that it was wholly legitimate to demoralise munitions workers and stevedores loading military supplies. Why should the person who made the gun be less a target than he who fired it? 'Moral effect is created by bombing in such circumstances but it is the inevitable result of a lawful operation

of war – the bombing of a military objective.'[22] Thus was developed
the official fig leaf used throughout the Second World War to justify
the area-bombing campaigns. But it does at least raise a legitimate
question: what is a 'military objective'? Where is the front line in
modern war – surely the armaments factory is on it too?

So far did the British believe their own theoreticians on the subject
of the effect of bombing that in 1939 the government made the
following preparations for London: it estimated 250,000 dead in the
first three weeks of suffering attack by bombers, with 3–4 million
refugees flooding into the surrounding countryside. It predicted three
million psychiatric cases from terror and confusion. It estimated that
50 per cent of London would be destroyed in that same first three
weeks. Even before then the mathematicians had been at work,
calculating the number of deaths and injuries per ton of bombs
dropped, on which basis they estimated a monthly need for 2.8
million hospital beds and twenty million square feet of coffin timber.
As part of the preparation for this horrendous disaster, the Ministry of
Health – in one of those gestures that amaze by their sheer futility –
issued an extra million death certificates to local authorities.[23]

It was not just the words of the theoreticians that convinced the
British government to think in these terms; it was the continued
trickle of apparent empirical confirmation from sites of conflict. The
Italians bombed Addis Ababa in 1936, the Japanese bombed Nanking in 1937, and in that same year the German Condor legion in
Spain carried out the Guernica bombing, killing a thousand people
and destroying 70 per cent of the town. Because Spain was close to
home in Europe, extreme shock was caused by reports of the
screaming Stuka dive-bombers and what they did to the town and
its people, whom they strafed as they fled into the surrounding fields.
The atrocities in Nanking, immensely greater but on the other side of
the world and anyway a matter between orientals, had nothing like
the same impact. Even so, the mere report of yet another demonstration of the horrors of air power fed into the fear everywhere felt. That
these attacks took place in 'ideal bombing conditions' – there was no

air defence, and the attacks took place in daylight – did not then make a difference to calculations. The corpses and the smoking ruins seemed to speak far too eloquently even for mildly sceptical voices to be heard.

All through the 1930s the British, and not them alone, were repeatedly told of the horrors of bombing and the immense threat it posed. Liddell Hart, not yet converted from his views, wrote a graphic account of terrified civilians fleeing bombed cities in the *Daily Telegraph* in November 1933.[24] In London the government decided to build up fighter defences against bomber attack. Bomber Command, so named, had come into official existence in 1936, but as described in chapter 2, although plans were simultaneously laid for a bomber force (including the large four-engined heavy bombers that eventually came into service when Sir Arthur Harris was chief of the Command) it now took second place to the urgent need for fighter defence. Moreover Bomber Command's first directive unequivocally stated that its role was not to enact the Trenchard–Douhet–Liddell Hart thesis, but to provide army support and to attack enemy airfields only. It was explicitly told 'to do nothing that might be construed as an attack on civilians and so to give the enemy an excuse to do likewise'.[25]

In fact so great was the desire not to provoke an enemy – now recognised to be Germany – into applying the Trenchard–Douhet thesis to British cities, that a special subcommittee of the Committee on Imperial Defence, assigned to examine the whole question of bombing, suggested that the government should publicly offer to refrain from bombing Germany's industrial Ruhr region, and also not to impose a naval blockade given that it would impose privations on German civilians, in the hope that Germany would reciprocate with restraint in the matter of bombing cities.

American air-power theory was wholly different. It was also aimed at causing an enemy collapse, but not by attacking civilians directly. Instead it focused on the idea of destroying key industrial links in the enemy economy, which would have the effect of disrupting supplies required to sustain the enemy population, and therefore its willingness to continue supporting a war. The doctrine was devised by a group of officers at the Air Corps Tactical School, the top American air-officer academy, during the 1930s. Four of the officers from this academy, Harold L. George, Haywood Hansell, Kenneth Walker and Laurence S. Kuter, wrote the first United States air-strategy plan in 1941, the 'Air War Plans Division Plan 1' (AWPD-1 for short).

The premise on which the theory underlying AWPD-1 turned was that the stresses imposed on an economy by war would be such that a relatively small number of bomber aircraft, dropping a relatively small quantity of bombs on carefully selected targets, would snap vital threads in the enemy's 'industrial web', and as a result secure a quick victory. The primary objectives specified by AWPD-1 were electricity, transport, and oil. Failure of these economic essentials, so the plan's authors claimed, would soon cause civilian discomfiture; indeed, they believed that the enemy would surrender within six months if fifty-four nominated targets in these sectors were hit. The plan recognised that accurate bombing required control of the air, and so as supplementary objectives it specified attacks on enemy air bases, on aircraft factories, and on sources of indispensable raw materials for aircraft production, such as aluminium and magnesium.

The credo at work in this view is expressed with commendable clarity in lectures given at the Air Corps Tactical School in 1939, quoted by Robert Pape in his study of the coercive use of air power. 'The ultimate object of all military operations . . . is to destroy the will of the people at home, for that is the real source of the enemy's national policy,' says a lecture entitled 'The Aim of War'; 'the loss of morale in the civilian population is far more conclusive than the defeat of the soldier on the battlefield . . . Air forces are capable of immediate employment towards accomplishing the ultimate aim. They can be used directly to break down the will of the mass of the enemy people.'[26]

Another lecture sets out the 'industrial web' thesis: 'Modern warfare places an enormous load upon the economic system of a nation, which increases its sensitivity to attack many-fold. Certainly a breakdown in any part of this complex interlocked organisation must seriously influence the conduct of war by that nation, and greatly interfere with the social welfare and morale of its nationals.' The lecture goes on to invite the audience to consider what would happen in the United States if 'section after section of our great industrial system [ceased] to produce all those numberless articles which are essential to life as we know it'.[27] A third lecture applies these tenets to a practical example: if New York City's water supplies were stopped, the city would soon have to be evacuated because of thirst, the danger of fire, and the undermining of sanitation. If railway bridges were wrecked by bombs, shortages in supplies of foodstuffs would quickly become apparent and make the city 'untenable' – so once again the population would have to be evacuated. This applies also to bombing of electric power stations: lack of electricity 'would cause refrigerated food to spoil'.[28]

In the light of what people can put up with in real rather than imagined war, it is obvious that the unwitting premise of these last remarks is that what would quickly end a war is a population's effeteness or softness, its inability to do without refrigerators or WCs. The lecturer had evidently forgotten that the majority of his contemporaries in the world lived reasonably happily without refrigerators and WCs. As the bombed civilians of the Second World War all over the world proved beyond a shadow of doubt, human beings are – short of devastating atomic bomb attack – much hardier than the Air Corps Tactical School lecturer seemed to realise.[29]

These remarks show a marked parallel, noticed by Pape, with the views of a Russian-born American theorist of air power called Alexander de Seversky, who argued in a book on the subject that the civilian will to support war would surely be broken by 'destroying effectively the essentials of their lives – the supply of food, shelter, light, water, sanitation, and the rest'.[30] Evidently there was a wide consensus among those in the United States applying their minds to the use of air power. On its merits the thesis seemed plausible, and the empirical evidence until then available appeared to support it.

But as always, the merits and evidence were not the only factors in play. Inter-service politics had their part in shaping the debate. Just as the Royal Air Force managed to maintain a separate identity after the First World War by appeal to the risks and promises of bombing – the risks implying a need for a separate fighter defence force against enemy bombers, the promise implying quicker and cheaper victories over enemies by bombing them first – so in America military fliers were able to compete for resources by emphasising the risks and promises of their craft likewise. They had long since been helped in this by their first and most enthusiastic prophet of bomber war, General William 'Billy' Mitchell, who in 1921 had given an apparently irrefutable demonstration of his thesis by sinking six surplus-to-requirement warships in a bombing demonstration that radically changed United States thinking about air power.[31] Mitchell later appeared to have hindered rather than helped the air-power cause by outspoken criticism of colleagues in the US Army and Navy who were sceptical about his views; indeed he succeeded in getting himself court-martialled and cashiered because of the heated and intemperate remarks he made about them. But by the time the Air Corps Tactical School was producing a cadre of air theoreticians of its own, they had arguments to bring to bear that the War Department in Washington could no long ignore.

Received wisdom in the US was that America was so far from potential major enemies, whether to the east or the west, that it was in no danger of aerial bombing. The risk, if it faced any, was from an enemy navy. To trump the US Navy's card on this score, the new theoreticians of air power pointed out – with Billy Mitchell's ringing lesson in mind – that bombers were the surest defence against naval attack. This of course meant precision bombing. One of the immediate effects of this tack was that the US Army Air Force therefore developed one of the first accurate bomb-sights, the famous Norden sight, and was so jealous of it that it refused to share it even with its

British friends. Happily for the air theoreticians, enemy warships and 'industrial web' targets both made the same demand for a precision-bombing capacity, so its proponents could offer Washington a compelling twin-track argument that offered both.[32]

In Pape's view there was an additional motivation for the precision-bombing strategy adopted by the US Army Air Force. This was that the constrained economic conditions in America in the 1930s made it necessary to devise strategies that would be relatively cheap.

> Attacking the enemy's will through the more humane and eco-nomic method of selective attack made sense in the 1930s [he writes], because the total budgets of the Army, of which the Air Corps was part, were in decline. Accordingly the Air Corps required a doctrine that promised victory not only at less cost relative to the Army and Navy but cheaply in absolute terms.[33]

Added to this was the thought that liberal sentiment in the United States would not readily tolerate 'the mass slaughter of civilians'. In an interestingly temporising remark, two men who were to have re-sponsibility for carrying out American air strategy in the coming war, General H. H. 'Hap' Arnold and General Ira Eaker, wrote in their jointly authored book *Winged Warfare* – published mere months before America entered the war – 'Human beings are not priority targets except in special situations. Bombers in far larger numbers than are available today will be required for wiping out people in sufficient numbers by aerial bombardment to break the will of a whole nation.'[34]

When AWPD-1 was presented to the War Department in Wa-shington in 1941, the Department's joint Army-Navy Board re-sponded with scepticism to its claim that air power could by itself bring victory, asserting that 'only land armies can finally win wars'. The Board therefore allocated to the Army air corps a lesser role, that of supporting the other forces by gaining air superiority, weakening the effectiveness of the enemy forces, reducing the capacity of the enemy economy, and (the last item on its list) undermining civilian morale. This response meant that American air units were to remain under the control of land-force commanders, something that the American fliers had hoped AWPD-1 would free them from. It was not until mid-1943 that the US air arm gained operational independence, as the result of the issue of a new Field Manual for the US Army, which gave much greater autonomy and flexibility to air commanders – a first major step to the ultimate independence of the American air arm as the United States Air Force (no longer the United States *Army* Air Force) after the end of the war.[35]

Because the new Field Manual's directions on the use of air power incorporated pre-war Air Corps Tactical School thinking, it can be regarded as a partial triumph for AWPD-1, and so it was. But the precision-bombing versus area-bombing argument had long been won by the draughtsmen of AWPD-1; in theory that had never been in question. This was so even though AWPD-1 had officially been abandoned in favour of a second air-war plan, called AWPD-42, as the result of AWPD-1 being leaked to the press soon after it was submitted to the War Department.[36] In most essentials the two plans were similar, the differences being mostly of emphasis in their respective lists of crucial targets. Whereas AWPD-1 had been drafted by fliers, AWPD-42 was drafted by a committee of economic experts and industrialists. In revising AWPD-1 the committee revisited the question of which bottle-necks in Germany's economy would be the right ones to target in order to strangle the German war effort. But as this implies, the official air strategy of US bomber forces remained – indeed, was reinforced in the direction of – precision bombing.

When the USAAF arrived in Britain to take its part in the attack on Nazi Germany, reality proved a harsh spoiler of hopes. Europe's weather – low cloud, rain, patchy mist, dense fog, hazy days, abrupt and unreliable changes from sun to showers – would by itself have made the ideal of precision daylight bombing a hard enough thing to achieve, if it were not for the added and infinitely worse disruptions of the Germans' anti-aircraft guns and Messerschmitt fighters. The fabled Norden bomb-sight required a straight and steady run of many miles with the bomb-aimer in clear visual command of the approaching target, no problem in training conditions in the United States but very hard to achieve in actual war conditions in European weather. In a deeply sceptical account of what really happened when the B-17s came to Europe, Stewart Ross – an academic historian with experience of analysing bombing-accuracy tests on behalf of the US Army Ordance Corps – claims that there was vastly more myth than fact in the accounts given of USAAF endeavours.[37] One of his conclusions is that although US bombers were officially required to attack only military or industrial targets and to avoid deliberate bombing of civilians, in practice any city with a population over 50,000 was regarded as likely to contain military or industrial assets and accordingly to be a legitimate target, and that therefore the USAAF not only conducted area bombing by default when 'blind bombing' (through cloud, at targets picked out by H2S radar), but when area bombing as such. He traces the Americans' increasing acceptance of area bombing in the European theatre to its logical conclusion in the explicit and open area bombing conducted by Curtis LeMay's XXI Bomber Command in its war over Japan.[38]

This suggests that the difference between RAF Bomber Command practice and USAAF practice in the European theatre was less than might be implied by the express rhetoric of USAAF bombing principles. But two points merit mention. The first is that the RAF always attempted to give the impression officially – as noted, to Harris's annoyance – that it was not indiscriminately bombing civilians, but attacking the enemy industrial capacity. The fact that it was doing so by bombing the workers (and everyone else around them) rather than their factories, and trying to undermine the German economy's effectiveness by demoralising, 'dehousing' and causing privations to those who survived bombing attacks, was cloaked in rhetoric similar to that used by the Americans. But whereas the Americans wanted to conduct precision bombing and were forced by circumstances to engage in area bombing, RAF Bomber Command wanted to engage in area bombing and used the rhetoric of attacking industrial and military targets as a conscious cover for what they were really doing.

The second point is that when the USAAF Eighth and Fifteenth Army Air Forces were able to engage in precision bombing, they did so; this happened principally in the closing months of the war when the Allies had greater command of the skies, and the Flying Fortresses had better 'bombing conditions' for their attacks on vital sectors of German war production, especially oil – with, as we have also seen, decisive effect. In that same period Bomber Command continued to carry out area bombing – in fact, Harris positively insisted on bombing those cities on his list which remained unbombed; and so his aircraft destroyed cities like Würzburg and Hildesheim, noted far more for their historical beauty than for their military importance.[39]

This fact, however, only increases the contrast between the American efforts in the European theatre and the area attacks carried out by XXI Bomber Command under Curtis LeMay in the Pacific theatre. Even here an effort, though not an especially great one, was made to disguise area bombing as directed at war production. Claiming that the Japanese produced military equipment on a cottage-industry basis, in which parts were manufactured in the little wooden houses of the civilians, LeMay said after the firebombing of Tokyo on 9–10 March 1945, 'There are no innocent civilians . . . The entire population got into the act and worked to make those aeroplanes or munitions . . . men, women, and children.'

The Mind of the Bomber II: The Fate of Gomorrah

All the theory and practice described in the last chapter had not been taking place in a vacuum. The efforts made at the Hague conferences of 1899 and 1907 to prevent the sky becoming another scene of war did not end there. It was the opinion of Sir Edward Grey, British Foreign Secretary from 1905 to 1916 and therefore one of those involved in – some say, one of those responsible for – the outbreak of the First World War, that the accumulation of armaments in the years prior to 1914 was a major factor in the war's occurrence.[40] The fourth of Woodrow Wilson's famous Fourteen Points iterated the need for limitation of armaments: 'Adequate guarantees [must be] given and taken that national armaments will be reduced to the lowest point consistent with domestic safety.' Throughout the inter-war years efforts were made to limit the size of armies and navies, and to place constraints on the kinds of weapons that might be used; and this included air power. This was an obligation to which all participating members of the League of Nations and signatories to the Treaty of Versailles committed themselves after the First World War.

Some success in limiting naval forces was reached in 1922, and an important rhetorical moment occurred when the Kellogg–Briand Pact was signed in 1928, this being the international treaty signed by many members of the League of Nations – chief among them the United States, Britain, France and Germany – renouncing war as an instrument of policy.[41] But the question of air power proved greatly more difficult to resolve. The fullest and most thoughtful attempt to provide rules for air warfare was made at a conference held at The Hague between December 1922 and February 1923. The then five major powers of Britain, France, the United States, Italy and Japan took part, neither Germany nor Russia then being in a position to count as such. The articles drawn up by the conference were never signed by the participating governments, so no Rules of Air Warfare came into existence; but the draft rules arrived at by the participants are fascinating, showing as they do how clearly the dangers of air power were foreseen. What happened in conflicts after the powers considered these rules, and especially what happened in the Second World War, has to be measured against the principles they embody.

ARTICLE XXII
Aerial bombardment for the purpose of terrorising the civilian population, of destroying or damaging private property not of a military character, or of injuring non-combatants, is prohibited.
[. . .]

ARTICLE XXIV

1) Aerial bombardment is legitimate only when directed at a military objective, that is to say, an object of which the destruction or injury would constitute a distinct military advantage to the belligerent.

2) Such bombardment is legitimate only when directed exclusively at the following objectives: military forces; military works; military establishments or depots; factories constituting important and well-known centres engaged in the manufacture of arms, ammunition, or distinctively military supplies; lines of communication or transportation used for military purposes.

3) The bombardment of cities, towns, villages, dwellings, or buildings not in the immediate neighbourhood of the operations of land forces is prohibited. In cases where the objectives specified in paragraph 2 are so situated, that they cannot be bombarded without the indiscriminate bombardment of the civilian population, the aircraft must abstain from bombardment.

4) In the immediate neighbourhood of the operations of land forces, the bombardment of cities, towns, villages, dwellings, or buildings is legitimate provided that there exists a reasonable presumption that the military concentration is sufficiently important to justify such bombardment, having regard to the danger thus caused to the civilian population.

ARTICLE XXV

In bombardment by aircraft all necessary steps must be taken by the commander to spare as far as possible buildings dedicated to public worship, art, science, or charitable purposes, historic monuments, hospital ships, hospitals, and other places where the sick and wounded are collected, provided such buildings, objects or places are not at the time used for military purposes. Such buildings, objects and places must by day be indicated by marks visible to aircraft. The use of marks to indicate other buildings, objects or places than those specified above is to be deemed an act of perfidy.

The marks used as aforesaid shall be in the case of buildings protected under the Geneva Convention the red cross on a white ground, and in the case of other protected buildings a large rectangular panel divided diagonally into two pointed triangular portions, one black and the other white.

A belligerent who desires to secure by night the protection for the hospitals and other privileged buildings above mentioned must take the necessary measures to render the special signs referred to sufficiently visible.

ARTICLE XXVI

The following special rules are adopted for the purpose of enabling States to obtain more efficient protection for important historic monuments situated within their territory, provided that they are willing to refrain from the use of such monuments and a surrounding zone for military purposes, and to accept a special regime for their inspection.

1) A State shall be entitled, if it sees fit, to establish a zone of protection round such monuments situated in its territory. Such zones shall in time of war enjoy immunity from bombardment.

2) The monuments round which a zone is established shall be notified to other Powers in peace time through the diplomatic channel; the notification shall also indicate the limits of the zones. The notification may not be withdrawn in time of war.

3) The zone of protection may include, in addition to the area actually occupied by the monument or group of monuments, an outer zone, not exceeding 500 meters in width, measured from the circumference of the said area . . .

The failure of this effort, and slow progress on other fronts, prompted the League of Nations to convene a full conference of all members in order to achieve disarmament – or more accurately, arms control, which is a different thing. A preliminary commission sat between 1925 and 1932, trying to establish a basis for discussion on which arms would be limited, and how.[42] When the Geneva Disarmament Conference officially began in February 1932, most of the attending powers were in agreement that air attacks on civilians were in violation of fundamental principles; but the conference as a whole quickly stalled on the political realities of the time. France did not wish to limit its forces, fearing hostilities from Germany. Germany stated that unless the rest of the world disarmed to its own level as specified by the terms of the Treaty of Versailles, it would regard itself as entitled to rearm to the point where it achieved equality with the other powers. During one of the adjournments of the deadlocked conference Hitler came to power, and not long afterwards withdrew Germany from the conference. Although officially the conference remained in (mainly adjourned) session until 1937, the hope of preventing war by limiting the means for making it had long since vanished.

When the conference began, with calls from various countries about abolishing submarines and limiting the armaments of battle-ships, Italy and Japan called for the outlawing of aerial bombardment. France wanted bombing to be forbidden beyond a radius of a given number of miles from the front lines – which assumed that there would be front lines, as in 1914–18; but the British were determined that there should be no repeat of such a thing. Both Britain and to a lesser extent France had far-flung empires, parts of which occasionally needed to be bombed in the interests of good order, so neither was keen on an outright bombing ban. The conference contemplated banning offensive weaponry but permitting defensive weapons, only to find that what counted as either was a matter of perspective: submarines for Germany were defensive weapons against British naval blockade, while for the British they were offensive weapons against Britain's sea trade routes. The same difficulty affected the question of bombs.

At one point it was (in the crazed way understandable among the impasses of a major international conference) mooted that flight itself should be banned, since while it existed – even for civilian purposes –

it was a certainty that someone would assuredly use it to bomb someone else. Stanley Baldwin, former British Prime Minister but at the time of the conference serving as President of the Board of Trade, was profoundly concerned about the threat of bombing. He told the US delegate that 'the course we are now following is straight toward the destruction of our civilisation and something radical has to be done unless we are all going down together'. His proposal, slightly less swingeing than the ban on flight as such, was the 'total abolition of all military aviation'.[43] When Sir Anthony Eden took over as representative at the conference he suggested instead severe limitations on when bombing would be permissible, but in any event he suggested a prohibition against air attacks on civilian populations. The RAF suspected that Eden was moving in the direction of a complete ban on bombing, and were very unhappy about it. The then chief of the RAF, Sir John Salmond, wrote to Eden with his 'deep misgivings' about the tendency of the British proposals, saying that in circumstances where a country is fighting for its very life it would be 'inconceivable' that it would not use bombing to defend itself; the idea 'has nothing in logic or common-sense to recommend it'.[44] Although he was opposed to the bombing of civilians – 'no military advantage is likely to accrue to a country which employs its bombing aircraft to terrorise rather than to disarm its opponent', Salmond wrote – he was adamant that bombing was a necessary weapon of war, and that therefore the main thrust of British efforts should go to defining what a 'military target' is, for in the absence of a definition belligerents would simply resort to indiscriminate bombing.[45]

At one point discussion at Geneva really did seem to be tending towards an outright ban on aerial bombing, and both the US and British governments, the latter in the teeth of RAF opposition, were in favour. But difficulties of detail kept arising, chief among them the position of civil aviation in the light of such a ban – for, again, it is easy to convert an airliner to a bomber, and no country, especially not the United States, was prepared to retrench on civil aviation. Disillusioned by the lack of progress, on 10 November 1932 Stanley

Baldwin made a famous speech. 'The bomber,' he said, 'will always get through . . . The only defence is offence. You have to kill more women and children more quickly than the enemy if you want to save yourselves.'[46] It is interesting to note that these remarks were then found highly offensive by the RAF, thus in effect accused of wishing to make war on women and children, whereas – so its leaders then passionately believed – bombing would shorten war and make it less costly in life overall, and perhaps even have the deterrent effect of preventing war altogether.

As usual, of course, RAF objections to banning bombers were intimately linked to the very survival of the RAF, for in the event of a ban the non-bombing remnants of the force would be returned to the Army and Navy for adjunctival roles. From the RAF point of view, therefore, it was as well that the conference collapsed in 1934; from the point of view of humanity it was not.

The failure of efforts to secure international agreement limiting bombers and restraining bombing meant that when a widening of hostilities threatened in 1939, Britain's then Prime Minister, Neville Chamberlain, was very anxious. The country was still under-strength in its air defences and its ability to retaliate if a bombing war started, and the government was alarmed by the propaganda that the British had themselves been promoting about the horrors of air war, horrors repeatedly insisted upon by the RAF in seeking to preserve not just its independence but its existence, and by politicians like Stanley Baldwin who saw all too clearly what unrestrained air war would be like. So when on 1 September 1939, two days before Britain declared war on Germany, President Roosevelt made his radio broadcast calling upon the European powers to promise not to bomb civilians, Chamberlain was eager to respond in the affirmative, as much out of conviction – he was by instinct a pacific man – as canniness, hoping to stave off devastating aerial bombardment of Britain at least until Britain was ready to counter such an attack. In his broadcast Roosevelt said that he was afraid 'hundreds of thousands of innocent human beings who have no responsibility for, and who are not even remotely participating in, the hostilities' would be killed. He asked the world's nations 'to affirm [a] determination that [their] armed forces shall in no event, and under no circumstances, undertake the bombardment from the air of civilian populations or of unfortified cities'.

Chamberlain was not alone in responding positively to the President's appeal; so did the French – and so did Hitler, at the very moment that the Luftwaffe's Stukas were bombing Warsaw. Even if there was a measure of calculation in Chamberlain's public pronouncements about abjuring the bombing of civilians, the frequency with which he made them and their emphatic character suggest an at least equal measure of genuine sentiment. In the House of Commons on 14 September 1939 he made his commitment in the clearest terms: 'His Majesty's Government will never resort to the deliberate attack on women and children and other civilians for the purpose of mere terrorism.'[47]

There was a greater victim of the failure of international efforts during the 1920s and 1930s to limit armaments and to outlaw bombing attacks on civilians. This victim, without overmuch drama, might be described as the future of mankind itself. For in the absence of agreements to restrict the development of new and more dangerous weapons, the race to produce atom bombs was by default allowed to go ahead. Not only were they used against the civilians of Hiroshima and Nagasaki, but they have held the world to ransom since, and it is only a matter of time before such a weapon is used – experts on conflict say: at the minimum either by terrorists, or in a regional war in (for example) south or east Asia.

From the outset the meaning of atomic weapons was clearly understood by those engaged in researching their production, and to many of these, in turn, their moral repugnance was equally clear. The Hungarian physicist Leo Szilard, who had fled his homeland in 1933, was so concerned by the possibilities that he urged his colleagues in the field of atomic research to keep their findings secret. When he discovered in March 1939 that a uranium nucleus would emit two neutrons if penetrated by one neutron, which meant that chain reactions are possible, he was filled with terrible foreboding. 'That night there was very little doubt in my mind that the world was headed for grief,' he said.[48] He and a colleague persuaded Einstein to write to Roosevelt to explain the dangers – and the possibilities; for Szilard and others thought that in the parlous international situation it was advisable for the democracies to develop atomic weapons before the dictatorships did. In one respect they were right; in Germany, despite the fact that its scientific community had been depleted by expulsion of 'non-Aryans' in the Civil Service Restoration Law of 1933, which removed Jewish scientists from the country's leading universities and laboratories (almost all went to Britain or America), work was under way on atomic weapons in a research project headed by Werner Heisenberg. (To a much lesser extent similar research programmes had also begun in Russia and Japan.) Some of the German scientists were as worried by the moral implications of atomic weapons as their colleagues elsewhere. But once the promise and dangers had been grasped by the politicians on both sides of a rapidly impending war, the production of atomic bombs had ceased to be a matter for moral anxiety, and had become an inevitability.

Before this, though, development of atomic weapons by the United States and Britain was almost stalled – not by moral scruples, but by bureaucracy; for in both countries committees were set up to evaluate the claims that scientists were making about atomic potential, and to consider the costs and benefits of experimental application of their theories. The US committee was especially sceptical; at its first meeting its members scornfully told the scientists presenting the possibilities of atomic weapons (Szilard among them) that it was the morale of troops, not the power of bombs, that eventually won wars. In Britain in 1940 a crucial breakthrough in the study of chain reactions in uranium-235 brought the reality of a bomb much closer, thereby prompting the setting-up of a British committee headed by the physicist G. P. Thomson. Although it agreed with its American counterpart in initially thinking that research into the possibility of a bomb was a 'wild goose chase', Thomson's committee changed its mind in the summer of 1941, and reported to Churchill that atom bombs were a genuine possibility and could have a decisive influence on the war. When this was communicated to Roosevelt in the early autumn of 1941 he immediately ordered a full-scale development effort. Thus the Manhattan Project came into existence; the rest is history.

The men who made the breakthrough in research into chain reactions in U-235 were Otto Frisch and Rudolph Peierls at the University of Birmingham in England. When they had made their calculations on the size of the critical mass required to produce reactions reaching temperatures equivalent to those in the centre of the sun, they were staggered: the required quantity was only two or three pounds of material rather than the tons they had expected. 'We stared at each other and realised that an atomic bomb might after all be possible,' Frisch said. Their figures told them that 2–3 lb of U-235 would cause an explosion equivalent to several thousand tons of TNT, and that the radiation released would be 'fatal to living beings even a long time after the explosion'. They further saw that nothing could resist the power of such an explosion, that wind would spread radiation far beyond the blast area and that therefore an atom bomb 'could not be used without killing large numbers of civilians' – which they therefore thought meant that 'this may make [atom bombs] unsuitable as a weapon for use by [Britain]'; and finally they concluded that if 'Germany is, or will be, in possession of this weapon [the] most effective reply would be a counter-threat with a similar weapon'.[49]

This memorandum by Frisch and Peierls succinctly and effectively covers the ground as regards atomic weapons: their immense danger, their moral repugnance, their inevitability, and the need to counter their threat with a threat of the same: a prefiguring of the doctrine of deterrence.

Whereas scientists were mainly thinking in terms of a deterrent, Roosevelt and his military advisers, and with them Churchill, thought explicitly in terms of a weapon for deployment when ready. Roosevelt's Secretary of War, Henry Stimson, said after the war that he never heard Roosevelt say that atomic bombs should not be used; rather, their role as a decisive war-winning instrument was alone what justified the effort and cost involved in developing them. Churchill concurred: 'the decision whether or not to use the atomic bomb,' he later wrote, '. . . was never an issue. There was unanimous, automatic, unquestioned agreement.'[50]

There was no 'unquestioned agreement' among those who really understood the implications. Niels Bohr managed to secure a personal meeting with Churchill on 16 May 1944 to press upon him how awful an atomic bomb attack would be, and to urge him not to allow one to be made. Churchill impatiently replied, 'I cannot see what you are talking about. After all this new bomb is just going to be bigger than our present bombs. It involves no difference in the principles of war. And as for any post-war problems there are none that cannot be amicably settled between me and my friend President Roosevelt.'[51] Bohr had no more luck with Roosevelt, whom he saw on 26 August 1944, and whom he urged to arrange for international controls on atomic weaponry and for the Russians to be included in knowledge about them. Roosevelt's friendly manner gave Bohr the impression that he had succeeded with the President where he had failed with the Prime Minister. But at a meeting between the two Allied leaders the following month it was Churchill's attitude that prevailed: the atom bomb was going to be kept secret, so no steps would be taken to institute international control of its use; the bomb would be used against Japan if 'after mature consideration' it was deemed necessary; and Professor Bohr was to be watched to ensure that he did not pass information about the atom bomb to the Russians. Churchill indeed thought he ought to be imprisoned as a security measure.[52]

Bohr was far from alone among scientists in campaigning to stop Washington's political and military leaders actually using the bomb, rather than brandishing it as a threat. In June 1944 a group of Chicago scientists lobbied Washington not just on the moral question, but on the pragmatic grounds that use of the atom bombs would trigger a disastrous arms race. They argued that the US government should announce to the world that it had the bomb but would not use it, and would indeed renounce it if everyone else would join them in forswearing the military use of atomic power.

In July 1944 Leo Szilard also renewed his efforts by submitting a petition, signed by himself and sixty-nine fellow physicists, insisting that the government had an 'obligation of restraint'. But the government had already resolved to use the atom bomb; its committee overseeing deployment of the new weapon noted the scientists' concerns in its minutes, but without further comment simply iterated its decision that the bomb should be deployed 'at the earliest opportunity . . . without warning'.[53]

There was one senior member of the Washington government who was not in favour of the bomb, and who used his position and influence first to try to stop its use, and when this failed, to try to mitigate its use. This was Henry Stimson, the Secretary of War to President Roosevelt and then to President Truman. One thing Stimson managed to do was to strike Kyoto off the list of possible targets. It had been selected as such along with Hiroshima, Kokura and Nigata, all of which were left unbombed by conventional means after the decision to use the atomic weapon had been taken, so that its effects on them could be measured more clearly. Kyoto was the capital of Japan from 794 until the seat of imperial government was moved to Edo, later called Tokyo, in 1868. A city of nearly 2,000 temples, monasteries and gardens, it was then as it is now the chief repository of Japan's culture and traditions, and Stimson was very much alive to its significance. General Leslie Groves, the military head of the Manhattan Project, was annoyed that Stimson had removed Kyoto from the list, but Stimson told him that 'such a wanton act' as dropping an atom bomb on Kyoto would make the post-war task of managing a conquered Japan vastly more difficult.

Stimson was also worried by the targeting policy adopted for the atom-bomb attack. The group of White House advisers considering this aspect of the matter, the Interim Committee, concluded that the bomb should be dropped over a city centre, not on the outskirts where industrial or military targets would usually be located, because there its effects would be diminished by the proximity of sparsely inhabited countryside. In any case, said the committee, industrial targets in large cities would be too small and insignificant as targets *per se*. Stimson objected to targeting city centres, arguing that it would give the United States a 'reputation for outdoing Hitler in atrocities'. He argued that the Japanese should be warned in advance of an attack so that the US could avoid 'the opprobrium which might follow from an ill-considered employment of such force'.[54] His efforts, together with those of several junior members of the government who agreed with him, were of course unavailing. President Truman was more inclined to listen to the man he had appointed as his Secretary of State, James Byrnes. In the Roosevelt administration Byrnes served as Director of the Office of War Mobilization, and as such had worked hard to ensure that the Manhattan Project received priority in money and manpower. Now he was determined that the effort should be seen to bear fruit. At a meeting of the Interim Committee on 1 June 1945 Byrnes strongly recommended that the atomic bomb should be used on an urban area, and very soon; and his principal reason was that the United States should demonstrate to Russia the considerable edge that possession of atomic weapons gave it, in order (as Leo Szilard observed) to 'make Russia more manageable in Europe'.

This motivation has been much discussed, and figures as part of the defence of the use of the atom bombs on Hiroshima and Nagasaki. The point therefore comes back into focus in chapter 7 below.

In a discussion of the 'mind of the bomber' – which is to say: the attitudes of those who planned and ordered bombing, especially of civilian targets – it is not possible to leave the story of the atom bomb without noting the effect of its dropping. One of the witnesses in the

B-29 that accompanied the *Enola Gay* on 6 August 1945 was Luis Alvarez, a Manhattan Project scientist. On the return flight from the sky above Hiroshima where the mushroom cloud still stood, he felt he had to write to his four-year-old son. 'What regrets I have about being party to killing and maiming thousands of Japanese civilians this morning,' he wrote, in stricken mood, 'are tempered with the hope that this terrible weapon we have created may bring the countries of the world together and prevent future wars.' Robert Lewis, a member of *Enola Gay*'s crew, shouted as he watched the effects of the explosion, 'Look at that! Look at that! Look at that! . . . My God! Look at that son-of-a-bitch go!' In his mission log shortly afterwards, when reflection had replaced excitement, he wrote, 'My God, what have we done?'[55]

Popular sentiment in America was one of exhilaration and triumph; polls showed 85 per cent of people in favour. But on both wings of the political spectrum there were grave regrets. A liberal commentator, Dwight McDonald, wrote sadly of America's 'decline to barbarism', while the conservative David Lawrence said, '[appeals to] military necessity . . . will never erase from our minds the simple truth that we, of all civilized nations . . . did not hesitate to employ the most destructive weapon of all times indiscriminately against men, women and children'.[56]

Of great interest is what President Truman thought and said at the time. In response to urging from a US Senator to use the toughest means possible to force Japan to surrender, Truman replied in a letter dated 9 August 1945 – that is, three days after the Hiroshima bomb and on the same day as the Nagasaki bomb – in the following terms:

I know that Japan is a terribly cruel and uncivilized nation in warfare but I can't bring myself to believe that, because they are beasts, we should ourselves act in the same manner. For myself, I certainly regret the necessity of wiping out whole populations because of the 'pigheadedness' of the leaders of a nation and, for your information, I am not going to do it unless absolutely necessary . . . my object is to save as many American lives as possible but I also have a humane feeling for the women and children in Japan.[57]

Next to this passage must be placed one from a speech broadcast by Truman on the radio that same day:

The world will note that the first atomic bomb was dropped on Hiroshima, a military base. That was because we wished in this first attack to avoid, insofar as possible, the killing of civilians. But that attack is only a warning of things to come. If Japan does not surrender, bombs will have to be dropped on her war industries and, unfortunately, thousands of civilian lives will be lost. I urge Japanese civilians to leave industrial cities immediately, and save themselves from destruction.[58]

As these passages show, the same official line was adopted by the United States for the atom-bomb attacks as by the British government for RAF area bombing of Germany: that the targets were industrial and military. It is significant to note that in *public* statements of this line, no effort was made to redefine civilians as legitimate military targets in circumstances of total war; that thought was reserved for discussions within government and high-command circles, and later among defenders of the bombing strategies adopted by the Allies in the Second World War.

A thorny problem now faces this examination of the attitudes of those who planned and directed Allied bombing campaigns. Why was it taken by Air Marshals Portal and Harris to be acceptable that, as a means of beating Germany, its cities should be destroyed? It cannot be that they saw nothing beyond the goal of victory in itself; they must have thought about how things would be in Germany after victory was secured. In the months following the D-Day landings they had direct knowledge of difficulties caused to Allied troops who were obliged to move – and more to the point, fight – across areas of France and the Low Countries which had been severely damaged by Allied bombing. Caen was a striking instance. Its streets were so piled with rubble that vehicles could not move through them until they had been cleared, and it was obvious that a part-demolished urban environment was excellent territory for defenders, who could only be defeated building by broken building. The Air Force chiefs, and their political masters, must assuredly have realised that a pulverised Germany was going to present an even more difficult task for troops on the ground.

But what about their forward planning for the situation when Allied forces would be in possession of Germany? Did it not occur to the Air Force chiefs and their political superiors that a defeated population would need to be governed and policed, and in the process at very least fed, watered, housed, and given medical attention? Portal and Harris themselves might have thought that this would be the responsibility of others, and that their task was solely to beat Germany into surrender, after which they could wash their hands of the affair. This would have involved taking a very limited view of matters. Suppose they did so; did not higher authority have a view on the matter? What was government on both sides of the Atlantic thinking about post-war affairs? What plans were being made, and why did they not take into account the potential difficulties represented by the immense material damage daily being made worse in Germany's main cities even as the war drew to a close?

Or were these considerations indeed being taken into account, and welcomed?

At the end of *The Natural History of Destruction* W. G. Sebald reports receiving a letter from one Dr H, a citizen of Darmstadt. 'I had to read it several times, because at first I could not believe my eyes,' Sebald tells us.

It propounds the theory that the Allies waged war in the air with the aim of cutting off the Germans from their origins and inheritance by destroying their cities, thus paving the way for the cultural invasion and general Americanisation that ensued in the post-war period. This deliberate strategy, continues the letter from Darmstadt, was devised by Jews living abroad, exploiting the special knowledge of the human psyche, foreign cultures and foreign mentalities that they are known to have acquired in their wanderings.[59]

Sebald was rightly disturbed by this letter, the anti-Semitism of which betrays its affinities with German neo-Nazism. Had Sebald consulted the internet he might have seen there that neo-Nazis everywhere, and not least their North American 'white supremacist' subset, make common cause in racism and conspiracy theories of the kind suggested by Dr H. Unhappily, some of the thinking put forward during the course of the Second World War about what to do with post-war Germany plays directly into their hands – just as it played into Goebbels' hands during the war, giving him a propaganda coup and the Nazi regime an excuse for encouraging Germany as a whole to fight to the very last ounce of its strength in 1945. For alas, responsible individuals in Roosevelt's government did indeed put forward a plan for post-war Germany that, if not quite Dr H's fantasy, was uncomfortably close to it. The area bombing of Germany's cities meant destroying its libraries, schools, universities, theatres, museums, art galleries, shops, monuments, architectural treasures, clinics, hotels, workshops, studios, concert halls – in short: its cultural fabric, its embodied memory and character. And this was in addition to the destruction of its houses and factories, municipal offices and waterworks, roads and bridges, to say nothing of its people – in short: its capacity to function. This pulverisation of the physical, cultural and human fabric of Germany was allowed to continue on a massive scale until the very last month of the war, not just unabated but with increasing intensity; which makes it natural to wonder whether it represented an intention to so cripple Germany that it could not revive to become yet again, as it had twice been in the preceding thirty years, a dangerous and oppressive destroyer of world peace.

For material destruction is merely instrumental to a more profound kind of destruction – the destruction of what has since come to be called 'social capital', in the form of the institutions and culture on the basis of which a society functions. No one wished Nazism and its institutions to survive, for very good reasons; but the question is, was the area-bombing campaign in any way an adjunct to a desire to put an end to Germany as such? Was it an attempt at what might be called 'culturecide'?

The controversial plan for post-war Germany briefly accepted by Roosevelt and Churchill is known as the Morgenthau Plan after the man who devised it, Henry Morgenthau Jr, Secretary of the Treasury to President Roosevelt for eleven years from 1934 to 1945, and therefore a key figure in Roosevelt's New Deal. As the war in Europe was reaching a climax Morgenthau put forward a plan to de-industrialise the Ruhr, reassigning parts of Germany to France and Poland, and divide the remainder of Germany into two purely agricultural states. The aim of weakening and 'pastoralising' Germany was of course to ensure that it could not again become powerful; and as Morgenthau's book *Germany Is Our Problem* (1945) argued, it was necessary to ensure this by institutional means, since the Germans were in his view by nature 'militaristic'.[60] After initial acceptance by both Roosevelt and Churchill at the second Quebec conference in 1944 it was abandoned by both, partly through the efforts of the indefatigable Henry Stimson, and partly because Churchill recognised that a restored Germany would be needed in the coming stand-off with the Soviet Union in Europe. At one point, indeed, he contemplated quickly allying the Allies with a post-Nazi Germany so that the Wehrmacht could be used in fighting back a Soviet advance which – so Churchill for a time feared – might go all the way to the Atlantic coast.

But the rejection of the Morgenthau Plan did not happen quickly enough to escape the notice of Goebbels, who made good use of it to stiffen German fighting resolve. Any Germans contemplating surrender to the Allies in the West, in order to forestall too great a conquest by the Soviets in the East, were discouraged by the 'apocalyptic vision' that Goebbels could now paint of life under Allied occupation, given the terms of the Plan.[61] Alluding also to suggestions put forward by others who thought that radical steps should be taken to prevent Germans from again being a threat to peace, he wrote:

[Our enemies say] that Germany had been treated too mildly by the Treaty of Versailles, and that it must be entirely beaten down after this war . . . A few days ago, the official English news agency Reuters carried a cable from an overseas émigré newspaper supported by the British government. It proposed that all German children between two and six years of age should be taken from their mothers and sent abroad for 25 years. This would lead the Germans, it said, to forget their nationality. A mixed ethnic brew would result that could no longer be called German. Had Reuters not carried this nonsense, one might have done the English government the favour of assuming that this outrageous proposal was the result of a deranged mind . . . Our women know what their sons are fighting for, and our women know what their husbands are fighting for. Each worker and each farmer is more certain than ever before of why he is swinging his hammer or standing behind his plough. Millions of children look to us. The enemy sees our future in them, and wants to destroy them. So let us get to work! The enemy has told us what is at stake.[62]

The Morgenthau Plan's negative effects seem to have been felt after the war, at least in an indirect and temporary way. They did this by influencing Roosevelt's attitude to the concessive plans drawn up by his State and War Departments for post-war Germany. These plans jointly envisaged a self-supporting Germany in which a reasonably high standard of living would be maintained, and for this to happen (so the State Department plan required) there should be 'no large-scale and permanent impairment of . . . German industry'. Roosevelt, apparently at Morgenthau's insistence, sent a highly critical memorandum to Stimson and Secretary of State Cordell Hull, saying that these plans were unacceptable because they would bring Germany too rapidly back to its pre-war state.[63]

Roosevelt and Churchill agreed to the Morgenthau Plan on 15 September 1944 at the second Quebec conference, initialling a draft of it which provided for 'eliminating the war-making industries in the Ruhr and the Saar' and 'looking forward to converting Germany into a country primarily agricultural and pastoral in character'. Anthony Eden, Churchill's Foreign Secretary, and Cordell Hull, his equivalent in the Roosevelt administration, were both horrified when they found this out. In his memoirs Eden wrote, 'I did not like the plan, nor was I convinced that it was to our national advantage.' Hull called it 'a plan of blind vengeance', and Stimson said it was 'just fighting brutality with brutality'.[64]

It seems that Churchill had at first been hostile to the idea, telling Morgenthau that it meant Britain would be 'chained to a dead body'; but he was then temporarily induced into accepting it by two considerations. One was that Britain was in desperate need of funds, and Morgenthau had given him to understand that 6.5 billion dollars' worth of post-war Lend-Lease arrangements were on offer. Since Roosevelt was in favour of the Plan, and since Churchill was the beggar not the chooser at the conference table, he felt that it would be politic to go along with it.

The other consideration was that his adviser Lord Cherwell (Professor Frederick Lindemann) persuaded him that the Morgenthau Plan would be to Britain's economic advantage in another way too. Cherwell claimed (in a communication to Churchill's physician Lord Moran) that Churchill began by saying that the plan was 'a cruel threat to the German people' – as indeed the Germans themselves did not need Goebbels' help to see – but that Cherwell had 'explained to Winston that the plan would save Britain from bankruptcy by eliminating a dangerous competitor . . . Winston had not thought of it in that way'.[65]

In the event Eden was able to dissuade Churchill, and more importantly Hull and Stimson were able to dissuade Roosevelt, and the plan was dropped.[66] In Churchill's case it did not take long to restore him to his first instinctive distrust of the idea of an economically inert Germany which could not be a trading partner for Britain and a market for British goods – to say nothing of needing profitable British input in the reconstruction process. But he had also quickly come to see the point earlier made, that a restored and viable Germany was needed for what would prove to be the coming Cold War, which Churchill foresaw with greater clarity than most, as his celebrated 'Iron Curtain' speech soon showed.

If the Morgenthau Plan had been a single instance of punitive thinking about Germany's post-war future, it might not be such fruitful terrain for far-right-wing apologists for Germany's Nazi past. But there were other advocates of a reduction of Germany, not a few of them calling for further and sometimes more extreme measures.[67] One was Bernadotte Schmitt, the Professor of Modern History at Chicago University, who specialised in Germany. He had first visited that country in 1906 while a Rhodes Scholar at Oxford, and had taken a profound dislike to it because of its militaristic character. 'I have never trusted Germany since', he wrote. In a speech to the National Council for Social Studies at Indianapolis in late November 1941, just over a week before the Japanese attack on Pearl Harbor, he called for a reduction of Germany's population from eighty million to thirty million, so that it would be less of a cuckoo in the European nest. He did not say how this was to be done.[68]

More extreme was Theodore Kaufman's *Germany Must Perish!*, self-published in 1940. It is an egregious example of the genre; it called for the systematic sterilisation of the German people so that once the existing German population died out there would no longer be an aggressive militaristic nation in the world to threaten its peace. 'Today's war is not a war against Adolf Hitler', the book begins.

Nor is it a war against Nazis. It is a war of peoples against peoples, of civilised peoples envisioning Light, against uncivilised barbarians who cherish Darkness . . . [Hitler, the Kaiser, Bismarck are] merely mirrors reflecting centuries-old inbred lust of the German nation for conquest and mass murder . . . This time Germany has forced TOTAL WAR upon the world. As a result, she must be prepared to pay a TOTAL PENALTY. And there is one, only one, such Total Penalty: Germany must perish forever! In fact – not fancy![69]

And so on. It is noteworthy that although this book was published by its own author, it was widely and on the whole positively reviewed; and this was before the United States entered the war, and before the mass murder of European Jewry in the Holocaust had fully begun.[70]

In 1944 a lawyer called Louis Nizer published (with a reputable publishing house, unlike Kaufman) *What to Do with Germany*, calling for the Nazi leadership, Gestapo and SS, army officers about the rank of colonel, officials of the German People's Courts (the kangaroo courts used for summary despatch of Nazism's opponents, 'defeatists', and others), and members of the Reichstag, to be put on trial for murder; and arguing that Germany should be de-industrialised, or at least that German industry be placed under foreign control. His indictment of the German character is uncompromising:

[N]o people can be innocent who have twice in one generation burst forth in aggression against all their neighbours, near and far. How is it that one spot on the surface of the earth, no larger than Texas, should so persistently explode and ravage the world?

And what were the toasts, the slogans, the anthems, the battle cries of this people? 'Der Tag' – when Germany will rule the world. 'Deutschland über Alles'. 'Tomorrow we will rule the world.' Rule the world! Rule the world! No people who can thrill to such a mission are innocent victims of wicked leaders.[71]

Worse, Nizer accused the Germans nation of being psychiatrically ill, suffering from a variety of sexually based disorders, principally sadism, homosexuality and bestiality. In a flight of rhetoric not entirely consistent with this thesis he asks, 'Is it possible that German cruelty and blood lust is traceable to sexual inhibitions? Is there significance in the pornographic tendencies of the German fed by such official documents as Streicher's Stuermer?'[72]

And so on again. But one refrain in Nizer's book, for all its mixture of intemperance and legalism – which no doubt struck a chord with many, given the degree of animosity against 'the Boche' during the war years – was the idea that the German people, not just its leaders but the people as a whole, bore a common responsibility for the engulfment of the world in war. This was because as a people – the generalisation comes all too naturally in such arguments – Germans are possessed of excessive characteristics that have always made them a menace to peace and stability. 'Under [Hitler, the Kaiser, Bismarck, Charlemagne] millions of Germans fought fanatically, heroically, sacrificially. Theirs was not conduct induced by compulsion,' Nizer argued, 'theirs was a will to execute a program and a readiness to die for it. The vaunted efficiency of German aggression depends on millions of little cogs acting in perfect co-ordination which involuntary compliance could not possibly produce.'[73]

The chorus of anti-German sentiment in the United States was a large one. Norman Cousins, editor of the *Saturday Review of Literature*, argued for the necessity of 'deep burning hatred' of Germans to potentiate the struggle against them.[74] The level of rhetoric rose when Rex Stout and Clifton Fadiman joined sixteen other literary figures on America's War Writers Board, a department of the Office of War Information responsible for propaganda. The Board provided the Office of War Information with supportive pens when skilful writing tasks needed to be done. According to James Martin, 'Fadiman was regarded by some as the most towering Germanophobe throughout the war, while others had as their outstanding figure in the field of action such as Lord Vansittart of

England, and such Americans as Shirer, Kaufman, Quentin Reynolds, Walter Winchell, Ben Hecht, Stout, Louis Nizer, and Henry Morgenthau, though a full roll-call would number in the hundreds.'[75]

The term 'collective guilt' as applied to the German people was coined by Robert, Lord Vansittart, who had been secretary to Stanley Baldwin and Ramsay MacDonald, and then Permanent Under-Secretary of State in the Foreign Office until his outspoken Germanophobia and his hostility to 'appeasers' led him to be sidelined in 1937 in a notional promotion to 'Foreign Office adviser'. (There is some suggestion that either then or during the course of the war he had a role in the intelligence services; he was described in the Canadian press in 1945 as 'a spokesman for British intelligence'.) In the mid-1930s British opinion about Hitler and Germany was deeply divided, and much acerbity infected the opposition between the two views. The *Times* newspaper was the flagship for pro-German and indeed pro-Hitler sentiment, while Churchill, Vansittart and others maintained a robust anti-German line, warning of the dangers posed by Hitler and the prospect of revived German military adventurism. In the event they were proved right, but in Vansittart's case the argument went beyond the need to defeat Nazi Germany; he wanted to see measures that would decisively and permanently prevent Germany from a second resurrection as a military menace.

Vansittart was raised to the peerage in 1940, and used the House of Lords as a platform for proposing harsh measures against Germany once the war was over. So uncompromising were his views that extremer versions of Germanophobia came to be called 'vansittartism'. In his book *Bones of Contention* (published just before the war's end, in March 1945) he wrote 'The Germans are savage to a degree almost inconceivable to anyone who has not had actual experience of them, and are a people born to deceit.' These were not his own words; he was quoting the first-century Roman historian Paterculus, and he went on to quote Tacitus, Seneca, Claudian, Nazarius, Ammianus, Marcellinus, Ennodius, Quintilian and Josephus to the same effect.[76]

In the House of Lords on 10 March 1943, during the course of a debate on the question of post-war Germany, he said,

> I am not wishing to destroy Germany. I desire only . . . to destroy Germany utterly and for ever as a military power; and I further desire . . . to make an end for ever of all German pretensions, intrigues and efforts to gain economical hegemony of Europe . . . Subject to those trifling reservations, I welcome the survival of Germany with one proviso only, and that is that it shall be a totally different Germany.[77]

Akin to the ideas of 'collective guilt' and 'flawed national character' is the premise for Daniel Goldhagen's *Hitler's Willing Executioners: Ordinary Germans and the Holocaust*, published in 1996, which imputes to the entire German people a practically genetic anti-Semitism and therefore capacity for genocide, in which any 'ordinary German' is by his nature capable of participating, and for which the character of the German people as a whole is responsible. Goldhagen's book was controversial not only for reviving this view, but for the questionable character of its scholarship, which is a separate matter.[78] The point of interest for present purposes is that if in 1996 such indictments of the German people *as a whole* were still possible, attitudes during the war itself to the question of post-war Germany were, obviously and at least, as likely to be coloured by generalised thinking of just that kind. The examples cited of extreme views such as Kaufman's and Nizer's, and views that almost translated into policy such as Morgenthau's, accordingly provide a background to under-standing the thinking of those directly engaged in the struggle with Germany. Army men had the opposing army to fight; the Navy had the opposing navy to fight; the RAF alone had the towns, cities and people of Germany deliberately and literally in its sights, and there-fore the question of what might be done during the course of the war to influence matters after it, was much more present for them than for those in the army and navy. (Given the precision-bombing aspirations of the USAAF in the European theatre, consideration of its leaders' attitudes are more relevant to the question of post-war Japan.)

A way of viewing this point from another perspective helps to clarify it further. In the Bosnian war of 1992–5, ultra-nationalist Serbs targeted Sarajevo's library in order to destroy the thousands of Ottoman, Persian and Arabic manuscripts held there. The Spanish writer Juan Goytisolo described this as an attempt to kill Bosnian Muslim memories and to make way for a new Serbian mythology of conquest. He called it 'memoricide'. In fact and legend alike the examples of memoricide, or what I suggest more generally and accurately might be called *culturecide*, are legion; history runs over with stories of the sack and destruction of cities, the extinction of cultures (think of native cultures in North and Central America, the ancient Celts of Western Europe, the aboriginals of India), iconoclasm (the Puritan destruction of murals, statuary and devotional objects), the burning of books and those who wrote them (by Qin Shi, the First Emperor of China; by the Inquisition) – examples are legion.

For some – and this does not include latter-day neo-Nazis and their like, for whom such questions are not matters of serious speculation but rabid certainty – it matters to ask how different was the attempt to raze Germany's major cities to the ground. Such an attempt was made: so much is fact. What was the intention? A city does not consist just of houses and factories (we are leaving aside for the moment the question of the people living there). To repeat and re-emphasise: it has libraries, schools, hospitals, universities, theatres, museums, monuments, churches, meeting halls, laboratories, concert halls with violins and pianos in them, art galleries with paintings and sculpture in them, craft workshops, antique shops, bookshops, newspaper offices, buildings of architectural importance, in fact the whole array and panoply of culture, education, literacy, artistic endeavour and civilised life. In the immediate aftermath of a bombing attack the survivors need victuals and shelter. But in the longer term, water, food and a place out of the rain are not enough for permanency, still less for revival and growth. And once the inheritance of a community has gone, it takes time to build a new one. Many of Germany's cities were places of beauty and charm before the Nazi period; when it was over, 40 per cent of the seventy largest cities had been demolished, mainly by bombing. Tracts of them are functional and visually rather sterile places now. Is it possible to believe that this programme of destruction was carried out without any thought of its effect on the post-war situation, and even the longer-term future of the country and its population?

As shown by how Eden, Cordell Hull, Stimson and eventually Churchill reacted to the Morgenthau Plan, there was in the end no serious possibility that a Morgenthau-style policy would be implemented in full for post-war Germany – although in the event Germany was indeed divided, a result that was accepted with a degree of satisfaction in some quarters, despite the Cold War implications. Correlatively, given the need seen by the Allied leadership for the eventual reconstruction of at least West Germany and its post-Nazi rehabilitation into the international order, there can also have been no intention to so pulverise Germany that recovery would be impossible. Yet the bombing of Germany gives every appearance to hindsight of a concerted smashing of as much of Germany, its people and its cultural heritage as possible. The same can be said of the USAAF's area bombing of Japan. If the war in either the European or the Pacific theatre had lasted months more, or another year, with the area-bombing campaigns continuing their intensifying curve, the impression given would be one of an attempt at annihilation. Harris, famously or notoriously, had a list of cities to be bombed, and which he insisted on bombing. In February and March of 1945 his bombers systematically sought them out and bombed them – which meant that they destroyed ancient and beautiful German towns with little or no military significance, as the destruction of Würzburg and Hildesheim shows.[79]

What explains the large and apparent discrepancy between the continued campaign of destruction and the fact that the thrust of official Allied policy on post-war Germany was that it would be de-Nazified, reconstructed, and returned to the international fold?

The answer I offer has to be tentative because it is speculative. In the case of RAF bombing in the European theatre, two factors were jointly operative. One was the relative autonomy of Bomber Command, and the other was the dynamic of its constantly growing number of bombers and bombs, all needing to be used, and in the closing period of the war in skies far less dangerous than in the early years. This gave an impetus to its campaign like the gathering speed of a lorry without brakes rolling down a hill. Until April 1945 the Wehrmacht was resisting on the Western Front with tenacity, and Allied progress was painfully slow. So the continued use of every available means of battering the enemy – even the bombing of unmilitary towns behind the front – continued to be permitted, though the strategic (as opposed to tactical, i.e. battlefield) bombing was not regarded by army commanders on the ground as having much relevance to their immediate task.

In the case of the USAAF in the Pacific theatre, the ferocity and destructiveness of its area-bombing campaign there is also explainable by two factors. One was the belief and hope that a bombing campaign could win the war against Japan without an invasion. The other was – to use blunt terms – racism towards and anger against the Japanese. There were at least four main reasons for this. One was the perfidy of the Pearl Harbor attack. Another was Japanese cruelty to American prisoners of war as testified by those liberated during the American advance along the Pacific islands. A third was the ferocity of the Japanese as fighters in contesting those advances. The fourth was the tactic of Kamikaze attacks, displaying what the Americans took to be a repugnant degree of weird oriental fanaticism. All these factors made the Japanese seem subhuman. American propaganda at the time portrayed them as such, in words and pictures, and the attitude was not merely rhetorical.

Ronald Schaffer remarks that American attitudes to the Japanese had begun to harden well before Pearl Harbor, not least because of stories about the atrocities they committed in China. They knew about the infamous Bataan Death March before their bombers had bases within range of the Japanese home islands, and they knew that captured American airmen had been executed by Japanese troops. All this made American military attitudes to the Japanese deeply hostile. General 'Tooey' Spaatz reported after the war that there was a widespread feeling in the US Army Air Force of repugnance for the Japanese; General Haywood Hansell said it was a 'universal feeling' among American airmen and troops that the Japanese were 'subhuman'.[80]

The USAAF's chief, General 'Hap' Arnold, shared this view. He wrote in his diary for 16 June 1945 after visiting Manila, lately liberated from the Japanese:

Apparently the atrocities by the Japs have never been told in the US – babies thrown up in the air and caught on bayonets – autopsies on living people – burning prisoners to death by sprinkling them with gasoline and throwing in a hand grenade to start a fire. If any tried to escape they were killed by machine guns as they came out of the door. More and more of the stories which can apparently be substantiated.[81]

He heard stories about rape and murder, and found that those who had suffered at the Japanese troops' hands had no thought of 'sparing any Japs, [whether] men, women or children', but instead a desire 'to use gas, fire, anything to exterminate the race'.[82]

The next entry in Arnold's diary is the sketch of a plan for the air attack on Japan, 'to completely destroy Jap industries and major cities' and 'complete destruction of Japan proper'. This was very different from the 'Hap' Arnold of the European theatre, one of the architects of precision bombing. Schaffer records a telling anecdote about a meeting after the Hiroshima bomb was dropped, at which Leslie Groves, the director of the Manhattan Project, was told by

General George Marshall not to rejoice too much about what had happened, because of the civilian deaths caused. Groves replied that his thoughts were not on the Japanese dead but the men of the Bataan March. Outside Marshall's office Arnold slapped Groves on the back and said, 'I'm glad you said that – that's just the way I feel.'[83]

General Curtis LeMay, in charge of the area bombing of Japan, felt the same way as his comrades did. He described the firebombing of Tokyo in uncompromising terms: 'We scorched and boiled and baked to death more people in Tokyo on that night of March 9–10 than went up in vapour in Hiroshima and Nagasaki combined.'[84] He is famous for saying, 'Killing Japanese didn't bother me very much at the time . . . I suppose if I had lost the war, I would have been tried as a war criminal . . . every soldier thinks something of the moral aspects of what he is doing. But all war is immoral and if you let that bother you, you're not a good soldier.' And he is equally famous for saying, when Chief of Staff of the US Air Force during the early years of the Vietnam War, that he planned to bomb the North Vietnamese 'back to the Stone Age'.[85]

It might seem odd to invoke the autonomy of RAF Bomber Command as an explanation for the unremitting character of its area bombing of Germany as the war approached an end. Two facts explain it. One is an examination of the diaries of Lord Alanbrooke, who as Field Marshal Sir Alan Brooke was Chief of the Imperial General Staff during the Second World War, and therefore chairman of the Chiefs of Staff (COS) committee comprising the heads of the British army, navy and air force. His diaries show – and they give one a frisson of surprise in doing so – how very little importance was attached by COS and the British government to the area-bombing campaign carried out by Bomber Command.[86] That is to say: COS and Churchill's war cabinet were content to let the entire apparatus of bombing continue to function, from aircraft and bomb production to Harris's almost independent direction of efforts at the sharp end, partly because they thought it kept general pressure on the enemy, and partly because it would have been more complicated to stop it than to leave it running.

In Alanbrooke's diary every COS meeting is mentioned, and its topic; these meetings were held on an almost daily basis. Air Marshal Sir Arthur Harris is mentioned just twice in the whole diary, both times disparagingly. On 13 October 1943, as Bomber Command's endeavours were gearing up towards the Battle of Berlin, Alanbrooke wrote (with his characteristic plethora of exclamation marks):

> Bert Harris came to see us this morning during the COS meeting. According to him the only reason why the Russian Army has succeeded in advancing is due to the results of the bomber offensive!! According to him I am certain that we are all preventing him from winning the war. If Bomber Command was left to itself it would make much shorter work of it all![87]

On 15 May 1944 Alanbrooke recorded the meeting at which General Eisenhower, King George VI, all the British and American Chiefs of Staff, and commanding officers in positions like Harris's, were present to review the D-Day plans. He writes, 'Bert Harris told us how well he might have won this war if it had not been for the handicap imposed by the existence of the other two services!'[88]

Sir Charles Portal figures much more in Alanbrooke's diaries, because the two were colleagues on the COS committee and therefore in continual contact. As shown in chapter 2 above, Portal began as an eager advocate of area bombing's war-winning potential, but in the later stages of the war he also saw the point of precision attacks on vital industries such as oil. As already noted, he conducted a long-running tussle with Harris to try to get the latter to redirect Bomber Command's energies towards this task. The very fact of this tussle is proof of the high degree of independence Harris enjoyed as a result of the relative irrelevance of his area-bombing campaign to the rest of the war effort. 'Spent afternoon in the office battling with Portal's latest ideas for the policy of conduct of this war. Needless to say it is based on bombing Germany at the expense of everything else,' Alanbrooke wrote on 29 September 1942.[89] Portal's commitment to the idea that bombing wins wars never diminished. Alanbrooke reports that at a 'long and difficult' COS meeting on 1 May 1945, devoted to discussion of the war in the East, Portal tabled a proposal 'to establish long range bomber groups on an island near Formosa'.[90]

It is clear that Alanbrooke and Churchill were in agreement about what could be expected from bombing, namely, that at most and best it was an 'annoyance' to Germany. Churchill, it will be remembered, said as much after receiving the Butt report on bombing accuracy (or more correctly, inaccuracy): 'It is very debatable whether bombing by itself will be a decisive factor in the present war . . . the most we can say is that it will be a heavy and I trust seriously increasing annoyance.'[91]

Bomber Command did have two other uses, though. One was its utility as a morale-booster on the home front, as shown by the excitement generated in the press by the 1,000-bomber attack on Cologne, the Dam Busters raid, the firebombing of Hamburg, and stories about the pounding given to Berlin in the winter before the invasion. There was nothing adventitious about the improvement in civilian morale thus generated. In a long war whose first years had been gloomy and fraught with danger, the knowledge that Britain was hitting back was a powerful psychological support. It released other feelings too, at least for some, of satisfaction that the Germans were being paid in kind, and more, for what they had done to British cities and towns in the Blitz of 1940–1.

The other major use of the area-bombing campaign was as a means of pacifying Stalin – at least to some extent – who was desperate for the western Allies to take action in their region of the war to ease the pressure on the Eastern Front. What he most wanted was a Second Front – an invasion of the European continent from the west – and he wanted it in 1942, long before it was possible for the western Allies to contemplate such a thing. Temporising, they made vague promises to the effect that a Second Front would be opened in that year, but what happened instead was that Rommel captured Tobruk, and Germany seemed poised for victory. The Russians by sheer blood and guts turned the balance of the war by themselves in the closing weeks of 1942. In the preceding summer of that year relations between Russia and the western Allies were strained by Stalin's accusations against them of bad faith, weakness and cowardice. Provoked by this, at the end of July Churchill suggested to Stalin that they meet face to face, and Stalin invited Churchill to the Kremlin. Churchill arrived in Moscow on 12 August 1942, and set about explaining to Stalin why nothing could be done about a Second Front in the remainder of that year.[92] It began as a bad-tempered meeting, with Stalin accusing the Allies of being afraid of the Germans and reluctant to take risks, without which, he said, wars cannot be won. But Churchill had two trump cards to play; one was the plan for Operation Torch, the Anglo-American landings in North Africa in the rear of Rommel's army; and the other was the plan for a massive assault on Germany by Bomber Command. Richard Overy describes what happened when Churchill told Stalin of these prospects:

> The mood of the meeting lightened. Stalin liked Torch. He saw straight away that it would secure the defeat of Rommel, and speed up the withdrawal of Italy from the war. But what he liked most was the bombing. The American envoy, Averill Harriman, who was present throughout the meeting, wired Roosevelt the next day that the mention of bombing elicited 'the first agreement between the two men'. Stalin came to life for the first time in the conference. He told Churchill to bomb homes as well as factories; he suggested the best urban targets. 'Between the two of them,' Harriman continued, 'they had soon destroyed most of the important industrial cities of Germany.' The tension eased. Stalin accepted that the British could, as Churchill put it, only 'pay our way by bombing Germany'. [Churchill] promised a 'ruthless' bombardment to shatter the morale of the German people.[93]

And so Bomber Command was set on its course, interrupted only by the temporary needs of the invasion in 1944, but able to return to the path Harris regarded as its destiny in the autumn of that year. It had already been given its area-bombing remit in the directive of 14 February 1942, and that remit was reinforced by the 'Pointblank' directive agreed between Britain and the United States at the Casablanca conference of January 1943, which outlined the direction of the combined offensive to be undertaken by the RAF and USAAF bomber forces: the former to continue its night attacks, the latter to seek its targets by day.[94]

Apart from the efforts made by Portal to engage Harris in attacks on oil late in the war, the only move made to redirect or limit area bombing thereafter came when Churchill issued his famous minute of 28 March 1945, at last questioning the area-bombing strategy.[95] A point not often stressed in connection with this minute relates to its concluding paragraph: 'The Foreign Secretary has spoken to me on this subject, and I feel the need for more precise concentration upon military objectives, such as oil and communications behind the immediate battle-zone, rather than on mere acts of terror and wanton destruction, however impressive.'[96] This minute was withdrawn after protests from Portal and the Air Ministry, but it had let a cat out of the bag. Sir Anthony Eden, the Foreign Secretary, had evidently become anxious about post-war reflection on the nature of the area-bombing campaign, perhaps as a result of discussions with Stimson, whose views on the subject were clear. Eden evidently therefore decided to urge Churchill to the same thoughts, and the 28 March minute was the result. Just before the Dresden bombing six weeks earlier, Churchill had been enthusiastic for a blow to show support for the Russian advance; and perhaps, in the same spirit as American use of atomic bombing to educate Russian sensibilities, he also wished to show the Russians what British bombing could do.[97] At the Yalta conference Stalin had asked for communications behind Germany's Eastern Front to be attacked, to interdict the movement of reinforcements. Berlin and Leipzig were mentioned as targets, but not

Dresden, one important reason being that the Russians 'clearly preferred to keep the RAF and USAAF away from territory they might soon be occupying'.[98] Whatever the logic, by the time Churchill came to write the 28 March minute, his attitude to the area-bombing campaign had changed. If beforehand it had been an alternating mixture of interest and relative indifference, it was now negative. In his victory broadcast on BBC radio on 13 May 1945 he did not mention Bomber Command. No campaign medal was struck for those who took part in Bomber Command's work, and Arthur Harris was not allowed to publish his final Despatch summarising his command's activities in the war.

The speculative conclusion that might be reached, in the light of all this, is that although there was no Allied policy to cripple Germany so badly that after the war it would be fit for nothing but 'pastoralisation', nevertheless the quasi-autonomy of Bomber Command meant that right until the last weeks of the war it continued to act in ways that gave every impression of trying to bring about just such a result. In the minds of Harris especially and of Portal too, a perhaps unspoken assumption seems to have operated: that a bombing strategy aimed at *destroying the will and capacity of the German people to wage war* easily translates into the thought that such bombing also ensures *the destruction of the will and capacity to be in a position to wage war again* or at least *later*, once the present war was over.

It would I think be too much to claim that RAF Bomber Command in a semi-autonomous way consciously attempted a kind of Morgenthau Plan of its own. But by default that is exactly what the tendency of massive urban destruction was. Note that this is a point still independent of the question whether the area-bombing campaign was morally right or wrong. After all, there were voices, among them Morgenthau's, arguing that this was the right thing to do. But Harris and Portal cannot themselves be blamed or praised alone – depending on point of view – for the Morgenthau-like tendency of the bombing campaign. The top level of Allied, and especially British, military and political leadership have to accept the major share of responsibility for initiating it and for letting it continue. Whether that responsibility is culpable is the chief point at issue in this book.

One very important point remains to be discussed to complete an understanding of the mind of the bombers, which is to comment on the war circumstances in which their thinking unfolded. These circumstances explain the reasons for the change in British and American thinking about air strategy, which in turn led to changes in practice from attempts at precision bombing to area bombing. For the British this change occurred in February 1942, and for the Americans it occurred in the Pacific theatre in late 1944. In the case of both countries the policy followed the facts rather than the other way round. Bomber Command's navigational and bomb-aiming difficulties meant that it had in practice been bombing civilian areas already, although trying to hit more specific targets, before the area-bombing directive of 14 February 1942. The same applies to the endeavours of the Eighth and Fifteenth Army Air Forces over Europe. But the practical difficulty of hitting precision targets was only one factor in forcing that change. More significant were the war situations in both Europe and the Pacific. It is these that are standardly invoked as part of the justification for area bombing in both theatres. A discussion of these factors is given in chapter 7 below.

5

Voices of Conscience

THERE WERE MORE conscientious objectors in the First than in the Second World War for the good reason that the latter was, from the Allied point of view, a justified war, and widely understood to be so. It was justified because it consisted in resistance to the unarguable fact of military aggression by jack-booted Fascism. But there were people for whom it mattered that the war should be not only a justified one, but a justly fought one, and to whom therefore some of the Allies' actions were unacceptable. One thing such people were concerned about was the blockade of continental Europe, in light of the suffering it caused to those in occupied countries such as Greece where, for a time, famine threatened.

But a much greater concern was the area-bombing campaign. In the summer of 1941 a Committee for the Abolition of Night Bombing was set up by the British Quaker pacifist Corder Catchpool, who had been a volunteer ambulance driver in the First World War until conscription was introduced. Then, because he refused to take part in any alternative to military duties which might aid the war effort, he was sent to prison for two years' hard labour. After the outbreak of the Second World War he was impelled by two things to set up his committee against night bombing: the experience of the Blitz, and a letter to *The Times* newspaper on 17 April 1941 from George Bell, Bishop of Chichester, who asked, 'if Europe is civilised at all, what can excuse the bombing of towns by night and terrorising of non-combatants?' In his letter Bell called on both Germany and Britain to forswear the tactic, and Catchpool decided to lobby to try to get at least his own country to comply.

Catchpool's commitment to the cause of peace was a deep and active one. While still in prison in 1918 he published an account of his experiences as both pacifist and prisoner.[1] After his release he went to Germany to work for the Friends War Victims Relief Committee, set up to further the task of reconciliation between the combatant nations. He remained in Germany for a time after the Nazi regime came to power, but his help for Jews attracted the attentions of the Gestapo, and he was arrested and interrogated by them. He returned to England soon afterwards. He had no illusions about Nazi Germany, but he adhered to his Quaker pacifist principles despite that.

Among those Catchpool invited to join his committee were Professor Stanley Jevons, T. C. Foley, Stuart Morris, and the novelist and eloquently vocal pacifist Vera Brittain. Not all of its members were pacifists like Vera Brittain and Catchpool himself, but they were all deeply opposed to bombing civilians. The committee's first endeavour was to organise a petition asking the British government to give up bombing by night; surprisingly for the time and circumstances, the petition gathered 15,000 names, among them those of three bishops, six Members of Parliament, and a mixture of pacifists and non-pacifists.

When it became clear in the spring of 1942 that the RAF was stepping up its bombing efforts – this was at the time of Arthur Harris's appointment – the Committee for the Abolition of Night Bombing reconfigured itself as the Bombing Restriction Committee, and redoubled its efforts. In her fortnightly *Letter* written and published for the peace movement, Vera Brittain wrote: '[We] must decide whether we want the government to continue to carry out through its Bomber Command a policy of murder and massacre in our name. Has any nation the right to make its young men the instruments of such a policy?'[2]

The committee's aim was to gather information about the status of area bombing in international law, to support the International Red Cross's efforts to designate 'sanctuary areas' free from bombing, and to provide data for Bishop Bell to use in his attacks on area bombing in the House of Lords. In the matter of data-gathering it was singularly successful.

George Bell's attitude to the conduct of the war was not a function of other-worldly innocence. He knew rather better than many what was at stake in Nazi Germany. Before the outbreak of hostilities in 1939 he was active in helping people of Jewish origin gain asylum in Britain, and he had maintained contact with people engaged in the opposition to Hitler, among them Dietrich Bonhoeffer and Martin Niemöller. In 1942 Bell and Bonhoeffer met in neutral Stockholm, and Bonhoeffer asked Bell to convey a message to the British government, asking for its support in a plot to overthrow Hitler. The German underground required that Britain would recognise a successor government to the Nazi regime, and agree to a truce. Bell told Anthony Eden and Stafford Cripps about the request when he returned home, and they in turn told Churchill. But the British government did not respond; it gave no assurances, and instead soon afterwards adopted the policy, devised in discussions with Roosevelt at the Casablanca Conference, of 'unconditional surrender'.

The disappointment of these endeavours did not stop Bell from trying to moderate Britain's bombing campaign, to which he gave the frank name of 'obliteration bombing'. He was almost a lone voice in the Church, which disapproved of his stance; it is commonly agreed that because of his repeated and outspoken criticism of the bombing he was not chosen to succeed William Temple as Archbishop of Canterbury when the latter died in October 1944.[3] He did however have one church ally in the House of Lords, in the form of Cosmo Lang, a former Archbishop of Canterbury. More representative of the Church's official line was the Archbishop of York, Cyril Foster Garbett, who went so far as to state his support for area bombing in print.

But Bell was not alone in Parliament as a whole. In the upper House his views were shared by Lord Addison and the Marquis of Salisbury as well as Lord Lang, and in the House of Commons by Richard Stokes, Reginald Sorensen and Rhys Davies.

In addition to providing parliamentarians with ammunition for their efforts, the Bombing Restriction Committee was concerned to keep the public informed of what was being done on its behalf and in its name, and to challenge the obfuscations and untruths in government statements about the aims and nature of the bombing offensive. The committee published posters and leaflets, and Vera Brittain began work on what was to be a pamphlet but turned into a short book which had an explosive impact on the debate about bombing: her *Seed of Chaos: What Mass Bombing Really Means*, published in the spring of 1944.

The immediate impulse for this remarkable little book was Operation Gomorrah – the firebombing of Hamburg in July 1943 – and the opening of the 'Battle of Berlin' in November 1943, together with the triumphalist tone of reports about these attacks in the British press. Angered and disgusted by this, and filled with a sense of urgency, Brittain set to work to digest the information amassed by the Bombing Restriction Committee so that the public could have a full picture of what was happening. She chose her title from Alexander Pope's *Dunciad* Book IV: 'Then rose the seed of Chaos, and of Night/ To blot out order and extinguish light', and her epigraph from the Book of Jeremiah 6: 15: 'Were they ashamed when they had committed abomination?'[4]

Despite both the fame of its author and the rage of controversy it caused, *Seed of Chaos* did not remain in print long because, no doubt, it was regarded merely as a book of its moment, and its polemical and exhortatory purpose is tied to that moment. But any discussion of the morality of war and the place of civilians in war is in fact its moment too, which is one good reason for summarising it here.[5] But a yet more compelling reason is that it is a truly invaluable resource for showing the nature and degree of contemporary understanding of the bombing campaign as it unfolded, for it wonderfully preserves a record of the intellectual battle Britain had with itself about the bombing campaign's justification and moral status, even at a period when the war's outcome – though looking more optimistic every day – was still uncertain, and when the comparative question of the heinousness of Nazi atrocities, not least against European Jewry, had not yet made it easier for people on the Allied side to forgo inspection of their own moral linen.

What is further remarkable about Brittain's little book is that its insights, judgements, and factual grasp would be commendable enough had it been written a decade after the war, and yet it was written in the winter of 1943–4, even as the bombing campaign it criticised was increasing in volume and power, though still a year away from its crescendo in the war's final months. The book's very existence, then, shows that there can have been no illusions in informed minds, at least, about the nature of the bombing campaign and its effects; which makes questions about the intentions and knowledge of those who conducted the campaign easy to answer.

Brittain's book begins by suggesting that the British public did not fully comprehend what was happening in the bombed cities of Germany and elsewhere in Europe. Because of a national lack of imagination, she says, 'Throughout our history wrongs have been committed, or evils gone too long unremedied, simply because we did not perceive the real meaning of the suffering which we had caused or failed to mitigate.' By telling the public what the true facts are, she is confident that they will 'rise and demand a change of policy on the part of our rulers'.[6]

The government, she continues, have been skilful in concealing from the public the true nature of 'obliteration bombing'. They use such phrases as 'softening-up an area', 'neutralising the target', 'area bombing', 'saturating the defences', and 'blanketing an industrial district'. Until the summer of 1943 reports of air attacks on Germany and German-occupied Europe received small notices on the back pages of newspapers; but then a change occurred, led by the *Daily Telegraph*. Full front-page coverage started to be given to bombing raids, and expert articles by pilots appeared on the inside pages. The first attacks of the Battle of Berlin in November 1943 'were apparently treated as gala occasions on which the whole Press was permitted to let itself go'. But when the facts are known, said Brittain, we realise the terrible sum of suffering this represents.[7]

People try to hide from the discomfort of this by using two main arguments. The first is that the bombing will shorten the war, 'a contention much favoured by Ministers, officials, Members of Parliament, and some leading Churchmen'. The second argument is that 'we too have suffered from obliteration bombing attacks', and are entitled to pay back in kind.

To the first argument Brittain gave four replies. First, there can be no certainty that bombing will shorten the war. But only absolute certainty could be invoked as a justification for what one commentator described as 'British boys being burnt to death in aeroplanes while they are roasting to death the population down below'. 'Mr Churchill himself has called the mass bombing an "experiment",' Brittain continued, thus showing that neither was he certain that it would shorten the war; but 'what does appear certain is the downward spiral in moral values, ending in the deepest abysses of the human spirit, to which this argument leads'. The Germans had argued in the First World War that their submarine blockade of Britain would shorten the war, but no one in Britain then thought this justified the policy.[8]

Churchill's 'experiment' remark had been reported in an article in *Time* magazine on 7 June 1943, which said that the commanders of the British and American bomber forces (Arthur Harris and Ira Eaker) had 'assured their military superiors that Germany can be bombed out of the war this year' but that Churchill had (as *Time* put it) 'stated the reaction of global strategists when he said, "The experiment is well worth trying so long as other measures are not excluded"'. The editor of *Time* had put Churchill's words in italics.

Brittain's second reply to the claim that bombing would shorten the war was that 'shorten' is a misleading concept in the circumstances. It implies the limiting or reduction of the total quantity of destruction and suffering that the war might cause, but 'in a vast, concentrated raid, lasting a few minutes, more persons may be killed or injured than in a modern major battle lasting two or three weeks'. And she added, this happens 'in addition to the destruction of an irreplaceable cultural heritage of monuments, art treasures and documents, representing centuries of man's creative endeavour. In fact, a mass bombing of great centres of population means *a speed-up of human slaughter, misery and material destruction imposed on that of the military fighting fronts*'.[9]

The third reply is that mass bombing does not cause revolt or the collapse of morale. The victims are too stunned and exhausted, too absorbed in the immediate tasks of survival, to start a revolution against their rulers. 'But when they recover, who can doubt that there will be, among the majority at any rate, the desire for revenge . . . thus we are steadily creating in Europe the psychological foundations for a third World War.'[10]

And fourth, the systematic demolition of German industry constitutes an injury to ourselves in the long term, given that the prosperity of the Continent has largely depended on it, and that Germany is one of Britain's best markets.[11] This argument, although doubtless from other sources, eventually weighed with Churchill a year later, after his Morgenthau lapse at the Quebec conference.

Brittain rebutteds the second argument – that the Germans had tried obliteration bombing on Britain first, and deserved to be repaid in kind – by quoting a characteristically sharp riposte to the idea from George Bernard Shaw: 'The blitzing of the cities has carried war this time to such a climax of infernal atrocity that all recriminations on that score are ridiculous. The Germans will have as big a bill of atrocities against us as we against them if we take them into an impartial international court.'[12] Here is one respect in which Shaw and Brittain were insufficiently informed, situated as they were in

1943: so far as a 'bill of atrocities' was concerned, Nazi Germany was going to outstrip all others by a very long way; so far as bombing was concerned, the Germans were already well behind the Allies.

But Brittain's book has other answers to the justified-reprisal argument. One is that the question of who started bombing civilians in areas far from the front lines of military conflict is not easy to answer. Bombs intended for industrial targets might be dropped by mistake on civilian areas; a reprisal raid is organised in kind; it provokes a further such reprisal – until eventually full-scale carpet bombing of cities is happening: 'the grim competition goes on, until the mass murder of civilians becomes part of our policy – a descent into barbarism which we should have contemplated with horror in 1939.'[13]

Moreover, although Britain suffered cruelly in the Blitz, the methods and weapons available to the RAF by the end of 1943 made mass bombing vastly worse. 'My own experience is relatively small, but as a Londoner who has been through about 600 raid periods and has spent 18 months as a volunteer fireguard, I have seen and heard enough to know that I at least must vehemently protest when this obscenity of terror is inflicted upon the helpless civilians of another country.' And she added, 'Nor do I believe that the majority of our airmen who are persuaded that mass bombing reduces the period of their peril really want to preserve their own lives by sacrificing German women and babies, any more than our soldiers would go into action using "enemy" mothers and children as a screen.'[14]

And third, retaliation 'in kind' simply reduces one to the level of one's enemies, and it is the perverted values of our enemies that made us fight them in the first place. Those in Britain who understood this most clearly were those who had most suffered from bombing. This was made plain by an opinion poll conducted in April 1941, when the Blitz was still happening, on the question: 'Would you approve or disapprove if the RAF adopted a policy of bombing the civilian population of Germany?' In heavily bombed areas such as inner London, 47 per cent disapproved of reprisals, 45 per cent approved, and the rest were undecided, whereas in the northernmost counties of England where there had been no bombing, 76 per cent approved.[15]

As Brittain then points out, this poll showed the inaccuracy of a claim made by Churchill just two months afterwards: 'If tonight,' he said in a speech at London's County Hall, 'the people of London were asked to cast their vote whether a convention should be entered into to stop the bombing of all cities, the overwhelming majority would cry, "No, we will mete out to the Germans the measure, and more than the measure, that they have meted out to us".'[16]

Brittain was anxious to show how the progress of the war had effected a regress in the moral standards of its conduct. She therefore contrasted Churchill's County Hall speech with one he made on 27 January 1940, before he became Prime Minister, condemning the German bombing of urban targets in Poland as 'a new and odious form of attack', and stating the government's refusal to follow its example when people called for the RAF's bombers to be loaded with bombs instead of leaflets.[17] Eighteen months later Churchill told the House of Commons, 'As the year advances, German cities, harbours and centres of war production will be subjected to an ordeal the like of which has never been experienced by any country in continuity, severity or magnitude.'[18] A year later again, in a speech to the US Congress in Washington, he said, 'It is the duty of those who are charged with the direction of the War to . . . begin the process so necessary and desirable of laying the cities and the other military centres of Japan in ashes, for in ashes they must surely lie before peace comes to the world.'[19] Press reports in London the following day said that members of Congress were so enthusiastic that they did not applaud but 'shouted their approval'; which, as Brittain dryly pointed out, was not entirely consistent with the speech made to the same august body by Roosevelt just four months later, on 8 September 1943, when he assured Congress that 'we [Americans] are not bombing tenements for the sadistic pleasure of killing as the Nazis did, but blowing to bits carefully selected targets – factories, ship-yards, munition dumps'.[20]

In the same month, on 21 September, Churchill told the House of Commons,

> The almost total systematic destruction of many of the centres of German war effort continues on a greater scale and at a greater pace. The havoc wrought is indescribable and the effect upon the German war production in all its forms . . . is matched by that wrought on the life and economy of the whole of that guilty organisation . . . There are no sacrifices we will not make, no lengths in violence to which we will not go, to destroy Nazi tyranny and Prussian militarism.

Shortly afterwards he sent a message of commendation to Bomber Command for its endeavours in 'beating the life out of Germany'.[21] As the record shows, he was quite wrong about the effect on German war production, which was still increasing year on year.

The rhetoric in play was an agreed one. Brendan Bracken, the Minister for Information, told the press in August 1943 while on a visit to Canada, 'Our plans are to bomb, burn, and ruthlessly destroy in every way available to us the people responsible for creating this war.' Sir Archibald Sinclair, the Minister for Air, told a public meeting in Cheltenham on 5 November 1943, 'We shall continue to hammer the enemy from the skies until we have paralysed their war industries, disrupted their transport system, and broken their will to war.'[22]

Most striking of all, perhaps, are the unwitting contradictions and ironies revealed by Brittain in the pro-bombing rhetoric of the British press. An editorial by John Gordon in the *Sunday Express* on 20 April 1942, written to comment on the content of the Bomber Command directive of 14 February once it had been made public, reads: 'Germany, the originator of war by air terror, is now finding that terror recoiling on herself with an intensity that even Hitler in his most sadistic dreams never thought possible.' On the next day the *News Chronicle* asserted that the German people must be made to feel in their own brick and bones the mad meaning of their rulers' creed of cruelty and destruction . . . if by the ferocity of our retribution we can convince them at last that violence does not pay and induce them to become good citizens of the world – then the loss of their monuments will be as nothing compared to the contribution to our common inheritance which their conversion to civilised conduct will make.[23]

And Brittain adds, after commenting on the contradictions in both editorials – British war by air terror will outstrip Hitler's most sadistic dreams; 'ferocious retribution' will convert Germans to civilised behaviour – 'A people who have been beaten into apathy and defeatism by their conquerors are hardly likely to conclude that violence does not pay.'

In August 1943, in the weeks following Operation Gomorrah, the British press publicised a government statement saying that 'at least 50 of Germany's main cities will meet the fate of Hamburg by Christmas'. The RAF employed some of its heroes in publicity roles to maintain public support and morale. One such was the Australian pilot Group Captain (later Air Commodore Sir) Hugh Edwards, VC DSO DFC, who won his VC for leading an intrepid bombing raid on Bremen in which, to his own great danger, he stayed over the target from first to last to direct his squadron's efforts, himself flying so low to place his bombs that telegraph wires were dangling from his bullet-riddled Blenheim when he returned to base. He made various radio broadcasts explaining the bombing campaign's aims, and on 13 October 1943 published an article in the *Daily Mail* in which he said, 'Bomber Command is obliterating vast areas of industrial Germany.'[24]

The official position of the government remained that the primary objects of Bomber Commands attentions were 'military'. In the House of Commons on 31 March 1943 the Minister for Air, Sir Archibald Sinclair, said 'The targets of Bomber Command are always military', thus implying that industrial and communication targets are military too, and with them workers, and with them again anyone living near the workers; for Sir Archibald continued, '. . . but night bombing of military objectives necessarily involves bombing the area in which they are situated.' This method of explaining why cities were being carpet-bombed gave the supporters of the bombing campaign ammunition of their own to attack those who were against area bombing of civilians; an editorial in the *Sunday Dispatch* for 21 March 1943 said, 'Bomber personnel, often in miserable weather, and under attack by vicious fighters, try to hit their targets. Any attempt to persuade them to worry unduly about civilians is an attempt to impair their military value.'[25] Not just truth but temperance is a victim of war; the fighters defending German cities were 'vicious', in contrast to the heroic Few who fought the Battle of Britain. The reference to weather is of great interest in this respect. In his autobiography Harris wrote that in the first four years of the war 'weather . . . had absolute power to make or mar an operation', which is why the navigational aid GEE was so important to Bomber Command hopes when first introduced, though in small numbers, in 1942. Harris wrote:

> [C]ould GEE be used for blind bombing, that is, would it give the bomb-aimer so accurate a fix that he could release the bombs on this alone, without sight of the target? Opinion at the Air Ministry was that GEE could definitely be used for the blind bombing of large industrial towns, though not of individual factories. It was believed that a large town could therefore be attacked through ten-tenths cloud; the estimate was that if Essen was attacked through cloud, nearly half of all the bombs dropped would fall on the city.[26]

These remarks sit very awkwardly next to Sir Archibald Sinclair's claim that 'all of Bomber Command's targets are military'.

Critics of the bombing campaign were aware, as Brittain showed, not just of the obvious point that Bomber Command's tactics and weapons were designed to maximise damage to targets, but of what some of those tactics and weapons were. Thus 'cascade bombing' or 'saturation bombing' – dropping as large a number as possible of high explosives and incendiaries in the shortest possible time over a wide urban area – was designed to overwhelm the emergency services on the ground. Part of the tactic involved bombing a ring around the main target area in order to prevent air-raid personnel and fire-fighters entering it.[27]

Describing the second, firebombing, raid of Operation Gomorrah on the night of 27–8 July 1943, the British press called it 'the heaviest air raid of all time'. One newspaper report said: 'A million fire-bombs and hundreds of huge two-ton "block-busters" were dropped in 45 minutes, five minutes quicker than in the 2,300 ton raid on the same target on Saturday. Every such cut in the bombing period means greater destruction and greater safety for men and aircraft. Defences are swamped.'[28]

What this meant on the ground was as clear to people in Britain as it had been to survivors in Hamburg itself. Less than two weeks after Operation Gomorrah was over, the *Daily Telegraph* helpfully described for its readers the firestorm and its effects:

The terrific heat [of the fires started by the bombing] causes a vacuum of air in the bombed districts, and air rushes from other parts of the town. In this way regular tornadoes arise. They are so strong that people were thrown flat on the ground, and the fire brigades cannot get to the blitzed area with their equipment. These violent currents of air help to spread the fire to surrounding districts . . . A number of people there died through lack of oxygen caused by the terrible heat . . . it was found on opening some [air raid shelters] that though [the shelters] were undamaged, many people had died from suffocation.[29]

The air correspondent of the *News Chronicle*, Ronald Walker, quoted Harris after Operation Gomorrah:

The six attacks on the city, port and U-boat yards of Hamburg during four nights and three days probably came nearer than any other series of attacks on Germany to the Harris aim of blotting out a target . . . Air Chief Marshal Sir Arthur Harris, RAF Bomber Command Chief, has made his bombing plan quite plain – the complete destruction of the German industrial cities and ports, one by one. His ideal is to pound them with blows of devastating weight and to keep up that pounding until there is no question of salvage or repair.[30]

The press portrayed Arthur Harris in commendatory terms as 'a tiger with no mercy in his heart'. They attributed to him the credit for forging Bomber Command as a weapon of formidable destructive power, and described his policy as 'the destruction of Germany's cities section by section'.[31] This portrait of Harris, together with the aggressive rhetoric of the press coverage given to the bombing campaign, was of course encouraged by everyone from Churchill down as part of the propaganda effort which, it was hoped, would frighten the German civilian population into surrendering, while at the same time persuading the Nazi leadership of their cause's hopelessness. But fearsome threats of total destruction of cities have to be carried out if surrender does not come, so the rhetoric created a self-imposed necessity to make it come true. And the less successful it proved, the harder became the efforts to make it succeed. Even before Operation Gomorrah – and long before the immense onslaught of the last six months of the war – *Time* magazine was therefore able to say: 'The air offensive against Germany and Axis Europe is suffering from understatement. The objective is not merely to destroy cities, industries, human beings and the human spirit on a scale never before attempted by air action. The objective is to defeat Hitler with bombs, and to do it in 1943.'[32]

To show the British public what this meant in practical terms, the air correspondent of the *Daily Telegraph* wrote in late October 1943 that 'Hamburg has had the equivalent of at least 60 "Coventries",

Cologne 17, Dusseldorf 12, and Essen 10 . . . from July 9th to October 17th no less than 74,000 tons of bombs were dropped on Germany and German-occupied Europe'.[33]

The response was not one of universal rejoicing. The *New Statesman* published a letter from six residents of Coventry on 30 November 1943 which read as follows:

Sir – Many citizens of Coventry who have endured the full horror of intense aerial bombardment would wish to dispute statements made in the *Daily Express* to the effect that all the people of Coventry expressed the opinion that they wished to bomb, and bomb harder, the peoples of Germany. This is certainly not the view of *all* or even the majority of the people of Coventry. The general feeling is, we think, that of horror, and a desire that no other peoples shall suffer as they have done. Our impression is that most people feel the hopelessness of bombing the working classes of Germany and very little satisfaction is attained by hearing that Hamburg is suffering in the same way as Coventry has suffered.'[34]

The citizens of Coventry who wrote in these terms were not alone. A letter from a resident of Southwark in London, one of the capital's most heavily bombed areas, appeared in the *Spectator* for 24 September 1943, asking, 'Why is it that so many religious leaders, politicians and journalists, who denounced German barbarism during the heavy raids on this country, now either applaud such methods when they are adopted in intensified form by the Allies, or acquiesce by their silence?'[35] From another heavily bombed city, Hull, came this:

When Hull was mercilessly blitzed and civilians were the chief sufferers, we condemned out of hand such barbarous methods of warfare; and what was wrong for Germany to do then does not become right for us to do now, merely by the passage of time and the fact that we seem to be 'on top'. You can't maintain that it is right for Britain to bomb whole areas indiscriminately without justifying the equally inhuman blitzing of Hull.[36]

What these expressions of dissent represented in general terms was a minority of public opinion. Rose Macaulay, dismayed by the 'lamentable lapse in the moral outlook of the British people', thought she was accurately reporting the national mood when she wrote to her sister about public reaction to George Bell's attack on the bombing campaign:

> I wonder what it is about any pleas for greater humanity or civilised care in war that makes so many people see red. I have heard the most passionate references to 'these old bishops' in shops; one woman said it was lovely to think of the way we 'gave Berlin a doing' on Tuesday night; and she'd like to 'throw old Chichester on the top of the bonfire'. It is nonsense of Lord Latham [leader of the London Country Council] to say 'there is no gloating or exaltation' among the English; he can't listen much.[37]

But although the dissenters were in a minority, it was a sizeable one. The Mass Observation Unit published a report in the *New Statesman* on 12 February 1944, describing what it found when canvassing opinion about bombing at various stages during the war. The report began with an account of opinion in 1940 at the height of the Blitz: 'It was regularly found that, after a blitz, people in bus, street and pub seldom talked of getting their own back.' Now, at the beginning of 1944, 'nearly one person in four expresses feelings of uneasiness or revulsion' about British methods of bombing the enemy.[38]

The opposition to the bombing campaign came from ordinary people with experience of being bombed, as the foregoing quotations show; and it came from those with military knowledge, and from leading cultural figures:

> In the last war it was the artillery battle [wrote Major-General J. F. C. Fuller]; in this war it is air bombardment. By means of the one

he obliterated entire battlefields, and by doing so denied to himself all possibility of exploiting the initial success gained by becoming bogged down in the slough he created. By means of the other he has annihilated great cities and vast industrial areas and in consequence has pulverised the very foundations upon which eventual peace must be made.[39]

'As to atrocities,' wrote George Bernard Shaw in January 1944,

> we have rained 200,000 tons of bombs on German cities; and some of the biggest of them have no doubt fallen into infants' schools or lying-in hospitals. When it was proposed to rule this method of warfare out, it was we who objected and refused. Can we contend that the worst acts of the Nazis whom our Russian allies have just hanged were more horrible than the bursting of a bomb as big as a London pillar-box in a nursery in Berlin or Bremen . . . German papers, please copy. Our enemies had better know that we have not all lost our heads, and that some of us will know how to clean our slate before we face an impartial international court.[40]

Opposition to Bomber Command's methods was not restricted to reflective minorities in the public at large. In Parliament the war-coalition government faced repeated questioning on the matter. On 14 March 1943 the *Sunday Times* reported debates in the Commons during the preceding week in terms calculated to give heart to the Bombing Restriction Committee:

> Our power continues to grow, and, to the lasting credit of the House of Commons, Members made it plain that they wanted a reassurance that the original clear distinction between military industrial objectives and the indiscriminate dropping of as much high explosive as possible on congested areas, was not being progressively abandoned, just as our superiority should remove any temptation to lower standards. Captain Balfour gave the

reassurance, but the Air Ministry can hardly make it too plain that we do not take our standards in these matters from the enemy; for we are fighting for the preservation of civilisation and he is not.[41]

Two months after this report, Clement Attlee was asked in the House of Commons whether the government had been approached by any of the Christian churches on the subject of bombing. He replied in the negative. Corder Catchpool called this 'a direct challenge, almost an invitation' from the government to the churches to say what they thought.[42] Apart from individual clergymen such as George Bell and a few others, the churches remained silent. William Temple, Archbishop of Canterbury, declined a request from an anti-bombing group to see him. One Canon Hannay wrote scornfully to the *Sunday Express* about German 'squealing' over Cologne. The churches might have been expected to show more interest when, in answer to a question in the House of Commons 'whether the same principles of discrimination that are applied to Rome are being and will be applied to other cities', Sir Archibald Sinclair replied, 'The same principles are applied to all centres. We must bomb important military objectives. We must not be prevented from bombing important military objectives because beautiful or ancient buildings are near them.'[43]

A good sense of the House of Commons atmosphere during discussions of bombing can be gathered from the *Evening Standard* report, on 1 December 1943, of the debate following Sir Archibald's announcement that, in the preceding month of November 1943, 13,000 tons of bombs had been dropped on Germany:

When Mr Stokes asked for the area, in square miles, in Berlin within which it was estimated that 100 per cent of the 350 block-buster bombs recently dropped in a single raid would fall, Sir Archibald said he could not reply without giving useful information to the enemy. Mr Stokes: Would not the proper answer be that the Government dare not give this information? Sir Archibald: No. Berlin is the centre of twelve strategic railways, it is the second largest inland port in Europe. In that city are AEG, the Rhein Metall, Siemens, Focke Wulf, Heinkel and Dornier factories. (Cheers). Mr Stokes: Do you not admit that the Government are now approving the indiscriminate bombing of Germany? Sir Archibald: You are incorrigible. I have mentioned a series of vitally important military targets. Mr Shinwell: Will you appreciate that much as we deplore the loss of civilian life we wish to encourage and applaud the efforts of your Ministry in trying to bring the war to a speedy conclusion? (Cheers). Mr Simmonds: Are not these bombings likely to reduce, vastly, our military casualties when we invade Europe? Sir Archibald: Yes. Mr Stokes also asked whether the policy of limiting objectives of Bomber Command to targets of military importance had or had not been changed to the bombing of towns and wide areas in which military targets are not situated. Sir Archibald: There has been no change of policy.

Hansard continues where the *Standard* leaves off:

Mr Stokes: May I say that the reply of my Right Hon. Friend does not answer this question. Am I to understand that the policy has changed, and that new objectives of Bomber Command are not specific military targets but large areas, and would it not be true to say that probably the minimum area of a target now is 16 square miles? Sir Archibald Sinclair: My Hon. Friend cannot have listened to my answer. I said there had been no change of policy.[44]

Debate in the House of Lords, both in fact and by tradition, is seemlier and more modestly phrased. George Bell's efforts to press questions about the bombing campaign there conform themselves to that model. *The Times* gave a full report of his speech to that House on 9 February 1944:

He [the Lord Bishop of Chichester] was not forgetting the Luftwaffe or its tremendous bombing of Belgrade, Warsaw, Rotterdam, London, Portsmouth, Coventry, Plymouth, Canterbury, and many other places of military, industrial, and cultural importance. Hitler was a barbarian. There was not a decent person on the allied side who was likely to suggest we should make him our pattern . . . The question with which he was concerned was this: Did the Government understand the full force of what our aerial bombardment was doing and what it was now destroying? Was it alive not only to the vastness of the material damage, much of which is irreparable, but also to the harvest it was laying up for the future relationships of the peoples of Europe? He recognised the legitimacy of concentrated attack on industrial and military objectives . . . He fully realised that any attacks on centres of war industry and transport inevitably carried with it the killing of civilians. But there must be a fair balance between the means employed and the purpose achieved. To obliterate a whole town because certain portions contained military and industrial objectives was to reject the balance.

He would instance Hamburg, with a population of between one and two millions. It contained targets of first-class military importance. It also happened to be the most democratic town in Germany, where the anti-Nazi opposition was strongest . . .

Berlin, the capital of the Reich, was four times the size of Hamburg. The military, industrial, and war-making establishments in Berlin were a fair target, but up to date half the city had been destroyed and it was said that 74,000 persons had been killed and 3,000,000 were already homeless. The policy was obliteration, openly acknowledged, and that was not a justifiable act of war. Berlin was one of the greatest centres of art galleries in the world. It had one of the best picture galleries in Europe, comparable to the National Gallery, and had one of Europe's finest libraries. All these non-industrial, non-military buildings were grouped together, and the whole of the area is reported to have been demolished. These works of art and libraries would be wanted for the re-education of the Germans after the war . . .

There were old German towns away from the great centres which almost certainly would be subjected to the raids of Bomber Command. In these places the historic and beautiful centres were well preserved and the industrial and military establishments were on the outskirts. We had destroyed much; we ought to think once, twice, three times, before we destroyed the rest . . .

He emphasised particularly the danger outside Germany, to Rome. The principle was the same . . . The history of Rome was our own history. Its destruction would rankle in the memory of every good European as the destruction of Rome by the Goths or the sack of Rome. The blame must not fall on those who were professing to create a better world. It would be the sort of crime which even in the political field would turn against the perpetrator.

It had been said that area bombing was definitely designed to diminish the sacrifice of British lives and to shorten the war. Everybody wishes with all his heart that these two objects could be achieved, but to justify methods inhumane in this way smacked of the Nazi philosophy of 'might is right'.[45]

The reply Bishop Bell received from the Government spokesman, Lord Cranborne, was brief and unconcessive. He said, 'These great war industries can only be paralysed by bringing the whole life of the cities in which they are situated to a standstill.'[46]

After setting out the facts and arguments, Brittain stated what the Bombing Restriction Committee proposed, which was that the belligerents should recognise 'sanctuary areas' to which women, children and the elderly could be evacuated, in advance of bombing, from towns containing military objectives. The Committee listed examples of towns without military significance which could be centres for sanctuary zones – among them Bonn, Heidelberg, Baden and Homburg. A corps of observers could be instituted, drawn from neutral countries and placed under Red Cross supervision, to ensure that no military or industrial assets were hidden in the sanctuary zones.

Independently of the Bombing Restriction Committee but with its full support, a group of notables led by the popular science-fiction writer J. D. Beresford presented a letter to the War Cabinet, asking for a moratorium on 'obliteration bombing', and for a debate to take place in Parliament and the country 'in order that this policy, by which the British nation will be judged in years to come, may have the free and considered verdict of the British people pronounced upon it'.[47]

In the closing pages of *Seed of Chaos*, as if wearied by all that she had to report in it, Vera Brittain wrote, 'From the story of our bombing during the past eighteen months only a mental or moral lunatic could fail to draw the conclusion that modern war and modern civilisation are utterly incompatible, and that one or the other must go.'[48]

As this extraordinary document shows, in the winter of 1943–4 the facts and the arguments about area bombing were as plain to anyone who then seriously enquired as they are to us now, even with today's added perspective, which includes Dresden, the massive tonnage of bombs dropped in the war's final months, the discovery of just how truly wicked Nazism was, and the analyses made after the war of the degree of significance that bombing had for the war effort. In the case assembled by the Bombing Restriction Committee and those who voiced its concerns, whether in letters to the press or in speeches in Parliament, are to be found some of the elements of an indictment that an accuser could lay against the bombing campaigns. In the answers given by ministers, airmen and the pro-area-bombing press, and in the aims of those who conducted the bombing campaigns, lie some of the elements of the defence. I return to each in the chapters to come.

An early draft of *Seed of Chaos* was taken to America before Christmas 1943 by one of the Bombing Restriction Committee's supporters, to show campaigners in America the facts and arguments that the

Committee had gathered in Britain. Without Vera Brittain's knowledge or permission the draft was published under the title 'Massacre by Bombing' in *Fellowship*, the magazine of an American peace organisation called the 'Fellowship of Reconciliation'. What drew public attention to Brittain's essay was the twenty-eight signatures of writers and – mainly – clergymen,[49] who endorsed the article and added to it a declaration that 'Christian people should be moved to examine themselves concerning their participation in this carnival of death, even though they be thousands of miles away'.[50]

The response to her pamphlet was a surprise and a shock to Vera Brittain. It is graphically described by the historian James Martin:

> Attacks on Miss Brittain occurred from coast to coast by the hundreds in every imaginable medium of communication; the printed condemnations alone would have filled a number of volumes. *The New York Times* reported its mail running fifty to one against it, and notables entered the arena repeatedly. Because so many of the signers of the preface of 'Massacre by Bombing' were renowned Protestant clergy, it appeared as though there were a compulsion on the part of those clergy of similar faith supporting the obliteration bombing to come out immediately in rejection of Miss Brittain and her small company of supporters. Famed Episcopal Bishop William T. Manning denounced Miss Brittain in a letter to *The New York Herald Tribune*, and the Rev. Daniel A. Poling, editor of the quarter-of-a-million circulation *Christian Herald*, a major in the Army Chaplain Corps and president of the International Christian Endeavour Society, was especially bitter, charging the entire group involved in the protest against bombing with 'giving comfort to the enemy,' which turned out to be a common, expectable, and widespread charge.[51]

A choice item of invective was provided by a Catholic priest in Connecticut, the Reverend Paul Koslowksi, who in the process of denouncing Brittain wrote, 'There is no other way but to attack these beasts in the lairs – that is, in the German cities – where they plan further mass murders of innocent people. Christ's saying, "if one smite thee on one cheek, give him the other" is a beautiful theory, but not with human beasts, drunk with vengeance and conquest.'[52] One of the few who supported Brittain among the American clergy was the editor of the *Catholic World*, Father Gillis, who pointed out that the logic of her critics' arguments came down to saying that 'missionaries should eat cannibals because cannibals eat missionaries'.[53]

Even the thoughtful journals in America, such as the *New Republic* and *Nation*, were against Brittain's stance, though phrasing their opposition more moderately. The *New Republic* said that 'those who take up arms to end aggression by others against humanity must do what is necessary to win', and it added that in contemporary war there were no longer any non-combatants. (James Martin, in a pertinent aside, remarks that this opinion was formed in the safety of a New York office block.)[54] The *Nation* claimed that Brittain's book (by now circulating as a self-standing reprint) was 'hardly objective or reliably documented' – its editors' grounds for this judgement being that they wondered whether 'obliteration bombing' was actually taking place at all – but they concluded that if it was indeed taking place, then although it was 'a revolting necessity' it was nevertheless a necessity.[55]

The celebrated American journalist Dorothy Thompson had a column in London's *Sunday Chronicle*, and she used it to tell the British public that 'British Woman Pacifist Rouses U.S. Fury'. Far from rousing opposition to the bombing campaign, Thompson wrote, Brittain had 'actually released a more furious defence of air warfare than any single political action to date'.[56]

Vera Brittain responded to only one of the US attacks on her, and even then only in private. It was by William Shirer, the foremost American journalist of his day, famous for his *Berlin Diary*, based on observations of Hitler and the Nazis during his time as a correspondent in Germany before the war. In the *New York Herald Tribune* on

12 March 1944, under the headline 'Rebuttal to the Protest Against Bombing', Shirer accused Brittain of being a mouth-piece for Nazi propaganda. To her husband George she wrote that Shirer had virtually accused her and the Bombing Restriction Committee of being not just 'Nazi dupes' but 'Nazi agents', and suggesting that all the information in the book came from Nazi sources. '[He] omits to mention that most of these sources were British newspaper correspondents and British papers – to say nothing of repatriated prisoners of war!' she wrote.[57]

The outcry in America went all the way up to the White House. The Under-Secretary of State for War, Robert Patterson, accused the Bombing Restriction Committee of 'giving encouragement to the enemy'; Eleanor Roosevelt, the President's wife, called Brittain's arguments 'sentimental nonsense'; and the President himself 'delivered a stinging rebuke' to the twenty-eight signatories to the original *Fellowship* appearance of Brittain's essay. On the President's behalf a letter had been sent to *Fellowship*, stating that although the President was 'disturbed and horrified' by the 'destruction of life' involved, the only way to save more lives was to compel the enemy to change their ways.[58]

When *Seed of Chaos* appeared in Britain in the spring of 1944, a few weeks after its controversial publication in America, it caused hardly a stir. Vera Brittain surmised that this was because Americans had not actually experienced bombing, and were therefore more ready to be bloodthirsty. As C. E. Montague once wrote, 'Hell hath no fury like a non-combatant.'[59] The only substantial response aroused by the book came from what might seem an unexpected quarter: George Orwell, who attacked it in *Tribune* on 19 May 1944.

> Miss Vera Brittain's pamphlet, *Seed of Chaos*, is an eloquent attack
> on indiscriminate or 'obliteration' bombing [Orwell wrote] [She is]
> not, however, taking the pacifist standpoint. She is willing and
> anxious to win the war, apparently. She merely wishes us to stick to

'legitimate' methods of war and abandon civilian bombing, which she fears will blacken our reputation in the eyes of posterity . . .

Now, no one in his senses regards bombing, or any other operation of war, with anything but disgust. On the other hand, no decent person cares tuppence for the opinion of posterity. And there is something very distasteful in accepting war as an instrument and at the same time wanting to dodge responsibility for its more obviously barbarous features. Pacifism is a tenable position; provided that you are willing to take the consequences. But all talk of 'limiting' or 'humanising' war is sheer humbug, based on the fact that the average human being never bothers to examine catchwords.[60]

The catchwords Orwell picks out for scrutiny are 'killing civilians', 'massacre of women and children' and 'destruction of our cultural heritage', and he challenges the assumptions they contain: that air bombing does more of these things than ground warfare, and that it is worse to kill civilians than soldiers.

Obviously one must not kill children if it is in any way avoidable [he says], but it is only in propaganda pamphlets that every bomb drops on a school or an orphanage. A bomb kills a cross-section of the population; but not quite a representative selection, because the children and expectant mothers are usually the first to be evacuated, and some of the young men will be away in the army. Probably a disproportionately large number of bomb victims will be middle-aged. (Up to date, German bombs have killed between six and seven thousand children in this country. This is, I believe, less than the number killed in road accidents in the same period.)[61]

A key to Orwell's attitude was his belief that the immunity of civilian populations in past wars is what made them possible – rather as with the bloodthirsty American enthusiasm, enjoyed at a safe distance, for area bombing. In 1937 he had written, 'Sometimes it is a comfort to me to think that the aeroplane is altering the conditions of war. Perhaps when the next great war comes we may see that sight unprecedented in all history, a jingo with a bullet hole in him.' But now the burden of war was being more equally shared by everyone in the combatant nations. 'The immunity of the civilian, one of the things that have made war possible, has been shattered. Unlike Miss Brittain, I don't regret that. I can't feel that war is "humanised" by being confined to the slaughter of the young and becomes "barbarous" when the old get killed as well.'[62]

Brittain sent a letter to *Tribune* in response, remarking that Orwell 'seems to assume that if pacifists do not succeed in preventing war, they just throw up the sponge and acquiesce in any excesses which war-makers choose to initiate'.[63] She might have added that air bombing does indeed kill more civilians, massacre women and children, and destroy more cultural heritage than ground war does; and that the reason why it is worse to kill civilians than soldiers is that the latter are contracted and trained to kill us and ours, and are armed for the purpose, whereas civilians are not. The point becomes moot when the civilian stands at a lathe, producing the weapons that the soldier will use against us; but then no one in the debate, then or now, who accepted the necessity for the war, ever said that the war industries and the workers in them should be immune, as George Bell's House of Lords speech illustrates.

Orwell went to Germany as a war correspondent in the spring of 1945 for the *Observer*. He was appalled by what he saw, and in what looks like a change of mind wrote, 'To walk through the ruined cities of Germany is to feel an actual doubt about the continuity of civilisation.'[64] Vera Brittain, meanwhile, had been receiving through her letter-box hate mail from all over North America and Britain, among it an envelope filled with dog faeces. She was relatively unconcerned about the opposition and vituperation she had aroused; she pointed out that when arguing for an unpopular cause, the worst thing is to be ignored, for if one gets a strong reaction it shows that one has managed to get under the opponent's skin.[65]

In any case, in such circumstances what matters is the opinion of those whose opinion is worth having. In July 1944 she received a letter from Basil Liddell Hart, many years before an eloquent proponent of air bombardment, now emphatically against it. His letter expressed 'profound respect for your courage in upholding the claims of human decency in a time when war fever is raging', and he added that his particular reason for writing was that 'since you are likely to have abundant evidence of the resentment you create, you may like to have some evidence of the respect you inspire'.[66]

Events stifled the controversy. In the summer of 1944 the V1 flying-bombs or 'doodlebugs' began to appear over London, at first not in sufficient numbers or with sufficient explosive power to be a serious menace to others than those they fell upon, but apt to cause anxiety, because people knew that when their engines cut out they were about to crash down on to the city, and it was very disconcerting to hear a V1 droning towards one and then suddenly going quiet. In June the D-Day landings occurred, and together with the flood of news from the invasion front, the fact that Bomber Command and the Eighth Army Air Force were busy on tactical duties meant that the area-bombing campaign left the news. When area bombing resumed with even greater intensity in the autumn, the land battles were still dominating the newspapers and radio broadcasts; and moreover London was suffering a serious area-bombing threat of its own again, with the arrival of the V2 rockets, which flew at faster than the speed of sound and therefore were not heard until they exploded. The V-weapons attack on London was not an insignificant one; it killed nearly 9,000 people in the final fourteen months of the war, with up to a hundred rockets a day falling on London at the peak of the attack in June and July 1944. This was Hitler's 'wonder weapon' riposte to the invasion, and one of the triumphs of Allied bombing was the July 1944 attack on V-weapon launch sites that reduced the intensity of attacks on London.[67]

And then there came the devastating footage of the concentration camps liberated by Allied troops in April 1945 – Bergen-Belsen,

Liberator B-24s in action.

Air Marshall Sir Arthur Harris.

Air Marshall Sir Charles Portal.

Crew of a Lancaster bomber walk away from their plane after a flight
while ground crew check it over, April 1943.

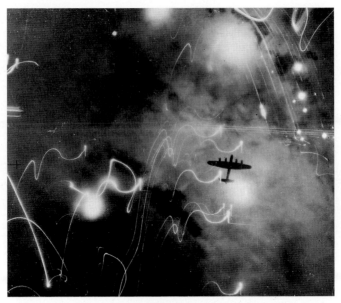

An Allied bomber above its target.

USAAF B-17 Flying Fortresses in 'box' formation, with fighter aircraft above.

Aachen in 1900.

Würzburg in 1938.

The rooftops of old Hamburg before the
Second World War.

Lübeck before 1900.

Berlin under attack in July 1944.

Hamburg burning during Operation Gomorrah, July 1943.

The Hamburg University bookshop after Operation Gomorrah.

Nuremberg, 1945.

Hannover, 1943.

Berlin, 1944.

Cologne, 1945.

Victims of the Dresden bombing, 14 February 1945.

Victims of the firebombing of Hamburg, Operation Gomorrah, July 1943.

Survivors of Operation Gomorrah, Hamburg, July 1943.

General Curtis Le May, Commander of USAAF XXI Bomb Group,
giving a press briefing, 3 August 1945.

A B-29 'bombing up', 24 November 1944.

A B-29 on a bombing run over Osaka, Japan.

Osaka under attack by 500 B-29 Superfortresses on 1 June 1945. Between them they dropped 3,000 tons of incendiary bombs.

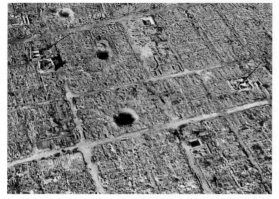

Osaka as it looked to aerial reconnaissance on 9 June 1945.

Tokyo's Ginza Street before being bombed in 1945.

Bombs falling on Kobe, 4 June 1945.

Kamamatsu destroyed by bombing, 9 June 1945.

The atom bomb exploding over Nagasaki.

Hiroshima after the explosion of the atom bomb, 1945.

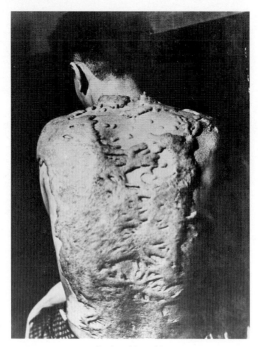

Survivor, Nagasaki.

Neuengamme, Ohrdruf, Buchenwald and Dachau – which produced such a feeling of revulsion against Germany that further discussion of moral duties owed to its civilians became impossible. British troops liberated Neuengamme and Bergen-Belsen, American troops the others. At Bergen-Belsen there were 60,000 prisoners, almost all in critical conditions of disease and starvation; 10,000 of them died in the weeks immediately following the liberation. Pictures of British Tommies using bulldozers to push piles of emaciated corpses into mass graves made discussion of morality in any other connection a nullity.

At the war's end the vast problems of a devastated Germany and Europe, and the need to arrest and put on trial as many of the Nazi leadership as could be found, consumed what attention was possible in the exhaustion and relief of the time. It is plausible to argue that the area bombing of Japan, and the dropping of the atom bombs, raised scarcely a flicker of negative public concern in either the United States or Europe for this very reason. Everyone wishes to move on as quickly as possible after such immense trauma; the immediate post-war years were not a time for self-examination and a clear-eyed adjustment of accounts. Even in the much larger and more significant matter of the Holocaust, time had to pass before survivors and witnesses were able to recover enough, after a time of forgetting and silence, to address the experience and its profound meanings. The right time for thinking about other aspects of the war's harms and wrongs, if such they were, was not yet, either for those who suffered under the terrific onslaught of area bombing in Germany and Japan, or for those in the victor nations whose air forces had executed it, week in and week out, for years.

The point of importance to be carried forward from this chapter is that the bombing campaigns were controversial even as they took place, and that anyone who was prepared to think about them and to look at what was said and known about them at the time could have been nearly as well informed about the facts, and as fully apprised of the arguments pro and con, as anyone today. This was certainly true of those charged with the conduct of the war in general and the bombing campaigns in particular; the relevant information crossed their desks daily, and the aims and intentions are on record, as quoted throughout here. From the point of view of the intentions and knowledge of those who planned and carried out area bombing on behalf of the Allied nations, there was therefore what the lawyers called *mens rea* in full and without qualification. At very least this means that no one can say, 'forgive them, for they knew not what they did.'

6

The Case Against the Bombing

To MAKE OUT the claim that the Allied practice of area bombing in the Second World War was wrong, two things are needful. One is to clarify the sense of 'wrong' at stake, and the other is to measure the facts of the bombing, and the knowledge and intentions of those who planned and directed the area-bombing campaigns, against the relevant principles of ethics and law. Previous chapters have sketched the area-bombing campaigns, their effects, and the background of knowledge and intentions on the part of those who devised and supervised them. Here I set out a case for saying that area bombing was wrong, and that its conductors committed wrong; and I do it by setting out the humanitarian and ethical considerations against which the facts of the preceding chapters are to be judged.

As this last point shows, by 'wrong' here I mean a moral wrong, a violation of humanitarian attitudes and civilised standards of treatment of human beings. In the seminars of philosophers it is easier to find objections, refutations and counter-examples to any proposed definition of morality – and of such associated concepts as 'the good' and 'right conduct' – than it is to secure general agreement about what any of these fundamentally important notions mean. This is not to claim that we do not know what 'right' and 'wrong' mean, it is instead an indictment of contemporary philosophy, which has allowed the term 'academic' in the phrase 'it's only academic' to mean 'empty and futile'. Once outside the seminar room and confronted with (say) a gang of thugs attacking an old lady, problems of definition evaporate. There are of course major disagreements within any society, and between societies, about fundamental matters of ethics, but there are also fundamental agreements; and it is easy to forget that the major ethical theories of the philosophical tradition, and the major world religions, have more in common on the question of what is good, than otherwise. Suffice it to say that if someone finds nothing wrong *per se* with dropping a bomb on a house in which unarmed and non-combatant women, children and elderly people are trying to shelter from harm – and leaving aside relevant complexities such as, for example, the possibility that all of the women, children and elderly huddled there are workers in an armaments factory – then that person is not going to get the point of efforts to devise humanitarian rules which protect civilians in wartime, and which thereby embody ethical principles of the kind that this chapter premises.

To anyone of humane and pacific instincts, the phrase 'a just war' looks like a contradiction. But a moment's thought shows otherwise. The idea that war, however ugly in itself, is sometimes unqualifiedly just is amply demonstrated by the example of Allied opposition to militaristic Fascism in the Second World War, a struggle which provides the focal case of a legitimate use of armed force to defend against aggression and to put an end to oppression and genocide. In this case the just war was the one waged by the Allies, not of course by the Axis, whose instigation and prosecution of war constituted aggression of an egregious kind, which few apart from the lunatic fringe of neo-Nazi apologists would regard as anything other than criminal and immoral.

But the fact that a war is just does not automatically make right every act committed during the fighting of it. Acts of injustice can be perpetrated in the course of a just war, and if the injustices committed are themselves very great, their commission can threaten the overall justice of the war in which they took place.

The theory of just war finds its first clear articulation in the writings of St Augustine and St Thomas Aquinas. In Part Two of his *Summa Theologica* Aquinas examined the proposition 'that it is always sinful to wage war', and argued to the contrary that, on three conditions, war can be justified. The conditions are, first, that there is a just cause of war, second, that it is begun on proper authority, and third, that it is waged with the right intention, meaning that it aims at 'the advancement of good, or the avoidance of evil'. The first two conditions constitute the *justum ad bellum*, the just cause for war, which Augustine centuries earlier had invoked to argue that having a just cause for going to war makes anything done in the course of it justified: 'When we do a thing for a good and lawful purpose, if thereby we unintentionally cause harm to anyone, it should by no means be imputed to us.'[1] But this leaves aside what later theorists regarded as a second kind of requirement for the *justum bellum*, namely, just conduct in the course of the war: *jus in bello*.

Aquinas's three conditions are clear and persuasive in themselves, offering what is from the point of view of ethics the unusual gift of an unambiguous set of principles. Difficulty enters when a case has to be made for whether the circumstances of a given prospective war are such that the principles apply to it, especially as regards the first and third, for the first always prompts the question: does such-and-such really count as a just cause for going to war? And the third always prompts the question, Are the aims for the intended war good ones?

There are clear examples of a just cause for going to war. Defence against aggression is one, as is going to the rescue of people being subjected to aggression. Is it equally just to engage in pre-emptive military action against a potential aggressor? The lesson of history teaches that appeasement and inaction are dangerous tactics; but how can one be sure that an unfulfilled threat is genuinely dangerous, and can one be sure that alleging a threat is not a mask for one's own aggression? On the other hand, a people has a right to defend itself, and the best form of defence is to prevent attack in the first place – by diplomacy if possible, but by force if necessary. A leadership fails its people if it does not do its best to prevent them from being harmed by aggressors, consistently with other values such as the liberty and privacy of its people.

What might count as just war aims? Aquinas said: promoting the good or avoiding evil. By this is meant that a war waged for such reasons as self-interest, *Lebensraum*, other people's oil fields, or pure aggrandisement, is not justified. 'Avoiding evil' can be invoked by those seeking to defend themselves preventatively, and – if they are right about the threat posed by a delinquent regime which is a danger to its neighbours – with justification. The positive aim, that of promoting good, which in the standard current view of the dominant Western world at least involves bringing about peace, stability, democracy, prosperity, and a situation in which both victor and defeated can cease to be enemies, is equally easy to identify. Too many wars, whether just in their inception or not, fail to achieve this outcome, because the harder struggle of 'winning the peace' is too often fudged or dodged.

Although the Aquinas conditions are clear and compelling, they can never, by themselves alone, count as sufficient conditions for going to war. Other considerations apply. Have all diplomatic means failed? Is there consensus over the 'just cause' and 'right intentions' requirements among all parties implicated on the side of the intending belligerent? Are there no means other than military action to bring about the desired aims? In practice, diplomacy and various forms of pressure, including sanctions, are the standard means for adjusting international disagreements (and those within a state that threaten civil war), and in most cases actual military conflict is a last resort, whether just or not. Certainly it seems hard to describe a war as just if it is not a last resort, that is, if further efforts could still be made to find other routes away from conflict.

To Aquinas's three conditions modern theorists have added two others: that to be just a war must have a reasonable chance of success, and that the means used to conduct it must be proportional to the ends sought. The first addition is a pragmatic one; it can be glossed as saying that a leadership commits an injustice against its own people if it leads them into a war they are sure to lose, in the process also causing harm and loss to those who, having been provoked into war, bring about their defeat. A problem with transforming this prudential consideration into a moral one is that it seems, by contrast, rather immoral, not to say spineless, to avoid engaging in an otherwise just war because it threatens to be too costly. When the Polish cavalry galloped towards Hitler's Panzers in defence of their homeland in the late summer of 1939, they were going futilely to war, but their courage gave them a moral victory, and was an inspiration to others.

The second addition – that the means used to conduct the war must be proportional to the ends sought – is one that matters centrally to my argument in this book. It is a controversial one; for as war leaders otherwise as different in outlook as Churchill and Mao Zedong both emphatically believed, it seems prudent to hold that, once involved in a war, there is no point in fighting with one hand tied behind one's back. As Mao succinctly put it, 'War is not crochet.' Whether this justifies using nuclear weapons, poison gas, or 'conventional' area bombing against civilian centres of population, is the very moot point at issue here. There is a view that if victory is the aim, and 'overwhelming force' is a sure means to attain it, then the use of overwhelming force is justified. But this in turn ignores a plethora of questions about the effects of its use, and especially about those on whom its effects fall.

So the question before us is not what makes a war a just war, nor whether the Allies' reasons for going to war in 1939 and 1941 respectively were such that their war was just or not; we can take that point as settled in the affirmative. In a different book questions might arise about a later matter – the Allied determination to settle for nothing less than unconditional surrender, thereby prolonging the war considerably, with consequent great destruction and loss of life. That topic might itself raise problems about the *justum ad bellum*. But in this book area bombing – a *jus in bello* point – is the focus, and the question being asked about it is whether the Allies, in carrying out area bombing, acted justly once engaged in their just war. Does British and American area bombing in the Second World War, in other words, constitute a failure of *jus in bello* in the midst of a *justum bellum*?

And what if it does constitute such a failure? Consider again the thought that it is not only the ends but the means which settle whether or not a war is just. Reflection suggests that questions of ends and means can and sometimes should be considered apart, as when for example one argues that ends do not justify certain means – as we are here considering in the case of area bombing. But even if we take it that means and ends must always be considered together, are we are bound to say that if the area-bombing campaign turns out on examination to be unjust, that detracts from the justice of the Allied cause?

I think not. It would be hard to conclude that opposing Nazism in particular and Axis aggression in general was anything but just in principle. And this is not a matter of hindsight only, to which the full extent of the Holocaust and other atrocities is clear: the nature of the Nazi regime was clear before the outbreak of war – and the outbreak of war itself made manifest its aggressions.[2]

One standard view offered in philosophical discussions about war is that if the practice of war is governed by rules, then whatever the rules are they must at least dictate what can be attacked and how it can be attacked (unless the rules are so permissive that they say 'anything' and 'anyhow' respectively, thus not really being rules at all). A straightforward principle might apply both to what counts as a legitimate target and what counts as a legitimate weapon or method of attack, namely, that whatever damage or loss of life is caused by military activities, it should be necessary to the attainment of the war's aims, and it should be proportionate to them. Thus, the definition of a just military action is any action *necessary and proportionate* to winning the war. By the same token, any unnecessary or disproportionate act is wrong.

An alternative view is that there are some things that should never be attacked or harmed even if doing so brings about or helps to bring about victory. The main such things are innocent persons and their property. The concept of 'innocence' is very important here: *nocens* is the Latin for 'engaged in harmful activity'; the prefix *in-* means 'not' or 'un'; thus *in-nocens* means 'not engaged in harmful activity'. This idea imposes an obligation on anyone engaged in fighting a war to distinguish between combatants and non-combatants, and they must not intend to cause harm to the latter either as a means to their ends, or as an end in itself, in their conduct of the war.

This formulation – 'they must not intend to harm the innocent' – accepts that innocents might be harmed in the course of military activity, as a by-product of it; the current euphemism for this is 'collateral damage'. No wrong is committed by the belligerent if the harm he does to innocents is an unavoidable ancillary to military operations – even if such harm can be foreseen. This is because the 'doctrine of double effect' applies here. This doctrine says that it is legitimate to do harm if the harm is the unintended side-effect of an effort to achieve a legitimate goal. Consider doctors who, by increasing morphine doses to control the pain of terminally ill patients, thereby shorten the lives of those patients. They foresee what effect the drug will have in this second respect, but their intention is not to kill but to palliate suffering. The 'double effect' is the palliation of suffering and the shortening of life; only the former is intended; and since it is a good and legitimate goal, the second effect, though foreseen, is accordingly not wrong.

The principle of double effect is controversial for various reasons, one being that it provides a ready mask for hypocrisy or dishonesty. It is easy to claim, hide or disavow intentions; we often recognise that whereas others may seem to have an identifiable intention, 'ulterior motives' can be in play. One control on the doctrine's applicability is the requirement that the foreseen but unintended effect should not only be a necessary concomitant of achieving the main and desired effect, but must just be sufficient – which is another way of saying, should be proportional. For example, if someone sought to cure another person's toothache by cutting off his head, the second effect, namely, the death of the toothache sufferer, is out of all proportion to achieving the intended effect, namely, ending the toothache.

A key question is this: suppose the threat posed by an adversary is mortal; is it not legitimate to use any means whatever of fighting him? Cannot one say that ordinary moral rules do not apply in extreme situations? If this is so, then we can say that in such situations even acts normally regarded as evil are permissible.

Some moral philosophers, chief among them Immanuel Kant, emphatically disagree with this view. They hold fast to the principle that it is never right to do evil in pursuit of a good, even if the good is one's own survival, or the defeat of a dangerous enemy. In its contrast to this absolute line, the thought that extreme situations license extreme remedies is part of an outlook which says that moral rules are instrumental – that is, are merely tools for realising such desiderata as the good ordering of relationships within a community. Accordingly they can be adjusted to circumstances, including being abandoned for the duration of an extremity such as war.

Both views have their obvious drawbacks. Strict rules easily prove ineffective by their rigidity; flexible rules might be made to bend before any glib tongue able to make a situation seem extreme enough for the purpose.

The foregoing remarks raise a few of the general moral considerations that need to be brought to bear. Ideas about 'laws of war' try to be more specific, bringing questions about just war down from the level of ethical abstraction to an attempt at stating concrete and definite principles.

The first systematic attempt to think about what is right and wrong in war is owed to the seventeenth-century Dutch philosopher Hugo Grotius, the effective founder of international law. His *De Jure Belli ac Pacis* (On the Law of War and Peace), published in 1625, is a major source for thinking about the difficult questions that war raises, not least because of his motivation in trying to bring some order, clarity, and moral principle to the problem. 'I saw in the whole Christian world a license of fighting at which even barbarous nations might blush,' he wrote. 'Wars were begun on trifling pretexts or none at all, and carried on without any reference to law, divine or human.' Moreover he took it that 'conscience [has] a judicial power to be the sovereign guide of human actions, by despising whose admonitions the mind is stupefied into brutal hardness'. Putting these two thoughts together explains his motivation for trying to systematise thinking about just war and just conduct of war. The first two books of his great work are devoted to the question of when a war is just; the third book addresses the question of what counts as just acts in the fighting of a war.

When Grotius wrote, the phrase 'laws of war' did not denote a body of agreed and binding rules dictating when wars are legitimate and what is permissible and impermissible in the course of them. Rather, it denoted an assemblage of assumptions and beliefs that had grown up by custom and usage, which generally permitted almost any treatment of prisoners, hostages, non-combatants, and property. As Grotius thought about the rights and wrongs of war he was presented with constant examples of the latter, for the terrible and bloody Thirty Years War was in progress, having begun in 1618. That war was about religion and power; the Holy Roman Emperor, a Habsburg prince, was trying to win back for Catholicism the small Protestant states, mainly of northern Europe, which had abandoned the Roman version of Christianity after the Reformation in the preceding century.

As too well illustrated by that war, which was by far the worst Europe had known to that date, the 'laws of war' were understood to mean something tough and uncompromising. They said such things as that if you put non-combatants to the sword during the course of sacking their town, you are not committing murder, for this is no less than their soldiers would do if matters were the other way round and they were sacking your town instead. In Grotius's lifetime there were some egregious examples of this view in practice; the most notorious was the sack of Magdeburg, which happened just five years after *De Jure Belli ac Pacis* was published. A famous account of it was given by Magdeburg's Bürgermeister, one of the few survivors of the atrocity:

> Thus it came about that the city and all its inhabitants fell into the hands of the enemy . . . Then was there naught but beating and burning, plundering, torture, and murder. Most especially was every one of the enemy bent on securing much booty . . . In this frenzied rage, the great and splendid city that had stood like a fair princess in the land was now, in its hour of direst need and unutterable distress and woe, given over to the flames, and thousands of innocent men, women, and children, in the midst of a horrible din of heartrending shrieks and cries, were tortured and put to death in so cruel and shameful a manner that no words would suffice to describe, nor no tears to bewail it.[3]

Eighty-five per cent of the citizens were slaughtered, and ashes from the fire that destroyed the town flew on the wind to neighbouring cities miles away.

Grotius accepted that 'an individual or belligerent power may, in the prosecution of a lawful object, do many things, which . . . in themselves it would not be lawful to do'; but that 'what is conformable to right taken in its strictest sense is not always lawful in a moral point of view. For there are many instances, in which the law of charity will not allow us to insist upon our right with the utmost rigour'. He quotes with approval Cicero's point that people are apt to call lawful what they can do with impunity – that is, what they can get away with – and and moreover that what one should consider is not what the utmost rigour of the law allows one to do, but what is 'becoming to one's character'.[4]

But the key question for Grotius is 'how far the power of lawfully destroying an enemy, and all that belongs to him, extends'. The answer is not a comforting one; the uses and customs of war throughout history suggest that combatants have always given themselves what license they choose, of whose extent, he writes,

> we may form some conception from the very circumstance, that even women and children are frequently subject to the calamities and disasters of war . . . The Psalmist's expression of the Babylonian children being dashed against the stones is a much stronger proof of the custom commonly prevailing among nations, in the use of victory, to which the language of Homer bears a close resemblance, where the poet says, that 'in the cruel rage of war, even the bodies of infant children were dashed against the ground'. Thucydides relates, that when Mycalessus was captured by the Thracians, they put all, even women and children to the sword. Arrian relates the same of the Macedonians, when they took the city of Thebes. And Germanicus Caesar, according to the account of Tacitus, laid waste whole cantons of the Marsians, a people of Germany, with fire and sword, to which the historian adds, 'without sparing either age or sex.' The Jewish women and children too were exposed by Titus, to be torn to pieces by wild beasts at a public spectacle. Yet neither of those generals were thought deficient in humanity, so much had custom reconciled the minds of men to this barbarous usage. So that the massacre of the aged, like that of Priam by Pyrrhus, is no way surprising.[5]

And to add to the discomfort, Grotius quotes Cicero as saying in the third book of his *Offices* 'that there is nothing repugnant to the law of nature in spoiling the effects of an enemy whom by the same law we are authorised to kill' – that is, to destroy or take possession of the enemy's property. Since that is so, it is not surprising that the laws of nations permit the same:

> Polybius, for this reason, in the fifth book of his history, maintains, that the laws of war authorise the destruction of an enemy's forts, harbours, and fleets, the seizure of his men, or carrying off the

produce of his country, and every thing of that description And we find from Livy that there are certain rights of war, by which an enemy must expect to suffer the calamities, which he is allowed to inflict, such as the burning of corn, the destruction of houses, and the plunder of men and cattle. Almost every page of history abounds in examples of entire cities being destroyed, walls levelled to the ground, and even whole countries wasted by fire and sword.[6]

To these despairing points Grotius opposes the answer of humanity, which Cicero likewise gave: 'some duties are to be observed even towards those, from whom you have received an injury. For even vengeance and punishment have their due bounds.' And Cicero praises those palmy periods of Rome's Republic when 'the events of war were mild, and marked with no unnecessary cruelty'. If this reads as milksop in the face of the acknowledged harshness that the right of might affords, Grotius has a slightly firmer answer. It is that

No one can justly be killed by design, except by way of legal punishment, or to defend our lives, and preserve our property, when it cannot be effected without his destruction . . . But to justify a punishment of that kind, the person put to death must have committed a crime, and such a crime too, as every equitable judge would deem worthy of death.

This is not a law of war but of morality as applied to law, a forbearance which is 'not only a tribute to justice, it is a tribute to humanity, to moderation, to greatness of soul. It was in this moderation, says Sallust, that the foundation of Roman greatness was laid'.[7]

The nobility of Grotius's endeavour to infuse considerations of humanity into the iron laws of war does him credit, but it is insufficient as a means of opposing the inhumanity which those iron laws represent. What people continued to mean by 'laws of war' was the custom and attitude that attended whatever sense of honour or humanity happened to subsist in individual commanders, officers and soldiers, and in regimental or national traditions about what counted as acceptable practice towards enemies, prisoners, non-combatants, and appropriate behaviour in occupied territories. There was often a lot of both honour and humanity in times of war; and as often – one suspects, more often – there was none of either. The description of what Voltaire's Candide saw as he decamped from the army of the 'Bulgarian King' is as true of the realities as if it were a despatch from the field, even in Enlightenment times:

At length, while the two kings were causing Te Deums to be sung in their camps, Candide took a resolution to go and reason somewhere else upon causes and effects. After passing over heaps of dead or dying men, the first place he came to was a neighbouring village, in the Abarian territories, which had been burned to the ground by the Bulgarians, agreeably to the laws of war. Here lay a number of old men covered with wounds, who beheld their wives dying with their throats cut, and hugging their children to their breasts, all stained with blood. There several young virgins, whose bodies had been ripped open, after they had satisfied the natural necessities of the Bulgarian heroes, breathed their last; while others, half-burned in the flames, begged to be dispatched out of the world. The ground about them was covered with the brains, arms, and legs of dead men.

Candide made all the haste he could to another village, which belonged to the Bulgarians, and there he found the heroic Abares had enacted the same tragedy.[8]

Actually the very first effort to say anything about restraint in war predates Grotius by a long way – in a classic Chinese text of the sixth century BC, Sun Tzu's *The Art of War*. In its second chapter, which cautions the would-be maker of war on its likely expense and the risks of a long campaign, Sun Tzu advises maintaining the morale of troops by allowing them booty, including the weapons and chariots of those they have defeated. But he adds, 'captured soldiers must be kindly treated and kept'.[9] In circumstances where war consisted almost exclusively in combat between armies, the first humanitarian restraint to come to mind naturally concerns defeated troops; and in most thinking about war from then until the nineteenth century the focus was on the idea that war is conducted by the armies of states, not by the whole peoples of states. It is doubtless for this reason that the first fully international agreement of a humanitarian kind relating to war is the 1864 Geneva Convention protecting sick and wounded soldiers. The person responsible for getting this convention accepted was Henri Dunant, founder of the Red Cross. His organisation has ever since played a major role as a neutral agency seeking to mitigate the harms of war, often in the very midst of it being waged.

Evidently the idea of controls by law or treaty on certain practices in circumstances of war had found its time. In 1865 an officer on the Confederate side of the American Civil War, Captain Henry Wirz, was tried and executed by the victorious Union government for the death of Union army soldiers at a prisoner-of-war camp at Andersonville in Georgia, of which he had been commandant.[10] He was the only person tried for war crimes in that bloody conflict. Summary accounts of the significance of his conviction usually point out that it set a precedent for war-crimes trials in the twentieth century, by establishing that a defence of 'I was only following orders' is not acceptable against a charge of acting in ways that violate the laws of war and humanity. From Wirz onwards it has been accepted that military personnel can be held personally liable for crimes committed as a result of following orders.

In the way of these things, Henry Wirz is a hero to some of a pro-Confederate persuasion, and books and articles in plenty have been written to refute allegations of cruelty at Andersonville stockade, at the same time defending Wirz as an upstanding officer.[11] The testimony in his trial is however conclusive, at least as regards the extremely bad conditions in the camp; of the 45,000 prisoners held at Andersonville in the fourteen months between February 1864 and

May 1865, nearly a third died of starvation and disease. Allegations of murder and such cruel practices as setting dogs on prisoners are controversial, and the testimony more ambiguous. Wirz claimed that everything he had done had been ordered by his superior, General John H. Winder. Winder died in February 1865 and so escaped trial, but Wirz's defence was rejected, thus establishing the key precedent in question.

The Wirz case was just one expression of the unprecedented degree of thinking in this period about laws of war. When the American Civil War broke out, the government of the North asked the jurist Franz Lieber to write a code-book for its army on the rules of war. One reason was that most of the pre-war professional officer corps were engaged on the Confederate side of the conflict, while the Union army was led by relatively inexperienced officers 'who would need all the instruction they could get about how to fight *comme il faut* . . . in a contest with Southern gentlemen'.[12] This was followed by the Brussels Project for an International Declaration on the Laws and Customs of War (1874) and the manual produced by the Institute of International Law at its Oxford meeting in 1880, *The Laws of War on Land*. Both sets of suggestions expressly included protections for non-combatants and – most importantly for our purposes – the outlawing of bombardment of towns other than fortified military places.

These efforts contributed significantly to the thinking of those engaged in the International Peace Conference at The Hague in 1899 (see chapter 4 above) as involving the first-ever effort to restrict aerial bombing. Both the Brussels Project and the Oxford manual provided much of the actual wording for the resulting convention relevant to present purposes, known as 'Hague IV'. The Hague Conference was a response to the obvious fact that war in the industrial age was a vastly more threatening prospect than at any previous point in history. Cynical comment then and now has it that one of the sponsors of the conference, Tsar Nicholas II, knew that Russia was so far behind the other major powers in military strength that he saw an arms-limitation agreement as a strategy of self-protection while Russia caught up.

Whatever the motive for the conference, the sentiments on which it was publicly premised were unimpeachable; its intention, as the then Russian Foreign Minister, Count Mikhail Nikolaevich Muraviev, expressed it, was 'a possible reduction of the excessive armaments which weigh upon all nations', and a revision of the existing principles, such as they were, governing war on land and sea.

After ten weeks of discussion the twenty-five participating governments adopted a number of conventions and agreed to a number of declarations. Among the former were the Convention for the Peaceful Adjustment of International Differences; the Convention Regarding the Laws and Customs of War on Land; and the Convention for the Adaptation to Maritime Warfare of the Principles of the Geneva Convention of the 22nd August, 1864.

The document that counts most for present purposes is the Convention Regarding the Laws and Customs of War on Land (Hague IV). It contains the following explicit provisions:

> Seeing that while seeking means to preserve peace and prevent armed conflicts between nations, it is likewise necessary to bear in mind the case where the appeal to arms has been brought about by events which their care was unable to avert;
>
> Animated by the desire to serve, even in this extreme case, the interests of humanity and the ever progressive needs of civilisation;
>
> Thinking it important, with this object, to revise the general laws and customs of war, either with a view to defining them with greater precision or to confining them within such limits as would mitigate their severity as far as possible [and] until a more complete code of the laws of war has been issued, the High Contracting Parties deem it expedient to declare that, in cases not included in the Regulations adopted by them, the inhabitants and the belligerents remain under the protection and the rule of the principles of the law of nations, as they result from the usages established among civilised peoples, from the laws of humanity, and the dictates of the public conscience . . .

The High Contracting Parties ... have agreed upon the following ...

SECTION II: HOSTILITIES

CHAPTER I: Means of injuring the enemy, sieges, and bombardments.

Article 22. The right of belligerents to adopt means of injuring the enemy is not unlimited.

Article 23. In addition to the prohibitions provided by special Conventions, it is especially forbidden:

(a) To employ poison or poisoned weapons;

(b) To kill or wound treacherously individuals belonging to the hostile nation or army ...

(d) To declare that no quarter will be given ...

(e) To employ arms, projectiles, or material calculated to cause unnecessary suffering ...

(g) To destroy or seize the enemy's property, unless such destruction or seizure be imperatively demanded by the necessities of war ...

Article 25. The attack or bombardment, by whatever means, of towns, villages, dwellings, or buildings which are undefended is prohibited.

Article 26. The officer in command of an attacking force must, before commencing a bombardment, except in cases of assault, do all in his power to warn the authorities.

Article 27. In sieges and bombardments all necessary steps must be taken to spare, as far as possible, buildings dedicated to religion, art, science, or charitable purposes, historic monuments, hospitals, and places where the sick and wounded are collected, provided they are not being used at the time for military purposes.

It is the duty of the besieged to indicate the presence of such buildings or places by distinctive and visible signs, which shall be notified to the enemy beforehand.

Article 28. The pillage of a town or place, even when taken by assault, is prohibited.[13]

If this document had been regarded as binding on the United Kingdom during the Second World War, any competent lawyer could easily defend the area-bombing campaign against imputations of having violated its provisions. Germany's cities were not undefended; their populations had been amply warned, both explicitly by leaflets and broadcasts, and by example; the destruction of enemy property was – so defenders of area bombing say – necessary to defeating him; and so on for all the provisions, even perhaps the one in Article 27, on the grounds that the enemy had not marked its culturally and morally important buildings clearly enough, and that anyway no bomb-aimer flying high above marker flares in the night would be deliberately seeking a church or hospital to bomb.

But of course such a defence is beside the main point; for the convention conveys a moral attitude towards the conduct of war which, however legalistically one might claim that its provisions were not violated in the letter, seems quite clearly and emphatically violated in spirit by area bombing.

The 1899 conventions and declarations sought to ban not only aerial bombardment but the use of asphyxiating gases and (iterating the provision of the 1864 conference) expanding bullets and other inhuman projectiles. These efforts reflected the ages-old anxiety felt about new weapons which conferred a disproportionate and, in the light of their efficacy, savage advantage on their first possessors. For example, in 1139 Pope Innocent II sought to ban the cross-bow as a weapon 'too murderous for Christian warfare'. This by implication contains the idea of proportionality, and of restriction to means minimally necessary for victory, that Aquinas made central to the idea of just war.

In 1907 most of the First International Peace Conference agreements were reasserted, and in 1925 they were followed by the Geneva Gas Protocol, which reconsidered the gas question in the light of First World War experience, and prohibited the use of poison gas and the practice of bacteriological warfare. This was one agreement that the combatant nations observed in the Second World War with respect to each other, though the Germans did not observe it with respect to Jews and others they sought to exterminate. Britain contemplated using gas in defending its coast in the event of a German invasion in 1940.[14]

As noted in chapter 4, at the General Conference for the Limitation and Reduction of Armaments held in Geneva between 1932 and 1934 efforts were made to restrict bombing from aircraft, and failed. In the opinion of some, this was because the British had found its twin-engined Vickers Virginia biplane bombers too useful in colonial policing. The relevant points discussed earlier concerned the question whether a bomber is an offensive or defensive aircraft; on this unresolvable question the conference failed. In the climate of the times a disarmament conference was never likely to get far anyway. Such good as had been done by earlier conferences attempting to introduce humanitarian restraint into war was, if anything, undone by the collapse of those discussions at Geneva in the 1930s, remembering that it was from this conference that both Germany and Japan withdrew, the latter for good measure resigning from the treaty reached in 1922 to limit naval armaments. A 1934 observer of the situation regarding humanitarian restraint in war would have had reason to think that scarcely any progress had been made since a sagacious Roman 2,000 years beforehand commented that *inter arma silent leges*: in time of war the laws are silent.

As this sketch shows, from Grotius's day until the outbreak of war in 1939 there was little success for those trying to establish binding international agreement on the laws of war, except in certain restricted respects such as the treatment of prisoners. In particular, these efforts were unavailing as regards the protection of civilians. In acknowledging that 'International law was not at that time copiously explicit about the protection of civilians', Geoffrey Best has argued that this was 'partly because . . . it was well understood that the conduct of some legitimate war operations precluded the separation of civilians from their country's posture of belligerence, and partly for the reason that the "standard of civilisation" so far accepted by the lawmaking States had made it seem unnecessary to elaborate legal instruments around so self-evident a principle'.[15] As this suggests, from the mid-nineteenth century onwards war had been changing in a way that implicitly called into question the assumption that 'civilians' – meaning, people not in the armed forces – were by definition 'non-combatants' or 'innocents' (recall the root in *innocens*), for in the industrial age the contribution made to the war effort by people in factories and railway depots, on farms and down mineshafts, in newspaper offices and even hospitals, was becoming more and more difficult to separate from that of the actual soldiery. In Britain part of the propaganda effort was directed at extolling the great contribution made by coal miners and 'Land Army' girls to winning the war. As this therefore implied, everyone was in fact or potentially on the front line of a war that had no traditional front lines. A term had come into menacing use to describe war in the mid-twentieth century, one part of whose definition embraced civilians in its scope. This term was 'total war'.[16]

But what these points do not acknowledge is that the efforts made at defining 'laws of war' assumed the principle that civilian populations should be treated as non-combatant, even if some of their members were engaged in producing weapons or food for troops, because others of their members, perhaps – and probably – the majority of them, would be innocent in the exact meaning of this term: namely, children, the elderly, the lame and ill, and at least many of the women. It was to these that the idea of 'standards of civilised treatment' were supposed to apply.

In the light of this, one can say that humane thinking wished to see civilians unharmed as far as possible in war, and (*pace* the implication of Best's remarks, which suggest that no great effort was being made to introduce protections for civilians) in fact a considerable effort was devoted to this aim before 1939. Anyone alert to civilised and informed opinion knew as much at the time, as is for example shown by the Geneva conference of 1932–4, and by the debate about the dangers anticipated from aerial bombing. Therefore to engage in activities which went deliberately against the principle at stake is a central point for the indictment sheet.

But even sharper points for the indictment sheet come from the laws of war and humanitarian declarations that followed the war, starting in the three years immediately after the war's end (1945–8). For these were framed expressly to address the atrocities that the war had seen, chief among them genocide. But they sought to address a number of other things besides: protection of the rights of the individual, outlawing of military aggression, outlawing of destruction of cultural heritage – and in the Geneva Convention of 1949 and its protocols, protection for civilians in time of war.

This thinking bears directly on the experience of the war and what, in its immediate aftermath, was thought about its moral character. So the protection of civilians against bombing included in these immediate post-war declarations and conventions constitutes a retrospective indictment of the practices they outlaw.

In late June 1945 delegates from the victorious powers – the United States, Britain, Russia and France – met in London to discuss the prosecution of Nazi leaders for what, from the outset, was described as 'war crimes', even before the Charter of the International Military Tribunal (IMT) was agreed. The chief problem facing the delegates was the unprecedented nature of their task. The Nazis had unquestionably done terrible things, from causing a worldwide war to committing genocide of European Jewry. The question was, under what laws were these atrocities to be prosecuted? In the absence of a clear pre-existing code of laws relevant to the circumstances, the IMT was open to the criticism that it was creating *ex post facto* law, laws devised after the commission of the crimes they themselves defined, thus breaching principles of natural justice.

In fact it was possible to argue that Germany's aggression brought it into breach of a number of conventions and treaties to which it was a signatory – the Hague rules of 1907, the Treaty of Versailles, the

Kellogg–Briand Pact of 1928 outlawing war, and the Locarno Pact. Its invasions of Poland, Norway, the Low Countries and France, Greece, Yugoslavia and Russia, multiply violated the terms and spirit of these agreements.[17]

Moreover, all civilised nations had laws against murder, torture and enslavement, and the drafters of the IMT's charter recognised that they would simply be applying them to the activities of the Nazi regime within the boundaries of its home and conquered territories. The IMT was not creating laws *ex post facto* – so it was therefore claimed – but bringing established law to bear in the special circumstances it faced. The IMT was in effect an instrument of enforcement, not of legislation.[18]

In the discussion that preceded the drafting of the IMT's charter it was agreed that the Wirz defence of 'following orders' would not be acceptable even in a regime where the *Führerprinzip* reigned, this being the principle that the leader has absolute authority and that subordinates must unhesitatingly and unquestioningly obey. It happened in any case that in the paybook of every German soldier was a clause stating that he was not required to obey an illegal order. And it transpired too that in cases where the Wehrmacht carried out executions or mass killings, for example on and behind the lines of the Eastern Front, individual soldiers could and did exempt themselves from involvement. These two facts undermined appeal to the *Führerprinzip* as an excuse.[19]

A further difficulty foreseen by the delegates to the London meeting was that the work of the IMT would appear to be 'victor's justice', given that atrocities had been committed by all sides in the conflict. Doubtless these were not specified in the meetings; the matter seems to have been discussed under the heading of an attempted defence of 'tu quoque' ('you also') by those indicted. But the truth was that in addition to the terrible crimes committed by Soviet troops as they fought their way westwards to and past Berlin – hundreds of thousands of acts of rape, to say nothing of other acts of brutality, murder and rapine – there was the unspoken fact of five years of increasingly heavy civilian-targeted bombing by the western Allies' air forces – most of it in Europe by the RAF, with the USAAF following suit in Japan. In the event it was decided that although there were arguments that could be adduced to counter a 'tu quoque' defence, the simplest and surest means was to make it impermissible in the terms of the charter.[20]

By the end of the first week in August 1945 the Charter of the International Military Tribunal was drafted, agreed and signed, and it specified four crimes for which Nazi leaders would be tried: conspiracy to carry out aggressive war, the launching of aggression, killing and destroying beyond the justification of military necessity, and 'crimes against humanity'.

The concept of crimes against humanity addressed the attempted extermination of the Jews, together with other crimes against civilians, and it was a novel concept, no older than the war just ended. In the Nuremberg Indictment 'crimes against humanity' was defined with precision to denote 'murder, extermination, enslavement, deportation, and other inhumane acts committed against any civilian population, before or during the war, or persecutions on political, racial or religious grounds in execution of or in connection with any crime within the jurisdiction of the Tribunal'.[21] These last fifteen words tie crimes against humanity to the war crimes being prosecuted by the IMT, and they have ambiguous scope: do they apply only to 'persecutions on political [etc.] grounds', or do they apply to all the crimes against humanity listed? The standard reading given by students of international law seems to be the latter; which restricts the concept's application. These same students of international law say that the concept now has little independent meaning given that its content is covered by the laws on war crimes, genocide and human rights that have since come into existence.[22] For present purposes, the inclusion of a specific indictment of 'inhumane acts committed against any civilian population' embodies an ethical spirit which is relevant to considering the moral status of area bombing.

The provisions of the Charter of the IMT that especially matter for present purposes are as follows:

ARTICLE 6 The following acts, or any of them, are crimes coming within the jurisdiction of the Tribunal for which there shall be individual responsibility:

(a) Crimes against Peace . . .

(b) War Crimes: namely, violations of the laws or customs of war. Such violations shall include, but not be limited to, murder, ill-treatment or deportation to slave labour or for any other purpose of civilian population of or in occupied territory, murder or ill-treatment of prisoners of war or persons on the seas, killing of hostages, plunder of public or private property, wanton destruction of cities, towns, or villages, or devastation not justified by military necessity;

(c) Crimes against Humanity: namely, murder, extermination, enslavement, deportation, and other inhumane acts committed against any civilian population, before or during the war, or persecutions on political, racial, or religious grounds in execution of or in connection with any crime within the jurisdiction of the Tribunal, whether or not in violation of domestic law of the country where perpetrated.

Leaders, organisers, instigators, and accomplices participating in the formulation or execution of a Common Plan or Conspiracy to commit any of the foregoing crimes are responsible for all acts performed by any persons in execution of such plan.

ARTICLE 7 The official position of defendants, whether as Heads of State or responsible officials in Government departments, shall not be considered as freeing them from responsibility or mitigating punishment.

ARTICLE 8 The fact that the defendant acted pursuant to order of his Government or of a superior shall not free him from responsibility, but may be considered in mitigation of punishment if the Tribunal determine that justice so requires.

The passages especially relevant here are *wanton destruction of cities, towns, or villages, or devastation not justified by military necessity,* and *inhumane acts committed against any civilian population.* The last two quoted articles unequivocally assign responsibility for the crimes identified by the charter to those who required and authorised them as well as those who, thus authorised, planned and executed them.

If the Allies were put on trial by the lights of their own Nuremberg Charter, how would they fare? Taken out of the specific context of Nazi-perpetrated aggression and its associated crimes, and considered purely as embodying ethical requirements to measure Allied area bombing against, the following immediately suggests itself. The second – *inhumane acts committed against any civilian population* applies to Allied area bombing without qualification. The first – *wanton destruction of cities, towns, or villages, or devastation not justified by military necessity* – invites defence on the grounds that area bombing was not 'wanton' but 'justified by military necessity', as we shall see in the next chapter. But among the answers this invites, the following is immediately pertinent: one does not have to appeal only to the smaller German towns and cities destroyed in the war's final months to contest this defence – the little Dresden of Würzburg among them. Massive bombing of civilian targets by any standard is disproportionate, which is what this indictment in effect charges. Take the atomic bombings of Hiroshima and Nagasaki: if these were claimed to be attacks on targets of military value, assuming there to have been industrial units or military barracks in these cities which 'military necessity' demanded should be destroyed, dropping an atom bomb on them is equivalent to chopping off a man's head to cure his toothache, such is the degree of disproportion involved. The same applies to the firebombing of Tokyo, Operation Gomorrah, the bombing of Berlin, Dresden, and indeed all aspects of the bomber war to which the description 'area bombing' applies. It is not a defence to say that there was no other way of destroying the militarily necessary target contained within the urban area, and that therefore the civilians killed and the collateral destruction caused is protected by the doctrine of double effect. Even if we did not have on record the public avowals – as we do – of the conductors of area bombing to the effect that they were specifically aiming at civilian morale, the degree of indifference to human life and suffering that would be involved in bombing a whole city in order to hit a barracks or factory within it, would remain culpable. But as it is, those avowals are indeed on record.

The moral culpability of area bombing was so well recognised during and immediately after the war that when at last an effort was made to arrive at a firm and binding statement of the laws of war, it was explicitly outlawed by them. This happened in the Fourth Geneva Convention of 1949 and the protocols subjoined to it afterwards. Its aim is to detail what counts as acceptable treatment of civilians during time of war, including hostages, diplomats, spies, bystanders, and populations under military occupation. The convention outlaws torture, collective punishment, and the introduction and settlement by occupying powers of their own civilians in the territories occupied. From the time of its adoption in 1949 until the time of writing these words, the Fourth Geneva Convention has never been invoked, though there have been a number of cases to which it clearly applies, such as Tibet, Bosnia, Rwanda, Kosovo and the Palestinian territories.

As with many of the earlier efforts at introducing humanitarian constraints into war, the mover of this Geneva Convention was the International Red Cross. And as with the contemporary endeavour to have the newly created United Nations commit itself to a declaration of universal human rights, the great powers of the United States, Britain, Russia and France were at first reluctant to sign up to it. In the case of human rights it was small countries, colonies and non-governmental organisations that insisted on the United Nations making an explicit commitment to the protection of human rights, against the reluctance of the great powers who saw it as posing obstacles to their international and imperial activities.

The same happened with the proposed new Geneva Convention. When the Red Cross invited the great powers to participate in a review of the laws of war and a discussion of how to protect civilians in future wars if any, the British government responded with impatience, saying that it was too busy to bother with such a thing for at least the next five years. The Soviet Union to begin with did not wish to participate at all.[23] What followed was a complicated and protracted story which, despite the convolutions of international diplomacy and internal Red Cross politics, eventually issued in 1949 in the Fourth Geneva Convention, and in 1977 in two Additional Protocols. Parts of the Convention and the first Additional Protocol are central to present purposes:

Geneva Convention relative to the Protection of Civilian Persons in Time of War. Adopted on 12 August 1949 by the Diplomatic Conference for the Establishment of International Conventions for the Protection of Victims of War, held in Geneva from 21 April to 12 August, 1949.

PART I GENERAL PROVISIONS

Article 3 Persons taking no active part in the hostilities, including members of armed forces who have laid down their arms and those placed hors de combat by sickness, wounds, detention, or any other cause, shall in all circumstances be treated humanely, without any adverse distinction founded on race, colour, religion or faith, sex, birth or wealth, or any other similar criteria.

To this end, the following acts are and shall remain prohibited at any time and in any place whatsoever with respect to the above-mentioned persons:

(a) Violence to life and person, in particular murder of all kinds, mutilation, cruel treatment and torture . . .

PART II GENERAL PROTECTION OF POPULATIONS AGAINST CERTAIN CONSEQUENCES OF WAR . . .

Article 14 In time of peace, the High Contracting Parties and, after the outbreak of hostilities, the Parties thereto, may establish in their own territory and, if the need arises, in occupied areas, hospital and safety zones and localities so organised as to protect from the effects of war, wounded, sick and aged persons, children under fifteen, expectant mothers and mothers of children under seven . . .

Article 15 Any Party to the conflict may, either directly or through a neutral State or some humanitarian organisation, propose to the adverse Party to establish, in the regions where fighting is taking place, neutralised zones intended to shelter from the effects of war the following persons, without distinction:

(a) Wounded and sick combatants or non-combatants;

(b) Civilian persons who take no part in hostilities, and who, while they reside in the zones, perform no work of a military character . . .

Article 16 The wounded and sick, as well as the infirm, and expectant mothers, shall be the object of particular protection and respect . . .

Article 18 Civilian hospitals organised to give care to the wounded and sick, the infirm and maternity cases, may in no circumstances be the object of attack, but shall at all times be respected and protected by the Parties to the conflict . . .

PART III STATUS AND TREATMENT OF PROTECTED PERSONS

SECTION I

Article 33 Reprisals against protected persons and their property are prohibited . . .

SECTION 111

Article 53 Any destruction by the Occupying Power of real or personal property belonging individually or collectively to private persons, or to the State, or to other public authorities, or to social or co-operative organisations, is prohibited, except where such destruction is rendered absolutely necessary by military operations . . .

The circumspect language of these provisions, which identify aerial bombing of civilian targets by what they do *not* say in providing protection for children, women, the wounded and the infirm, and for safe places for such individuals to be housed away from attack, is explainable by immediate post-war sensitivities and politics. The two countries that had most experience to offer in drafting provisions to protect civilians from aerial attack, namely Germany and Japan, were not at the conference table because they were the defeated parties to the war; while the two countries who had most to gain from not mentioning aerial bombing of civilians as something so wrong as to require being outlawed, namely the victor nations of Britain and the United States, were very much present. So it took until 1977, a further quarter of a century, for the required explicit wording to appear, in the form of the first Additional Protocol to the 1949 Convention. This document at long last clearly and unequivocally states that area bombing is unacceptable, and outlaws it. It is a retrospective condemnation of area bombing, a passing of judgement by history on the area-bombing campaigns of the Second World War. It merits full quotation therefore. It reads as follows:

Protocol Additional to the Geneva Conventions of 12 August 1949, and relating to the Protection of Victims of International Armed Conflicts (Protocol 1). Adopted on 8 June 1977 by the Diplomatic Conference on the Reaffirmation and Development of International Humanitarian Law applicable in Armed Conflicts.

PART III METHODS AND MEANS OF WARFARE

SECTION I. Article 35. Basic rules

1. In any armed conflict, the right of the Parties to the conflict to choose methods or means of warfare is not unlimited.

2. It is prohibited to employ weapons, projectiles and material and methods of warfare of a nature to cause superfluous injury or unnecessary suffering.

3. It is prohibited to employ methods or means of warfare which are intended, or may be expected, to cause widespread, long-term and severe damage to the natural environment.

Article 36. New weapons

In the study, development, acquisition or adoption of a new weapon, means or method of warfare, a High Contracting Party is under an obligation to determine whether its employment would, in some or all circumstances, be prohibited by this Protocol or by any other rule of international law applicable to the High Contracting Party.

Article 40. Quarter

It is prohibited to order that there shall be no survivors, to threaten an adversary therewith or to conduct hostilities on this basis.

PART IV CIVILIAN POPULATION

SECTION I.-GENERAL PROTECTION AGAINST EFFECTS OF HOSTILITIES

CHAPTER 1. Article 48. Basic rule

In order to ensure respect for and protection of the civilian population and civilian objects, the Parties to the conflict shall at all times distinguish between the civilian population and combatants and between civilian objects and military objectives and accordingly shall direct their operations only against military objectives.

CHAPTER 11.-CIVILIANS AND CIVILIAN POPULATION

Article 50. Definition of civilians and civilian population

1. A civilian is any person who does not belong to one of the categories of persons referred to in Article 4 A (1), (2), (3) and (6) of the Third Convention and in Article 43 of this Protocol. In case of doubt whether a person is a civilian, that person shall be considered to be a civilian.

2. The civilian population comprises all persons who are civilians.

3. The presence within the civilian population of individuals who do not come within the definition of civilians does not deprive the population of its civilian character.

Article 51.-Protection of the civilian population

1. The civilian population and individual civilians shall enjoy general protection against dangers arising from military operations. To give effect to this protection, the following rules, which are

additional to other applicable rules of international law, shall be observed in all circumstances.

2. The civilian population as such, as well as individual civilians, shall not be the object of attack. Acts or threats of violence the primary purpose of which is to spread terror among the civilian population are prohibited . . .

4. Indiscriminate attacks are prohibited. Indiscriminate attacks are:

(a) Those which are not directed at a specific military objective;

(b) Those which employ a method or means of combat which cannot be directed at a specific military objective; or

(c) Those which employ a method or means of combat the effects of which cannot be limited as required by this Protocol; and consequently, in each such case, are of a nature to strike military objectives and civilians or civilian objects without distinction.

5. Among others, the following types of attacks are to be considered as indiscriminate:

(a) An attack by bombardment by any methods or means which treats as a single military objective a number of clearly separated and distinct military objectives located in a city, town, village or other area containing a similar concentration of civilians or civilian objects; and

(b) An attack which may be expected to cause incidental loss of civilian life, injury to civilians, damage to civilian objects, or a combination thereof, which would be excessive in relation to the concrete and direct military advantage anticipated.

6. Attacks against the civilian population or civilians by way of reprisals are prohibited.

CHAPTER III.-CIVILIAN OBJECTS

Article 52.-General protection of civilian objects

1. Civilian objects shall not be the object of attack or of reprisals. Civilian objects are all objects which are not military objectives as defined in paragraph 2.

2. Attacks shall be limited strictly to military objectives. In so far as objects are concerned, military objectives are limited to those

objects which by their nature, location, purpose or use make an effective contribution to military action and whose total or partial destruction, capture or neutralisation, in the circumstances ruling at the time, offers a definite military advantage.

3. In case of doubt whether an object which is normally dedicated to civilian purposes, such as a place of worship, a house or other dwelling or a school, is being used to make an effective contribution to military action, it shall be presumed not to be so used.

Article 53.-Protection of cultural objects and of places of worship [I]t is prohibited:

(a) To commit any acts of hostility directed against the historic monuments, works of art or places of worship which constitute the cultural or spiritual heritage of peoples . . .

(c) To make such objects the object of reprisals.

Article 54.-Protection of objects indispensable to the survival of the civilian population

2. It is prohibited to attack, destroy, remove or render useless objects indispensable to the survival of the civilian population, such as foodstuffs, agricultural areas for the production of foodstuffs, crops, livestock, drinking water installations and supplies and irrigation works, for the specific purpose of denying them for their sustenance value to the civilian population or to the adverse Party, whatever the motive, whether in order to starve out civilians, to cause them to move away, or for any other motive . . .

4. These objects shall not be made the object of reprisals.

CHAPTER IV.-PRECAUTIONARY MEASURES

Article 57.-Precautions in attack

1. In the conduct of military operations, constant care shall be taken to spare the civilian population, civilians and civilian objects.

2. With respect to attacks, the following precautions shall be taken:

(a) Those who plan or decide upon an attack shall:

(i) Do everything feasible to verify that the objectives to be attacked are neither civilians nor civilian objects and are not subject to special protection but are military objectives within the meaning of paragraph 2 of Article 52 and that it is not prohibited by the provisions of this Protocol to attack them;

(ii) Take all feasible precautions in the choice of means and methods of attack with a view to avoiding, and in any event to minimising, incidental loss of civilian life, injury to civilians and damage to civilian objects;

(iii) Refrain from deciding to launch any attack which may be expected to cause incidental loss of civilian life, injury to civilians, damage to civilian objects, or a combination thereof, which would be excessive in relation to the concrete and direct military advantage anticipated;

(b) An attack shall be cancelled or suspended if it becomes apparent that the objective is not a military one or is subject to special protection or that the attack may be expected to cause incidental loss of civilian life, injury to civilians, damage to civilian objects, or a combination thereof, which would be excessive in relation to the concrete and direct military advantage anticipated . . .

3. When a choice is possible between several military objectives for obtaining a similar military advantage, the objective to be selected shall be that attack which may be expected to cause the least danger to civilian lives and to civilian objects.

4. In the conduct of military operations at sea or in the air, each Party to the conflict shall, in conformity with its rights and duties under the rules of international law applicable in armed conflict, take all reasonable precautions to avoid losses of civilian lives and damage to civilian objects.

5. No provision of this Article may be construed as authorising any attacks against the civilian population, civilians or civilian objects.

This protocol now has the force of law. Britain is a party to it, as it is to the main convention itself. The United States is party to the main convention, but not to its additional protocols, having refused to sign them. But this does not exempt the United States from the requirements of the convention and its additional protocols, because they are considered part of customary international law, and therefore as binding on all countries whether signatories or not.

In practice, if a country fails in its obligations under the convention, the High Contracting parties to it can be called on to 'take action to ensure respect for international humanitarian law', a phrase vague enough to encompass everything from diplomatic notes of protest to armed intervention. Enforcement of international humanitarian law has been the Achilles heel of efforts to introduce a global regime of such law since the end of the Second World War; but one aspect of it has been the institution of special tribunals to try those who have violated human rights, as with those for Nuremberg and the former Yugoslavia, and the International Criminal Court.

The basic demands of the fourth Geneva Convention and its protocols come down to requiring that states must give unequivocal instructions to their armed forces not to mount direct attacks against civilians or civilian targets; not to mount indiscriminate attacks, that is, they must first seek to distinguish between military targets and civilians or civilian objects; not to mount attacks which, though aimed at legitimate military objectives, have a disproportionate impact on civilians in the vicinity; not to use weapons that are inherently indiscriminate in their effects; and otherwise to take all necessary measures to protect civilian populations from the effect of military operations.

As each and every one of these provisions shows, if this Geneva Convention had been in force during the Second World War, the British and American conductors of area bombing would have been straightforwardly liable for prosecution under its terms. It was not of course then in force, so this is not the point of quoting it here; and no suggestion is being offered that it should be made to apply *ex post facto* – apart from anything else, none of the individuals responsible are alive to be indicted. Rather, the point of quoting it, as with the other instruments and efforts made to protect civilians in war, is to reveal the ethical thrust that underlies it, and to measure area bombing against it. The claim that area bombing manifestly fails when measured against it is strengthened by noting, also once again, that the principles enunciated in the first protocol were clearly present to the minds of British leaders before the outbreak of the Second World War, and to some of them indeed those principles already seemed to have the force of customary international law. 'In the first place,' said Prime Minister Neville Chamberlain in the House of Commons on 21 June 1938,

> it is against international law of bomb civilians as such and to make deliberate attacks upon civilian populations. That is undoubtedly a violation of international law. In the second place, targets which are aimed at from the air must be legitimate military objectives and must be capable of identification. In the third place, reasonable care must be taken in attacking these military objectives so that by carelessness a civilian population in the neighbourhood is not bombed.[24]

That the British government then took this seriously is attested by the restrictions on bombing applied throughout the opening phase of the war, as shown in the account of the bombing war given in chapter 2. And as that chapter shows, this was a policy which, in part through sheer ineffectiveness, was explicitly abandoned in February 1942, with the consequences we all know. When Sir Arthur Harris came to write his memoirs immediately after the war, he felt able to say,

> Whenever the fact that our aircraft occasionally [*sic*] killed women and children is cast in my teeth I always produce this example of the blockade, although there are endless others to be got from the wars of the past. I never forget, as so many do, that in all normal warfare of the past, and of the not distant past, it was the common practice to besiege cities and, if they refused to surrender when called upon with due formality to do so, every living thing in them was in the end put to the sword . . . And as to bombardment, what city in what war has ever failed to receive the maximum bombard-

ment from all enemy artillery within range so long as it has continued resistance? International law can always be argued pro and con, but in this matter of the use of aircraft in war there is, it so happens, no international law at all.[25]

In the opinion of Geoffrey Best, Harris's claim that there was 'no international law at all' applicable to aerial bombing goes too far; 'but he would not have gone too far if he had restricted himself to saying that there was not much of it, and that what there was lay mostly in the realm of principles' – after which Best immediately adds the point that will be central, as we shall see in the next chapter, to the defence of area bombing: 'as to whose practical application in circumstances of desperate total war against an exceptionally nasty enemy there was bound to be much controversy'.[26]

For present purposes it is enough that there is a recognised ethical principle at stake. If there was in addition a principle of customary international law present to the minds of competent persons before and during the Second World War, then there is indeed a debate to be had about the use that should have been made of it during the lifetimes of Presidents Roosevelt and Truman, Winston Churchill, their war cabinets, and the senior officers commanding their bombing forces – General Hap Arnold, General Curtis LeMay, Lord Portal and Sir Arthur Harris not least among them.

Much of the discussion here has been about 'laws of war', conventions, treaties, declarations, all straining towards the status of binding laws that could be invoked to indict, try, and if they are found guilty punish, those who violate them. The question whether there was anything in force having the status of law in this sense, at the time that Allied area bombing was carried out, was, as we see, moot; but that is not the point here. The effort made from the time of Grotius onwards to outlaw unnecessary and disproportionate conduct in war, and to avoid harm to non-combatants and their cultural treasures, their schools and their hospitals, embodies an ethical spirit whose character and intention is crystal clear. In the light of it, the question being asked here is whether Allied area bombing was contrary to that ethical spirit; and the indictment is, that it was.

The point about strict legality matters in one respect. If all those efforts from Grotius onwards had translated into actual law, then as we see there would be a proper question about whether Allied area bombing broke that law. From a juridical point of view this matters because in the absence of such law, no crime as such was committed: as an ancient principle of Roman law states, *nullum crimen et nulla poene sine lege*, there is no crime and no punishment without a law. So if there was no law in existence which Allied area bombing broke, then it is not strictly correct to describe area bombing as a 'war crime', and those who planned and conducted it as 'war criminals'.

One way of viewing the Nuremberg procedure is to say that it involved taking certain acts not previously proscribed by laws, and saying of them that their egregious nature required that they be regarded as crimes, and those charged with perpetrating them tried and, if found guilty, punished accordingly. On this view, because of the particular nature of the offence done to humanitarian instincts and ideals of natural right and justice, the offence itself was seen as creating the law it breaks; it taught observers that there is an implicit law in the case, and that in these special circumstances it accords with natural justice that that implicit law should be made explicit, and applied.

If this was indeed the idea at work at Nuremberg, then – as mentioned already – it risks contravening the fundamental principle whose shadow hung over the International Military Tribunal at Nuremberg: the principle that laws should not be created retrospectively. Hereby hangs an opportunity for much debate. But here the crucial point is different: it concerns the fundamental *ethical* thrust that lay behind Nuremberg as behind all the efforts to infuse humanitarian considerations into the conduct of war. This ethical point includes saying, among other things, that deliberately bombing cities and towns to kill and terrorise civilians, not all of whom were engaged in manufacturing arms or aiding their country's military, and many of whom were children and elderly folk – and at the same time, destroying much that belongs to the culture and necessities of those people, including schools and hospitals – contravenes every moral and humanitarian principle debated in connection with the just conduct of war.

This, then, is the indictment of British and United States area-bombing activities in Europe and Japan in the Second World War: that it was a moral crime. The next task is to see if this accusation survives the defence now to be offered to it.

7

The Defence of Area Bombing

IN HIS MEMOIR of the bombing war Sir Arthur Harris wrote,

> In spite of all that happened at Hamburg, bombing proved a comparatively humane method. For one thing, it saved the flower of the youth of this country and of our allies from being mown down by the military in the field, as it was in Flanders . . . But the point is often made that bombing is specially wicked because it causes casualties among civilians. This is true, but then all wars have caused casualties among civilians. For instance, [in] the last war . . . our blockade of Germany . . . caused nearly 800,000 deaths – naturally these were mainly of women and children and old people because at all costs the enemy had had to keep his fighting men adequately fed.[1]

There is a double defence of Bomber Command's war in this paragraph, though both parts are aimed at supporting the conclusion that bombing is 'relatively humane' as a weapon of war. Harris's claim that bombing saved Allied military lives is the same justification given by the United States for its area bombing of Japanese cities, and constitutes the main defence of its atom-bomb attacks. Harris's second claim, that civilians have always been targeted in war, has the merit of being true; the figure he cites for civilian deaths by blockade-induced starvation in Germany during the First World War is likewise correct.

These are just two of the arguments deployed by defenders of the Allied area-bombing campaigns. They offer at least five others. They say that area bombing undermined enemy civilian morale; that it reduced the capacity and efficiency of enemy war industries; that it created logistical difficulties for the German economy and administration by obliging them to deal constantly with repairs and refugees; that it kept soldiers, guns and fighter planes away from the battle-fronts to protect the cities instead; and that it distracted enemy soldiers at the front by making them worry about what was happening to their families at home.

Officially it was easy to claim that area bombing's main aim was the enemy's war industry, and that civilian casualties were an unavoidable side-effect. When challenged on the disproportion of this side-effect, defenders of the strategy were apt to say that the enemy started it first, that the enemy's crimes deserved punishment, that it was 'them or us', and that war is not a place for sentiment but requires resolution and tough choices in the effort to survive and win. This, after all, was a war against a formidable and dangerous enemy, and – for the British – well into 1942 the outcome was not merely uncertain, but threatening, for although the United States had entered the war in December 1941 – which meant that in the longer term victory was more likely than not – in 1942 the forces of the United States were not yet mustered in sufficient strength in the European theatre to help protect against, for example, another attempt by Germany to invade the British Isles. At that point practically the only means available to Britain for fighting back against Germany was bombing. Thus a strongly urged argument was that the resort to area bombing was the result of the necessities of war, implying that it was crucial that enemy morale and industry should be attacked, and that civilian casualties were an unavoidable outcome of doing so.

Among these arguments the four that are especially relied upon by post-war defenders of the area-bombing campaigns are: the effect on enemy war industry, the logistical difficulties created for the economy and administration, the holding-back of military resources from the battle-fronts, and the fact that area bombing was a major means, and for a time the only means, of 'carrying the war to Germany'.

Before turning to these, let us consider Harris's two arguments first, since evidently they were the ones that sustained him, as Bomber Command's chief, during the arduous years of sending bombers over Germany on every night that the weather allowed.

The answer to the first point he offers – that bombing civilians saved soldiers' lives – was given by Vera Brittain in her *Seed of Chaos*. It is that saving military lives by substituting civilian deaths for them is no different morally from a soldier on the battlefield using a civilian as a shield. Soldiers are contracted, trained and armed for battle, and although they are placed in danger, their commanders usually try to keep as many of them unharmed as possible, by appropriate tactics. Civilians are in a very different situation from soldiers. Many, whether or not in a minority, will not be willing parties to the war that affects them. Civilians also have efforts made on their behalf to protect them, but the conditions of modern war – especially in respect of bombs and missiles from the air – place them in great hazard despite all that defence measures can do.

The defender of bombing can reply to this, in turn, that an army is equipped, fed, and otherwise supported by the civilian population at home, and there is in principle no difference between the civilian factory worker who makes a gun and the soldier who fires it. Therefore the civilian armaments worker is a legitimate target. And if he is a legitimate target in his factory, why is he not a legitimate target in his home?

This answer is in part right. War industries are certainly a legitimate target for military action. But it is obviously better to destroy the factory than to kill the people who work in it; and if their deaths are covered by the principle of double effect – as the 'collateral damage' done in the process of the factory being destroyed – killing their families and neighbours is not. Killing their families and neighbours instead violates the principle established by Aquinas and Grotius that a just action in war is a proportionate one. To stop guns being made by killing an armaments worker *and* his family and neighbours is disproportionate.

Sometimes the argument about the relation of civilians to war is extended to the limit, by saying that in modern war there are no non-combatants: 'everyone is in the front line'. This assertion is alas true, but not because infants and the elderly are somehow indistinguishable from armed and trained infantrymen or bomber crews in their aeroplanes. Rather it is because civilians are placed on the front line by having military attacks launched at them. If any civilians are involved in working to support the military efforts of their country, it is because they are specifically the workers and technicians in the industries crucial to the military effort; they and they alone are legitimate targets for attack therefore; and they are certain to be a minority of the civilian population as a whole.

The question of proportion is a major one for the area-bombing war. Bomber Command sought to demoralise the German population by killing as many of its members as possible, and by 'dehousing', terrorising, and causing hardship to the survivors. That was a direct assault on non-combatants, unacceptable on moral grounds even allowing that living among them they had that minority directly engaged in war-supporting activities. But in claiming that this was not only damaging the will but the ability to continue the war – that is, that it was reducing the capacity of Germany's war industries – the means was obviously disproportionate to this latter end. This is not a point about the fact – though fact it is – that area bombing did not reduce German war production; it is a point about the fact that there were other ways of aiming to hurt war production that greatly lessened impact on civilians, for example precision bombing, as with the American endeavour in the European theatre, which in the end – in its attack on oil – proved highly effective. The American oil attack was proportionate and pertinent; it could also legitimately claim to be a necessary part of the effort to defeat Germany. The area bombing of civilian populations was not necessary.

Harris's attempt to defend the area-bombing strategy by saying that civilians always die in war – his second argument – is no defence, nor is the game of numbers he adds to it. He says in effect that his killing civilians was licensed by the fact that civilians have always been killed in war; and anyway he killed fewer than were killed by the First World War blockade. To see what is wrong with this argument, imagine someone who has done something wrong and who asks to be let off on the grounds that wrongs have always been done, and that some of them were greater wrongs. For a robust example: imagine a murderer defending himself by saying that there have always been murders, and that anyway he only murdered two people when someone else had murdered five. Would this argument exonerate him? It would not. But this is exactly the form of Harris's 'blockade' argument; and these analogies dispose of it. A shorter way of putting the point is to recall that a greater wrong does not excuse a lesser; and that two such do not make a right.

Harris also claimed, in connection with his blockade example, that the means by which civilians died in previous wars was sometimes crueller than death by bombing. But it is debatable whether starvation is a crueller form of death than being blown up, burned, crushed under a fallen building, or asphyxiated in a cellar.[2]

One point that Harris mentions by implication rather than directly, and which post-war defenders of area bombing no longer mention much if at all, is the once-vaunted bombing aim of 'undermining civilian morale'. This was thought to be a key part of the aim of shortening the war, and that is what Harris meant in talking of saving young soldiers' lives. As we saw, it turned out that heavy bombing did not undermine civilian morale – where it did not buoy it, it numbed it – nor therefore did it cause a collapse in the will to fight or work, nor did it precipitate a revolution. But a thought canvassed earlier was that this perhaps was because the weight of bombing was still insufficient, even by the measure of the closing months of the war in Europe. By contrast, the claim is often made that the atom-bomb attacks on Hiroshima and Nagasaki were the last straw for Japanese morale, and that it was these particular instances of area bombing that won the war in the East.

If civilian morale were a decisive factor, was it necessary to kill so many residents of Hiroshima and Nagasaki? Could not the same result have been attained by means of dropping a demonstration bomb, either within sight of a major Japanese population centre, or showing this on film to the Japanese? It might well have been enough to give a demonstration of the atom bomb to the Japanese forces.

In his account of the American bombing war over Japan, Ronald Schaffer notes that at first this was precisely the intention. Truman at one point instructed his Secretary of War, Henry Stimson, to arrange matters so that 'military objectives and soldiers and sailors are the target and not women and children . . . The target will be a purely military one and we will issue a warning statement asking the Japs to surrender and save lives'.[3] There was quite a wide consensus among scientists working on the bomb, and among some of the military high command, that this was the appropriate way to proceed.

And indeed half of this way of proceeding was to some extent implemented. At the Potsdam Conference on 26 July 1945 a warning was issued to Japan that if they continued with the war they would meet with the 'utter destruction of their homeland'.[4] Nothing was said about a new kind of weapon being used, and by this time the decision to opt for a demonstration explosion rather than an attack on a city had been changed – in favour of the latter. The Japanese had for some time already been making tentative approaches to end the war, not directly but through the Russians (who were then not yet at war with Japan); but some commentators allege that Russian designs on Japanese-controlled territory in the East meant that they delayed passing on to the western Allies details of Japan's approaches, and misrepresented them when they did.

In the event, when the order reached General Carl 'Tooey' Spaatz, now in command of the USAAF strategic bombing in the Pacific, to drop an atom bomb on Hiroshima, he requested the order in writing, not wanting an imputation of responsibility on his own head. He did not believe that dropping an atom bomb was necessary; like his colleagues in RAF Bomber Command, although as a late and surprising convert, he believed that massive conventional bombing was enough. Still, he carried out his orders. He then suggested that the second bomb be dropped on an unpopulated area 'so that it would not be so devastating to the city and the people'.[5] His orders were otherwise, and the Nagasaki bomb was duly dropped.

It is very hard now to see what possible *justification* can be given for the atom-bomb attacks, though *explanations* abound: among them the desire to make a demonstration to the Russians of the new access to American power, and the frank desire to wreak retribution on Japan, perceived as an evil and brutal aggressor which had given America a humiliating surprise at Pearl Harbor, threatened to dominate America's Pacific back-yard, and needed to be taught a severe lesson. The atom bombings were intended to be that lesson – though many would judge the Tokyo firebombing, the devastation of other Japanese cities, and the imminence of total defeat, as more than enough punishment already.

Harris's conception of a bombing war, as we have seen, was to have forces so overwhelming that every night they could reproduce an Operation Gomorrah, or more than an Operation Gomorrah, destroying one major city after another until the population of Germany could take it no longer. He fervently believed that bombing was a war-winning weapon, and he did everything possible – to the point of near-insubordination – to prove the point right.

And some, to repeat, might argue that he was indeed right. They might point at Hiroshima and Nagasaki to show that he was right, and that the reason why people thought he was mistaken was that even at the war's end he still did not have enough pulverising power available. If he had possessed atom bombs, and had dropped them on Berlin, Hamburg, Munich, Cologne, the Ruhr cities, one per night, night after night, the war would have ended very quickly. In the big attacks he mounted, the 1,000-bomber raids and the repeated attacks on Berlin, he was seeking to bring about the crushing effect that was only achieved when atomic bombs were available.

The biggest problem with the idea of winning a war by city bombing, however, is that it involves the mass killing of civilians to do so. And if winning by the means just described – a series of atom-bomb attacks until either the enemy surrenders or there is no enemy left – is the logical extension of the belief that bombing can win war, then it offers an appalling prospect of what such bombing would have to be like to make this belief true. As argued in chapter 4, this technique at least would be self-defeating: the saying 'to make a wasteland and call it peace', with 'victory' substituted for or added to 'peace', applies here.

Let us now examine the other main arguments offered by area bombing's defenders, returning to the European theatre in search of justifications because that is where the area-bombing campaign was carried out if not more comprehensively, then for longer.

One of the arguments is that area bombing prevented Germany's 88-mm. anti-aircraft guns and Messerschmitt fighters from being used on the battle-fronts. This is a significant matter, for the 88-mm. guns could have been used as highly effective anti-tank guns against the Russians on the Eastern Front, and 70 per cent of the Luftwaffe's fighter force was detained in the home arena to defend against the bombers. Because it was recognised by the Eighth Army Air Force that the key to the success of their precision-bombing efforts was control of the skies – a mirror-image of the situation in 1940 and the Battle of Britain – a major effort was made to achieve exactly that. In the closing months of 1943 the long-range Mustangs, Lightnings and Thunderbolts quadrupled in number; the Luftwaffe losses grew alarmingly, and began to outstrip production. The Eighth Army Air Force attacked the Luftwaffe on the ground too – its factories and airfields, its fuel, the aircraft factories' component suppliers – and the result was that by the time D-Day arrived, the Luftwaffe had 300 operational aircraft to pit against 12,000 Allied aircraft.[6] On the Eastern Front 500 Luftwaffe fighters faced 13,000 Soviet aircraft. This is one good reason why an observer in the summer of 1944 could see that the war was won.

It is therefore true to say that the bomber campaign kept the 88-mm. guns and the Messerschmitts in Germany instead of the battle-fronts. But note that what kept the Luftwaffe at home was the presence of bombers in the German sky, whether they were bombing precision targets as the Eighth Army Air Force attempted to do, or whether they were bombing urban areas as the RAF did. It was not necessary that the bombers were seeking to attack cities; it was sufficient that they were there at all. If a principal aim of the bombing campaigns was to anchor defensive resources to Germany, then however inaccurate the attempts to bomb factories, power stations, railway lines and marshalling yards, airfields, canals, bridges, harbours, dams and coal mines, the mere effort would have been enough to achieve this aim.

Moreover, the troops who manned searchlights and anti-aircraft batteries in Germany were not front-line troops. Many of them were youths and older men. The airmen in the fighter-defence force were certainly front-line material; and doubtless their absence from the Eastern Front made a difference. But they were not absent from the Western Front during the crucial invasion period, because Bomber Command and the Eighth Army Air Force were busy at the Western Front too. So the argument that the bombing campaign kept military resources confined in Germany is, though true up to a point, not quite the truth defenders of bombing wish it to be, and anyway – as just noted – would have happened whether or not the bombing attempted to be precise.

Mention of the anti-aircraft guns and Luftwaffe fighters reminds one that Bomber Command turned to area bombing because it found precision bombing too dangerous by day and too difficult by night. Is this fact a moral defence against the charge that deliberately targeting civilians is wrong? It is not. Consider an analogy: politicians have sometimes failed to persuade their publics by argument, and have therefore resorted to coercing them instead, by imprisoning and even shooting them, as in Stalin's Russia and Pinochet's Chile. This in effect is what Bomber Command did, and with the same degree of moral justification. Arguably, its action in this respect was worse, because its early precision-bombing efforts were expressly premised on the attempt to avoid or at least limit civilian casualties; so the switch to area bombing was a complete reversal of policy and an abandonment of avowed principle. The discovery of its inability to achieve its ends without performing a moral volte-face as to means comes nowhere near a defence of those means.

The argument that area bombing put logistical pressure on German resources because of the need for burying the dead, caring for the injured, housing those whose homes had been demolished, dealing with refugees, clearing rubble, restoring electricity, water and sewerage services, and getting food and clothing to those who had been bombed out, is not a strong one. As shown in connection with the efficient management of affairs after the 1,000-bomber raid on Cologne, Germany was well able to deal with the problems caused by bombing until the last months of the war, when the overall degree of social disorganisation swiftly reached critical levels. This was in large part a result of the remorseless bombing of the last months, but also because of the approach of hostile armies and the final breakdown of supplies.

Germany had an abundance of slave and prisoner labour available for the disagreeable task of clearing corpses and shovelling rubble, and an army of foreign workers for repair and restoration work. The capacity of its economy (as discussion of the next point shows) was such that it could absorb and deal with bomb damage without major distraction from either the military or the industrial tasks it faced; in the latter sense it had surplus capacity.

This leads directly to the argument that area bombing affected German industry in general and its war industry in particular. The argument was discussed and dismissed in chapter 3. As there shown, the rate of output of German industry increased until the last months of the war, and it was precision bombing not area bombing that then had an impact – on oil certainly, and on the movement of coal from the mines to the industrial plants that needed them. When Albert Speer was in prison in Nuremberg, awaiting trial, he was invited to give a lecture to an Allied group interested in German industrial activity during the war. What he told them about the way industry in the Third Reich continued to increase output despite years of bombing should not have surprised them; with the possible exception of the Soviet Union, all the major combatants had spare industrial capacity – and in the United States, spare manpower – throughout the war, which if necessary could have been adapted to meet military demand. 'Throughout the war,' writes Richard Overy, 'the German economy produced fewer weapons than its raw resources of materials, manpower, scientific skill and factory floor space could have made possible.'[7]

This point is cited by Roger Chickering and Stig Forster in questioning the concept of 'total war' as applied to the Second World War, a pertinent challenge given that area bombing is sometimes exempted from moral critique on the grounds that it was one element in a 'total war' with all the implications of this for seeing every individual member of a society as pitched in battle against every member of the enemy society. The phrase 'total war' implies just that: that everyone was in fact or potentially on the front line of a war that had no traditional front lines.[8]

The shocking figures bear out the fact that the Second World War was certainly a war of peoples even more than of armies: an estimated 15 million soldiers, sailors and airmen were killed in all theatres of the war between 1939 and 1945, whereas in excess of 45 million civilians were killed. 'The preponderance of civilians was no accidental or peripheral feature of this war; it reflected the central significance of civilians in the conflict, the indispensable roles that they played in the war's outcome, as well as the vulnerabilities that they shared, as a direct consequence, with the soldiers.'[9]

But there is of course an elision of ideas here. Even if 'total war' means that everyone in a society is affected or involved in some way by the fact of their country's being at war – and this was certainly so in the belligerent nations of Europe, far less so in the United States, and only so in the last six months of the war in Japan itself – it does not make every individual himself or herself a combatant. But the fact is that the Second World War was not a 'total war' in this or indeed any sense, as Chickering and Forster argue. Most of the land surface of the world was unaffected, many nations were bystanders merely, and the engaged nations (other possibly than Russia) had not put their every last tooth-pick and shoe-horn to the struggle.[10]

Industry was a legitimate target, yes. The move from this to seeing the workers as legitimate targets too, given the difficulty of hitting their factories, meant a slide to accepting that their families and neighbours were legitimate targets. This was the point at which moral trespass occurred, because it is where disproportion enters. It is sometimes said that we make virtues of our necessities; in this case we allowed what we mistakenly supposed was a necessity to make our vices.

A defender of area bombing might be prepared to concede that bombing the whole city where an industry was located, rather than trying to hit the industry itself, is questionable; but he might then say: what if the city was full of troops on the move towards a front line, contained many refugees who if caught up in bombing attacks might create serious difficulties for military movement and for logistics, and also had several crucial war-industry plants, and was an equally crucial transport hub? Would not such a target be a legitimate and indeed important one, if it was located close to an important stretch of the front?

Just this argument has been offered in defence of the bombing of Dresden on 14 February 1944, in the outstanding book by Frederick Taylor which examines the attack in detail, and offers the fullest picture of the circumstances yet given.[11] Taylor points out that the degree of devastation suffered by Dresden was partly the result of unfortunate weather conditions – the prevailing wind helped create the firestorm that did much of the damage and caused many of the deaths, so this aspect of the raid's consequences was not intended by the attackers, who, at the request of the advancing Russian forces, had seen Dresden as an important choke-point for supplies and troops moving east, and refugees streaming west. Moreover, says Taylor, the air-raid precautions were inadequate, and the city's residents were inexperienced at being bombed; and the absence of fighter defences, and the presence of good luck for the attackers, for whom everything went smoothly, made this 'the raid which went horribly right'.[12]

Taylor agrees with the conclusion reached by the distinguished historian Richard Overy in his *Why the Allies Won*, that Allied bombing was a decisive factor in the victory over Germany and Japan (Overy says that 'bombing mattered most' in the victory over Germany). It is interesting therefore to note that Overy's analysis of how this was so focuses on the two points that, first, the bombing campaign kept guns and fighter aircraft away from the fronts to defend the homeland, and second, that by January 1945 bombing had at last so depleted Germany's industrial capacity that Speer was moved to write to Hitler saying that 'realistically, the war is over in this area of heavy industry and armaments'.[13]

This however is not a vindication of area bombing. For once again one has to point out that precision-bombing efforts against industry, transport, power and military targets would have kept those guns and fighter planes in Germany; and once again one has to point out that it was precision-bombing endeavours against oil and transport, not area bombing, that forced German war production to diminish and at last falter in the closing months of the war.

In this sense bombing was decisive; but not area bombing. And it is area bombing which is the moral issue at stake here.

Among the questions that might be asked about the bombing of Dresden are these. Given that the chief point of bombing Dresden was its importance as a transport hub close to a region where crucial military events were unfolding, why was the bombing effort not directed at the railways and roads in the environs of the city, or leading to and from the city along the crucial west–east axis? The aiming-point issued to Bomber Command crews was not the railway yards, but a stadium close to the city centre.

The city was known to be full of tens of thousands of refugees fleeing the approach of the Soviet troops. Was this a reason to bomb the city? Why was it not, on humanitarian grounds, a reason not to bomb the city?

Indeed, instead of asking what the reasons were for bombing the city (rather than others near by also involved in the movement of troops and refugees), one might ask for the reasons not to bomb it, and the answer might have been the same that America's Secretary of State Henry Stimson gave when he struck Kyoto off the list of possible targets for atom-bomb attack.

It is recognised that one of the main motives for the atom-bomb attacks on Hiroshima and Nagasaki was to demonstrate to the Russians the superiority in weaponry that the United States had attained. In the case of Dresden something similar is regrettably true. Max Hastings, a trenchant critic of the area-bombing campaigns carried out by the Allies, quotes a briefing note sent out to Bomber Command squadrons detailed for the attack on Dresden. Its final paragraph reads: 'The intention of the attack is to hit the enemy where he will feel it most, behind an already partially collapsed front, to prevent the use of the city in the way of further advance, and incidentally to show the Russians when they arrive what Bomber Command can do.'[14] Considered in hindsight, the degree of moral set-aside obvious here in the idea of 'hitting the enemy where he will feel it most' – that is, a civilian population in an iconic city – and the calculation involved in using civilian lives and the precipitates of history to make a gesture in a game of diplomatic politics, is breathtaking.

*   *   *

Another argument offered in defence of area bombing is that for the first half of the war at least it was the only means Britain had of 'carrying the war to Germany', and since precision bombing was impracticable, area bombing had to be the means employed.

The phrase 'carrying the war to the enemy' is not a very clear one, though at the least it means 'reminding the enemy that there is a war on', and perhaps also reminding the enemy 'that we are still here and in pugnacious mood', which is certainly the message Britain wished to convey in the perilous period between the summer of 1940 and the turn of the tide in late 1942. Because this aim was not being realised by precision attacks, in February 1942 the fateful decision was taken to switch to area attacks. Was area bombing the only way to 'carry the war to the enemy' in this sense? Obviously not. Almost any belligerent act, such as attacking the enemy's navy and harbours, and harassing its military dispositions in the occupied territories of France and the Low Countries, as well as attempting precision attacks on important industrial and transport targets, would have constituted 'carrying the war to the enemy'. Area bombing was not exclusively the right way to do it, though it perhaps carried the satisfaction that it was causing pain, grief and damage to part of the enemy's corporate being, however little real impact it was having on the course of the war.

The war situation was a factor in the bombing campaign in a number of ways. From the summer of 1940, when the British army was rescued without its equipment from the beaches of Dunkirk, until the tide of war began to turn strongly and permanently against Germany in late 1942, Britain was in a perilous state. It had seen off the invasion threat of 1940, and Germany's attack on Russia in 1941 meant that there was unlikely to be a repeat of that threat at least for a year or two. But the 'Battle of the Atlantic' was a serious worry; throughout the period between Dunkirk and the crisis of this battle on the high seas in early 1943, the threat to Britain's lifeline across the ocean to America was very real. In reminiscing about the war once it was safely over, Churchill said 'the only thing that ever really frightened me was the U-boat peril'. A combination of factors won the Battle of the Atlantic for the Allies, after a terrible struggle in which millions of tons of shipping were sent by U-boats to the sea-bed. The principal ones were British decipherment of the Enigma code, the development of long-range aircraft for anti-submarine operations, and the fact that the Americans built ships (the famous 'Liberty' ships) faster than Germany's U-boats could sink them. In the end this last factor was by far the most important; once again, the war was a matter of numbers: industrial output, shipping tonnages, personnel, resources in general.

In this period Britain carried the struggle against Germany alone. The United States presence in the European theatre began in a small way with advance units of its Army Air Force in 1942, but it was well into 1943 before the American bomber force began to have the numbers and the right methods to make an impact on the aerial campaign over Germany. By this time the Allies were fighting their way up Italy, albeit slowly and painfully; Germany was in retreat from Russia; and the build-up had begun towards the continental invasion that took place on D-Day. Harris himself nominated 5 March 1943 as the moment that Bomber Command was at last ready to get down to the kind of work he wanted from it; that was the date on which the navigational aid OBOE was at last fully operational, and when Harris was beginning to have the kind of aircraft in the kind of numbers he saw as desirable.[15]

But it is an interesting fact that Bomber Command's readiness for its major area-bombing campaign coincided with the turn of the tide in the Allies' favour. The argument that says that Bomber Command was the only means of 'carrying the war to Germany' during Britain's time of greatest weakness, when it was alone in the struggle and woefully undermanned and under-equipped for the task, overlooks the fact that during that fragile time Bomber Command was itself very limited in both respects, meagre in capacity and range, and ineffective as an instrument of war.[16] And for a large part of that period anyway – from the outbreak of hostilities until February 1942 at the earliest – Bomber Command was still 'hamstrung' (as Portal and Harris saw it) by not having *carte blanche* to conduct area bombing of German towns and cities by night.

When that *carte blanche* was given in February 1942, Harris began preparing the three 1,000-bomber raids of the coming summer. The raids effectively shot Bomber Command's bolt for that year, and were propaganda successes merely; Cologne was badly damaged, but its civilian casualties were low, and the two succeeding big raids did little harm because they were so off-target. As far as 1942 was concerned, on a few occasions Bomber Command's activities managed a certain amount of sound and fury, but with disappointing results in concrete terms.

So the anomaly is that area bombing began in full earnestness only when the tide of the war had already begun to run against Germany, and it reached its most devastating proportions when Germany's defeat was recognised to be a matter of time only – in the last six months of the war.

As the discussion of America's air war over Japan has already shown, the same applies. The defeat of Japan was not in question when the Tokyo firebombing happened in March 1945, and it was certainly not in question when the atom bombs were dropped in August of that year. Victory in the war as a whole was a matter of numbers – of industrial capacity and manpower reserves – and once America was in the war, the Allies were in effect guaranteed victory. The Axis powers' only hope was to induce a favourable early ending to hostilities by some decisive or lucky stroke that would make the Allied powers decide that the process of gaining victory would be too long or costly, even though inevitable in the long run. That eventuality was made unlikely by the Allied decision at the Casablanca Conference in early 1943 to seek nothing less than unconditional surrender from the Axis powers; but the combination of hope for a lucky break, and having nothing to lose given the unconditional terms, kept the Axis powers going until the last drop of fuel – in Germany's case – and in Japan's case, the last drop of hope. Japan's military command had come to recognise, by the spring of 1945, that the defence of the home islands was a lost cause, and from then on – four months before the atom-bomb attacks – they began to send out feelers to discover what the prospects were for an end to the war.

These points – that the defeat of Germany and Japan were seen to be inevitable, months if not indeed years before they actually happened – is vigorously contested by some, who say that the outcome of the war was in doubt in both theatres until close to the end, and that continued assault from all quarters on all aspects of the military, civil and administrative organisation of the Axis powers was required to realise the overwhelming necessity of the war, which was to defeat them.

Does this objection have weight? On the question whether it was unclear that the Allies had won until close to the end, one need only quote the agreement of the historians. Robin Neillands says that by September 1944 'Germany was going to lose the war, and quite soon – that much was clear'.[17] John Terraine agrees; 'By the end of August, 1944, Germany was palpably defeated.'[18] One could quote the same from many sources, and for Japan too.

The point about the 'overwhelming necessity of the war was to win' is a good one. In light of it, it is often argued that the greatest immorality would have been to lose the war, and that since this is so, anything and everything done to win it was legitimated by this overriding aim.

It can certainly be granted that the overwhelming aim was to defeat the Axis powers, and it is surely right that it would have been an act of immorality not to strive fully and effectively to achieve that goal. But it is wrong to use this to justify indiscriminate bombing of towns and cities, for the familiar reason that ends do not automatically justify means. Suppose that the Axis powers had won the war: would that fact justify everything they did in the course of it? Obviously not. In practice victory tends to provide absolution for all wrongs, since the victor is the judge and jury in his own behalf – and history is written by victors. In the same way, the victor nations of the Second World War have allowed their victory to excuse them from self-examination over some aspects of their behaviour. But that is a wrong in itself.

Let us for a moment suppose that all the arguments of the defenders of area bombing are correct, namely, that it damaged enemy morale, reduced enemy industrial capacity, kept enemy military resources away from battle-fronts, reduced military deaths, and 'carried the war' to the enemy. We have seen that these arguments do not persuade; but let us for a moment accept them. Do they make area bombing morally acceptable? One thing would be needed to make an affirmative answer more likely, namely, the claim that there was no other way to survive against the Axis powers than by carrying out area bombing. Is this true? Manifestly not. For one thing, Britain survived its greatest threat from Nazi Germany in the two years before area bombing became its policy. For another, the effects claimed by defenders of area bombing, and which we are temporarily granting, could have been gained, as we have seen, by efforts at precision-bombing – and may indeed have been more successfully gained by it. This too shows that area bombing was not necessary.

Remember the criteria for *jus in bello*: that the means employed be necessary, and proportional. Area bombing was neither necessary nor proportional, and it was neither of these things by quite a long way.

It is striking to notice the judgements made by historians, even those sympathetic to the endeavours and sufferings of Bomber Command, about the merits of its campaigns in the Second World War. In his excellent history of Bomber Command's war, Denis Richards lists its outstanding achievements as follows. First, there were its mine-laying activities, which interrupted the movement of merchant ships supplying Germany, kept U-boats in their bases at the time of critical operations such as Operation Torch in North Africa in 1942, and Operation Overlord on 6 June 1944. Moreover, the mine-laying interfered with U-boat training in the Bay of Danzig when Admiral Dönitz was trying to bring his new large submarines into service for the Atlantic struggle.[19] Bomber Command also sank or put out of action six of Germany's twelve major warships; its epic sinking of the *Tirpitz* involved three raids, one from temporary bases in Russia which the attacking Lancasters had to use as a staging post before trying to bomb the battleship in its hiding place in Kaafiord. The same Lancasters eventually sank the *Tirpitz* on 12 November 1944 at moorings near Tromsø. Finally, Bomber Command delayed and reduced V-weapon production by its attacks of Peenemunde and rocket-launch sites, making a valuable impact on the missile attacks on London in the summer and autumn of 1944.[20]

Note that these are all precision attacks. To them can be added Bomber Command's help in preventing the threatened invasion of 1940, and its contribution to the strangulation of Germany's fuel supplies in the last months of the war – though this was chiefly an American success. These again were precision attacks. The only recognition given by Richards to area bombing is its role in helping to persuade the Italian populace to change sides in the war. Almost any of the military actions of the Allies in the Italian theatre could be praised for this, but it is only fair to include Bomber Command, whose crews found that attacks on Milan, Genoa and Turin were relatively safe in comparison to the danger posed by fighter planes and anti-aircraft defences in Germany. It is easy to be dismayed by the thought of the indifference thus displayed to the centuries of cultural treasures cavalierly subjected to bombing, though the indifference to the possibility of civilian deaths – children, women and the elderly almost certainly the majority among them – is infinitely worse.

Naturally, and rightly enough, the defender of bombing will respond to all the foregoing criticisms of the area-bombing campaign by asking: what should the Allies have done instead? The answer is given in the mere process of making the question itself more precise: what should the Allies have done *instead of area bombing*? The answer is: Bomber Command should have continued its efforts at precision bombing, and devoted its energies to making this tactic safer for its bombers and more effective. The fact that precision bombing proved highly dangerous in the early years of the war was the practical reason for switching to area bombing, but there was an alternative which, if the principle of limiting harm to civilians had been maintained, could and doubtless would have been taken: namely, seeking remedies to the danger – as the Eighth Army Air Force did, finding their answer in long-range fighter escorts. The RAF made no efforts in this direction, because it chose to concentrate on night area bombing. But the same quantum of effort could have been devoted to making daylight precision bombing practicable, exactly as the Americans did.

All four of the desiderata specified by the main defence of the bombing campaign would have been realised by a precision bombing effort. Anti-aircraft guns and fighter planes would have had to remain in Germany. The war would have been 'carried to' Germany. A concentrated effort at precision bombing of crucial industrial and economic targets might have reduced the capacity of Germany's war industries far earlier than the actual precision-bombing efforts by the Eighth Army Air Force did – and as area bombing did not – thus perhaps genuinely shortening the war. And this in turn might have had an impact on morale too, and where it mattered most: not so much the morale of the civilian population, but of the troops kept short of equipment and fuel and thus made more vulnerable to their enemies.

And all this would have been achieved without the deliberate targeting of civilians, and therefore with lower civilian casualties. The Allies could accordingly have maintained moral standards through-out, consistently with their professions before and at the beginning of the war that they would never stoop to deliberate bombing of civilians.

A point that defenders of area bombing might make at this juncture is to say that it was not obvious, at the time that the bombing campaign was actually going on, that it was having little effect on Germany's war industry or on the population's morale. The hope that it would shorten the war by making German civilians demand that their leaders end it, was a real hope, and if it does not justify area bombing at the very least it excuses it, or allows a plea of mitigation to be entered on its behalf.

To this the answer is that the conductors of area bombing knew, from pre-war discussions and widely advertised fears, and from the pre-war efforts to limit civilian bombing by international agreement, that the very act of targeting civilians was wrong. Indeed at the outset of war the British government had repeatedly and pointedly forsworn the idea of targeting civilians as a barbarous and uncivilised technique of war. So not being aware of its ineffectiveness, yet hoping that it was effective enough that it might shorten the war, cannot be invoked as a justification nor even as an excuse. The combination of ignorance and hope might be an *explanation* of why the conductors of area bombing chose it as a strategy and allowed it to continue; but an explanation is not an excuse.

For a perspective on the standards Roosevelt, Chamberlain and others sought to uphold in respect of bombing at the outbreak of the Second World War – in Chamberlain's case, as earlier chapters showed, partly out of conviction and partly out of a pragmatic desire to dissuade Germany from area-bombing Britain – a much more recent example might be given. Writing in the spring of 2005 on the subject of US treatment of prisoners in Afghanistan and Iraq, the American commentator Thomas Friedman said:

Yes I know war is hell and ugliness abounds in every corner. I also understand that in places like Iraq and Afghanistan, America is up against a vicious enemy, which, if it had the power, would do great harm to the United States. You do not deal with such people with kid gloves. But killing prisoners of war, presumably in the act of torture, is an inexcusable outrage. The fact that Congress has just shrugged this off, and no senior official or officer has been fired, is a travesty.[21]

The comment can be applied retrospectively to the Second World War, with a few changes of names and nouns, and exactly the same principle holds: civilised standards have to be made to apply even in severe situations, both for intrinsic reasons and because there is, properly, a reckoning always to come.

There is one final throw of the dice for defenders of area bombing, and that, with respect to the points just made, is to ask, 'Has morality any place in war at all?' If it does not, then anything goes, and with it area bombing of civilian targets. This would be the ultimate defence of anything done under the cloak of war – and alas, it often is, given the frightful facts of war, from terrible battles like Stalingrad, to the atrocities, bombing victims, Japanese prisoner-of-war camps, men dying in submarines at the bottom of the sea or burning in the cockpits of aeroplanes – and so on and on – the list is ghastly and endless, and as one contemplates it, the refined nuances of ethical debate seem wholly out of place.

Robin Neillands, whose question 'Has morality any place in war at all?' I quote, cites both Clausewitz and Macaulay in support of the idea that once war has broken out the only aim is to win it 'at any cost, and especially if that cost can be met by the enemy'.[22] Clausewitz says that the will of the enemy is a legitimate target: 'the destruction of his capacity to resist, the killing of his courage rather than his men' is what warfare is about. For Macaulay, writing in 1831, 'The essence of war is violence; moderation in war is imbecility'.[23] For Neillands, the idea that war is something to be won at any cost, preferably to be paid by the enemy, is 'a point that can be endlessly debated by moral philosophers, who tend to find so blunt a point unacceptable; but wars are not usually fought by moral philosophers'.[24] Interestingly, the convergence between the views of moral philosophers, on the one hand, and on the other hand soldiers who have seen the battlefield, tends to be greater than between the latter and the historians of their doings. Hereby hangs a tale. But Neillands continues, '[Wars] are fought by ordinary people . . . once they are in it they find moral questions largely academic; their main aim is to stay alive, and to win.' This is doubtless true. But the high command in wars, both military and political – the people who make the choices and take the decisions – are not the ordinary soldiers who find themselves reluctantly at war. This implies an important difference. Greater responsibility demands a more encompassing view not just of the strategic but of the political, diplomatic, and finally human implications of what is involved in going to war, and in the conduct of war.

Yet even the ordinary people who get caught up in war might find themselves doing some moral philosophy after all, as Neillands now changes tack to acknowledge:

> To win, these people may be obliged to do dreadful things to their fellow men, often in the interests of personal survival, but most of these ordinary people would agree that even in war some actions are beyond the pale. The killing of prisoners or women and children is certainly among them. In short, there has to be morality in war; to suppose otherwise is to condone barbarism.[25]

This last remark, I think, says it all. It is of course infinitely easier to say than to apply in times of dreadful emergency. But it is the mark of a truly civilised arrangement that in even such emergency, the effort is made, not abandoned.

I conclude that the defences offered for area bombing are unpersuasive, and that therefore the indictment stands.

8

Judgement

THROUGHOUT THIS BOOK the principal example I have cited of a
bombing assault on civilians is Operation Gomorrah, the Hamburg raids of July–August 1943. I could have cited Dresden and the
atom-bomb attacks on Hiroshima and Nagasaki as my central
examples; but I chose Hamburg. Why?

Readers will note that with one exception all my sources for this
discussion have been works in English. I could have given attention to
the recent spate of publications in German about the experience of
German civilians under bombing in the Second World War, but I
chose to approach the question of the morality of Allied area bombing
from the point of view of the literature on the subject in the language
of the victor nations. Why?

My reasons for both these things are conscious and deliberate, and
they are as follows.

The bombing of Dresden and the atom-bomb attacks on Hiroshima and Nagasaki are, for very good reason, obvious targets for
moral disapprobation when area bombing is criticised. Earlier I
offered reasons why they are special. They took place when the
war was effectively over, and each has a particular claim to notice.
Dresden's claim is the terrible casualties suffered by its residents, and
the horror of the way they were crushed, asphyxiated and burned to
death by the attack, so at odds with the great beauty and cultural

significance of their city. The atom-bombed cities' claim is that they were destroyed by a horrific new weapon, and remain unique – at time of writing – in being so; and that the attacks left a poison in the survivors, which killed them over the months, years and decades following, a hellish legacy that seems unjustifiable on any grounds.

However, I choose Operation Gomorrah as the principal example of an area-bombing atrocity because it took place when the war was, although running in the Allies' favour, by no means securely won. It was conducted by means that were 'conventional' for the Second World War, at least until August 1945; that is, a mixture of incendiary and high-explosive bombs. It clearly and unequivocally targeted the civilian population of a large city, which was carpet-bombed at night to fulfil the aim, graphically described in Sir Arthur Harris's own words, quoted earlier, of 'crushing Boche, killing Boche, terrorising Boche'.

If Operation Gomorrah was an immoral act, then how much more so were Dresden, Hiroshima and Nagasaki. If Operation Gomorrah was *unnecessary* and *disproportionate*, to use the language of just-war theory, then how much more so were the attacks on Dresden, Hiroshima and Nagasaki – and indeed the firebombing of Tokyo and other Japanese cities, the bombing of Berlin, and the destruction of Würzburg and so many other German towns indiscriminately bombed in the very last months of the war for no better reason than that they were unbombed, and that there were many bombers and bombs waiting to be used.

If Operation Gomorrah was a moral crime, then the area-bombing campaigns of the Second World War were as a whole morally criminal. Bombing attacks that were genuine attempts at precision bombing – targeting oil, V-weapon launch sites, railway lines, U-boat pens – killed people too; but here the defence applies that there was a war on, and that these things happen in war. It cannot be said that deliberately targeting civilians and dropping thousands of tons of bombs on them remorselessly over many years is a side-effect of war.

The second point is that I have used only English-language sources in compiling this account. Most of these, it is true, themselves rely partly on German sources in their turn, and facts, figures and anecdotal material culled from German sources therefore finds its way into these pages by their means. And a couple of my sources are books by Germans either written in English or translated into English. But I have deliberately avoided drawing on such recent publications as Jorg Friedrich's *Der Brand* and *Brandstatten*, or the collection edited by Volker Hage, *Hamburg 1943: Literarische Zeugnisse zum Feuersturm*, or Christoph Kucklick's *Feuersturm: Der Bombenkrieg gegen Deutschland*. These books invite their German readers to set alongside the national sense of guilt for the Nazi era a second thought, which is that hundreds of thousands of Germans suffered in the war years from the area-bombing attacks, which not only killed over 300,000 people but did immense damage to the built fabric and cultural heritage of Germany. Two of these books, Friedrich's *Brandstatten* and Kucklick's *Feuersturm*, provide photographic evidence of the devastation and the torment of the casualties, some of it never seen before; and the first of them constitutes a photographic essay on the architectural treasures that were lost under the bombs, and by implication what they contain – for in *Der Brand* Friederich gives an account of the cultural losses too, in the form of the contents of historic buildings, churches, palaces, museums, and libraries.

These books seem to me to be legitimate and now timely contributions to the process of discussion required for putting the Second World War into proper proportion. I neither expect nor wish that this will change anything on the question of Nazi war crimes and crimes against humanity, which so weigh against the Germany of the time that nothing can excuse or abate what happened in it, or in its name. The point is not to make up a balance sheet, and by entering into it the sufferings of Germans under area bombing, thereby to diminish the culpability of Nazism. This is what neo-Nazis try illegitimately to do. I do not think that Germany's responsible historians are seeking to do this. But at any rate, what I have written here, and what I judge on the basis of it, is independent of their view of the matter, however closely in many points their conclusions and mine converge. In writing this book I wished to view the matter solely from the standpoint of someone in one of the victor nations, who inherited the benefits of that victory, but hopes that by now there is enough perspective available for a frank acknowledgement of the wrongs done in the course of how it was won.

There are two major reasons why it matters to recognise and accept that the Allied bomber forces' area-bombing campaigns constitute moral crimes. One is so that we in the victor nations can face up to our part in committing crimes in the course of that terrible war; crimes by a long way far less in magnitude than those committed by Nazism, though in the matter of comparisons the culpability of Allied area bombing should prompt uncomfortable reflections about the moral company it keeps, given that it is more akin to Japanese actions in their infamous attack on Nanking than it is to, say, Henry Stimson's withdrawal of Kyoto from the list of atom-bomb targets. It is an obvious enough comment that only if a civilisation looks at itself frankly and accepts what it sees, can it hope to learn from the exercise, and progress in the right way and direction thereafter. The cliché, no less true and pertinent for being one, that applies here is that we owe it to our future to get matters straight about the past.

The second reason is that we are at risk of repeating mistakes if we do not face up to their commission in the past. There is a very particular reason for being anxious about this. Look at what the United States military forces recently have to say in their interpretation of those aspects of International Humanitarian Law (the Geneva 1949 conventions and their two protocols) which protect civilians. The Geneva Convention Protocol 1 of 1977 forbids military attacks upon civilians and civilian targets, and these latter are defined in Protocol I, Article 52 (1) as follows: 'Civilian objects are all objects which are not military objectives.' Article 52 (2) defines military objectives as 'those objects which by their nature, location, purpose or use make an effective contribution to military action and whose total or partial destruction, capture or neutralisation, in the circumstances ruling at the time, offers a definite military advantage'. Now observe the very wide latitude that US military manuals apply here: 'Military advantage may involve a variety of considerations, including the security of the attacking force . . . Economic targets of the enemy that indirectly but effectively support and sustain the enemy's war-fighting capability may also be attacked' (Annotated Supplement to the Commander's Handbook on the Law of Naval Operations, 8.1.1.); 'The official US Air Force doctrine suggests that the morale of the civilian population may, in itself, legitimately be targeted since weakening of the will to fight would offer a military advantage' (Air Force Doctrine Document 1: Air Force Basic Doctrine, AFDD-1 (1997)). In other words, the US Navy and Air Force still think in Second World War terms about 'civilian morale' and the legitimacy of attacking what can be described as 'economic' targets – not, note, 'war industries' or some more closely defined economic target such as oil, electricity, transport or water. 'Economic targets' covers far too much.

Such interpretations of the Geneva Convention and protocols are not permissible in the light of an acceptance that Allied area bombing in the Second World War was a moral crime. This acceptance places much sharper constraints on such interpretations. It therefore matters.

To see the hard truth about the morality of Allied area bombing, we need only ask the relevant questions. Was it necessary? Was it proportionate? Is it really true that all civilians without exception belong in the front line of war? Why do Western militaries try so hard now – even if only in theory; even if it is only a matter of lip-service or propaganda – to avoid 'collateral damage'? Why did we come up with the Geneva Convention provisions in 1949 to protect civilians in time of war, and more explicitly so in the protocols to that convention? Does the Allies' Second World War area bombing pass the test of the Nuremberg principles drawn up by the Allies themselves? How does Allied area bombing square with the sentiment behind the United Nations' Universal Declaration of Human Rights?

Talk of declarations and conventions on rights and on lawful practice in war in the wake of 1945 was the result of a determination to try to avoid the gross human-rights violations that had taken place during the war. They came in the immediate wake of the war's horrors as a judgement on them, and as a statement of what was unacceptable in what had happened. The Holocaust properly occupied centre stage in thinking about these matters; but that thinking also embraced other atrocities of the war, and as the evolution of the fourth Geneva Convention shows, area bombing was a part of that, though its chief perpetrators – the British and Americans – did not permit a specific reference to it. The history behind the provisions of the 1977 first protocol to the Geneva Convention of 1949 is left in silence by it. But its meaning is crystal clear: as a retrospective judgement on area bombing, it nominates it as a crime.

The questions can go on, adding to the discomfiture they cause. What is the moral difference between bombing women and children and shooting them with a pistol? Is it that when you bomb them you cannot see them – you did not intend *that* particular woman and *that* particular child to die – and anyway they might escape the bombing, perhaps by reaching a shelter? But if they are here against a wall just feet away from the muzzle of your pistol they cannot escape: it is more personal; you can see their eyes. Is that the difference – the anonymity of the act of killing from 20,000 feet?

On the basis of the foregoing chapters the answer I give to the following questions are these:

Was area bombing necessary? No.

Was it proportionate? No.

Was it against the humanitarian principles that people have been striving to enunciate as a way of controlling and limiting war? Yes.

Was it against general moral standards of the kind recognised and agreed in Western civilisation in the last five centuries, or even 2,000 years? Yes.

Was it against what mature national laws provide in the way of outlawing murder, bodily harm, and destruction of property? Yes.

In short and in sum: was area bombing wrong? Yes.

Very wrong? Yes.

And now there come some very hard questions for us to ask ourselves about our own airmen – our own kinsmen.

Should airmen have refused to carry out area-bombing raids? Yes. In the hypothetical ideal world which does not exist and certainly not in wartime, they should have insisted on being sent against genuine industrial and military targets, and unavoidable 'collateral damage' should have been the worst they accepted as regards the effects of their actions on civilians. Doubtless many thought or made themselves think that this was what they were doing anyway; and standardly they were told as much, and doubtless some chose to believe the line in psychological self-defence. But many also knew full well what they were doing, and accepted it, or suffered silently because of it, or regretted it. But in wartime people are taught to hate their enemy, and in the Second World War the Allied fliers had good reason to believe that the enemy regime was a bad lot. Bomber Command crews, and in the Pacific theatre USAAF crews, had the backing of most of the public and their seniors for their area bombing of civilian populations, and they needed both, together with the conviction that they were fighting a just war – which was true – to give them the courage to go and do a job which, whatever else might be said about it with this comfort of hindsight, was a very dangerous one.

In warfare, the 'element of surprise' is regarded as a valuable tactic, and all military planning is kept secret unless the threat of an attack has propaganda value or is aimed at distracting enemy resources. When Japan attacked Pearl Harbor in 1941 the Unites States forces were wholly unprepared, and suffered major losses. A student of Japanese military strategy would have known that the sudden surprise attack was a Japanese speciality – in 1905 the Russian fleet in Port Arthur was surprised by Japanese forces in a manner closely pre-figuring Pearl Harbor. Naturally, the United States represented the Japanese attack as 'perfidy'. This is not a rhetorical notion only; perfidy is forbidden by the laws of war, though rather futilely so, given what war is. By a superb act of historical management, and by its resounding victory in the war, the United States has changed perceptions of Pearl Harbor from an ignominious defeat into a noble national tragedy.

But at least the Pearl Harbor attack was aimed at military assets. On the second night raid of Operation Gomorrah, the one that created the horrific firestorm, Bomber Command created the equiva-lent of the element of surprise by flying past Hamburg to its north, as if proceeding to targets deeper into Germany; only to swing round and unexpectedly attack the city from the east. Here the target was the civilian population. Similarly, the lone aircraft droning above Hiro-shima on 6 August 1945 gave no cause for alarm to the hundreds of thousands of people below, who accordingly went about their normal business, taking no precautions. When the first atom bomb exploded in the sky above the city's centre, not one individual in the purlieus of the blast expected it.

A surprise attack on a civilian population aimed at causing maximum hurt, shock, disruption, and terror: there comes to seem very little difference in principle between the RAF's Operation Gomorrah, or the USAAF's atom bomb attacks on Hiroshima and Nagasaki, and the destruction of the World Trade Center in New York by terrorists on 11 September 2001. And this latter, prescinding from differences in scale and the drama of the target, is no different in turn from terrorist bombings carried out in Madrid by Basque separatists or in London by the IRA. All these terrorist attacks are atrocities, consisting in deliberate mass murder of civilians to hurt and coerce the society they belong to. To say that the principle underlying

'9/11', Hamburg and Hiroshima is the same is to say that the same moral judgement applies to all three.

No doubt these will seem unduly provocative comparisons. It can be pointed out that the Allied bombings were carried out in time of declared war, in which offensive operations are in effect a form of defensive operation, given that the enemy will seek to do the same if given an opportunity; whereas Pearl Harbor and 9/11 were perfidious attacks on unprepared targets, the first military and the second civilian.

This point is a good one, for there is indeed a difference here, though some will attempt to make it a debating point whether those who carry out terrorist attacks believe that they are at war and that their offence is in the same way a form of pre-emptive defence. Very well: grant the difference; yet focus on the net effect. In all these cases the centre-piece is an attack on a civilian population aimed at causing maximum hurt, shock, disruption and terror. This is what these events have in common, whether in the midst of declared war or not, and so far as this core point is concerned, adjustments of fine moral calibration are at best irrelevant. All such attacks are moral atrocities.

Recognising this ought to bring home with full force the degree of moral concern raised by Allied area bombing in the Second World War. It should by now be time for a mature and dispassionate acceptance of this point. The benefit of accepting it is that it secures the importance of the 1977 first protocol to the fourth Geneva Convention protecting civilians, one day perhaps enforceable in an international court; and explains why it is genuinely important that so much attention is paid to avoiding 'collateral damage' in wartime – again: no doubt too often as lip service merely; but the aspiration is what matters as a start.

Above all it will help to infuse a more honest appreciation of the character of the war fought by the Allies against the Axis between 1939 and 1945: a just war against morally criminal enemies, in which in some important respects the eventual victors allowed themselves to join their enemies in the moral depths, a fact which should be profoundly and frankly regretted.

Getting the record straight is all that can be done now. But it is far from little. Speaking from the point of view of an inheritor of the triumph of morally better forces over worse in the epic conflict of 1939–45, I think it places on even firmer footing our just condemnation of the atrocities of Nazism in particular and Axis aggression in general, because we do not pretend to have clean hands ourselves. What we can claim is that they were far cleaner than those of the people who plunged the world into war and carried out gross crimes under its cover, and that the explanation – not the excuse – for why we allowed our own hands to get dirty at all is because of what we had to clean up.

A fitting conclusion to the debate is provided by someone who was a participating witness to the Second World War, and whose judgement about the use of area bombing was made in an interesting context. This was a navy airman, Admiral Ralph Ofstie of the United States Navy, who contributed to the post-Second World War debate in his country about the role of atomic weapons in its future military arrangements. Part of his qualification for doing so – and it was an excellent one – was that he had served on the US Strategic Bombing Survey. He told a hearing of the House Armed Services Committee that as the Allied bombing campaigns of the war had shown, strategic bombing was 'inherently inaccurate' and no matter how its objectives were defined it inevitably involved 'mass slaughter of men, women and children in the enemy country'. It was not only militarily ineffective but with its 'ruthless, barbaric methods' it lowered the moral standards of the society whose forces carried it out. 'Must we,' asked Admiral Ofstie, 'translate the historical mistake of World War II into a permanent concept merely to avoid clouding the prestige of those who led us down the wrong road in the past?'[1]

And a fitting *envoi* is provided by the closing words of Vera Brittain's *Seed of Chaos*. From the very midst of war she prophesied with 'complete confidence that the callous cruelty which has caused us to destroy innocent human life in Europe's most crowded cities, and the vandalism which has obliterated historic treasures in some of her loveliest, will appear to future civilisation as an extreme form of criminal lunacy with which our political and military leaders deliberately allowed themselves to become afflicted'.

Postscript

THE QUESTION EXAMINED IN the previous chapters – did the United Kingdom and the United States commit what we would now call a war crime by 'area bombing' civilian populations in the cities of Germany and Japan during the Second World War? – is given an unequivocally affirmative answer in the final chapter. This conclusion predictably caused controversy for and against, both among historians who specialise in the Second World War and veterans of the Allied air forces who took part in it.

Two equally controversial corollaries that also drew attention were, first, that if given the choice, Allied aircrews should have elected to attack genuine military and industrial targets exclusively, rather than to participate in indiscriminate attacks on civilian populations in urban areas; and second, that in a single crucial respect the terrorist atrocities of 11 September 2001 and others like them resemble 'area bombings' of civilians, namely, in their aim of assaulting and undermining the morale of the attacked population by hurting and terrorising it.

In this postscript I take the opportunity to reflect on the debate generated by my arguments here, and especially these main points of contention.

One premise of this book is that the Second World War was a just war for the Allied side – one of the very few just wars in history –

fought against dangerous and wicked aggressors whose atrocities far outweigh anything that the Allies might or might not have done in the course of it. Losing the war would have been a disaster of epochal proportions for the Allied nations and the world at large. And yet, if the Allies did indeed do anything questionable in the course of fighting that just war, we as the survivors, veterans and descendants of the Allied side should have the maturity and moral courage to acknowledge the fact and learn from it, because we are still fighting wars, and may have to fight yet more – and we should wish to fight them justly even if we fight them with all our might and determination.

Indeed, a primary motivation for writing this book was that too many parts of the world were (and, as this postscript is written, still are) convulsed in military and terrorist violence, including acts that horrify one's conscience. I thought that one of many needful tasks was that of recalling and fully understanding the lessons of crucial aspects of past conflicts, for our own sakes and that of the future.

Among those who contacted me to express support for my conclusions were veteran airmen, both British and American, who typically reported the doubts they felt about area bombing even at the time they participated in it. One, Harold Nash, told me a touching story. He was shot down while on a bombing raid over Hanover, captured the next morning, and taken under guard to Hanover train station where refugees from his bombing raid were assembling to leave the ravaged city. In his state of anxious trauma he expected that the German civilians, recognising his RAF flying gear despite its dirt and disarray, would turn on him in anger. Instead, two women gave him bread.

There is an analogue of this in the attitudes of British victims of the Blitz in 1940–1, which was an aerial assault of traumatic proportions despite being tiny in comparison to the years of massive obliteration bombing unleashed by RAF Bomber Command on Germany and by the single horrifically intense year of bombing of Japan carried out by the USAAF. This was that people in the bombed cities of Britain were far less keen, when asked by the British government's polling organisation, to see German cities bombed than were the residents of unbombed cities. The Allied civilians most keen on bombing Germany and Japan were American, whose cities were not bombed in World War II. There is a speaking moral in these facts, and they go some way to explaining why Harold Nash was given bread by refugees whose homes he had participated in destroying the previous night.

My critics focus on three main areas. They defend the bombing campaign against Germany by saying that it hampered the Nazi war effort because it kept troops, guns and aircraft on the home front, thus weakening the eastern and western military fronts, and at the same time slowing industrial production. The bombing of Japan, and particularly the atom bombing of Hiroshima and Nagasaki, is defended on the grounds that it shortened the war against Japan and saved the lives of many thousands of American troops who might otherwise have had to engage in a land invasion.

The critics next say that to describe area bombing of civilians as any kind of crime is to make a judgement of hindsight, using concepts – particularly that of a 'war crime' – which did not exist until later.

The historians among my critics say that because they have touched on the bombing controversy in their own books, the matter has already been addressed and that therefore there is nothing new to add. The implication is that the tacit prevarications of debate subsequent to World War II have effectively put the area bombing question to rest in the consciences of the Western allies.

These criticisms are wrong on all counts. Consider the last point first. As the preceding chapters show, a vigorous debate about bombing had started as early as 1899, even before manned flight began, when the Hague Conference outlawed throwing grenades from balloons. The experience of the First World War, in which German Zeppelins and Gothas bombed a number of British towns, made international fears about bombing so acute that during the Geneva disarmament conferences of the 1920s and 1930s some delegates went so far as to suggest banning flight itself. The reason for this anxiety was that bombing theory, from Douhet and Tren-chard onwards, was unequivocal in predicting that bombing would cause terrible casualties and destruction, threatening civilisation itself. Historians of the Second World War ignore this background because it places Allied decisions to commence area bombing in a very exposed position: the planners of area bombing well knew what they were doing – and hoping.

The historians also often ignore the fact that during the first three years of war the British government publicly foreswore any plans to bomb civilian populations, and changed tack only in the third year of war – in February 1942 – when whole urban areas and their civilian inhabitants were nominated as the primary target for Bomber Command efforts. The historians ignore the Morgenthau Plan for a divided, de-industrialised, entirely rural post-war Germany. The bombing campaign tacitly served this aim by destroying the libraries, schools, universities, archives, concert halls, art galleries, studios, monuments and architectural treasures that sustained German cul-ture. They also ignore the anti-bombing campaign in Britain itself, and play down Winston Churchill's own ambiguous attitude – and his eventual serious doubts – about its legitimacy.

Until now, discussion of the Allied bombing campaigns has focused on a few egregious events, such as the attacks on Dresden and Hiroshima. The foregoing chapters here put the morality of the entire bombing war under scrutiny, and bring in to relief not just the forgotten great pre-war debate about bombing and the Morgenthau Plan, but also the nature of the attacks and the weapons used in them, such as an early form of napalm and the phosphorus bombs whose use is now outlawed.

This book is the first to bring all the foregoing points together, and they throw the question of area bombing into a sharp new light. We do not like to admit that we took decisions to employ bombing as a tactic of terror and mass civilian death, but so we did; and we did so despite – and in important senses because of – the background of decades of debate and anxiety about doing so. This is precisely the fact that has to be confronted and honestly acknowledged if we are to recognise why we are under an obligation to adjust our moral attitude to how we conduct ourselves in times of conflict hereafter.

The first of the critics' points mentioned above was that the bombing kept substantial German forces on the home front. This is true, but it is not quite the truth that the critics wish it to be. The same effect would have been achieved if, instead of indiscriminately targeting the civilian populations of cities, the bombing effort had been directed at transport links, factories, airfields, harbours and, above all, coal, gas and oil plants. This is just what, in the European theatre, the USAAF did, and it was their tactical (as opposed to area) bombing that had a real effect on Germany's war effort, as the post-war bombing surveys of the UK and US governments found. By the most conservative calculations, if all the bombing effort had been directed at these crucial targets, the war might have been shortened by a year or more.

This same effect might have been achieved if RAF bombing efforts had focused on long-range anti-submarine search and destroy missions in the north Atlantic, protecting that vital supply route. This is a major point. Churchill wrote that the only thing that kept him awake at night with anxiety was the Battle of the Atlantic. In *The War at Sea 1939–45*, S. W. Roskill wrote, 'In the early spring of 1943 we had a very narrow escape from defeat in the Atlantic; had we suffered such a defeat, history would have judged the main cause had been the lack of two more squadrons of very long range aircraft for convoy escort duties.'[1]

The historians correctly point out that the RAF switched to night bombing, with its necessary corollary of imprecision in targeting, because bombing by day was highly dangerous and costly. This is an explanation not an excuse; the USAAF persisted in seeking ways to make daylight bombing safer and more effective, and eventually succeeded, to greatly important effect in the European theatre. This route was open to RAF Bomber Command too, and it was not chosen. Instead it bombed civilians by night.

Moreover, area bombing of cities did not harm civilian morale in Germany, as it was intended to do: rather, it strengthened it, an effect that many in Britain recognised from their own experience of the Blitz. Thus it was that Joseph Goebbels was cheered in the streets of Berlin (a hitherto largely anti-Nazi city) in early 1944 after the winter-long 'Battle of Berlin' waged by seemingly endless fleets of RAF bombers – a battle lost by the RAF on more than just the morale front, at great sacrifice to our own courageous airmen.

Those who manned the searchlights and 88mm anti-aircraft guns in Germany were boys and older men, not front-line troops. On the day that Berlin fell in 1945, Germany still had ten million men between the ages of 18 and 35, booted and fully equipped, in service on the eastern and western fronts. Yes, the Luftwaffe had been defeated by USAAF daylight forces principally, but indiscriminate bombing of cities had given Germany more reason to fight to the end than otherwise.

As for the question of German war production, the plain fact is that German output increased every year of the conflict until the end of 1944, and the country's economy was never put on a full war footing. With the manpower and resources of vast conquered territories in Europe, Germany was in a position to sustain the war for a number of years. What won the war in Europe for the Allied powers was Russian infantry and tanks, and USAAF daylight precision bombing of Germany's energy supplies, aircraft factories and (with the RAF) transport links. The interdiction of fuel supplies was one of the single most important successes of the bombing war. In Europe the USAAF aimed for the jugular vein of the Nazi war machine – energy supplies – and succeeded in slashing it. The critics' claim that area bombing 'slowed the rate of increase' of Germany's industrial output is an unquantifiable surmise, for all its plausibility, whereas the effect of attacks on fuel supplies was palpable and decisive.

If anything further needed to be said on this point, the magisterial examination of Germany's wartime economy by Adam Tooze in *The Wages of Destruction*, published after this book was completed, should put the matter to rest. His book shows two things: the importance of the bombing effort specifically directed against industrial, military and fuel targets, and the ineffectiveness of area bombing. 'The correlation between the area bombing of Germany's cities and the collapse of its war production was loose, at best,' he writes. 'The wanton destruction of German cities could disrupt production, but it could not bring it to a complete standstill. The way in which the bombers achieved that effect was by severing rail links and waterways between the Ruhr and the rest of Germany.'[2] Tooze describes the 'Battle of Berlin' – the months of attacks on Berlin between the autumn of 1943 and the spring of 1944 – as 'perverse', and it stands in sharp contrast to the major utility of the kind of bombing that really had an impact, such as USAAF bombing of German oil refineries and aircraft factories. As regards this last, the 'Big Week' American air raids of 20–25 February 1944 dealt a heavy blow to German aircraft production from which it struggled to recover. Along with the attrition of Luftwaffe forces in the air, now that the American raids had superb fighter cover, the ability of Germany to defend itself in the air was fast collapsing.[3]

The critics' remaining main point, concerning hindsight, is the least cogent. One wonders where the world would be without hindsight, which is the principal resource for learning from experience. In the case of area bombing there is much to profit from it. For one thing, it reminds us that there had been 40 years of pre-Second World War debate about the morality and legality of area bombing, a fact that explains why Neville Chamberlain, while Prime Minister, twice told MPs that bombing civilians was not British government policy because – as he himself put it – it would constitute a crime in international law.

But in fact one scarcely needs hindsight if one knows anything about the St Petersburg Declaration of 1868, or has read Hugo Grotius' 1625 book on the morality and laws of war, or Thucydides' account of the Mytilenean Debate, in which the Athenians discussed a plan to massacre the entire population of an enemy city. The place of civilians in war has been debated in the Western tradition for 2,500 years, and for the past 300 years has turned on the notion of international norms. How, therefore, can assessing our deliberate mass bombing of civilian populations for its morality and its status in international law be considered as mere hindsight? By this reasoning, we would be obliged to say that the Nazis did not commit horrendous crimes against humanity because the concept of crimes against humanity was not defined until the post-war Nuremberg Principles.

One of the most contentious points in the whole bombing debate is the USAAF atom bombing of Hiroshima and Nagasaki, still vigorously defended on the grounds of saving US military lives and 'shortening the war'. But the key point here is that Japan had been suing for peace for months before the atom bomb attacks took place. The US government refused to talk on the grounds that it would accept nothing less than unconditional surrender, whereas the Japanese asked for one condition: retention of their Emperor. The US refusal was in line with the Casablanca agreement between Roosevelt and Churchill that only unconditional surrender would be accepted. The Japanese request concerning their Emperor was eventually granted, but not before the atom bombs were dropped. The reasons for the delay, and the suspicions it invites, constitute serious questions against US conduct in this regard, and this book is not alone in questioning it: perhaps the single most telling revelation in this arena is what Robert S. McNamara had to say in the compelling documentary film *The Fog of War*.

One point of surmise in the preceding chapters concerns the apparent autonomy of RAF Bomber Command in the prosecution of its own war, at times in direct opposition to demands for redirection of its efforts, as in the tactical bombing campaign associated with the D-Day landings, and the attack on enemy oil installations. Since pointing out in these pages what looks almost like indifference on the part of Churchill and Sir Alan Brooke, Chief of the Imperial General Staff, to Sir Arthur Harris's endeavours, an interesting hint arrived in a letter from R. E. George concerning the role of Churchill's scientific advisor, Viscount Cherwell (Frederick A. Lindemann). It would seem that Cherwell was as persuaded as were Portal and Harris about the war-winning potential of bombing, and his support must therefore have been a factor in the independence of Sir Arthur Harris at Bomber Command, and the continued volume of resources poured into its efforts. P. M. S. Blackett, who had served on the Tizard Committee on early air warning systems before the outbreak of war (Cherwell did not believe in their efficacy and argued that efforts to develop radar should cease), reported a discussion with Cherwell in 1942 in which the latter said 'that he considered any diversion of aircraft production and supply to the anti-submarine campaign, to army co-operation, or even to fighter defence, in fact to anything but bombing, as being a disastrous mistake.' This view so closely parallels Sir Arthur Harris' own that it is hard not to believe that either Cherwell or Harris was quoting the other here. Almost certainly it was the advisor quoting the Air Marshall, but the advisor had the ear of Churchill and the War Cabinet.

As noted, controversy was also generated by two corollaries to my conclusion that, in fighting a just and justifiable war against the criminal Nazi regime and Japanese aggression, the Allied air forces committed a wrong by engaging in area bombing of civilian populations. One corollary was that in ideal circumstances Allied aircrews should, had they been given the choice, have elected to attack genuine military and industrial targets only, rather than participating in indiscriminate attacks on civilian populations. The other was that in a crucial respect the terrorist atrocities of 11 September 2001 in New York and Washington and others like them (for example, the subsequent terrorist bombings in Madrid, London and Bombay) resemble 'area bombing' of civilians, namely, in their goal of assaulting and undermining the morale of the attacked population, by hurting and terrorising it.

On the first point all that is needed is iteration of what is said about it in the final chapter, which is that of course this would be the ideal option, but that it is understandable and highly mitigatable that most aircrew did not even consider this option. In large part this was because their duties were presented to them as genuinely aiding the war effort against a pernicious enemy, and moreover they were under military discipline in doing so, a point worth acknowledging despite the fact that international law since the American Civil War has not recognised a defence of 'following orders' in the commission of crimes. A dispassionate consideration of the point would recognise the joint validity of saying this is what in the ideal aircrew should have done, and that aircrew are nevertheless not individually culpable for being required to carry out the plans and directions of those focally responsible for it – in the UK, Sir Charles Portal and Sir Arthur Harris, with the morally lax supervision of Sir Alan Brooke, the equivocal position of Sir Winston Churchill, and the questionable agreement of the War Cabinet. In the US a similar distribution of responsibility could be made, reaching from Presidents Roosevelt and Truman down to General Curtis Le May.

And even at this level of responsibility a far bigger picture is required: whereas Sir Arthur Harris and General Curtis Le May were the principal hands-on architects of campaigns of mass murder by bombing, the others to whom responsibility also devolves were responsible for a broader and more complex set of urgencies aimed at defeating wicked aggressor regimes, and it would be nothing more than naive puritanism to say that the wrong of area bombing trumps the claim of overall victory. What is needed is an ability to hold together in one's mind all the elements of the picture, and to see the rights and wrongs in their due proportion and relationship. Simple finger-pointing gets us nowhere.

The 9/11 point is a different matter. Those who have most belligerently opposed the comparison, such as Christopher Hitchins, are right to point out that whereas World War II area bombing occurred in the setting of declared war between states whose military forces were engaged in combat to the death, the 9/11 attacks were acts of terrorism carried out not by one state against another, but by an egregiously nasty private organisation with no interest in anything other than the unrestrained furtherance of its agenda. I grant this, and indeed all the other differences, and acknowledge that there is no moral equivalence between Allied military endeavours against the Nazi and Japanese regimes, and the 9/11 attacks, both taken on their own inclusive terms. Instead I argued that in one crucial respect – one respect only – there is a dismaying similarity between area bombing and terrorist bombings: namely, that they both seek to coerce a people by blowing up as many of them as possible and thereby terrorising and demoralising the rest. In this single respect, all acts of mass murder are indeed morally equivalent: and their equivalence lies in their being great wrongs. That was my point; and I adhere to it, because it is surely a profoundly educative one, since it allows one to make a simple but profound emotional connection between one's horror at the 9/11 attacks in which 3000 people died in a single atrocity, to one's horror at the deaths of ten and sometimes twenty times as many in each of the bombings of such places as Hamburg, Dresden, Tokyo, Hiroshima and Nagasaki. This way of grasping the purport of what area bombing meant, really meant, is vital to making a difference to how we behave and what we accept today in the conduct of conflicts. There is nothing abstract or theoretical about the mass murder in which bombing consists: it is real and terrible, and anything that drives the point home has its place in the debate, for in the end the effect on victims, and the atrocity of the act, are indeed one and the same in all cases – in this one crucial, central respect.

Appendix

Schedule of RAF bombing attacks on Germany, with civilian casualties caused and RAF loses sustained.

1940

11/12 May
Mönchengladbach
19 Hampdens, 18 Whitleys (2
Hampdens, 1 Whitley lost)

15/16 May
Ruhrgebiet
(first strategic bombing of German
industry)
39 Wellingtons, 36 Hampdens, 24
Whitleys (1 Wellington crashed in France)

17/18 May
Hamburg, Bremen, Cologne
48 Hampdens to Hamburg, 24 Whitleys
to Bremen, 6 Wellingtons to Cologne (no
losses)

21/22 May
between Mönchengladbach and
Euskirchen, Münster
52 Whitleys, 47 Wellingtons, 25
Hampdens (3 Wellingtons, 1 Hampden, 1
Whitley lost)

22/23 May
Merseberg
35 Hampdens (all but one recalled)

5/6 June
Hamburg
36 Hampdens, 34 Wellingtons, 22
Whitleys, some to the Somme (1
Hampden, 1 Wellington lost)

6/7 June
Hamburg
24 Hampdens (no losses)

14/15 June
Ruhrgebiet, Süddeutschland, Konstanz
24 Wellingtons, 5 Hampdens

17/18 June
Cologne, Ruhrgebiet, Norddeutschland
51 Whitleys, 49 Wellingtons, 39
Hampdens (2 Whitleys lost)

18/19 June
Ruhrgebiet, Mannheim, Bremen,
Hamburg
38 Whitleys, 26 Wellingtons, 5
Hampdens 2 Whitleys, 1 Wellington lost)

19/20 June
between Hamburg and Mannheim
53 Hampdens, 37 Wellingtons, 22
Whitleys (1 Wellington, 1 Whitley lost)

20/21 June
Rheinland
39 Whitleys, 17 Hampdens (1 Hampden,
1 Whitley lost)

21/22 June
Ruhrgebiet, Nord-/Mittel-deutschland
42 Hampdens, 33 Wellingtons, 30
Whitleys (1 Hampden, 1 Wellington lost)

23 June
Osnabrück, Soest, Hamm
26 Blenheims (3 lost)

23/24 June
Bremen, Ruhrgebiet, Rheinland
53 Hampdens, 26 Whitleys (no losses)

30 June/1 July
Darmstadt, Hamburg, Hamm, Hanau
88 aircraft (no losses)

1/2 July
Osnabrück, Kiel
73 aircraft (1 Hampden and 1 Whitley
lost)

3 July
Hamburg
33 Blenheims

5/6 July
Kiel
51 aircraft despatched, did not all bomb
Kiel (1 Wellington lost)

15/16 July
Hamborn, Hannover, Osnabrück,
Paderborn
33 Hampdens (no losses)

17/18 July
Gelsenkirchen
7 Wellingtons to Gelsenkirchen, 3
Hampdens (mine-laying)

26/27 July
Hamm, Ludwigshafen
18 Wellingtons, 9 Whitleys (1 lost)

27/28 July
Hamburg, Bremen, Willhelmshaven,
Borkum
24 Wellingtons, 19 Hampdens (no losses)

29/30 July
Homburg, Cologne, Hamm
76 Hampdens, Wellingtons and Whitleys
(no losses)

5/6 August
Hamburg, Kiel, Willhelmshaven, Wismar
85 Hampdens, Wellingtons and Whitleys
(no losses)

6/7 August
Homburg, Reisholz
26 Wellingtons, also to Holland

7/8 August
Emmerich, Hamm, Soest, Kiel
50 Hampdens and Wellingtons (no losses)

9/10 August
Cologne, Ludwigshafen
38 Wellingtons and Whitleys, also to
Dutch airfields (no losses)

10/11 August
Hamburg
57 Hampdens, Wellingtons and Whitleys
to 9 targets (1 Hampden lost)

11/12 August
Ruhrgebiet
59 Hampdens, Wellingtons and Whitleys
to 6 targets (1 Whitley lost)

16/17 August
Ruhrgebiet, Frankfurt, Augsburg, Jena,
Leuna
150 Blenheims, Hampdens, Wellingtons
and Whitleys, also to Dutch airfields (4
Whitleys, 2 Hampdens, 1 Wellington lost)

17/18 August
Brunswick
102 Blenheims, Hampdens and
Wellingtons to 5 targets, also to Holland,
Belgium and France (no losses)

18/19 August
Rheinfelden, Freiburg
20 Whitleys (no losses)

24/25 August
Stuttgart
68 Wellingtons and Whitleys to 5 targets
(2 Whitleys lost)

25/26 August
Berlin, Bremen, Cologne, Hamm
103 aircraft despatched, with about half
going to Berlin (6 Hampdens, 3
Blenheims lost)

26/27 August
Hannover, Leipzig, Leuna, Nordhausen
99 Blenheims, Hampdens and
Wellingtons (1 Hampden lost)

28/29 August
Berlin
79 Blenheims, Hampdens, Wellingtons
and Whitleys to 6 targets in Germany and
French airfields (1 Blenheim, 1 Hampden
lost)

29/30 August
Bottrop, Essen, Mannheim, Soest
81 Blenheims, Hampdens, Wellingtons
and Whitleys, also to Dutch and French
airfields (1 Blenheim, 1 Hampden lost)

31 August
Berlin, Cologne
77 Blenheims, Hampdens, Wellingtons
and Whitleys, also to Belgian airfields (1
Hampden lost)

3/4 September
Berlin, Magdeburg, Ruhrgebiet
90 Blenheims, Hampdens, Wellingtons
and Whitleys, also to French airfields (no
losses)

4/5 September
Stettin, Magdeburg, Berlin
86 Blenheims, Hampdens, Wellingtons
and Whitleys, also to French airfields (1
Hampden, 1 Whitley lost)

8/9 September
Hamburg, Bremen, Emden
133 Blenheims, Hampdens, Wellingtons
and Whitleys, also to Holland (1
Hampden lost)

10/11 September
Berlin, Bremen
17 Whitleys (2 lost)

23/24 September
Berlin
129 Hampdens, Wellingtons and Whitleys
(1 Hampden, 1 Wellington, 1 Whitley
lost)

26/27 September
Dortmund, Kiel
77 Blenheims, Hampdens, Wellingtons
and Whitleys, also to Channel ports (1
Blenheim, 1 Hampden lost)

5/6 October
Cologne, Gelsenkirchen, Hamm,
Osnabrück, Soest
20 Hampdens (1 lost)

7/8 October
Berlin
140 Blenheims, Hampdens, Wellingtons
and Whitleys (1 Wellington lost)

13/14 October
Ruhrgebiet, Willhelmshaven, Kiel
125 Battles, Blenheims, Hampdens and
Wellingtons (1 Wellington lost)

14/15 October
Berlin, Stettin, Magdeburg, Böhlen
78 Hampdens, Wellingtons and Whitleys,
also to France (2 Hampdens, 1 Wellington
lost, 1 Whitley crashed in England)

16/17 October
Bremen, Kiel, Merseburg
73 Hampdens and Wellingtons, also to
France (2 Hampdens, 1 Wellington lost.
10 Hampdens and 4 Wellingtons crashed
on return)

18/19 October
Hamburg, Lünen
28 Blenheims, Hampdens and Whitleys
(no losses)

19/20 October
Osnabrück
2 Whitleys, 1 Hampden (no losses, 1
Whitley crashed in England)

20/21 October
Berlin
139 Blenheims, Hampdens, Wellingtons
and Whitleys to various targets in
Germany, Italy and occupied countries (1
Hampden and 3 Whitleys lost)

21/22 October
Cologne, Hamburg, Stuttgart, Reisholz
31 Wellingtons, 11 Whitleys (1 Whitley
lost)

28/29 October
Hamburg
97 aircraft to various targets, with 20
Hampdens going to Hamburg (1
Blenheim, 1 Whitley lost)

30/31 October
Duisburg, Emden
28 Blenheims and Wellingtons, also to Belgium and Holland (no losses)

1/2 November
Berlin, Gelsenkirchen, Magdeburg
81 Blenheims, Hampdens, Wellingtons and Whitleys, also to Belgian, Dutch and French airfields (2 Hampdens lost)

6/7 November
Berlin
64 Hampdens, Wellingtons and Whitleys to various targets, with 18 Wellingtons going to Berlin (1 Wellington and 1 Whitley lost)

7/8 November
Essen, Cologne
91 Blenheims, Hampdens, Wellingtons and Whitleys, also to occupied countries (no losses)

12/13 November
Gelsenkirchen
77 Blenheims, Hampdens, Wellingtons and Whitleys to various targets, with 24 Wellingtons to Gelsenkirchen (1 Whitley lost)

14/15 November
Berlin, Hamburg
82 Hampdens, Wellingtons and Whitleys (4 Hampdens, 4 Whitleys, 2 Wellingtons lost)

15/16 November
Hamburg
67 Hampdens, Wellingtons and Whitleys (no losses)

16/17 November
Hamburg, Kiel
130 Blenheims, Hampdens, Wellingtons and Whitleys (2 Wellingtons, 1 Blenheim lost)

17/18 November
Gelsenkirchen, Hamm
49 Wellingtons and Whitleys (no losses)

18/19 November
Merseburg
11 Whitleys (no losses)

20/21 November
Duisburg
68 Blenheims, Hampdens, Wellingtons and Whitleys, with 43 going to Duisburg (1 Whitley lost)

22/23 November
Dortmund, Duisburg, Wanne-Eickel
95 Blenheims, Hampdens, Wellingtons and Whitleys, also to Bordeaux (1 Hampden lost)

24/25 November
Hamburg
42 Blenheims, Hampdens and Wellingtons (1 Blenheim, 1 Hampden lost)

25/26 November
Wilhelmshaven
36 Hampdens, Whitleys and Wellingtons (1 Wellington lost)

27/28 November
Cologne
62 Blenheims, Hampdens, Wellingtons and Whitleys (1 Whitley lost)

28/29 November
Düsseldorf
24 Blenheims (1 lost)

29/30 November
Bremen, Cologne
42 Blenheims, Hampdens, Wellingtons and Whitleys, also to Channel ports (1 Blenheim lost)

3/4 December
Duisburg, Essen, Mannheim
20 Blenheims and Whitleys (1 Blenheim lost, 4 aircraft crashed in England)

4/5 December
Düsseldorf
83 Blenheims, Hampdens, Wellingtons and Whitleys, also to Turin (1 Blenheim and 1 Wellington lost)

5/6 December
Gelsenkirchen
5 Whitleys (no losses)

7/8 December
Düsseldorf
69 Blenheims, Hampdens, Wellingtons and Whitleys, mostly to Düsseldorf (3 Wellingtons, 1 Hampden and 1 Whitley lost)

8/9 December
Düsseldorf
90 Blenheims, Hampdens, Wellingtons
and Whitleys, also to France and airfields
(1 Hampden and 1 Wellington lost)

9/10 December
Bremen
39 Blenheims and Wellingtons, also to
Holland and France (1 Blenheim lost)

11/12 December
Mannheim
42 Blenheims, Wellingtons and Whitleys,
also to France (1 Blenheim and 1
Wellington lost)

13/14 December
Bremen, Kiel
33 Wellingtons and Whitleys (1 Whitley lost)

15/16 December
Berlin, Frankfurt, Kiel
71 Hampdens, Wellingtons and Whitleys
(3 Whitleys lost)

16/17 December
Mannheim (first RAF area bombing)
61 Wellingtons, 35 Whitleys, 29
Hampdens and 9 Blenheims (2
Hampdens and 1 Blenheim lost, 4 aircraft
crashed in England)

17/18 December
Mannheim
9 Whitleys (no losses)

18/19 December
Mannheim
17 Wellingtons and 9 Whitleys (1
Wellington lost)

19/20 December
Cologne, Duisberg, Gelsenkirchen
85 Blenheims, Hampdens, Wellingtons
and Whitleys, also to France (1 Blenheim
lost)

20/21 December
Berlin, Gelsenkirchen
125 Blenheims, Hampdens, Wellingtons
and Whitleys, also to Channel ports (no
losses)

23/24 December
Mannheim, Ludwigshafen
43 Blenheims, Hampdens and
Wellingtons, also to Holland and France
(1 Wellington lost)

29/30 December
Frankfurt/M., Hamm
27 Blenheims, Wellingtons and Whitleys,
also to Boulogne and French airfields (2
Wellingtons lost)

1941

1/2 January
Bremen
141 Blenheims, Hampdens, Wellingtons
and Whitleys, also to Belgian, Dutch and
French ports (no losses, 4 aircraft crashed
in England)

2/3 January
Bremen, Emden
47 Hampdens, Wellingtons and Whitleys,
also to Amsterdam (1 Whitley lost)

3/4 January
Bremen
71 Blenheims, Hampdens, Wellingtons
and Whitleys (1 Whitley lost)

8/9 January
Wilhelmshaven, Emden
48 Hampdens, Wellingtons and Whitleys
(no losses)

9/10 January
Gelsenkirchen
60 Wellingtons, 36 Blenheims, 20
Hampdens, 19 Whitleys (1 Whitley lost)

11/12 January
Wilhelmshaven
35 Hampdens and Wellingtons (no losses)

13/14 January
Wilhelmshaven
24 Wellingtons and Whitleys, also to
French ports (no losses)

15/16 January
Wilhelmshaven
96 Blenheims, Hampdens, Wellingtons
and Whitleys (1 Whitley lost)

16/17 January
Wilhelmshaven
81 Blenheims, Hampdens, Wellingtons
and Whitleys (2 Wellingtons, 2 Whitleys,
1 Hampden lost)

22/23 January
Düsseldorf
28 Wellingtons, 12 Blenheims (no losses)

26/27 January
Hannover
10 Whitleys, 7 Wellingtons (no losses)

29/30 January
Wilhelmshaven
25 Wellingtons, 9 Hampdens (no losses)

4/5 February
Düsseldorf
30 Hampdens (1 lost)

10/11 February
Hannover
112 Wellingtons, 46 Hampdens, 34
Blenheims, 30 Whitleys (2 Wellingtons, 1
Blenheim, 1 Hampden lost, 3 aircraft shot
down in England by German intruders)

11/12 February
Bremen
79 Hampdens, Wellingtons and Whitleys
(no losses, 11 Wellingtons, 7 Whitleys, 4
Hampdens crashed in England)

14/15 February
Gelsenkirchen, Homburg
44 Wellingtons to Gelsenkirchen, 22
Blenheims and 22 Wellingtons to
Homburg (no losses)

15/16 February
Homburg
37 Blenheims and 33 Hampdens (no
losses)

21/22 February
Wilhelmshaven
34 Wellingtons (1 lost), 7 Whitleys to
Düsseldorf

25/26 February
Düsseldorf
43 Wellingtons, 22 Hampdens, 15
Whitleys (1 Wellington lost)

26/27 February
Cologne
126 aircraft

28 February
Wilhelmshaven
116 Blenheims, Hampdens, Wellingtons
and Whitleys (1 Blenheim lost)

1/2 March
Cologne
131 Blenheims, Hampdens, Wellingtons
and Whitleys (5 Whitleys and 1
Wellington lost, 14 aircraft crashed in
England)

3/4 March
Cologne
71 Hampdens, Wellingtons and Whitleys
(1 Hampden lost)

10/11 March
Cologne
19 Hampdens (1 lost)

11/12 March
Kiel
27 Wellingtons (no losses)

12/13 March
Hamburg, Bremen, Berlin
Hamburg: 40 Hampdens, 25 Whitleys, 16
Wellingtons, 4 Manchesters, 3 Halifaxes
(no losses)
Bremen: 54 Wellingtons, 32 Blenheims (1
Blenheim lost)
Berlin: 30 Hampdens, 28 Wellingtons, 14
Whitleys (1 of each lost)

13/14 March
Hamburg
53 Wellingtons, 34 Hampdens, 24
Whitleys, 21 Blenheims, 5 Manchesters, 2
Halifaxes (2 Wellingtons, 2 Whitleys, 1
Blenheim, 1 Hampden lost. 1 Manchester
shot down by intruder in England)

14/15 March
Gelsenkirchen, Düsseldorf
Gelsenkirchen: 61 Wellingtons, 21
Hampdens, 19 Whitleys (1 Wellington
lost)
Düsseldorf: 24 Blenheims (no losses)

15/16 March
Düsseldorf
21 Hampdens (no losses)

17/18 March
Bremen, Wilhelmshaven
57 Hampdens, Wellingtons, Whitleys and
1 Stirling to Bremen, 21 Blenheims to
Wilhelmshaven (no losses, 1 Wellington
shot down by intruder)

18/19 March
Kiel, Wilhelmshaven
Kiel: 40 Hampdens, 34 Wellingtons, 23
Whitleys, 2
Manchesters (no losses)
Wilhelmshaven: 44 Blenheims (1 lost)

19/20 March
Cologne
36 Wellingtons (no losses)

23/24 March
Berlin, Kiel, Hannover
Berlin: 35 Wellingtons and 28 Whitleys
(no losses)
Kiel: 31 Hampdens (no losses)
Hannover: 26 Blenheims (1 lost)
5 Hampdens mine-laying off Kiel

27/28 March
Cologne, Düsseldorf
Cologne: 38 Wellingtons and 1 Stirling (1
Wellington lost)
Düsseldorf: 22 Hampdens. 13 Whitleys, 4
Manchesters (1 Manchester and 1 Whitley
lost)

31 March/1 April
Bremen
28 Wellingtons (1 lost)

7/8 April
Kiel, Bremerhaven
Kiel: 117 Wellingtons, 61 Hampdens, 49
Whitleys, 2 Stirlings (2 Wellingtons, 2
Whitleys lost)
Bremerhaven: 24 Blenheims (no losses)
9 aircraft to Emden

8/9 April
Kiel, Bremerhaven
Kiel: 74 Wellingtons, 44 Whitleys, 29
Hampdens, 12 Manchesters, 1 Stirling (2
Wellingtons, 1 Hampden, 1 Manchester

lost, 9 aircraft crashed in England)
Bremerhaven: 22 Blenheims (no losses)
2 Blenheims to Emden

9/10 April
Berlin
36 Wellingtons, 24 Hampdens, 17
Whitleys, 3 Stirlings (3 Wellingtons, 1
Stirling, 1 Whitley lost)
7 aircraft to Emden

10/11 April
Düsseldorf
29 Hampdens and 24 Whitleys (5
Hampdens lost)

15/16 April
Kiel
49 Wellingtons, 21 Whitleys, 19
Hampdens, 5 Halifaxes, 2 Stirlings (1
Wellington lost)

16/17 April
Bremen
62 Wellingtons, 24 Whitleys, 21
Hampdens (1 Whitley lost)

17/18 April
Berlin
50 Wellingtons, 39 Hampdens, 28
Whitleys, 1 Stirling (5 Whitleys, 2
Hampdens, 1 Wellington lost)

20/21 April
Cologne
37 Wellingtons, 12 Whitleys, 11
Hampdens, 1 Stirling (2 Hampdens, 1
Wellington lost)

24/25 April
Kiel
39 Wellingtons, 19 Whitleys, 10
Hampdens, 1 Stirling (1 Whitley lost)
9 aircraft to Wilhelmshaven

25/26 April
Kiel
38 Wellingtons, 14 Whitleys, 10
Hampdens (1 Wellington lost)
5 aircraft to Bremerhaven, 4 to Emden, 3
to Berlin (no losses)

26/27 April
Hamburg
28 Hampdens and 22 Wellingtons (1
Hampden lost)
4 Wellingtons to Emden (no losses)

29/30 April
Mannheim
42 Wellingtons, 15 Whitleys, 14
Hampdens (1 Wellington lost)

30 April/1 May
Kiel
43 Wellingtons, 25 Whitleys, 13
Hampdens (no losses)

2/3 May
Hamburg
49 Wellingtons, 21 Whitleys, 19
Hampdens, 3 Manchesters, 3 Stirlings (1
Hampden, 1 Manchester, 1 Whitley lost)
17 Wellingtons and 6 Whitleys to Emden
(1 Wellington lost)

3/4 May
Cologne
37 Wellingtons, 35 Whitleys, 27
Hampdens, 2 Manchesters (no losses)

5/6 May
Mannheim
70 Wellingtons, 33 Hampdens, 30 Whitleys,
4 Manchesters, 4 Stirlings (no losses)

6/7 May
Hamburg
50 Wellingtons, 31 Whitleys, 27
Hampdens, 4 Manchesters, 3 Stirlings (no
losses)

8/9 May
Hamburg, Bremen, Bremerhaven, Kiel
Hamburg: 100 Wellingtons, 78
Hampdens, 9 Manchesters, 1Stirling (3
Wellingtons, 1 Hampden lost)
Bremen: 78 Whitleys, 55 Wellingtons (3
Wellingtons, 2 Whitleys lost)
Kiel: 23 Blenheims (no losses)
Bremerhaven: 4 Blenheims (no losses)

9/10 May
Mannheim, Ludwigshafen
69 Wellingtons, 42 Whitleys, 24
Hampdens, 11 Manchesters (1
Wellington, 1 Whitley lost)

10/11 May
Hamburg, Berlin
Hamburg: 60 Wellingtons, 35 Hampdens,
23 Whitleys, 1 Manchester (3
Wellingtons, 1 Whitley lost)
Berlin: 23 aircraft (2 Stirlings, 1
Manchesters lost) 6 Wellingtons to
Emden (no losses)

11/12 May
Hamburg, Bremen
Hamburg: 91 Wellingtons, 1 Stirling (3
Wellingtons lost)
Bremen: 48 Whitleys, 31 Hampdens, 2
Manchesters (1 Hampden lost)

12/13 May
Mannheim, Ludwigshafen, Cologne
42 Wellingtons, 41 Hampdens, 18
Whitleys, 4 Manchesters, with 65 going
to Mannheim and 40 to Ludwigshafen.
16 aircraft reported bombing Cologne (no
losses)

15/16 May
Hannover
55 Wellingtons, 27 Hampdens, 18
Whitleys, 1 Stirling (2 Wellingtons, 1
Hampden lost)
14 Manchesters to Berlin (1 lost)

16/17 May
Cologne
48 Wellingtons, 24 Hampdens, 20
Whitleys, 1 Stirling (1 Whitley lost)

17/18 May
Cologne, Kiel
Cologne: 44 Wellingtons, 28 Whitleys, 23
Hampdens (1 Hampden, 1 Whitley lost)
Kiel: 33 Wellingtons, 19 Whitleys, 18
Hampdens (no losses)

23/24 May
Cologne
24 Hampdens, 22 Wellingtons, 5 Stirlings
(no losses)

27/28 May
Cologne
46 Whitleys, 18 Wellingtons (no losses)

28/29 May
Kiel
14 Whitleys (1 lost)

2/3 June
Düsseldorf, Duisburg, Berlin
Düsseldorf: 68 Wellingtons, 43
Hampdens, 39 Whitleys (2 Hampdens, 1
Whitley lost)
Duisburg: 25 Wellingtons (no losses)
Berlin: 8 Stirlings, 3 Wellingtons (1
Stirling lost)

11 June
Bremerhaven
25 Blenheims (1 lost, 19 turned back)

11/12 June
Düsseldorf, Duisburg
Düsseldorf: 92 Wellingtons, 6 Stirlings (6
Wellingtons lost)
Duisburg: 36 Whitleys, 35 Hampdens, 9
Halifaxes (1 Whitley lost)
20 Hampdens mine-laying in Kiel Bay (1
lost)

12/13 June
Soest, Schwerte, Hamm, Osnabrück, Hüls
Soest: 91 Hampdens (2 lost)
Schwerte: 80 Whitleys, 4 Wellingtons (3
Whitleys lost)
Hamm: 82 Wellingtons (no losses)
Osnabrück: 61 Wellingtons (1 lost)
Hüls: 11 Halifaxes, 7 Stirlings (no losses)

14/15 June
Cologne
29 Hampdens (no losses)

15/16 June
Cologne, Düsseldorf, Hannover
Cologne: 49 Wellingtons, 42 Hampdens
(1 Hampden lost)
Düsseldorf: 31 Whitleys, 28 Wellingtons
(no losses)
Hannover: 16 aircraft (no losses)

16/17 June
Cologne, Düsseldorf, Duisburg
Cologne: 47 Hampdens, 39 Whitleys, 16
Wellingtons, 3 Halifaxes (1 Whitley, 1
Wellington lost)
Düsseldorf: 65 Wellingtons, 7 Stirlings
(no losses)
Duisburg: 39 Wellingtons (1 lost)

17/18 June
Cologne, Düsseldorf, Duisburg
Cologne: 43 Hampdens, 33 Whitleys (1
Whitley lost)
Düsseldorf: 57 Wellingtons (no losses)
Duisburg: 26 Wellingtons (no losses)
11 aircraft to Hannover (no losses)

19/20 June
Cologne, Düsseldorf
Cologne: 28 Wellingtons (1 lost)
Düsseldorf: 20 Whitleys (1 lost)

20/21 June
Kiel
47 Wellingtons, 24 Hampdens, 20
Whitleys, 13 Stirlings, 11 Halifaxes (2
Wellingtons lost)

21/22 June
Cologne, Düsseldorf
Cologne: 68 Wellingtons (no losses)
Düsseldorf: 28 Hampdens, 28 Whitleys
(no losses)

22/23 June
Bremen, Wilhelmshaven
Bremen: 45 Wellingtons, 25 Hampdens
(1 of each lost)
Wilhelmshaven: 16 Wellingtons, 11
Whitleys
3 Wellingtons to Emden, 1 Hampden to
Düsseldorf (no losses)

23/24 June
Cologne, Kiel, Düsseldorf
Cologne: 44 Wellingtons, 18 Whitleys (1
Wellington lost)
Düsseldorf: 30 Hampdens, 11
Manchesters (no losses)
Kiel: 13 Stirlings, 10 Halifaxes, 3
Wellingtons (1 Halifax lost)
1 aircraft to each of Bremen, Emden and
Hannover (no losses)

24/25 June
Cologne, Kiel, Düsseldorf
Cologne: 32 Whitleys, 22 Wellingtons (no
losses)
Kiel: 25 Hampdens, 23 Wellingtons (1
Wellington lost)
Düsseldorf: 23 Wellingtons, 8
Manchesters (no losses)

25/26 June
Bremen, Kiel
Bremen: 56 Wellingtons, 8 Whitleys (1
Wellington lost)
Kiel: 30 Hampdens, 17 Wellingtons (1
Hampden lost)
1 aircraft each to Cologne and Düsseldorf
(no losses)

26/27 June
Cologne, Düsseldorf, Kiel
Cologne: 32 Wellingtons, 19 Whitleys (1
Wellington lost)
Düsseldorf: 30 Hampdens, 14
Wellingtons (1 Wellington lost)
Kiel: 18 Manchesters, 15 Stirlings, 8
Halifaxes (2 Manchesters lost)

27/28 June
Bremen
73 Wellingtons, 35 Whitleys (11
Whitleys, 3 Wellingtons lost)
3 aircraft to Emden, 1 to Cologne, 1 to
Düsseldorf (no losses)

29/30 June
Bremen, Hamburg
Bremen: 52 Wellingtons, 30 Hampdens,
24 Whitleys (4 Wellingtons, 2 Hampdens,
1 Whitley lost)
Hamburg: 13 Stirlings, 7 Wellingtons, 6
Manchesters, 2 Halifaxes (4 Stirlings, 2
Wellingtons lost)

30 June/1 July
Ruhrgebiet
32 Wellingtons, 18 Whitleys, 14
Hampdens (2 Hampdens, 2 Whitleys lost)

2/3 July
Bremen, Cologne, Duisburg
Bremen: 57 Wellingtons, 6 Stirlings, 4
Halifaxes (1 Wellington lost)
Cologne: 33 Whitleys, 9 Wellingtons (1
Wellington lost)
Duisburg: 39 Hampdens (2 lost)

3/4 July
Essen, Bremen
Essen: 61 Wellingtons, 29 Whitleys (2 of
each lost)
Bremen: 39 Hampdens, 29 Wellingtons
(2 Wellingtons, 1 Hampden lost)

5/6 July
Münster, Osnabrück, Bielfeld
Münster: 65 Wellingtons, 29 Whitleys (1
Whitley lost)
Osnabrück: 39 Hampdens (3 lost)
Bielfeld: 33 Wellingtons (no losses)
13 Halifaxes, 3 Stirlings to Magdeburg
(no losses)

6/7 July
Münster, Dortmund
Münster: 47 Wellingtons (2 lost)
Dortmund: 31 Whitleys, 15 Wellingtons
(2 Whitleys lost)
2 Wellingtons to Emden

7/8 July
Cologne, Osnabrück, Münster
Cologne: 114 Wellingtons (3 lost)
Osnabrück: 54 Whitleys, 18 Wellingtons
(3 Whitleys lost)
Münster: 49 Wellingtons (3 lost)
40 Hampdens to Mönchengladbach (2
lost)
14 Halifaxes, 3 Stirlings to Frankfurt

8/9 July
Hamm, Münster, Bielefeld, Merseburg
Hamm: 45 Hampdens, 28 Whitleys (4
Whitleys, 3 Hampdens lost)
Münster: 51 Wellingtons (1 lost)
Bielefeld: 33 Wellingtons (no losses)
Merseburg: 13 Halifaxes, 1 Stirling (1
Halifax lost)

9/10 July
Aachen, Osnabrück
Aachen: 39 Hampdens, 27 Whitleys, 16
Wellingtons (1 Hampden, 1 Whitley lost)
Osnabrück: 57 Wellingtons (2 lost)

10/11 July
Cologne
98 Wellingtons, 32 Hampdens (2
Wellingtons lost)

11/12 July
Wilhelmshaven
36 Hampdens (no losses)

12/13 July
Bremen
33 Hampdens, 28 Wellingtons (no losses)

14/15 July
Bremen, Hannover
Bremen: 78 Wellingtons, 19 Whitleys (4
Wellingtons lost)
Hannover: 44 Hampdens, 21
Wellingtons, 14 Halifaxes, 6 Stirlings (2
Wellingtons lost)

16/17 July
Hamburg
51 Wellingtons, 32 Hampdens, 24
Whitleys (3 Wellingtons, 1 Hampden
lost)

17/18 July
Cologne
50 Wellingtons, 25 Hampdens (no losses)

19/20 July
Hannover
20 Whitleys, 17 Wellingtons, 12
Hampdens (1 Wellington, 1 Whitley lost)

20/21 July
Cologne
46 Wellingtons, 39 Hampdens, 25
Whitleys, 3 Stirlings (no losses)

21/22 July
Frankfurt, Mannheim
Frankfurt: 37 Wellingtons, 34 Hampdens
(no losses)
Mannheim: 36 Wellingtons, 8 Halifaxes
(1 Wellington lost)

22/23 July
Frankfurt, Mannheim
Frankfurt: 34 Hampdens, 16 Whitleys, 13
Wellingtons (no losses)
Mannheim: 29 Wellingtons (no losses)

23/24 July
Mannheim, Frankfurt
Mannheim: 51 Wellingtons (no losses)
Frankfurt: 33 Hampdens (1 lost)

24/25 July
Kiel, Emden
Kiel: 34 Wellingtons, 30 Hampdens (1 of
each lost)
Emden: 31 Whitleys, 16 Wellingtons (2
Wellingtons lost)

25/26 July
Hannover, Hamburg
Hannover: 30 Hampdens, 25 Whitleys (4
Whitleys, 1 Hampden lost)
Hamburg: 43 Wellingtons (2 lost)

30/31 July
Cologne
62 Wellingtons, 42 Hampdens, 7
Halifaxes, 5 Stirlings (2 Hampdens, 1
Wellington lost, 6 aircraft crashed in
England)

2/3 August
Hamburg, Berlin, Kiel
Hamburg: 58 Wellingtons, 21 Whitleys, 1
Stirling (2 Wellingtons lost)
Berlin: 40 Wellingtons, 8 Halifaxes, 5
Stirlings (3 Wellingtons, 1 Stirling lost)
Kiel: 50 Hampdens (5 lost)
5 Hampdens mine-laying off Kiel (no
losses)

5/6 August
Mannheim, Karlsruhe, Frankfurt
Mannheim: 65 Wellingtons, 33
Hampdens (2 Wellingtons, 1 Hampden
lost)
Karlsruhe: 50 Hampdens, 28 Wellingtons,
11 Halifaxes, 8
Stirlings (1 Halifax, 1 Hampden, 1
Wellington lost)
Frankfurt: 46 Whitleys, 22 Wellingtons (2
Whitleys, 1 Wellington lost)
13 Wellingtons to Aachen (2 lost)

6/7 August
Frankfurt, Mannheim, Karlsruhe
Frankfurt: 34 Whitleys, 19 Wellingtons (2
of each lost)
Mannheim: 38 Wellingtons (no losses)
Karlsruhe: 38 Hampdens (1 lost)

7/8 August
Essen, Hamm, Dortmund
Essen: 54 Hampdens, 32 Wellingtons, 9
Halifaxes, 8 Stirlings, 3 Manchesters (2
Hampdens, 1 Stirling lost)
Hamm: 45 Welingtons, 1 Stirling (no
losses)
Dortmund: 20 Wellingtons, 20 Whitleys
(no losses)

8/9 August
Kiel, Hamburg
Kiel: 50 Hampdens, 4 Whitleys (2
Hampdens, 1 Whitley lost)
Hamburg: 44 Wellingtons (1 lost)

11/12 August
Krefeld, Mönchengladbach
Krefeld: 20 Hampdens, 9 Whitleys (no
losses)
Mönchengladbach: 29 Wellingtons (no
losses)

12/13 August
Berlin, Hannover, Magdeburg, Essen
Berlin: 40 Wellingtons, 12 Halifaxes, 9
Stirlings, 9 Manchesters (3 Manchesters, 3
Wellingtons, 2 Halifaxes, 1 Stirling lost)
Hannover: 65 Wellingtons, 13 Hampdens
(4 Wellingtons lost)
Magdeburg: 36 Hampdens (no losses)
Essen: 30 Wellingtons, 3 Stirlings, 2
Halifaxes (1 Wellington shot down in
England by an intruder)

14/15 August
Hannover, Brunswick, Magdeburg
Hannover: 96 Wellingtons, 55 Whitleys,
1 Stirling (5 Wellingtons, 4 Whitleys lost)
Brunswick: 81 Hampdens (1 lost)
Magdeburg: 27 Wellingtons, 9 Halifaxes,
9 Stirlings, 7 Manchesters (2 Wellingtons,
1 Halifax, 1 Stirling lost)

16/17 August
Cologne, Düsseldorf, Duisburg
Cologne: 37 Wellingtons, 29 Whitleys, 6
Halifaxes (7 Whitleys, 1 Wellington lost)
Düsseldorf: 52 Hampdens, 6 Manchesters
(3 Hampdens, 2 Manchesters lost)
Duisburg: 54 Wellingtons (1 lost)

17/18 August
Bremen, Duisburg
Bremen: 39 Hampdens, 20 Whitleys (2
Hampdens lost)
Duisburg: 41 Wellingtons (no losses)

18/19 August
Cologne, Duisburg
Cologne: 42 Hampdens, 17 Whitleys, 3
Wellingtons (5 Whitleys, 1 Wellington
lost)
Duisburg: 41 Wellingtons (2 lost)

19/20 August
Kiel
54 Wellingtons, 41 Hampdens, 7
Stirlings, 6 Halifaxes (3 Wellingtons, 1
Hampden lost)

22/23 August
Mannheim
51 Wellingtons, 41 Hampdens (1
Hampden lost)

24/25 August
Düsseldorf
25 Whitleys, 12 Hampdens, 7 Halifaxes
(2 Whitleys, 1 Halifax lost)

25/26 August
Karlsruhe, Mannheim
Karlsruhe: 37 Wellingtons, 12 Stirlings (2
Wellingtons, 1 Stirling lost)
Mannheim: 38 Hampdens, 7 Manchesters
(3 Hampdens lost)

26/27 August
Cologne
47 Wellingtons, 29 Hampdens. 22
Whitleys, 1 Manchester (1 Wellington, 1
Whitley lost)

27/28 August
Mannheim
35 Hampdens, 41 Wellingtons, 15
Whitleys (no losses. 7 Wellingtons, 1
Whitley crashed in England)

28/29 August
Duisburg
60 Wellingtons, 30 Hampdens, 13
Stirlings, 9 Halifaxes, 6 Manchesters (3
Wellingtons, 1 Halifax, 1 Hampden, 1
Stirling lost)
6 Hampdens on searchlight-suppression
duty (2 lost)

29/30 August
Frankfurt, Mannheim
Frankfurt: 73 Hampdens. 62 Whitleys, 5
Halifaxes, 3 Manchesters (2 Hampdens, 1
Whitey lost)
Mannheim: 94 Wellingtons (2 lost)

31 August
Cologne, Essen
Cologne: 45 Wellingtons, 39 Hampdens, 7 Halifaxes, 6 Manchesters, 6 Stirlings (3 Hampdens, 1 Manchester, 1 Wellington lost. 1 Wellington shot down by an intruder in England)
Essen: 43 Whitleys, 28 Wellingtons (1 Whitley lost)

2/3 September
Frankfurt, Berlin
Frankfurt: 71 Wellingtons, 44 Whitleys, 11 Hampdens (3 Wellingtons, 1 Hampden lost)
Berlin: 32 Hampdens. 7 Halifaxes, 6 Stirlings, 4 Manchesters (2 Halifaxes, 2 Hampdens, 1 Manchester lost)

6/7 September
Hüls
41 Whitleys, 27 Wellingtons, 18 Hampdens (5 Whitleys, 2 Wellingtons lost)

7/8 September
Berlin, Kiel
Berlin: 103 Wellingtons, 43 Hampdens, 31 Whitleys, 10 Stirlings, 6 Halifaxes, 4 Manchesters (8 Wellingtons, 2 Hampdens, 2 Whitleys, 2 Stirlings, 1 Manchester lost)
Kiel: 30 Wellingtons, 18 Hampdens, 3 Stirlings (2 Hampdens, 1 Wellington lost)

8/9 September
Kassel
52 Wellingtons, 27 Hampdens, 16 Whitleys (no losses)

11/12 September
Rostock, Kiel, Warnemünde
Rostock: 39 Hampdens, 12 Wellingtons, 5 Manchesters (2 Hampdens lost)
Kiel: 55 Wellingtons (2 lost)
Warnemünde: 32 Whitleys (1 lost)

12/13 September
Frankfurt
71 Wellingtons, 31 Hampdens, 18 Whitleys, 9 Stirlings (2 Wellingtons lost)

15/16 September
Hamburg
169 aircraft (3 Wellingtons, 2 Hampdens, 1 Halifax, 1 Stirling, 1 Whitley lost)

16/17 September
Karlsruhe
55 Wellingtons (no losses)

17/18 September
Karlsruhe
38 Wellingtons (1 lost)

19/20 September
Stettin
72 aircraft, mostly Wellingtons (1 Wellington, 1 Whitley lost)

20/21 September
Berlin, Frankfurt
Berlin: 74 aircraft, all recalled due to weather. 10 did not receive signal and carried on, none reached Berlin. (3 Wellingtons, 1 Whitley lost. 12 aircraft crashed in England)

26/27 September
Cologne, Emden, Mannheim
104 aircraft, all recalled due to fog. 23 aircraft carried on. (1 Wellington lost. 4 Wellingtons crashed in England)

28/29 September
Frankfurt
30 Hampdens, 14 Wellingtons (1 Hampden, 1 Wellington lost. 5 aircraft crashed in England)
6 Wellingtons, 1 Stirling to Emden (no losses)

29/30 September
Stettin, Hamburg
Stettin: 67 Wellingtons, 56 Whitleys, 10 Stirlings, 6 Halifaxes (4 Whitleys, 2 Wellingtons, 2 Stirlings lost)
Hamburg: 93 aircraft, most Hampdens and Wellingtons (2 Wellingtons lost, 2 Hampdens crashed in England)

30 September/1 October
Hamburg, Stettin
Hamburg: 48 Hampdens, 24 Wellingtons, 10 Whitleys (1 Wellington lost)
Stettin: 40 Wellingtons (no losses)

1/2 October
Karlsruhe, Stuttgart
Karlsruhe: 44 Hampdens, 1 Wellington, all recalled due to fog. 3 flew on to Karlsruhe, 23 bombed alternative targets (1 Wellington lost)
Stuttgart: 27 Whitleys, 4 Wellingtons (no losses)

10/11 October
Essen, Cologne
Essen: 78 aircraft (2 Hampdens, 2 Whitleys lost)
Cologne: 69 aircraft (5 Wellingtons lost)
5 Hampdens on searchlight-suppression raids in Essen and Cologne

12/13 October
Nuremberg, Bremen, Hüls
Nuremberg: 82 Wellingtons, 54 Whitleys, 9 Halifaxes, 7 Stirlings (5 Wellingtons, 1 Halifax, 1 Stirling, 1 Whitley lost. 5 aircraft crashed in England)
Bremen: 99 aircraft, mostly Wellingtons and Hampdens (2 Wellingtons, 1 Hampden lost)
Hüls: 79 Hampdens, 11 Manchesters (1 of each lost)

13/14 October
Düsseldorf, Cologne
Düsseldorf: 53 Wellingtons, 7 Stirlings (1 Wellington lost)
Cologne: 30 Hampdens, 9 Manchesters

14/15 October
Nuremberg
58 Wellingtons, 13 Whitleys, 5 Halifaxes, 4 Stirlings (4 Wellingtons lost)

15/16 October
Cologne
27 Wellingtons, 7 Stirlings (3 Wellingtons lost)

16/17 October
Duisburg
47 Wellingtons, 26 Hampdens, 14 Whitleys (1 Wellington lost)
8 Hampdens on searchlight-suppression flights

20/21 October
Bremen, Wilhelmshaven, Emden
Bremen: 82 Hampdens, 48 Wellingtons, 15 Stirlings, 8b Manchesters (2 Hampdens, 2 Wellingtons, 1 Manchester lost)
Wilhelmshaven: 40 Whitleys, 4 Wellingtons, 3 Hampdens (no losses)
Emden: 35 Wellingtons, 1 Halifax (1 Wellington lost)

21/22 October
Bremen
136 aircraft (2 Wellingtons, 1 Hampden lost)
4 Manchesters to Kiel Bay

22/23 October
Mannheim
50 Wellingtons, 45 Hampdens, 22 Whitleys, 6 Halifaxes (3 Wellingtons, 1 Hampden lost)

23/24 October
Kiel
43 Wellingtons, 38 Hampdens, 27 Whitleys, 6 Manchesters (1 Hampden lost)

24/25 October
Frankfurt
70 aircraft (2 Wellingtons, 1 Hampden, 1 Whitley lost)

26/27 October
Hamburg
115 aircraft (3 Wellingtons, 1 Hampden lost)
5 Hampdens mine-laying at Kiel Bay

31 October
Hamburg, Bremen
Hamburg: 123 aircraft (4 Whitleys lost)
Bremen: 40 Wellingtons, 8 Stirlings (1 Wellington lost)

1/2 November
Kiel
72 Wellingtons, 32 Hampdens, 30 Whitleys (2 Whitleys, 1 Hampden lost)
5 Hampdens, 2 Manchesters mine-laying in Kiel Bay

4/5 November
Essen
28 Wellingtons (no losses)

7/8 November
Berlin, Cologne, Mannheim
Berlin: 101 Wellingtons, 42 Whitleys, 17
Stirlings, 9 Halifaxes (10 Wellingtons, 9
Whitleys, 2 Stirlings lost)
Cologne: 61 Hampdens, 14 Manchesters
(no losses)
Mannheim: 53 Wellingtons, 2 Stirlings (7
Wellingtons lost)
30 Halifaxes, Hampdens, Wellingtons,
Whitleys on rover patrols in Essen and
other areas (6 aircraft lost)

8/9 November
Essen
54 aircraft (3 Wellingtons, 2 Whitleys, 1
Hampden lost)
8 Hampdens on searchlight-suppression
flights (1 lost)

9/10 November
Hamburg
103 aircraft (1 Wellington lost)

15/16 November
Emden, Kiel
Emden: 49 aircraft (4 Wellingtons lost)
Kiel: 47 aircraft (4 Wellingtons lost)

26/27 November
Emden
80 Wellingtons, 20 Hampdens (2
Wellingtons, 1 Hampden lost)

27/28 November
Düsseldorf
41 Wellingtons, 34 Hampdens, 6
Manchesters, 5 Stirlings (1 Hampden, 1
Wellington lost)

30 November/1 December
Hamburg, Emden
Hamburg: 92 Wellingtons, 48 Hampdens,
24 Whitleys, 11 Halifaxes, 4 Manchesters,
2 Stirlings (6 Wellingtons, 4 Whitleys, 2
Hampdens, 1 Halifax lost)

7/8 December
Aachen
130 aircraft (1 Halifax, 1 Hampden lost)

11/12 December
Cologne
60 aircraft (1 Halifax lost)

16/17 December
Wilhelmshaven
57 Wellingtons, 14 Hampdens, 12
Whitleys (no losses)

22/23 December
Wilhelmshaven
12 Whitleys, 10 Wellingtons (no losses)

23/24 December
Cologne
33 Wellingtons, 20 Hampdens, 15
Whitleys (no losses)

27/28 December
Düsseldorf
66 Wellingtons, 30 Hampdens, 29
Whitleys, 7 Manchesters (5 Whitleys, 2
Wellingtons lost)

28/29 December
Wilhelmshaven, Hüls, Emden
Wilhelmshaven: 86 Wellingtons (1 lost)
Hüls: 81 Hampdens (4 lost)
Emden: 25 Wellingtons, 14 Whitleys, 1
Stirling (1 Whitley lost)

1942

10/11 January
Wilhelmshaven
124 aircraft (3 Wellingtons, 2 Hampdens
lost)

14/15 January
Hamburg
95 aircraft (2 Hampdens, 2 Wellingtons lost)

15/16 January
Hamburg, Bremen
Hamburg: 96 aircraft (3 Wellingtons, 1

Hampden lost, 8 aircraft crashed in
England)
Emden: 50 aircraft (1 Wellington, 1
Whitley lost)

17/18 January
Bremen
83 aircraft (3 Wellingtons lost, 1 Stirling
crashed in England after being fired on)
24 aircraft to Emden

20/21 January
Emden
20 Wellingtons, 5 Hampdens (3
Wellingtons, 1 Hampden lost)

21/22 January
Emden, Bremen
Bremen: 54 aircraft (2 Hampdens, 1
Wellington lost)
Emden: 38 aircraft (3 Hampdens, 1
Whitley lost)

22/23 January
Münster
47 aircraft (1 Wellington lost)

26/27 January
Hannover, Emden
Hannover: 71 aircraft (no losses)
Emden: 31 aircraft (2 Whitleys lost)
2 Whitleys to Germany on leaflet flights

28/29 January
Münster
55 Wellingtons, 29 Hampdens (4
Hampdens, 1 Wellington lost)

11/12 February
Mannheim
49 aircraft (no losses)

14/15 February
Mannheim
98 aircraft (1 Hampden, 1 Whitley lost)

22/23 February
Wilhelmshaven
31 Wellingtons, 19 Hampdens (no losses)
7 aircraft to Emden, 5 Manchesters mine-
laying off Wilhelmshaven (no losses)

25/26 February
Kiel
43 Wellingtons, 12 Manchesters, 6
Stirlings (3 Wellingtons lost)

8/9 March
Essen
115 Wellingtons, 37 Hampdens, 27
Stirlings, 22 Manchesters, 10 Halifaxes (5
Wellingtons, 2 Manchesters, 1 Stirling lost)

9/10 March
Duisburg, Essen
Essen: 136 Wellingtons, 21 Stirlings, 15
Hampdens, 10 Manchesters, 5 Halifaxes
(2 Wellingtons, 1 Halifax lost)

10/11 March
Essen
56 Wellingtons, 43 Hampdens, 13
Manchesters, 12 Stirlings, 2 Lancasters (2
Hampdens, 1 Stirling, 1 Wellington lost)

12/13 March
Kiel
68 Wellingtons (5 lost)
Emden: 20 Wellingtons, 20 Whitleys (3
Whitleys lost)

13/14 March
Cologne
135 aircraft, 6 types (1 Manchester lost)

25/26 March
Essen
192 Wellingtons, 26 Stirlings, 20
Manchesters, 9 Hampdens, 7 Lancasters
(5 Manchesters, 3 Wellingtons, 1
Hampden lost)

26/27 March
Essen
104 Wellingtons, 11 Stirlings (10
Wellingtons, 1 Stirling lost)
36 aircraft mine-laying off Wilhelmshaven

28/29 March
Lübeck
320 dead
39,000 bombed out
146 Wellingtons, 41 Hampdens, 26
Stirlings, 21 Manchesters (7 Wellingtons,
3 Stirlings, 1 Hampden, 1 Manchester
lost)

1/2 April
Hanau
35 Wellingtons, 14 Hampdens (12
Wellingtons, 1 Hampden lost)

5/6 April
Cologne
179 Wellingtons, 44 Hampdens, 29
Stirlings, 11 Manchesters (4 Wellingtons,
1 Hampden lost)

6/7 April
Essen
110 Wellingtons, 19 Stirlings, 18
Hampdens, 10 Manchesters (2
Hampdens, 1 Manchester, 1 Stirling, 1
Wellington lost)

8/9 April
Hamburg
177 Wellingtons, 41 Hampdens, 22
Stirlings, 13 Manchesters, 12 Halifaxes, 7
Lancasters (4 Wellingtons, 1 Manchester
lost)

10/11 April
Essen
167 Wellingtons, 43 Hampdens, 18
Stirlings, 10 Manchesters, 8 Halifaxes, 8
Lancasters (7 Wellingtons, 5 Hampdens, 1
Halifax, 1 Manchester lost)

12/13 April
Essen
171 Wellingtons, 31 Hampdens, 27
Stirlings, 13 Halifaxes, 9 Manchesters (7
Wellingtons, 2 Hampdens, 1 Halifax lost)

14/15 April
Dortmund
142 Wellingtons, 34 Hampdens, 20
Stirlings, 8 Halifaxes, 4 Manchesters (5
Wellingtons, 4 Hampdens lost)

15/16 April
Dortmund
111 Wellingtons, 19 Hampdens, 15
Stirlings, 7 Manchesters (3 Wellingtons, 1
Stirling lost)

17/18 April
Hamburg
134 Wellingtons, 23 Stirlings, 11
Halifaxes, 5 Manchesters (7 Wellingtons,
1 Manchester lost)

22/23 April
Cologne
64 Wellingtons, 5 Stirlings (2 Wellingtons
lost)

23/24 April
Rostock
93 Wellingtons, 31 Stirlings, 19 Whitleys,
11 Hampdens. 6 Manchesters, 1 Lancaster
(2 Wellingtons, 1 Manchester, 1 Whitley
lost)

24/25 April
Rostock
125 aircraft, 6 types (1 Hampden lost)

25/26 April
Rostock
128 aircraft, 6 types (no losses)

26/27 April
Rostock
200 dead
30,000 bombed out
106 or 109 aircraft, 7 types (1 Stirling, 1
Wellington, 1 Whitley lost)

27/28 April
Cologne
76 Wellingtons, 19 Stirlings. 2 Halifaxes
(6 Wellingtons, 1 Halifax lost)

28/29 April
Kiel
62 Wellingtons, 15 Stirlings, 10
Hampdens, 1 Halifax (5 Wellingtons, 1
Hampden lost)

3/4 May
Hamburg
43 Wellingtons, 20 Halifaxes, 13 Stirlings,
5 Hampdens (3 Halifaxes, 2 Wellingtons
lost)

4/5 May
Stuttgart
69 Wellingtons, 19 Hampdens, 14
Lancasters, 12 Stirlings, 7 Halifaxes (1
Stirling lost)

5/6 May
Stuttgart
49 Wellingtons, 13 Stirlings, 11 Halifaxes,
4 Lancasters (3 Wellingtons, 1 Stirling
lost)

6/7 May
Stuttgart
55 Wellingtons, 15 Stirlings, 10
Hampdens, 10 Lancasters, 7 Halifaxes (5
Wellingtons, 1 Halifax lost)

8/9 May
Warnemünde
98 Wellingtons, 27 Stirlings, 21
Lancasters, 19 Halifaxes, 19 Hampdens, 9
Manchesters (8 Wellingtons, 4 Lancasters,
3 Hampdens, 2 Halifaxes, 1 Manchester,
1 Stirling lost)

19/20 May
Mannheim
105 Wellingtons, 31 Stirlings, 29
Halifaxes, 15 Hampdens, 13 Lancasters, 4
Manchesters (4 Halifaxes, 4 Stirlings, 3
Wellingtons lost)

30/31 May
Cologne
486 dead
45,000 bombed out
602 Wellingtons, 131 Halifaxes, 88
Stirlings. 79 Hampdens, 73 Lancasters, 46
Manchesters, 28 Whitleys (29
Wellingtons, 4 Manchesters, 3 Halifaxes,
2 Stirlings, 1 Hampden, 1 Lancaster, 1
Whitley lost)

1/2 June
Essen
545 Wellingtons, 127 Halifaxes, 77
Stirlings, 74 Lancasters, 71 Hampdens, 33
Manchesters, 29 Whitleys (15
Wellingtons, 8 Halifaxes, 4 Lancasters, 1
Hampden, 1 Manchester, 1 Stirling, 1
Whitley lost)

2/3 June
Essen
97 Wellingtons, 38 Halifaxes, 27
Lancasters, 21 Stirlings, 12 Hampdens (7
Wellingtons, 2 Halifaxes, 2 Lancasters, 2
Stirlings, 1 Hampden lost)

3/4 June
Bremen
170 aircraft, all types (4 Wellingtons, 2
Halifaxes, 2 Lancasters, 2 Stirlings, 1
Manchester lost)

5/6 June
Essen
98 Wellingtons, 33 Halifaxes, 25 Stirlings,
13 Lancasters, 11 Hampdens (8
Wellingtons, 2 Stirlings, 1 Halifax, 1
Lancaster lost)

6/7 June
Emden
124 Wellingtons, 40 Stirlings, 27
Halifaxes, 20 Lancasters, 15 Hampdens, 7
Manchesters (3 Manchesters, 3
Wellingtons, 2 Stirlings, 1 Halifax lost)

8/9 June
Essen
92 Wellingtons, 42 Halifaxes, 14 Stirlings,
13 Lancasters, 9 Hampdens (7
Wellingtons, 7 Halifaxes, 3 Lancasters, 1
Hampden, 1 Stirling lost)

16/17 June
Essen
40 Wellingtons, 39 Halifaxes, 15
Lancasters, 12 Stirlings (4 Halifaxes, 3
Wellingtons, 1 Stirling lost)

19/20 June
Emden
112 Wellingtons, 37 Halifaxes, 25
Stirlings, 11 Hampdens, 9 Lancasters (6
Wellingtons, 2 Stirlings, 1 Halifax lost)

20/21 June
Emden
185 aircraft, 5 types (3 Wellingtons, 2
Stirlings, 1 Halifax, 1 Lancaster lost)

22/23 June
Emden
144 Wellingtons, 38 Stirlings, 26
Halifaxes, 11 Lancasters, 8 Hampdens (4
Wellingtons, 1 Lancaster, 1 Stirling lost)

25/26 June
Bremen
472 Wellingtons, 124 Halifaxes, 96
Lancasters, 69 Stirlings, 51 Blenheims, 50
Hampdens, 50 Whitleys, 24 Bostons, 20
Manchesters, 4 Mosquitoes
(also 102 Hudsons and Wellingtons from
Coastal Command and 5 aircraft from
Army Co-operation Command) (48
aircraft lost)

27/28 June
Bremen
55 Wellingtons, 39 Halifaxes, 26 Stirlings,
24 Lancasters (4 Wellingtons, 2 Halifaxes,
1 Stirling lost)

29/30 June
Bremen
108 Wellingtons, 64 Lancasters, 47
Stirlings, 34 Halifaxes (4 Stirlings, 4
Wellingtons, 3 Halifaxes lost)

2/3 July
Bremen
175 Wellingtons, 53 Lancasters, 35
Halifaxes, 34 Stirlings, 28 Hampdens (8
Wellingtons, 2 Hampdens, 2 Stirlings, 1
Halifax lost)

8/9 July
Wilhelmshaven
137 Wellingtons, 52 Lancasters, 38
Halifaxes, 34 Stirlings, 24 Hampdens (3
Wellingtons, 1 Halifax, 1 Lancaster lost)

11 July
Danzig
44 Lancasters (2 lost)

13/14 July
Duisburg
139 Wellingtons, 33 Halifaxes, 13
Lancasters, 9 Stirlings (3 Wellingtons, 2
Stirlings, 1 Lancaster lost)

19/20 July
Bremen
40 Halifaxes, 31 Stirlings, 28 Lancasters,
also to Vegesack (3 Halifaxes lost)

21/22 July
Duisburg
170 Wellingtons, 39 Halifaxes, 36
Stirlings, 29 Lancasters, 17 Hampdens (10
Wellingtons, 1 Halifax, 1 Hampden lost)

23/24 July
Duisburg
93 Wellingtons, 45 Lancasters, 39
Stirlings, 38 Halifaxes (3 Wellingtons, 2
Lancasters, 2 Stirlings lost)

25/26 July
Duisburg
177 Wellingtons, 48 Stirlings, 41
Halifaxes, 33 Lancasters, 14 Hampdens (7
Wellingtons, 2 Halifaxes, 2 Lancasters, 1
Stirling lost)

26/27 July
Hamburg
337 dead
14,000 bombed out
181 Wellingtons, 77 Lancasters, 73
Halifaxes, 39 Stirlings, 33 Hampdens (15
Wellingtons, 8 Halifaxes, 2 Hampdens, 2
Lancasters, 2 Stirlings lost)

28/29 July
Hamburg
161 Wellingtons, 71 Stirlings, 24
Whitleys (20 Wellingtons, 9 Stirlings, 4
Whitleys lost. 1 Whitley crashed in the
sea)

29/30 July
Saarbrücken
291 aircraft, 5 types (3 Wellingtons, 2
Halifaxes, 2 Lancasters, 2 Stirlings lost)

31 July/1 August
Neuss
279 dead
12,000 bombed out
Düsseldorf
308 Wellingtons, 113 Lancasters, 70
Halifaxes, 61 Stirlings, 54 Hampdens, 24
Whitleys (16 Wellingtons, 5 Hampdens, 4
Halifaxes, 2 Lancasters, 2 Whitleys lost)

6/7 August
Duisburg
216 aircraft, 5 types (2 Halifaxes, 2
Stirlings, 1 Wellington lost)

9/10 August
Osnabrück
91 Wellingtons, 42 Lancasters, 40
Stirlings, 19 Halifaxes (3 Halifaxes, 3
Wellingtons lost)

11/12 August
Mainz
68 Wellingtons, 33 Lancasters, 28
Stirlings, 25 Halifaxes (3 Wellingtons, 2
Halifaxes, 1 Lancaster lost)

12/13 August
Mainz
138 aircraft, 4 types (2 Lancasters, 1
Hampden, 1 Stirling, 1 Wellington lost)

15/16 August
Düsseldorf
131 aircraft, 5 types (2 Lancasters, 1
Hampden, 1 Wellington lost)

17/18 August
Osnabrück
139 aircraft, 5 types (3 Wellingtons, 1
Lancaster, 1 Stirling lost)

18/19 August
Flensburg
118 aircraft, including 31 Pathfinders (2
Wellingtons, 1 Halifax, 1 Stirling lost)

24/25 August
Frankfurt/M.
104 Wellingtons, 61 Lancasters, 53
Stirlings, 8 Halifaxes (6 Lancasters, 5
Wellingtons, 4 Stirlings, 1 Halifax lost)

27/28 August
Kassel
306 aircraft, 5 types (21 Wellingtons, 5
Stirlings, 3 Lancasters, 1 Halifax, 1
Hampden lost)

28/29 August
Nuremberg, Saarbrücken
Nuremberg: 71 Lancasters, 41 Wellingtons,
34 Stirlings, 13 Halifaxes (14 Wellingtons,
4 Lancasters, 3 Stirlings, 2 Halifaxes lost)
Saarbrücken: 71 Wellingtons, 24
Halifaxes, 17 Hampdens, 1 Stirling (4
Hampdens, 2 Halifaxes, 1 Wellington lost)

1/2 September
Saarbrücken
231 aircraft, 5 types (1 Halifax, 1
Lancaster, 1 Stirling, 1 Wellington lost)

2/3 September
Karlsruhe
200 aircraft, 5 types (4 Wellingtons, 2
Lancasters, 1 halifax, 1 Stirling lost)

4/5 September
Bremen
98 Wellingtons, 76 Lancasters, 41
Halifaxes, 36 Stirlings (7 Wellingtons, 3
Lancasters, 1 Halifax, 1 Stirling lost)

6/7 September
Duisburg
207 aircraft, 6 types (5 Wellingtons, 2
Halifaxes, 1 Stirling lost)

8/9 September
Frankfurt M., Rüsselsheim
249 aircraft, 5 types (5 Wellingtons, 2
Halifaxes lost)

10/11 September
Düsseldorf
242 Wellingtons, 89 Lancasters, 59
Halifaxes, 47 Stirlings, 28 Hampdens, 14
Whitleys (20 Wellingtons, 5 Lancasters, 4
Stirlings, 3 Halifaxes, 1 Hampden lost)

13/14 September
Bremen
446 aircraft (15 Wellingtons, 2 Lancasters,
1 Halifax, 1 Hampden, 1 Stirling, 1
Whitley lost)

14/15 September
Wilhelmshaven
202 aircraft, 5 types (2 Wellingtons lost)

16/17 September
Essen
369 aircraft (21 Wellingtons, 9 Lancasters,
5 Stirlings, 3 Halifaxes, 1 Whitley lost)

19/20 September
Saarbrücken, Munich
Saarbrücken: 72 Wellingtons, 41
Halifaxes, 5 Stirlings (3 Wellingtons, 2
Halifaxes lost)
Munich: 68 Lancasters, 21 Stirlings (3 of
each lost)

23/24 September
Wismar
83 Lancasters (4 lost)
24 Stirlings to Vegesack (1 lost)

1/2 October
Wismar
78 Lancasters (2 lost)
25 Stirlings to Lübeck (3 lost)

2/3 October
Krefeld
95 Wellingtons, 39 Halifaxes, 31
Lancasters, 23 Stirlings (3 Halifaxes, 2
Wellingtons, 1 Lancaster, 1 Stirling lost)

5/6 October
Aachen
101 Wellingtons, 74 Lancasters, 59
Halifaxes, 23 Stirlings (5 Halifaxes, 2
Stirlings, 2 Wellingtons, 1 Lancaster lost)

6/7 October
Osnabrück
101 Wellingtons, 68 Lancasters, 38
Stirlings, 30 Halifaxes (2 Halifaxes, 2
Lancasters, 2 Stirlings lost)

13/14 October
Kiel
100 Wellingtons, 82 Lancasters, 78
Halifaxes, 28 Stirlings (5 Wellingtons, 1
each of the others lost)

15/16 October
Cologne
109 Wellingtons, 74 Halifaxes, 62
Lancasters, 44 Stirlings (6 Wellingtons, 5
Halifaxes, 5 Lancasters, 2 Stirlings lost)

9/10 November
Hamburg
74 Wellingtons, 72 Lancasters, 48
Halifaxes, 19 Stirlings (5 Lancasters, 4
Stirlings, 4 Wellingtons, 2 Halifaxes lost)

22/23 November
Stuttgart
97 Lancasters, 59 Wellingtons, 39
Halifaxes, 27 Stirlings (5 Lancasters, 3
Wellingtons, 2 Halifaxes lost)

2/3 December
Frankfurt/M.
48 Halifaxes, 27 Lancasters, 22 Stirlings,
15 Wellingtons (3 Halifaxes, 1 each of the
others lost)

6/7 December
Mannheim
101 Lancasters, 65 Halifaxes, 57
Wellingtons, 49 Stirlings (5 Wellingtons,
3 Halifaxes, 1 Lancaster, 1 Stirling lost)

20/21 December
Duisburg
111 Lancasters, 56 Halifaxes, 39
Wellingtons, 26 Stirlings (6 Lancasters, 4
Wellingtons, 2 Halifaxes lost)

21/22 December
Munich
119 Lancasters, 9 Stirlings, 9 Wellingtons
(8 Lancasters, 3 Stirlings, 1 Wellington
lost)

1943

3/4 January
Essen
3 Pathfinder Mosquitoes, 19 Lancasters (3
Lancasters lost)

4/5 January
Essen
4 Pathfinder Mosquitoes, 29 Lancasters (2
Lancasters lost)

7/8 January
Essen
3 Pathfinder Mosquitoes, 19 Lancasters
(no losses)

8/9 January
Duisburg
3 Pathfinder Mosquitoes, 38 Lancasters (3
Lancasters lost)

9/10 January
Essen
2 Pathfinder Mosquitoes, 50 Lancasters (3
Lancaster lost)

11/12 January
Essen
4 Pathfinder Mosquitoes, 72 Lancasters (1
Lancaster lost)

12/13 January
Essen, Remscheid, Solingen, Wuppertal
4 Pathfinder Mosquitoes, 55 Lancasters (1
Lancaster lost)

13/14 January
Essen
3 Mosquitoes, 66 Lancasters (4 Lancasters
lost)

16/17 January
Berlin
190 Lancasters, 11 Halifaxes (1 Lancasters
lost)

17/18 January
Berlin
170 Lancasters, 17 Halifaxes (19
Lancasters, 3 Halifaxes lost)

27/28 January
Düsseldorf
124 Lancasters, 33 Halifaxes, 5
Mosquitoes (3 Halifaxes, 3 Lancasters lost)

30/31 January
Hamburg
135 Lancasters, 7 Stirlings, 6 Halifaxes (5
Lancasters lost)

2/3 February
Cologne
116 Lancasters, 35 Halifaxes, 8 Stirlings,
2 Mosquitoes (3 Lancasters, 1 Halifax, 1
Stirling lost)

4 February
Emden, Hamm
No aircraft data

3/4 February
Hamburg
84 Halifaxes, 66 Stirlings, 62 Lancasters,
51 Wellingtons (8 Stirlings, 4 Halifaxes, 3
Wellingtons, 1 Lancaster lost)

11/12 February
Wilhelmshaven
129 Lancasters, 40 Halifaxes, 8 Stirlings (3
Lancasters lost)

14 February
Hamm
No aircraft data

14/15 February
Cologne
90 Halifaxes, 85 Wellingtons, 68 Stirlings
(3 of each lost)

18/19 February
Wilhelmshaven
127 Lancasters, 59 Halifaxes, 9 Stirlings
(4 Lancasters lost)

19/20 February
Wilhelmshaven
120 Wellingtons, 110 Halifaxes, 56
Stirlings, 52 Lancasters (5 Stirlings, 4
Lancasters, 3 Wellingtons lost)

21/22 February
Bremen
130 Lancasters, 7 Stirlings, 6 Halifaxes
(no losses)

24/25 February
Wilhelmshaven
71 Wellingtons, 27 Halifaxes, 9 Stirlings,
8 Lancasters (no losses)

25/26 February
Nuremberg, Fürth
169 Lancasters, 104 Halifaxes, 64 Stirlings
(6 Lancasters, 2 Stirlings, 1 Halifax lost)

26/27 February
Cologne
145 Lancasters, 126 Wellingtons, 106
Halifaxes, 46 Stirlings, 4 Mosquitoes (4
Wellingtons, 3 Lancasters, 2 Halifaxes, 1
Stirling lost)

1/2 March
Berlin
709 dead
64, 909 bombed out
156 Lancasters, 86 Halifaxes, 60 Stirlings
(7 Lancasters, 6 Halifaxes, 4 Stirlings lost)

3/4 March
Hamburg, Duisburg
Hamburg: 149 Lancasters, 123
Wellingtons, 83 Halifaxes, 62 Stirlings,
also bombed Wedel (4 Lancasters, 2
Wellingtons, 2 Halifaxes, 2 Stirlings lost)

4 March
Hamm
No aircraft data

5/6 March
Essen
461 dead
30,000 bombed out

8/9 March
Nuremberg
170 Lancasters, 103 Halifaxes, 62 Stirlings
(4 Stirlings, 2 Halifaxes, 2 Lancasters lost)

9/10 March
Munich
142 Lancasters, 81 Halifaxes, 41 Stirlings
(5 Lancasters, 2 Halifaxes, 1 Stirling lost)

11/12 March
Stuttgart
152 Lancasters, 109 Halifaxes, 53 Stirlings
(6 Halifaxes, 3 Stirlings, 2 Lancasters lost)

12/13 March
Essen
158 Wellingtons, 156 Lancasters, 91
Halifaxes, 42 Stirlings, 10 Mosquitoes (8
Lancasters, 7 Halifaxes, 6 Wellingtons, 2
Stirlings lost)

18 March
Bremen
No aircraft data

22 March
Wilhelmshaven
No aircraft data

26/27 March
Duisburg
173 Wellingtons, 157 Lancasters, 114
Halifaxes, 9 Mosquitoes, 2 Stirlings (3
Wellingtons, 1 Halifax, 1 Lancaster, 1
Mosquito lost)

27/28 March
Berlin
191 Lancasters, 124 Halifaxes, 81 Stirlings
(4 Halifaxes, 3 Lancasters, 2 Stirlings lost)

29/30 March
Berlin, Bochum
Berlin: 162 Lancasters, 103 Halifaxes, 64
Stirlings (11 Lancasters, 7 Halifaxes, 3
Stirlings lost)
Bochum: 8 *Oboe* Mosquitoes, 149
Wellingtons (12 Wellingtons lost)

3/4 April
Essen
225 Lancasters, 113 Halifaxes, 10
Mosquitoes (12 Halifaxes, 9 Lancasters
lost, 2 Halifaxes crashed in England)

4/5 April
Kiel
203 Lancasters, 168 Wellingtons, 116
Halifaxes, 90 Stirlings (5 Lancasters, 4
Halifaxes, 2 Stirlings, 1 Wellington lost)

8/9 April
Duisburg
156 Lancasters, 97 Wellingtons, 73
Halifaxes, 56 Stirlings, 10 Mosquitoes (7
Wellingtons, 6 Lancasters, 3 Halifaxes, 3
Stirlings lost)

9/10 April
Duisburg
5 Mosquitoes, 104 Lancasters (8
Lancasters lost)

10/11 April
Frankfurt
144 Wellingtons, 136 Lancasters, 124
Halifaxes, 98 Stirlings (8 Wellingtons, 5
Lancasters, 5 Stirlings, 3 Halifaxes lost)

14/15 April
Stuttgart
619 dead
146 Wellingtons, 135 Halifaxes, 98
Lancasters, 83 Stirlings (8 Stirlings, 8
Wellingtons, 4 Halifaxes, 3 Lancasters
lost)

16/17 April
Mannheim
159 Wellingtons, 95 Stirlings, 17
Halifaxes (9 Wellingtons, 7 Stirlings, 2
Halifaxes lost)

17 April
Bremen
No aircraft data

20/21 April
Stettin
586 dead
Rostock
194 Lancasters, 134 Halifaxes, 11 Stirlings
(13 Lancasters, 7 Halifaxes, 1 Stirling lost)

26/27 April
Duisburg
215 Lancasters, 135 Wellingtons, 119
Halifaxes, 78 Stirlings, 14 Mosquitoes (7
Halifaxes, 5 Wellingtons, 3 Lancasters, 2
Stirlings lost)

30 April/1 May
Essen
190 Lancasters, 105 Halifaxes, 10
Mosquitoes (6 Halifaxes, 6 Lancasters lost)

4/5 May
Dortmund
693 dead
40,000 bombed out
255 Lancasters, 141 Halifaxes, 110
Wellingtons, 80 Stirlings, 10 Mosquitoes
(12 Halifaxes, 7 Stirlings, 6 Lancasters, 6
Wellingtons lost)

12/13 May
Duisburg
238 Lancasters, 142 Halifaxes, 112
Wellingtons, 70 Stirlings, 10 Mosquitoes
(10 Lancasters, 10 Wellingtons, 9
Halifaxes, 5 Stirlings lost)

13/14 May
Bochum
302 dead
135 Halifaxes, 104 Wellingtons, 98
Lancasters, 95 Stirlings, 10 Mosquitoes
(13 Halifaxes, 6 Wellingtons, 4 Stirlings,
1 Lancaster lost)

14 May
Kiel
No aircraft data

16/17 May
Möhnetalsperre
1,294 dead
The Dams Raid: 19 Lancasters

19 May
Kiel
No aircraft data

23/24 May
Dortmund
599 dead
343 Lancasters, 199 Halifaxes, 151
Wellingtons, 120 Stirlings, 13 Mosquitoes
(18 Halifaxes, 8 Lancasters, 6 Stirlings, 6
Wellingtons lost)

25/26 May
Düsseldorf
323 Lancasters, 169 Halifaxes, 142
Wellingtons, 113 Stirlings, 12 Mosquitoes
(9 Lancasters, 8 Stirlings, 6 Wellingtons, 4
Halifaxes lost)

27/28 May
Essen
274 Lancasters, 151 Halifaxes, 81
Wellingtons, 12 Mosquitoes (11 Halifaxes,
6 Lancasters, 5 Wellingtons, 1 Mosquito
lost)

29/30 May
Wuppertal
3,400 dead
130,000 bombed out

11 June
Wilhelmshaven, Cuxhaven
No aircraft data

11/12 June
Düsseldorf
1,292 dead

140,000 bombed out
326 Lancasters, 202 Halifaxes, 143
Wellingtons, 99 Stirlings, 13 Mosquitoes
(14 Lancasters, 12 Halifaxes, 10
Wellingtons, 2 Stirlings lost)
Münster
29 Lancasters, 22 Halifaxes, 21 Stirlings
(2 Halifaxes, 2
Lancasters, 1 Stirling lost)

12/13 June
Bochum
312 dead
323 Lancasters, 167 Halifaxes, 11
Mosquitoes (14 Lancasters, 10 Halifaxes
lost)

13 June
Bremen
No aircraft data

14/15 June
Oberhausen
197 Lancasters, 6 Mosquitoes (17
Lancasters lost)

16/17 June
Cologne
202 Lancasters, 10 Halifaxes (14
Lancasters lost)

20/21 June
Friedrichshafen
60 Lancasters (no losses)

21/22 June
Krefeld
1,056 dead
72,600 bombed out
262 Lancasters, 209 Halifaxes, 117
Stirlings, 105 Wellingtons, 12 Mosquitoes
(17 Halifaxes, 9 Lancasters, 9
Wellingtons, 9 Stirlings lost)

22 June
Hüls
No aircraft data

22/23 June
Mülheim
578 dead
242 Lancasters, 155 Halifaxes, 93
Stirlings, 55 Wellingtons, 12 Mosquitoes
(12 Halifaxes, 11 Stirlings, 8 Lancasters, 4
Wellingtons lost)

24/25 June
Wuppertal
1,800 dead
112,000 bombed out
251 Lancasters, 171 Halifaxes, 101
Wellingtons, 98 Stirlings, 9 Mosquitoes
(10 Halifaxes, 10 Stirlings, 8 Lancasters, 6
Wellingtons lost)

25 June
Wangerooge
No aircraft data

25/26 June
Gelsenkirchen, Solingen, Düsseldorf
214 Lancasters, 134 Halifaxes, 73
Stirlings, 40 Wellingtons, 12 Mosquitoes
(13 Lancasters, 7 Halifaxes, 6 Stirlings, 4
Wellingtons lost)

28/29 June
Cologne
4,377 dead
230,000 bombed out
267 Lancasters, 169 Halifaxes, 85
Wellingtons, 72 Stirlings, 12 Mosquitoes
(10 Halifaxes, 8 Lancasters, 5 Stirlings, 2
Wellingtons lost)

3/4 July
Cologne
588 dead
72,000 bombed out
293 Lancasters, 182 Halifaxes, 89
Wellingtons, 76 Stirlings, 13 Mosquitoes
(9 Halifaxes, 8 Lancasters, 8 Wellingtons,
5 Stirlings lost)

8/9 July
Cologne
502 dead
48,000 bombed out
282 Lancasters, 6 Mosquitoes (7
Lancasters lost)

9/10 July
Gelsenkirchen
218 Lancasters, 190 Halifaxes, 10
Mosquitoes (7 Halifaxes, 5 Lancasters lost)

13/14 July
Aachen
294 dead
40,000 bombed out

214 Halifaxes, 76 Wellingtons, 55
Stirlings, 18 Lancasters, 11 Mosquitoes
(15 Halifaxes, 2 Lancasters, 2
Wellingtons, 1 Stirling lost)

24/25 July
Hamburg
1,500 dead
380,000 bombed out
347 Lancasters, 246 Halifaxes, 125
Stirlings, 73 Wellingtons (4 Halifaxes, 4
Lancasters, 3 Stirlings, 1 Wellington lost)

25 July
Hamburg, Kiel
No aircraft data

25/26 July
Essen
More than 500 dead
100,000 bombed out
294 Lancasters, 221 Halifaxes, 104
Stirlings, 67 Wellingtons, 19 Mosquitoes
(10 Halifaxes, 7 Stirlings, 5 Lancasters, 4
Wellingtons lost)

26 July
Hannover
No aircraft data

27/28 July
Hamburg
35,000 dead
800,000 bombed out
353 Lancasters, 244 Halifaxes, 116
Stirlings, 74 Wellingtons (11 Lancasters, 4
Halifaxes, 1 Stirling, 1 Wellington lost)

29 July
Kiel
No aircraft data

29/30 July
Hamburg
1,000 dead
150,000 bombed out
340 Lancasters, 244 Halifaxes, 119
Stirlings, 70 Wellingtons, 4 Mosquitoes
(11 Halifaxes, 11 Lancasters, 4 Stirlings, 2
Wellingtons lost)

30 July
Kassel
No aircraft data

30/31 July
Remscheid
1,120 dead
40,000 bombed out
95 Halifaxes, 87 Stirlings, 82 Lancasters,
9 Mosquitoes (8 Stirlings, 5 Halifaxes, 2
Lancasters lost)

2/3 August
Hamburg
329 Lancasters, 235 Halifaxes, 105
Stirlings, 66 Wellingtons, 5 Mosquitoes
(13 Lancasters, 10 Halifaxes, 4
Wellingtons, 3 Stirlings lost)

9/10 August
Mannheim
269 dead
286 Lancasters, 171 Halifaxes (6
Halifaxes, 3 Lancasters lost)

10/11 August
Nuremberg
585 dead
28,000 bombed out
318 Lancasters, 216 Halifaxes, 119
Stirling (7 Halifaxes, 6 Lancasters, 3
Stirlings lost)

12 August
Bochum, Recklinghausen, Gelsenkirchen
No aircraft data

17 August
Regensburg
No aircraft data

17/18 August
Peenemünde
780 dead
324 Lancasters, 218 Halifaxes, 54 Stirlings
(2 aircraft lost)

22/23 August
Leverkusen, Düsseldorf, Solingen
257 Lancasters, 192 Halifaxes, 13
Mosquitoes (3 Lancasters, 2 Halifaxes lost)

23/24 August
Berlin
899 dead
103,558 bombed out
335 Lancasters, 251 Halifaxes, 124
Stirlings, 17 Mosquitoes (23 Halifaxes, 17
Lancasters, 16 Stirlings lost)

27/28 August
Nuremberg
349 Lancasters, 221 Halifaxes, 104
Stirlings (11 of each lost)

30/31 August
Mönchengladbach
297 Lancasters, 185 Halifaxes, 107
Stirlings, 57 Wellingtons, 14 Mosquitoes
(8 Halifaxes, 7 Lancasters, 6 Stirlings, 4
Wellingtons lost)

31 August/1 September
Berlin
331 Lancasters, 176 Halifaxes, 106
Stirlings, 9 Mosquitoes (20 Halifaxes, 17
Stirlings, 10 Lancasters lost)

3/4 September
Berlin
623 dead
39,844 bombed out
316 Lancasters, 4 Mosquitoes (22
Lancasters lost)

5/6 September
Ludwigshafen
127 dead
20,000 bombed out
299 Lancasters, 195 Halifaxes, 111
Stirlings (13 Halifaxes, 13 Lancasters, 8
Stirlings lost)

6 September
Stuttgart
No aircraft data

6/7 September
Munich
257 Lancasters, 147 Halifaxes (13
Halifaxes, 3 Lancasters lost)

22/23 September
Hannover
322 Lancasters, 226 Halifaxes, 137
Stirlings, 26 Wellingtons, also 5 American
B-17s (12 Halifaxes, 7 Lancasters, 5
Stirlings,
2 Wellingtons lost)

23/24 September
Mannheim, Ludwigshafen, Darmstadt
Mannheim: 312 Lancasters, 193 Halifaxes,
115 Stirlings, 8 Mosquitoes (18
Lancasters, 7 Halifaxes, 7 Wellingtons lost)
Darmstadt: 21 Lancasters, 8 Mosquitoes
(no losses)

27 September
Emden
No aircraft data

27/28 September
Hannover, Brunswick
Hannover: 312 Lancasters, 231 Halifaxes,
111 Stirlings, 24 Wellingtons, also 5
American B-17s (17 Halifaxes, 10
Lancasters, 10 Stirlings, 1 Wellington lost)
Brunswick: 21 Lancasters, 6 Mosquitoes
(1 Lancaster lost)

29/30 September
Bochum
213 Lancasters, 130 Halifaxes, 9
Mosquitoes (5 Halifaxes, 4 Lancasters lost)

1/2 October
Hagen
266 dead
30,000 bombed out
243 Lancasters, 8 Mosquitoes (1 Lancaster
lost)

2 October
Emden
No aircraft data

2/3 October
Munich
294 Lancasters (8 lost)

3/4 October
Kassel
223 Halifaxes, 204 Lancasters, 113
Stirlings, 7 Mosquitoes (14 Halifaxes, 6
Stirlings, 4 Lancasters lost)

4 October
Frankfurt/M., Wiesbaden, Saarbrücken
No aircraft data

4/5 October
Frankfurt/M.
529 dead
162 Lancasters, 170 Halifaxes, 70

Stirlings, 4 Mosquitoes (5 Halifaxes, 3
Lancasters, 2 Stirlings lost)
Ludwigshafen
66 Lancasters (no losses)

7/8 October
Stuttgart, Böblingen
343 Lancasters (4 lost)
16 Lancasters to Friedrichshafen (no
losses)

8 October
Bremen
No aircraft data

8/9 October
Hannover
1,200 dead
282 Lancasters, 188 Halifaxes, 26
Wellingtons, 8 Mosquitoes (14 Lancasters,
13 Halifaxes lost)
Bremen
95 Stirlings, 17 Halifaxes, 7 Lancasters (3
Stirlings lost)

9 October
Anklam, Marienburg, Danzig
No aircraft data

10 October
Münster
473 dead
20,000 bombed out
No aircraft data
Coesfeld
No aircraft data

14 October
Schweinfurt
No aircraft data

18/19 October
Hannover
360 Lancasters (18 lost)

20 October
Düren
No aircraft data

20/21 October
Leipzig
358 Lancasters (16 lost)

22/23 October
Kassel
7,000 dead
53,800 bombed out
322 Lancasters, 247 Halifaxes (25
Halifaxes, 18 Lancasters lost)

3 November
Wilhelmshaven
No aircraft data

3/4 November
Düsseldorf
622 dead
344 Lancasters, 233 Halifaxes, 12
Mosquitoes (11 Lancasters, 7 Halifaxes lost)
Cologne
52 Lancasters, 10 Mosquitoes (no losses)

5 November
Gelsenkirchen, Münster
No aircraft data

11 November
Münster
No aircraft data

13 November
Bremen
No aircraft data

17/18 November
Ludwigshafen
66 Lancasters, 17 Halifaxes (1 Lancaster lost)

18/19 November
Berlin, Mannheim, Ludwigshafen
Berlin: 440 Lancasters, 4 Mosquitoes (9
Lancasters lost)
Mannheim/Ludwigshafen: 248 Halifaxes,
114 Stirlings, 33 Lancasters (12 Halifaxes,
9 Stirlings, 2 Lancasters lost)

19/20 November
Leverkusen
170 Halifaxes, 86 Stirlings, 10 Mosquitoes
(4 Halifaxes, 1 Stirling lost)

22/23 November
Berlin
2,000 dead
175,000 bombed out
469 Lancasters, 234 Halifaxes, 50
Stirlings, 11 Mosquitoes (11 Lancasters,
10 Halifaxes, 5 Stirlings lost)

23/24 November
Berlin
1,000 dead
100,000 bombed out
365 Lancasters, 10 Halifaxes, 8
Mosquitoes (20 Lancasters lost)

25/26 November
Frankfurt/M.
236 Halifaxes, 26 Lancasters (11
Halifaxes, 1 Lancaster lost)

26 November
Bremen
No aircraft data

26/27 November
Berlin, Stuttgart
Berlin: 443 Lancasters, 3 Mosquitoes (28
Lancasters lost)
Stuttgart: 157 Halifaxes, 21 Lancasters (6
Halifaxes lost)

29 November
Bremen
No aircraft data

30 November
Solingen
No aircraft data

1 December
Leverkusen
No aircraft data

2/3 December
Berlin
425 Lancasters, 18 Mosquitoes, 15
Halifaxes (37 Lancasters, 2 Halifaxes, 1
Mosquito lost)

3/4 December
Leipzig
1,717 dead
114,000 bombed out
307 Lancasters, 220 Halifaxes (15
Halifaxes, 9 Lancasters lost)

11 December
Emden
No aircraft data

13 December
Kiel, Hamburg
No aircraft data

16 December
Bremen
No aircraft data

16/17 December
Berlin
628 dead
30,063 bombed out
483 Lancasters, 10 Mosquitoes (25 Lancasters lost)

20 December
Bremen
No aircraft data

20/21 December
Frankfurt/M.
390 Lancasters, 257 Halifaxes, 3 Mosquitoes (27 Halifaxes, 14 Lancasters lost)

23/24 December
Berlin
364 Lancasters, 8 Mosquitoes, 7 Halifaxes (16 Lancasters lost)

29/30 December
Berlin
457 Lancasters, 252 Halifaxes, 2 Mosquitoes (11 Lancasters, 9 Halifaxes lost)

30 December
Ludwigshafen
No aircraft data

1944

1/2 January
Berlin
421 Lancasters (28 lost)

2/3 January
Berlin
362 Lancasters, 12 Mosquitoes, 9 Halifaxes (27 Lancasters lost)

4 January
Kiel, Neuss, Düsseldorf
No aircraft data

5/6 January
Stettin
348 Lancasters, 10 Halifaxes (14 Lancasters, 2 Halifaxes left)

7 January
Ludwigshafen
No aircraft data

11 January
Oschersleben, Halberstadt, Brunswick, Osnabrück, Meppen
No aircraft data

14/15 January
Brunswick
496 Lancasters, 2 Halifaxes (38 Lancasters lost)

20/21 January
Berlin
306 dead

20/21 January
Berlin
306 dead
20,938 bombed out
495 Lancasters, 264 Halifaxes, 10 Mosquitoes (22 Halifaxes, 13 Lancasters lost)

21/22 January
Magdeburg
421 Lancasters, 224 Halifaxes, 3 Mosquitoes (35 Halifaxes, 22 Lancasters lost)

24 January
Eschweiler
No aircraft data

27/28 January
Berlin
426 dead
19,945 bombed out
515 Lancasters, 15 Mosquitoes (33 Lancasters lost)

28/29 January
Berlin
531 dead
69,466 bombed out
432 Lancasters, 241 Halifaxes, 4 Mosquitoes (26 Halifaxes, 20 Lancasters lost)

29 January
Frankfurt/M.
903 dead
No aircraft data

30 January
Brunswick, Hannover
No aircraft data

30/31 January
Berlin
582 dead
82,980 bombed out
440 Lancasters, 82 Halifaxes, 12
Mosquitoes (32 Lancasters, 1 Halifax lost)

3 February
Wilhelmshaven
No aircraft data

4 February
Frankfurt/M.
No aircraft data

8 February
Frankfurt/M.
No aircraft data

10 February
Brunswick
No aircraft data

11 February
Frankfurt/M.
No aircraft data

15/16 February
Berlin
302 dead
561 Lancasters, 314 Halifaxes, 16
Mosquitoes (26 Lancasters, 17 Halifaxes
lost)

19/20 February
Leipzig
817 dead
30,000 bombed out
561 Lancasters, 255 Halifaxes, 7
Mosquitoes (44 Lancasters, 34 Halifaxes
lost)

20 February
Rostock, Leipzig, Gotha, Helmstedt
No aircraft data

20/21 February
Stuttgart
460 Lancasters, 126 Halifaxes, 12
Mosquitoes (7 Lancasters, 2 Halifaxes lost)

21 February
Diepholz, Verden, Brunswick, Lingen,
Rheine
No aircraft data

22 February
Aschersleben, Bernburg, Halberstadt,
Magdeburg
No aircraft data

24 February
Rostock, Schweinfurt, Gotha
No aircraft data

24/25 February
Schweinfurt
554 Lancasters, 169 Halifaxes, 11
Mosquitoes (26 Lancasters, 7 Halifaxes
lost)

25 February
Regensburg, Augsburg, Fürth
No aircraft data

25/26 February
Augsburg
720 dead
85,000 bombed out
461 Lancasters, 123 Halifaxes, 10
Mosquitoes (16 Lancasters, 5 Halifaxes
lost)

29 February
Brunswick
No aircraft data

1/2 March
Stuttgart
415 Lancasters, 129 Halifaxes, 13
Mosquitoes (3 Lancasters, 1 Halifax lost)

2 March
Frankfurt/M., Offenbach
No aircraft data

3 March
Wilhelmshaven
No aircraft data

4 March
Bonn, Cologne
No aircraft data

6 March
Berlin, Potsdam, Wittenberg
No aircraft data

8 March
Berlin
No aircraft data

9 March
Berlin, Hannover, Brunswick, Nienburg/
Weser
No aircraft data

10 March
Münster
No aircraft data

15 March
Brunswick
No aircraft data

15/16 March
Stuttgart
617 Lancasters, 230 Halifaxes, 16
Mosquitoes (27 Lancasters, 10 Halifaxes
lost)

16 March
Augsburg, Ulm, Friedrichshafen
No aircraft data

18 March
Oberpfaffenhofen, Landsberg, Munich,
Memmingen, Friedrichshafen
No aircraft data

18/19 March
Frankfurt/M.
421 dead
55,000 bombed out
620 Lancasters, 209 Halifaxes, 17
Mosquitoes (12 Halifaxes, 10 Lancasters
lost)

20 March
Frankfurt/M., Mannheim, Bingen
No aircraft data

22/23 March
Frankfurt/M.
1,001 dead
120,000 bombed out

620 Lancasters, 184 Halifaxes, 12
Mosquitoes (26 Lancasters, 7 Halifaxes
lost)

23 March
Brunswick, Münster, Osnabrück
No aircraft data

24 March
Schweinfurt, Frankfurt/M.
No aircraft data

24/25 March
Berlin
577 Lancasters, 216 Halifaxes, 18
Mosquitoes (44 Lancasters, 28 Halifaxes lost)

26/27 March
Essen
550 dead
476 Lancasters, 207 Halifaxes, 22
Mosquitoes (6 Lancasters, 3 Halifaxes lost)

29 March
Brunswick
No aircraft data

30/31 March
Nuremberg, Schweinfurt
572 Lancasters, 214 Halifaxes, 9 Mosquitoes
(64 Lancasters, 31 Halifaxes lost)

1 April
Pforzheim
No aircraft data

6/7 April
Hamburg
35 Mosquitoes (1 lost)

8 April
Brunswick, Oldenburg, Rheine
No aircraft data

9 April
Marienburg, Warnemünde, Parchim
No aircraft data

11 April
Oschersleben, Bernburg, Sorau, Stettin,
Rostock
No aircraft data

11/12 April
Aachen
1,525 dead

13 April
Schweinfurt, Lechfeld, Augsburg
No aircraft data

18 April
Oranienburg, Perleberg, Wittenberg,
Brandenburg, Rathenow
No aircraft data

19 April
Kassel, Lippstadt, Werl, Paderborn,
Gütersloh
No aircraft data

20/21 April
Cologne
664 dead
20,000 bombed out
357 Lancasters, 22 Mosquitoes (4
Lancasters lost)
Stettin

22 April
Hamm, Koblenz, Bonn
No aircraft data

22/23 April
Düsseldorf
1,200 dead
20,500 bombed out
323 Lancasters, 254 Halifaxes, 19
Mosquitoes (16 Halifaxes, 13 Lancasters
lost)
Brunswick
238 Lancasters, 17 Mosquitoes (4
Lancasters lost)

24 April
Friedrichshafen
No aircraft data

24/25 April
Munich
136 dead
70,000 bombed out
234 Lancasters, 16 Mosquitoes (9
Lancasters lost)
Karlsruhe
269 Lancasters, 259 Halifaxes, 9 Mosquitoes
(11 Lancasters, 8 Halifaxes lost)

26 April
Brunswick, Hildesheim
No aircraft data

26/27 April
Essen
313 dead
342 Lancasters, 133 Halifaxes, 18
Mosquitoes (6 Lancasters, 1 Halifax lost)
Schweinfurt
206 Lancasters, 11 Mosquitoes (21
Lancasters lost)

27/28 April
Friedrichshafen
322 Lancasters, 1 Mosquito (18
Lancasters lost)

29 April
Berlin
No aircraft data

7 May
Berlin, Münster, Osnabrück
No aircraft data

8 May
Berlin, Brunswick
No aircraft data

11 May
Saarbrücken, Völklingen
No aircraft data

12 May
Merseburg, Zwickau, Chemitz, Gera, Hof,
Zeitz, Böhlen
No aircraft data

13 May
Stettin, Stralsund, Tutow, Osnabrück
No aircraft data

19 May
Berlin, Brunswick
No aircraft data

20/21 May
Düsseldorf
30 Mosquitoes (no losses)

21/22 May
Duisburg
510 Lancasters, 22 Mosquitoes (29
Lancasters lost)

22 May
Kiel
No aircraft data

22/23 May
Dortmund
361 dead
361 Lancasters, 14 Mosquitoes (18
Lancasters lost)
Brunswick
225 Lancasters, 10 Mosquitoes (13
Lancasters lost)

24 May
Berlin
No aircraft data

24/25 May
Aachen
264 Lancasters, 162 Halifaxes, 16
Mosquitoes (18 Halifaxes, 7 Lancasters lost)

27 May
Ludwigshafen, Mannheim, Karlsruhe,
Saarbrücken, Neunkirchen
No aircraft data

27/28 May
Aachen
162 Lancasters, 8 Mosquitoes (12
Lancasters lost)

28 May
Dessau, Zwickau, Meißen, Leipzig,
Magdeburg
No aircraft data

29 May
Pölitz, Tutow, Leipzig, Schneidmühl,
Posen, Sorau, Cottbus
No aircraft data

30 May
Dessau, Halberstadt, Oldenburg,
Rotenburg/Wümme, Bad Zwischenahn
No aircraft data

31 May
Osnabrück, Schwerte, Gütersloh
No aircraft data

12/13 June
Gelsenkirchen
293 dead
286 Lancasters, 17 Mosquitoes (17
Lancasters lost)

18 June
Hamburg, Bremerhaven, Hannover,
Bremen, Stade, Brunsbüttel
No aircraft data

20 June
Magdeburg, Fallersleben, Hamburg, Pölitz
No aircraft data

21 June
Ruhland, Berlin
No aircraft data

29 June
Böhlen, Leipzig, Wittenberg, Bernburg,
Magdeburg
No aircraft data

7 July
Merseburg, Leipzig
No aircraft data

11/13/16 July
Munich
1,471 dead
200,000 bombed out
No aircraft data

13 July
Saarbrücken
No aircraft data

16 July
Stuttgart, Augsburg, Saarbrücken
No aircraft data

18 July
Kiel, Cuxhaven, Peenemünde
No aircraft data

18/19 July
Wesseling
No aircraft data

19 July
Augsburg, Kempten, Böblingen,
Schweinfurt, Saarbrücken, Koblenz
No aircraft data

20 July
Dessau, Merseburg, Leipzig, Erfurt,
Schmalkalden, Gotha
No aircraft data

21 July
Munich, Saarbrücken, Regensburg,
Schweinfurt
No aircraft data

23/24 July
Kiel
315 dead
20,000 bombed out
519 Lancasters, 100 Halifaxes, 10
Mosquitoes (4 Lancasters lost)

24/25 July
Stuttgart
461 Lancasters, 153 Halifaxes (17
Lancasters, 4 Halifaxes lost)

25/26 July
Stuttgart, Wanne-Eickel
Stuttgart: 412 Lancasters, 138 Halifaxes (8
Lancasters, 4 Halifaxes lost)
Wanne-Eickel: 114 Halifaxes, 11
Lancasters, 10 Mosquitoes (no losses)

28/29 July
Hamburg
265 dead
187 Halifaxes, 106 Lancasters, 14
Mosquitoes (18 Halifaxes, 4 Lancasters
lost)
Stuttgart
494 Lancasters, 2 Mosquitoes (39
Lancasters lost)

29 July
Merseburg, Bremen
No aircraft data

31 July
Munich, Ludwigshafen
No aircraft data

4 August
Hamburg, Bremen, Peenemünde, Anklam,
Kiel, Wismar, Rostock, Schwerin
No aircraft data

5 August
Magdeburg, Halberstadt, Brunswick,
Hannover
No aircraft data

6 August
Brandenburg, Berlin, Hamburg
No aircraft data

9 August
Ulm, Pirmasens, Karlsruhe, Saarbrücken
No aircraft data

12/13 August
Brunswick, Rüsselsheim
Brunswick: 242 Lancasters, 137 Halifaxes
(17 Lancasters, 10 Halifaxes lost)
Rüsselsheim: 191 Lancasters, 96 Halifaxes,
10 Mosquitoes (13 Lancasters, 7 Halifaxes
lost)

14 August
Mannheim, Ludwigshafen
No aircraft data

15 August
Wiesbaden, Frankfurt, Cologne
No aircraft data

16 August
Delitzsch, Schkeuditz, Halle/S., Zeitz,
Rositz, Dessau, Köthen, Magdeburg
No aircraft data

16/17 August
Stettin
1,117 dead
461 Lancasters (5 lost)

16/17 August
Kiel
195 Lancasters, 144 Halifaxes, 9
Mosquitoes (3 Halifaxes, 2 Lancasters lost)

18/19 August
Bremen
1,300 dead
30,000 bombed out
216 Lancasters, 65 Halifaxes, 7
Mosquitoes (1 Lancaster lost)

23/24 August
Cologne
46 Mosquitoes (no losses)

24 August
Brunswick, Weimar, Merseburg
No aircraft data

25 August
Rostock, Schwerin, Wismar, Rechlin,
Pölitz, Peenemünde, Anklam,
Neubrandenburg
No aircraft data

25/26 August
Rüsselsheim, Darmstadt
Rüsselsheim: 412 Lancasters (15 lost)
Darmstadt: 190 Lancasters, 6 Mosquitoes
(7 Lancasters lost)

26 August
Gelsenkirchen
No aircraft data

26/27 August
Kiel, Königsberg
Kiel: 371 Lancasters, 10 Mosquitoes (17
Lancasters lost)
Königsberg: 174 Lancasters (4 lost)

29/30 August
Königsberg
500 dead
189 Lancasters (15 lost)
Stettin
1,033 dead
402 Lancasters, 1 Mosquito (23
Lancasters lost)

30 August
Kiel, Bremen
No aircraft data

3 September
Ludwigshafen
No aircraft data

5 September
Stuttgart, Karlsruhe
No aircraft data

6 September
Emden
No aircraft data

8 September
Ludwigshafen, Kassel, Karlsruhe
No aircraft data

9 September
Mannheim, Mainz, Düsseldorf
No aircraft data

9/10 September
Mönchengladbach
113 Lancasters, 24 Mosquitoes (no losses)

10 September
Ulm, Heilbronn, Nürnberg, Fürth,
Gaggenau, Sindelfingen, Zuffenhausen
No aircraft data

11 September
Fulda, Merseburg, Eisenach, Magdeburg
No aircraft data

11/12 September
Darmstadt
10,550 dead
49,000 bombed out
226 Lancasters, 14 Mosquitoes (12
Lancasters lost)

12 September
Münster, Magdeburg
No aircraft data

12/13 September
Frankfurt/M.
957 dead
50,000 bombed out
378 Lancasters, 9 Mosquitoes (17
Lancasters lost)
Stuttgart
469 dead
204 Lancasters, 13 Mosquitoes (4
Lancasters lost)

13 September
Osnabrück, Gelsenkirchen, Stuttgart,
Schwäbisch Hall, Ulm, Merseburg
No aircraft data

14 September
Wilhelmshaven
No aircraft data

15/16 September
Kiel
310 Lancasters, 173 Halifaxes, 7
Mosquitoes (4 Halifaxes, 2 Lancasters lost)

18/19 September
Bremerhaven
618 dead
30,000 bombed out
206 Lancasters, 7 Mosquitoes (1
Lancaster, 1 Mosquito lost)

19 September
Koblenz, Limburg, Hamm, Dortmund,
Unna
No aircraft data

19/20 September
Mönchengladbach, Rheydt
227 Lancasters, 10 Mosquitoes (4
Lancasters, 1 Mosquito lost)

21 September
Ludwigshafen, Mainz, Koblenz
No aircraft data

22 September
Kassel
No aircraft data

23/24 September
Neuss, Dortmund, Münster
Neuss: 378 Lancasters, 154 Halifaxes, 17
Mosquitoes (5 Lancasters, 2 Halifaxes lost)
Dortmund: 136 Lancasters, 5 Mosquitoes
(14 Lancasters lost)
Münster: 107 Lancasters, 5 Mosquitoes, 1
Lightning (1 Lancaster lost)

25 September
Ludwigshafen, Frankfurt, Koblenz
No aircraft data

26 September
Osnabrück, Hamm, Bremen
No aircraft data

26/27 September
Karlsruhe
226 Lancasters, 11 Mosquitoes (2
Lancasters lost)

27 September
Cologne, Ludwigshafen, Kassel
No aircraft data

27/28 September
Kaiserslautern
144 dead
30,000 bombed out
217 Lancasters, 10 Mosquitoes (1 of each
lost)

28 September
Magdeburg, Merseburg, Kassel
No aircraft data

30 September
Bielefeld, Münster, Hamm
No aircraft data

30 September
Bottrop
No aircraft data

2 October
Kassel, Cologne, Hamm
No aircraft data

3 October
Nuremberg, Gaggenau
No aircraft data

5 October
Wilhelmshaven, Cologne, Lippstadt,
Münster
No aircraft data

5/6 October
Saarbrücken
344 dead
25,000 bombed out
531 Lancasters, 20 Mosquitoes (3
Lancasters lost)

6 October
Stargard, Neubrandenburg, Stralsund,
Hamburg
No aircraft data

6/7 October
Dortmund
258 dead
100,000 bombed out
248 Halifaxes, 46 Lancasters, 20
Mosquitoes (4 Halifaxes, 2 Lancasters lost)
Bremen
65 dead
37,700 bombed out
246 Lancasters, 7 Mosquitoes (5
Lancasters lost)

7 October
Emmerich
641 dead
Kleve, Zwichau, Merseburg, Kassel,
Clausthal
No aircraft data

9 October
Bochum, Schweinfurt, Mainz, Koblenz
Bochum: 375 Halifaxes, 40 Lancasters, 20
Mosquitoes (4 Halifaxes, 1 Lancaster lost)

12 October
Wanne-Eickel, Osnabrück
Wanne-Eickel: 11 Halifaxes, 26 Lancasters

14 October
Duisburg
519 Lancasters, 474 Halifaxes, 20
Mosquitoes (13 Lancasters, 1 Halifax lost)

14/15 October
Brunswick
561 dead
80,000 bombed out
233 Lancasters, 7 Mosquitoes (1 Lancaster lost)
Duisburg
2,541 dead
498 Lancasters, 468 Halifaxes, 39 Mosquitoes (5 Lancasters, 2 Halifaxes lost)

15/16 October
Wilhelmshaven
257 Halifaxes, 241 Lancasters, 8 Mosquitoes

16/17 October
Cologne
39 Mosquitoes (no losses)

18 October
Bonn
313 dead
20,000 bombed out
128 Lancasters (1 lost)

19/20 October
Stuttgart
338 dead
565 Lancasters, 18 Mosquitoes (6 Lancasters lost)
Nuremberg, Karlsruhe
Nuremberg: 263 Lancasters, 7 Mosquitoes (2 Lancasters lost)

21/22 October
Hannover
242 Halifaxes, 21 Pathfinder Lancasters, all recalled

22 October
Neuss, Brunswick, Hannover, Hamm, Münster
Neuss: 100 Lancasters (no losses)

23/24 October
Essen
662 dead
561 Lancasters, 463 Halifaxes, 31 Mosquitoes (5 Lancasters, 3 Halifaxes lost)

25 October
Essen
820 dead
508 Lancasters, 251 Halifaxes, 12 Mosquitoes (2 Halifaxes, 2 Lancasters lost)
Homburg, Neumünster
Homburg: 199 Halifaxes, 32 Lancasters, 12 Mosquitoes (no losses)

26 October
Leverkusen, Bielefeld, Münster, Hannover
Leverkusen: 105 Lancasters (no losses)

28 October
Cologne
630 dead
20,000 bombed out
428 Lancasters, 286 Halifaxes, 19 Mosquitoes (4 Halifaxes, 3 Lancasters lost)
Münster, Hamm

30 October
Hamm, Münster
No aircraft data

30/31 October
Cologne
550 dead
438 Halifaxes, 435 Lancasters, 32 Mosquitoes (no losses)

31 October/1 November
Cologne
331 Lancasters, 144 Halifaxes, 18 Mosquitoes (2 Lancasters lost)

1 November
Gelsenkirchen
No aircraft data

1/2 November
Oberhausen
202 Halifaxes, 74 Lancasters, 12 Mosquitoes (3 Halifaxes, 1 Lancaster lost)

2 November
Merseburg, Bielefeld, Castrop-Rauxel
No aircraft data

2/3 November
Düsseldorf
748 dead
15,000 bombed out
561 Lancasters, 400 Halifaxes, 31 Mosquitoes (11 Halifaxes, 8 Lancasters lost)

4 November
Neunkirchen, Saarbrücken, Hannover, Hamburg, Gelsenkirchen
No aircraft data

4/5 November
Bochum
984 dead
10,000 bombed out
384 Halifaxes, 336 Lancasters, 29
Mosquitoes (23 Halifaxes, 5 Lancasters lost)

5 November
Solingen
1,882 dead
20,000 bombed out
173 Lancasters (1 lost)
Frankfurt/M., Ludwigshafen, Karlsruhe

6 November
Gelsenkirchen
518 dead
383 Halifaxes, 324 Lancasters, 31
Mosquitoes (3 Lancasters, 2 Halifaxes lost)
Hamburg, Miden, Bottrop, NeuMünster

6/7 November
Koblenz
104 dead
25,000 bombed out
128 Lancasters (2 lost)
Merseburg

8 November
Merseburg, Homburg
Homburg: 136 Lancasters (1 lost)

9 November
Wanne-Eickel
256 Lancasters, 21 Mosquitoes (2
Lancasters lost)

10 November
Saarbrücken, Hanau, Wiesbaden, Cologne
No aircraft data

11 November
Oberlahnstein, Gelsenkirchen, Bottrop
No aircraft data

11 November
Castrop-Rauxel
122 Lancasters (no losses)

11/12 November
Harburg, Dortmund
Harburg: 237 Lancasters, 8 Mosquitoes (7
Lancasters lost)
Dortmund: 209 Lancasters, 19
Mosquitoes (no losses)

16 November
Düren
2,900 dead
485 Lancasters, 13 Mosquitoes (3
Lancasters lost)
Eschweiler
No aircraft data

18 November
Münster
367 Halifaxes, 94 Lancasters, 18
Mosquitoes (1 Halifax crashed in Holland)

18/19 November
Wanne-Eickel
285 Lancasters, 24 Mosquitoes (1
Lancaster lost)

20/21 November
Koblenz
43 Lancasters (no losses)

21 November
Merseburg, Gießen, Westlar, Osnabrück,
Hamburg
No aircraft data

21/22 November
Aschaffenburg
344 dead
274 Lancasters, 9 Mosquitoes (2
Lancasters lost)
Castrop-Rauxel
176 Halifaxes, 79 Lancasters, 18
Mosquitoes (4 Halifaxes lost)

23 November
Gelsenkirchen
168 Lancasters (lost)

25 November
Merseburg, Bingen
No aircraft data

26 November
Fulda, Bielefeld, Hamm, Misburg
Fulda: 75 Lancasters (no losses)

26/27 November
Munich
270 Lancasters, 8 Mosquitoes (1 Lancaster
crashed in France)

27 November
Bingen, Offenburg
No aircraft data

27/28 November
Freiburg i. Br.
2,700 dead
40,000 bombed out
341 Lancasters, 10 Mosquitoes (1
Lancaster lost)
Neuss
173 Halifaxes, 102 Lancasters, 15
Mosquitoes (1 Mosquito lost)

28/29 November
Essen, Neuss
Essen: 270 Halifaxes, 32 Lancasters, 14
Mosquitoes (no losses)
Neuss: 153 Lancasters (no losses)

29 November
Dortmund, Duisburg
Dortmund: 294 Lancasters, 17
Mosquitoes (6 Lancasters lost)
Duisburg: 30 Mosquitoes (no losses)

30 November
Zeitz, Merseburg, Neunkirchen, Homburg
No aircraft data

30 November/1 December
Duisburg
425 Halifaxes, 126 Lancasters, 25
Mosquitoes (3 Halifaxes lost)

2 December
Bingen
No aircraft data

2/3 December
Hagen
583 dead
20,000 bombed out
394 Halifaxes, 87 Lancasters, 23
Mosquitoes (1 Halifax and 1 Lancaster
crashed in France)

4 December
Oberhausen, Kassel, Mainz
Oberhausen: 160 Lancasters (1 lost)

4/5 December
Karlsruhe
357 dead
20,000 bombed out
369 Lancasters, 154 Halifaxes, 12
Mosquitoes (1 Lancaster, 1 Mosquito lost)
Heilbronn
7,000 dead

50,000 bombed out
282 Lancasters, 10 Mosquitoes (12
Lancasters lost)

5 December
Berlin, Münster
No aircraft data

5 December
Hamm
1,000 dead
20,000 bombed out
94 Lancasters (no losses)

5/6 December
Soest
385 Halifaxes, 100 Lancasters, 12
Mosquitoes (2 Halifaxes lost)

6 December
Merseburg, Bielefeld
No aircraft data

6/7 December
Gießen
813 dead
30,000 bombed out
255 Lancasters, 10 Mosquitoes (8
Lancasters lost)
Osnabrück
363 Halifaxes, 72 Lancasters, 18
Mosquitoes (7 Halifaxes, 1 Lancaster lost)

9 December
Stuttgart
No aircraft data

10 December
Bingen, Koblenz
Koblenz: 8 Mosquitoes (no losses)

11 December
Frankfurt/M., Mannheim, Hanau, Gießen
No aircraft data

12 December
Witten
409 dead
20,000 bombed out
140 Lancasters (8 lost)
Merseburg, Hanau, Darmstadt
No aircraft data

12/13 December
Essen
349 Lancasters, 163 Halifaxes, 28
Mosquitoes (6 Lancasters lost)

15 December
Kassel, Hannover
Hannover: 62 Mosquitoes

15/16 December
Ludwigshafen
327 Lancasters, 14 Mosquitoes (1
Lancaster lost)

16 December
Siegen
348 dead
108 Lancasters (1 lost)

17/18 December
Ulm
606 dead
50,000 bombed out
317 Lancasters, 13 Mosquitoes (2
Lancasters lost)
Duisburg, Munich
Duisburg: 418 Halifaxes, 81 Lancasters,
24 Mosquitoes (8 Halifaxes lost)
Munich: 280 Lancasters, 8 Mosquitoes (4
Lancasters lost)

18 December
Mainz, Koblenz, Kaiserslautern
No aircraft data

19 December
Trier
32 Lancasters (no losses)

21 December
Trier
113 Lancasters (no losses)

21/22 December
Cologne, Pölitz, Bonn
Cologne: 67 Lancasters, 54 Halifaxes, 15
Mosquitoes (no losses)
Pölitz: 207 Lancasters, 1 Mosquito (3
Lancasters lost. 5 Lancasters crashed in
England)
Bonn: 97 Lancasters, 17 Mosquitoes (no
losses)

22/23 December
Bingen, Koblenz
Bingen: 90 Halifaxes, 14 Lancasters, 2
Mosquitoes (2 Halifaxes, 1 Lancaster lost)
Koblenz: 166 Lancasters, 2 Mosquitoes
(no losses)

24 December
Babenhausen, Groß Ostheim, Zellhausen,
Biblis, Darmstadt, Frankfurt/M.,
Merzhausen
No aircraft data

27 December
Fulda
No aircraft data

27/28 December
Opladen
227 Halifaxes, 66 Lancasters, 35
Mosquitoes (2 Lancasters lost)

28 December
Kaiserslautern, Koblenz
No aircraft data

28/29 December
Bonn
486 dead
162 Lancasters, 16 Mosquitoes (1
Lancaster lost)
Mönchengladbach
129 Lancasters, 46 Halifaxes, 11
Mosquitoes (no losses)

29 December
Koblenz
162 Halifaxes, 107 Lancasters, 8
Mosquitoes (no losses)

30/31 December
Cologne
356 Halifaxes, 93 Lancasters, 21
Mosquitoes (1 Halifax, 1 Lancaster lost)

31 December
Hamburg, Neuss, Krefeld,
Mönchengladbach, Remagen, Koblenz
No aircraft data

31 December
Vohwinkel
155 Lancasters (2 lost)

1945

1 January
Kassel, Göttingen, Koblenz, Andernach
No aircraft data

2 January
Gerolstein, Mayen, Daun, Bitburg, Koblenz,
Bad Kreuznach, Kaiserslautern, Lebach
No aircraft data

2/3 January
Nürnberg
1794 dead
100,000 bombed out
514 Lancasters, 7 Mosquitoes (4
Lancasters lost. 2 Lancasters crashed in
France)
Ludwigshafen
351 Halifaxes, 22 Lancasters, 16
Mosquitoes (1 Halifax crashed in France)

3 January
Fulda, Aschaffenburg, Gemünd, Schleiden,
Koblenz, Pforzheim, Homburg,
Zweibrücken, Neunkirchen, Landau,
Pimasens, St Vith, Cologne
No aircraft data

5 January
Neustadt/W., Sobernheim, Pirmasens,
Hanau, Neunkirchen, Frankfurt/M.,
Kaiserslautern, Heilbronn, Niederbreisig,
Niedermendig, Koblenz
No aircraft data

5 January
Ludwigshafen
160 Lancasters (2 lost)

5/6 January
Hannover
340 Halifaxes, 310 Lancasters, 14
Mosquitoes (23 Halifaxes, 8 Lancasters lost)

6 January
Worms, Kaiserslautern, Ludwigshafen,
Cologne, Bonn, Koblenz
No aircraft data

6/7 January
Hanau
90 dead
20,000 bombed out
314 Halifaxes, 154 Lancasters, 14
Mosquitoes (4 Halifaxes, 2 Lancasters lost)

7 January
Hamm, Paderborn, Bielefeld, Cologne,
Landau, Kaiserslautern, Zweibrücken,
Rastatt
No aircraft data

7/8 January
Munich
505 dead
70,000 bombed out
645 Lancasters, 9 Mosquitoes (11
Lancasters lost. 4 Lancasters crashed in
France)

8 January
Speyer, Frankfurt/M.
No aircraft data

10 January
Cologne, Düsseldorf, Bonn, Euskirchen
No aircraft data

11 January
Krefeld
152 Lancasters (no losses)

13 January
Mainz, Worms, Kaiserslautern,
Rüdesheim, Germersheim, Mannheim
No aircraft data

14 January
Derben, Magdeburg, Cologne
No aircraft data

15 January
Ingolstadt, Freiburg/Br., Reutlingen,
Augsburg
No aircraft data

16/17 January
Magdeburg
16,000 dead
190,000 bombed out
320 Halifaxes, 44 Lancasters, 7
Mosquitoes (17 Halifaxes lost)
Zeitz
328 Lancasters (10 lost)

17 January
Hamburg, Paderborn
No aircraft data

18 January
Kaiserslautern
No aircraft data

20 January
Rheine, Heilbronn, Mannheim
No aircraft data

21 January
Aschaffenburg, Mannheim, Heilbronn
No aircraft data

22/23 January
Duisburg
286 Lancasters, 16 Mosquitoes (2
Lancasters lost)

23 January
Neuss
No aircraft data

28 January
Cologne, Duisburg
Cologne: 153 Lancasters (3 lost. 1 crashed
in France)

28/29 January
Stuttgart
316 Halifaxes, 258 Lancasters, 28
Mosquitoes (6 Lancasters, 4 Halifaxes, 1
Mosquito lost)

29 January
Siegen, Koblenz, Bad Kreuznach, Kassel,
Bielefeld, Hamm, Münster
No aircraft data

1 February
Mannheim, Ludwigshafen, Wesel
No aircraft data

1/2 February
Mainz, Ludwigshafen, Siegen
Mainz: 293 Halifaxes, 40 Lancasters, 8
Mosquitoes (no losses)
Ludwigshafen: 382 Lancasters, 14
Mosquitoes (6 Lancasters lost)
Siegen: 271 Lancasters, 11 Mosquitoes (3
Lancasters, 1 Mosquito lost)

2/3 February
Wiesbaden
1,000 dead
20,000 bombed out
495 Lancasters, 12 Mosquitoes (3
Lancasters crashed in France)
Wanne-Eickel, Karlsruhe
Wanne-Eickel: 277 Halifaxes, 27
Lancasters, 19 Mosquitoes (4 Halifaxes lost)

Karlsruhe: 250 Lancasters, 11 Mosquitoes
(14 Lancasters lost)

3 February
Berlin
2,541 dead
119,057 bombed out
Magdeburg
No aircraft data

3/4 February
Bottrop, Dortmund
Bottrop: 192 Lancasters, 18 Mosquitoes (8
Lancasters lost)
Dortmund: 149 Lancasters (4 lost)

6 February
Chemnitz, Gotha, Gießen, Magdeburg
No aircraft data

9 February
Magdeburg, Weimar, Gießen, Fulda,
Bielefeld, Paderborn, Dülmen
No aircraft data

13/14 February
Dresden
More than 30,000 dead
250,000 bombed out
796 Lancasters, 9 Mosquitoes (6
Lancasters lost. 2 Lancasters crashed in
France, 1 in England)
Böhlen
326 Halifaxes, 34 Lancasters, 8 Mosquitoes
(1 Halifax lost)

14 February
Dresden, Chemnitz, Bamberg,
Magdeburg, Wesel, Dülmen
No aircraft data

14/15 February
Chemnitz
499 Lancasters, 218 Halifaxes (8
Lancasters, 5 Halifaxes lost)

15 February
Cottbus, Dresden, Magdeburg, Rheine
No aircraft data

16 February
Hamm, Dortmund, Münster, Osnabrück,
Rheine, Wesel
Wesel: 100 Lancasters, 1 Mosquito (no
losses)

16/17 February
Wesel
562 dead
No aircraft data

17 February
Frankfurt/M., Gießen
No aircraft data

19 February
Osnabrück, Meschede, Siegen, Dortmund,
Bochum, Gelsenkirchen, Münster, Rheine,
Wesel
Wesel: 168 Lancasters (1 lost)

20 February
Nürnberg
No aircraft data

20/21 February
Dortmund, Düsseldorf
Dortmund: 514 Lancasters, 14
Mosquitoes (14 Lancasters lost)
Düsseldorf: 156 Halifaxes, 11 Mosquitoes,
6 Lancasters (4 Halifaxes, 1 Lancaster lost)

21 February
Nürnberg
1,356 dead
69,385 bombed out
No aircraft data

21/22 February
Worms
239 dead
35,000 bombed out
288 Halifaxes, 36 Lancasters, 25
Mosquitoes (10 Halifaxes, 1 Lancaster lost)

22 February
Bamberg, Ansbach, Ulm, Halberstadt,
Nordhausen, Peine, Hildesheim,
Wittenberg, Stendal, Uelzen, Ludwigslust
No aircraft data

23 February
Treuchtlingen, Crailsheim, Plauen,
Meiningen, Kitzingen, Weimar, Gera,
Osnabrück, Paderborn
No aircraft data

23 February
Essen
1,555 dead
297 Halifaxes, 27 Lancasters, 18

Mosquitoes (1 Halifax crashed in
Holland)
Gelsenkirchen
133 Lancasters (no losses)

23/24 February
Pforzheim
Up to 20,000 dead
50,000 bombed out
367 Lancasters, 13 Mosquitoes (10
Lancasters lost. 2 crashed in France)

24 February
Kamen
290 Halifaxes, 26 Lancasters, 24
Mosquitoes (1 Halifax lost)

24 February
Hamburg, Lehrte, Bielefeld, Bremen,
Wesel
No aircraft data

25 February
Friedrichshafen, Munich, Ulm,
Aschaffenburg, Schwäbisch
Hall
No aircraft data

26 February
Berlin
636 dead
71,283 bombed out
No aircraft data

27 February
Leipzig
677 dead
Halle
No aircraft data

27 February
Mainz
311 Halifaxes, 131 Lancasters, 16
Mosquitoes (1 Halifax, 1 Mosquito lost)

28 February
Soest, Hagen, Siegen, Meschede,
Arnsberg, Bielefeld, Kassel
No aircraft data

1 March
Mannheim
372 Lancasters, 90 Halifaxes, 16
Mosquitoes (3 Lancasters lost)

1 March
Bruschal
1,000 dead
30,000 bombed out
Reutlingen, Neckarsulm, Ulm, Heilbronn,
Ingolstadt, Augsburg
No aircraft data

2 March
Chemnitz, Magdeburg
No aircraft data

2 March
Cologne
500 dead
531 Lancasters, 303 Halifaxes, 24
Mosquitoes (6 Lancasters, 2 Halifaxes lost.
1 Halifax crashed in Belgium)

3 March
Hannover, Chemnitz, Bielefeld, Herford,
Magdeburg, Brunswick
No aircraft data

3/4 March
Kamen, Dortmund
Kamen: 201 Halifaxes, 21 Lancasters, 12
Mosquitoes (no losses)
Dortmund: 212 Lancasters, 10
Mosquitoes (7 Lancasters lost)

4 March
Ulm, Ingolstadt
No aircraft data

5 March
Chemnitz, Hamburg
No aircraft data

5/6 March
Chemnitz
498 Lancasters, 256 Halifaxes, 6
Mosquitoes (14 Lancasters, 8 Halifaxes
lost, 9 aircraft crashed in England)

7 March
Soest, Bielefeld, Dortmund, Siegen,
Gießen, Datteln
No aircraft data

7/8 March
Dessau
600 dead
20,000 bombed out
526 Lancasters, 5 Mosquitoes (18
Lancasters lost)

Harburg
422 dead
234 Lancasters, 7 Mosquitoes (14
Lancasters lost)

8 March
Siegen, Dortmund, Gießen, Essen, Hüls
No aircraft data

8/9 March
Hamburg
241 Halifaxes, 62 Lancasters, 9
Mosquitoes (1 Halifax lost)

9 March
Frankfurt/M., Kassel, Münster, Rheine,
Osnabrück
No aircraft data

10 March
Arnsberg, Paderborn, Bielefeld, Soest,
Dortmund, Schwerte
No aircraft data

11 March
Essen
897 dead
750 Lancasters, 293 Halifaxes, 36
Mosquitoes (3 Lancasters lost)

11 March
Kiel, Hamburg, Bremen
No aircraft data

12 March
Dortmund
895 dead
748 Lancasters, 292 Halifaxes, 68
Mosquitoes (2 Lancasters lost)

12 March
Swinemünde
Up to 23,000 dead
Wetzlar, Friedberg, Marburg, Siegen,
Betzdorf, Dillenburg
No aircraft data

13 March
Wuppertal
562 dead
310 Halifaxes, 24 Lancasters, 20
Mosquitoes (no losses)

14 March
Hannover, Hildesheim, Gütersloh, Gießen
No aircraft data

15 March
Zossen, Oranienburg
No aircraft data

15/16 March
Hagen
505 dead
32,500 bombed out
134 Lancasters, 122 Halifaxes, 11
Mosquitoes (6 Lancasters, 4 Halifaxes lost)

16/17 March
Nuremberg
517 dead
35,000 bombed out
277 Lancasters, 16 Mosquitoes (24
Lancasters lost)
Würzburg
225 Lancasters, 11 Mosquitoes (6
Lancasters lost)

17 March
Ruhland, Bitterfeld, Plauen, Böhlen,
Mölbis, Jena, Erfurt,
Münster, Hannover
No aircraft data

18 March
Berlin
336 dead
79,785 bombed out
No aircraft data

18/19 March
Witten
500 dead
20,000 bombed out
259 Halifaxes, 45 Lancasters, 20
Mosquitoes (6 Halifaxes, 1 Lancaster, 1
Mosquito lost)
Hanau
2,000 dead
30,000 bombed out
277 Lancasters, 8 Mosquitoes (1 Lancaster
lost)

19 March
Zwickau, Jena, Plauen, Neuburg,
Leipheim, Bäumenheim
No aircraft data

20 March
Hamburg
No aircraft data

22 March
Hildesheim
1,645 dead
40,000 bombed out
227 Lancasters, 8 Mosquitoes (4
Lancasters lost)

23/24 March
Wesel
195 Lancasters, 23 Mosquitoes (no losses)

24 March
Gladbeck
3,095 dead
40,000 bombed out
153 Halifaxes, 16 Halifaxes (1 Halifax
lost)

25 March
Osnabrück
143 dead
20,000 bombed out
132 Halifaxes, 14 Lancasters, 10
Mosquitoes (no losses)
Hannover, Münster
Hannover: 267 Lancasters, 8 Mosquitoes
(1 Lancaster lost)
Münster: 151 Halifaxes, 14 Lancasters, 10
Mosquitoes (3 Halifaxes lost)

27 March
Paderborn
330 dead
30,000 bombed out
268 Lancasters, 8 Mosquitoes (no losses)

31 March
Hamburg
361 Lancasters, 100 Halifaxes, 8
Mosquitoes (8 Lancasters, 3 Halifaxes lost)

3 April
Kiel
624 dead
No aircraft data

3/4 April
Nordhausen
8,800 dead
20,000 bombed out
3 April: 247 Lancasters, 8 Mosquitoes (2
Lancasters lost)
4 April: 243 Lancasters, 1 Mosquito (1
Lancaster lost)

4/5 April
Leuna, Harburg, Lützkendorf
Leuna: 327 Lancasters, 14 Mosquitoes (2
Lancasters lost)
Harburg: 277 Halifaxes, 36 Lancasters, 14
Mosquitoes (2 Lancasters, 1 Halifax lost)
Lützkendorf: 258 Lancasters, 14
Mosquitoes (6 Lancasters lost)

6 April
Leipzig
733 dead
No aircraft data

8 April
Halberstadt
1,866 dead
25,000 bombed out
No aircraft data

8/9 April
Hamburg
263 Halifaxes, 160 Lancasters, 17
Mosquitoes (3 Lancasters lost)

9/10 April
Kiel
591 Lancasters, 8 Mosquitoes (3
Lancasters lost)

10 April
Leipzig
134 Lancasters, 90 Halifaxes, 6
Mosquitoes (1 Halifax, 1 Lancaster lost)

10/11 April
Plauen
20,000 bombed out
307 Lancasters, 8 Mosquitoes (no losses)

11 April
Bayreuth, Nuremberg
Nuremberg: 129 Halifaxes, 14 Lancasters
(no losses)
Bayreuth: 100 Halifaxes, 14 Lancasters, 8
Mosquitoes (no losses)

13/14 April
Kiel
377 Lancasters, 105 Halifaxes (2
Lancasters lost)

14/15 April
Potsdam
5,000 dead
40,000 bombed out
500 Lancasters, 12 Mosquitoes (1
Lancaster lost)
Zerbst
No aircraft data

18 April
Helgoland
617 Lancasters, 332 Halifaxes, 20
Mosquitoes (3 Halifaxes lost)

20 April
Regensburg
100 Lancasters (1 lost)

20/21 April
Berlin
76 Mosquitoes (no losses)

21/22 April
Kiel
107 Mosquitoes (2 lost)

22 April
Bremen
651 Lancasters, 100 Halifaxes, 16
Mosquitoes (2 Lancasters lost)

24 April
Bad Oldesloe
700 dead
110 Lancasters (no losses)

25 April
Wangerooge, Berchtesgaden
Wangerooge: 308 Halifaxes, 158
Lancasters, 16 Mosquitoes (5 Halifaxes, 2
Lancasters lost)
359 Lancasters, 16 Mosquitoes (2
Lancasters lost)

2/3 May
Kiel
126 Mosquitoes (no losses)

Notes

Abbreviations Used in the Notes

BCWD Bomber Command War Diaries
OH   Official History, from Charles Webster and Noble Frankland, *The Strategic Air Offensive Against Germany 1939–45*, HMSO, 1961
USSBS United States Strategic Bombing Survey AHB
AHB   Air Historical Branch

2 The Bomber War

1 W. G. Sebald, *The Natural History of Destruction*, London, 2003, pp. 27–29.
2 Ibid.
3 The story of Operation Gomorrah is told in detail by Martin Middlebrook in his *The Battle of Hamburg*, London, 1980, one in his excellent series of volumes on aspects of the bomber war.
4 *The Firestorm Raid*, OH, vol. II, pp. 154–5. For casualty figures and Bomber Command losses see Henry Probert, *Bomber Harris His Life and Times*, London, 2001, p. 261.
5 Quoted by Middlebrook, *Battle of Hamburg*, p. 251.
6 See chapter 3 below for a discussion of the significance of the post-Hamburg panic in Germany, and the degree to which it confirmed Sir Arthur Harris's belief about the 'moral effect' of large-scale targeting of civilian populations by bombers.
7 Chapter and verse for this claim occurs in the appropriate places below, where the effects of the bombing campaigns are discussed. See especially chapters 3 and 8.
8 The idea that Allied thinking canvassed the idea of an effective 'culturecide' of Germany by means of bombing all its major cities and turning the country into a farm must not be taken as an excuse for forgetting that the Nazi regime in Germany, with the active support of many among its population, not only contemplated but enacted an actual genocide against European Jewry, and had plans to do the same for East Europe's Slavic population too, except in so far as it could be useful as slave labour. I repeat the point, however, that the fact that a wrong is less than a competing wrong does not make it a

right; and the fact that the Allies seriously contemplated permanently crippling German – and Japanese – culture, and set about doing so by means of the area-bombing campaigns, is one that must be looked squarely in the face.

9 This shows how much emphasis was placed on naval considerations in war planning before the outbreak of hostilities. Some argue that over-concentration on naval planning was typical of British thinking, given the country's splendid naval history and the great power of its fleets, but was not tailored to the realities, as they proved, of the Second World War. This is so even when one considers the importance of the war at sea; if Britain had lost the Battle of the Atlantic it would have lost the war as surely as if it had lost the Battle of Britain. But the war at sea was only marginally about great battleships and cruisers – it was much more about long-distance aircraft hunts for submarines, the technique of convoy sailings, the courage and endurance of merchant crews, and the weather.

10 In 1918 the newly formed RAF consisted of 188 operational and 194 training squadrons.

11 Denis Richards, *The Hardest Victory: RAF Bomber Command in the Second World War*, London, 1994, chapter 1 *passim*.

12 Ibid., p. 4.

13 It was followed by further schemes, not all accepted; for example, Scheme H was put before the British Cabinet in 1937, calling for 2,500 front-line aircraft of which 1,659 were to be bombers. The figures were arrived at by looking at what the Luftwaffe had available, and aimed at parity. The scheme was rejected, because the British government, on the basis more of wishful thinking than clarity of vision, believed German assurances that Luftwaffe strength would not be so great that such an expansion of British air power would be needed.

14 The new bomber specifications that eventuated in the Halifaxes and Lancasters that became the mainstay of Bomber Command – this especially true of the latter, a magnificent aircraft ideally suited to the task and the conditions of the time – were laid down in 1936.

15 The fighter specifications had been laid down in 1934.

16 See Robert Jackson, *Before the Storm: The Story of Bomber Command 1939–42*, London, 1972, chapter 2 *passim*.

17 In the period of expansion before the war the RAF also had, among other quickly obsolescent types, the Handley Page Harrow and the Wellesley long-range bomber. The latter saw some service in the early part of the war in the Middle East, and because of its geodetic design (one of its designers was the remarkable Barnes Wallis) it was 40 per cent lighter than it would have been if conventionally constructed. This is what helped to give it an enormous range. Both types would have been a terrible liability in the air war as it evolved from 1940 onwards.

18 Quoted in Jackson, *Before the Storm*, p. 76. The preceding account is based on *Before the Storm*, pp. 70–5.

19 Ibid., p. 89.

20 Robert Jackson, *Bomber! Famous Bomber Missions of World War II*, London, 1980, pp. 21–8.

21 Of these bombing episodes and their effect on modern consciousness, more below.

22 In the first five days of Germany's invasion of the Low Countries and France, the Luftwaffe lost over 539 aircraft, while the RAF lost 205 of all types. At that point in the war, however, the relative rates of attrition were not the concern; that was a consideration for the longer term. Rather, as Dowding's worries showed, it was the absolute rate of the RAF's own losses that mattered for the immediate future: the days, weeks, and at most months ahead in 1940.

23 Admittedly, sometimes by single aircraft.

24 See Denis Richards, *Portal of Hungerford*, London, 1977, p. x.

25 T. Taylor, *The Breaking Wave*, London, 1957, p. 157–8; newsreel footage.

26 General Paul Deichmann (ex-Luftwaffe), The Karlsruhe Studies; 'Reasons of the Luftwaffe for changing over to mass attacks on London' 1953–8; reprint of USAF Historical Studies.

27 USSBS interviews with Werner Junck, 20–4 April 1945.

28 T. Taylor, *Breaking Wave*, p. 44. See the excellent account given by John Ray in *The Night Blitz 1940–41*, London, 1996, which has been a helpful guide here.

29 Quoted in Ray, *Night Blitz*, p. 103.

30 This much-rehearsed accusation is discussed at length in (e.g.) Group Captain F. W. Winterbotham, *The Ultra Secret*, New York, 1974; Cave Brown, *Bodyguard of Lies* (2 vols) New York, 1974; William Stevenson, *A Man Called Intrepid*, New York, 1976; etc. An apparently definitive statement of the case is given by one who was intimately in the know: John Colville, who worked in Downing Street in the war years. In his *The Churchillians* (London, 1981, p. 62) he writes: 'All concerned with the information gleaned from the intercepted German signals were conscious that German suspicions must not be aroused for the sake of ephemeral advantages. In the case of the Coventry raid no dilemma arose, for until the German directional beam was turned on the doomed city nobody knew where the great raid would be. Certainly the Prime Minister did not. The German signals referred to a major operation with the code name "Moonlight Sonata". The usual "Boniface" secrecy in the Private Office had been lifted on this occasion and during the afternoon before the raid I wrote in my diary (kept under lock and key at 10 Downing Street), "It is obviously some major air operation, but its exact destination the Air Ministry find it difficult to determine".'

31 BCWD, p. 103.

32 Official Narrative.

33 As an indication of the relative inefficacy of aerial bombing at this juncture of the war, the figures scrupulously kept by the city of Cologne – subject of the devastating 1,000-bomber attack in July 1942 – showed that in the period June 1941 to February 1942 the city was bombed 33 times, but that only 17 per cent of the tonnage dropped fell within the city limits. Although houses and factories had been damaged, and over 13,000 people temporarily dehoused, only 138 people had died in all those raids.

34 Quoted Richards, *The Hardest Victory*, p. 97.

35 OH, vol. IV, pp. 135–40.

36 On the night of 16–17 December 1940, as a retaliation for the Coventry raid, an area-bombing attack was carried out on Mannheim. The largest assembly of RAF bombers so far gathered for a single mission – 134 aircraft – took part in the attack, which killed forty-seven people and demolished nearly 500 buildings. But this raid, although 'Coventry-style', did not by itself herald the onset of area bombing, though of course it made the later acceptance of the policy easier.

37 Edmund Fawcett drew my attention to the fact that the striking photograph showing the dome of St Paul's floating in a sea of fire was in fact concocted for propaganda purposes; it was by Harry Morgan, as reported in *St Paul's: The Cathedral Church of London 604–2004* edited by Derek Keene, Arthur Burns and Andrew Saint, New Haven, CT, 2004.

38 Sir Arthur Harris, *Bomber Offensive*, London, 1947, pp. 51–2.

39 OH, vol. IV, pp 143–8.

40 Harris, *Bomber Offensive*, pp. 115–17.

41 Ibid., p. 115.

42 Richards, *The Hardest Victory*, p. 120.

43 Other towns are sometimes included in the Baedeker raid story: Ipswich, Cambridge, Bury

St Edmunds and Great Yarmouth; but these were small raids and did nowhere near as much damage as the principal Baedeker attacks.

44   Quoted Richards, *The Hardest Victory*, p. 127.

45   Harris, *Bomber Offensive*, p. 113.

46   BCWD, p. 297.

47   This crucial point is discussed along with others in the next chapter.

48   Harris believed that the formation of an élite corps would damage Bomber Command morale, and in this he was supported by all of his Group commanders. In the event a force was constituted by having the best crews nominated by Groups themselves, and it was placed under the charge of an extremely able Australian airman, Donald Bennett, an expert in navigation as in other aspects of the air arts. Harris devised the name 'Pathfinder Force' (abbreviated to 'PFF') and invented a badge for it: an eagle.

49   The superb Mosquito was also in service with Bomber Command by now too, flying with the Pathfinder Force and also able to bomb and photograph by day, because its speed and altitude were able to keep it for the most part away from fighters.

50   Probert, *Bomber Harris*, pp. 252–3.

51   Ibid., p. 253.

52   Richards, *The Hardest Victory*, pp. 172–3.

53   OH, vol. II, p. 291.

54   Richards, *The Hardest Victory*, p. 196.

55   Quoted in Probert, *Bomber Harris*, p. 263.

56   Ibid., p. 266.

57   OH, vol. II, p. 193.

58   The statistics are these: the sixteen major raids between mid-November and the end of March involved 8,700 sorties, from which about 500 bombers failed to return. This is a loss rate of 5.8 per cent, above the 'acceptable' upper limit of 5 per cent. In the view of commentators favourable to Harris, he did not call off the 'Battle of Berlin' because he felt, as the official historians did, that it was a defeat, but because preparations for Operation Overlord – the D-Day landings – and the Combined Offensive required the attention of Bomber Command elsewhere. One possibility is that if Overlord had not been imminent, and if the USAAF had not still been having doubts about deep-penetration attacks into Germany, Harris might have continued – with yet worsening results. The German defences were at this stage more than equal to the challenge, though very soon they were to suffer defeats, and continuing attrition, as the Allied offensives on all fronts wore with increasing effectiveness on their capacity.

In a detailed account of the bomber war, there would appear at this juncture an account of a catastrophically unsuccessful raid on Nuremberg at the end of March 1944 which cost Bomber Command many aircraft and air crews for scarcely any return, most of the bomber force being blown far off target by unexpectedly strong winds, and finding navigation difficult because of adverse weather generally. Harris never spoke of this débâcle, but it is likely that if the Combined Offensive had not begun at about the same time, with some major successes to show for itself, this single disaster might well have cost Harris his job.

59   Quoted Richards, *The Hardest Victory*, p. 217.

60   Probert, *Bomber Harris*, p. 293.

61   Ibid., p. 291.

62   Ibid., pp. 291–2.

63   Richards, *The Hardest Victory*, p. 233.

64   Ibid., p. 239.

65   Quoted Probert, *Bomber Harris*, p. 305.

66 Ibid., p. 308.

67 Ibid., p. 311.

68 Richards, *The Hardest Victory*, p. 270.

69 Widely divergent figures are given for the dead in the Dresden raid, from 25,000 to 150,000. I give the most conservative figure, though the number of unrecognisable bodies, and the number of refugees, probably means that the figure should be higher. See Frederick Taylor, *Dresden*, London, 2004, pp. 370–1.

70 AHB Narrative, vol. IV, p. 203.

71 See Hermann Knell, *To Destroy a City: Strategic Bombing and its Human Consequences in World War II*, Cambridge, MA, 2003, p. 17 *et. seq.* Knell was a boy in Würzburg when it was destroyed in air raids in February and March 1945. The main reason for its being a target seems to be that its population was just over 100,000, and hence 'on the list' of cities to be destroyed.

72 OH, vol. III, p. 112.

73 US Strategic Bombing Survey Summary Report (USSBS) (Pacific War), Washington DC, 1 July 1946, p. 16.

74 Ibid.

75 The USSBS said 185,000 dead; see ibid., p. 20; subsequent reports lower the figure to 100,000. The exact number will of course never be known, but it is likely to be somewhere between these figures, perhaps in the region of the lower of them.

76 Ibid., p. 20.

77 Ibid., p. 24.

78 I return to all these points in later chapters.

3 The Experience of the Bombed

1 Quoted Middlebrook, *Battle of Hamburg*, p. 257.

2 Ibid., p. 258.

3 Ibid., pp. 258–9.

4 In London such an area lies between King's Cross, Hyde Park, the Thames and the Tower of London; in New York it would be all of Lower Manhattan from Madison Square Park to Battery Park. See ibid., p. 263.

5 Ibid., p. 265.

6 Earl R. Beck *Under the Bombs: The German Home Front 1943–45*, Lexington, KY, 1986, p. 69.

7 Ibid., p. 70.

8 W. G. Sebald, *Natural History of Destruction*, p. 29.

9 Middlebrook, *Battle of Hamburg*, pp. 264–5.

10 Ibid., p. 266.

11 Ibid., p. 268.

12 Ibid., p. 274.

13 Ibid., p. 275.

14 Ibid., p. 276.

15 Quoted in Christoph Kucklick, *Feuersturm: Der Bombenkrieg gegen Deutschland*, Hamburg, 2003, p. 32.

16 See Churchill's 'exterminating attack' remark.

17 Beck, *Under the Bombs*, p. 60.

18 Ibid., p. 62; Beck is here describing the experiences reported by Josef Fischer, a citizen of Cologne who made a record of his experience under bombing.

19 See chapter 7 below, where I discuss the question of when the Allies knew that victory, even if it still had to be fought for, was inevitable given their industrial and manpower superiority over the Axis.

20 Kurt Vonnegut, *Slaughterhouse 5*, New York, 1969, p. 157.

21 John Hersey, *Hiroshima*, London, 1946, p. 68.

22 USSBS Pacific, p. 17.

23 Ibid., p. 20.

24 Hersey, *Hiroshima*, p. 182.

25 USSBS Pacific, p. 21.

26 The figures are quoted in Beck, *Under the Bombs*, pp. 8–9.

27 Ibid., p. 9.

28 Ibid., p. 111.

29 Richard Overy, *War and the Economy in the Third Reich*, Oxford, 1994, p. 312. Overy's book is an excellent study of the German war economy, and provides correctives to what had hitherto been a number of misconceptions about it. See also Gitta Sereny, *Albert Speer: His Battle with Truth*, New York, 1995; Joachim Fest, *Speer: The Final Verdict*, London, 2001.

30 USSBS Europe, p. 2.

31 The photographs in Antony Beevor's marvellous *Berlin – The Downfall 1945*, London, 2002, reveal as much; the text testifies to the ferocity of the German resistance, impossible without at least the basic equipment.

32 It is a fact forgotten by many that the giant Skoda armaments works in Czechoslovakia, and the separate Skoda automative works, were leaders in their fields in central Europe, for the country had been the industrial powerhouse of the Austro-Hungarian empire, and its genius for design was second to none.

33 In Britain the labour shortfall occasioned by men going into the armed forces was made up by women entering the workforce. In Germany this did not happen; the percentage of women in work in Germany was the same before and after 1939. Contract and prisoner labour in wartime Germany included women, but the proportions of them depended on the status of the group from which they came. Thus, Jewish and Slav women were allowed, or made, to work, whereas French and Dutch women were not.

34 Richard Bessel, *Nazism and War*, London, 2004, pp. 132–3. The prisoners of Mittelbau-Dora remind one of the Earthmen in C. S. Lewis's *The Silver Chair*, slaves of the Lady of the Green Kirtle.

35 Richards, *The Hardest Victory*, p. 194.

36 Ibid., p. 195.

37 Robin Neillands, *The Bomber War: The Allied Air offensive Against Germany*, New York, 2001, p. 343.

38 Richards, *The Hardest Victory*, p. 301.

39 *The Goebbels Diaries*, London, 1948, p. 113.

40 Ibid., p. 393.

41 Ibid., pp. 496–8.

42 Ibid., pp. 425–7.

43 Ibid., p. 485, and Richards p. 212.

44 Quoted Beck, *Under the Bombs*, pp. 87–8.

45 Middlebrook, *Battle of Hamburg*, p. 360.

46 Princess Marie Vassiltchikov, *The Berlin Diaries*, London, 1985. Admittedly, 'Missie' Vassiltchikov had aristocratic and well-placed friends, and after being bombed out could resort to the commodious hospitality in Potsdam of Count Gottfried Bismarck-Schonhausen. But the contrast between this and families sharing a cellar is one of degree not kind: the point was that everyone pulled together, even those who – like

Count Bismarck-Schonhausen, shortly afterwards put on trial for anti-Hitler activities – had no interest in a German victory in the war.

47 Beck, *Under the Bombs*, p. 108.
48 The horrific story of the Russian advance at the end of the war is told by Antony Beevor in his excellent and excoriating *Berlin*, London, 2002.
49 USSBS Europe, p. 15.
50 Ibid., p. 14.
51 Richards, *The Hardest Victory*, p. 303.
52 John Terraine gives a graphic account of the Typhoon attacks on Panzer divisions in the attempted counter-thrust by the Wehrmacht on 7 August 1944 westward from Mortain. As the rocket-firing Typhoons of the Second Tactical Air Force defeated the tanks, fighters from the Ninth Air Force kept the Luftwaffe fighters away. Terraine quotes Sir A. M. Coningham: 'This was to date one of the best demonstrations of the tactical use of air power which had been given in this war. It showed that a Tactical Air Force may be a decisive battle winning factor, and it showed the smooth co-ordination of air effort which could be achieved at short notice by the team work which had been perfected between the Ninth Air Force and the second Tactical Air Force.' John Terraine, *The Right of the Line: The Royal Air Force in the European War 1939–1945*, London, 1985, p. 661.
53 Probert, *Bomber Harris*, p. 293. In May 1944 Harris told a meeting at Montgomery's HQ: 'it can be stated without fear of contradiction that the heavy bomber is a first-class strategic weapon and one of the least effective tactical weapons.'
54 Ibid., p. 297.
55 Beck, *Under the Bombs*, pp. 130–1.
56 Neillands, *The Bomber War*, p. 336.
57 USSBS Europe, p. 8.
58 Harris, *Bomber Offensive*, p. 233.
59 USSBS Europe, p. 9.
60 Ibid.
61 Figures quoted in Richards, *The Hardest Victory*, pp. 301–2.
62 Alfred Mierzejewski, *Collapse of the German War Economy 1944–1945: Allied Air Power and the German National Railway* Chapel Hill, NC, 1988, p. 192.
63 Robert A. Pape, *Bombing to Win: Air Power and Coercion in War*, Ithaca, NY, 1996.
64 Ian Buruma *The Wages of Guilt Memories of War in Germany and Japan*, London, 1994.
65 During a spell as Visiting Professor at Tokyo University I had the opportunity to visit Nagasaki and Hiroshima, and heard this view at first hand in conversations in both cities. What is said in the course of such conversations might be demurred in more public contexts, but the sense that at least some Japanese have of Japanese victims of area bombing being *victims* is not equally the default attitude among Germans of the war and immediately post-war generations, at least in anything like the same straightforward way. That attitude is now changing.
66 Buruma, *Wages of Guilt*, p. 12.
67 Ibid., p. 11.
68 Ibid., p. 162.

4 The Mind of the Bomber

1 Beck, *Under the Bombs*, p. 64.
2 Henry Probert's *Bomber Harris* is a sympathetic portrayal, intended – and with a good measure of success – to redress the balance of hostile opinion that Harris attracted

whenever the ethics of Bomber Command's activities in the war was at issue. Whatever else might be said about Harris, he was clearly an outstanding leader, and his concern for the welfare and proper reward of those under his command does him credit. He had his callous and uncompromising side, he was arguably wrong-headed in his larger theories, and he was not an easy subordinate for the Air Staff to manage, to the point of reducing the effectiveness of the air contribution to the war. But most men are of mixed alloy, and Probert does a masterly job in leaving one with a sense of Harris's large qualities while not masking his warts and failings.

3 No doubt some would say that being cultured and yet still able to carry out such policies is worse; the thought has weight – for this must have been true of many German SS personnel.

4 Probert, *Bomber Harris*, pp 154–5.

5 Ibid., p. 223.

6 Ibid., pp. 193–4, 227.

7 Ibid., p. 208.

8 See A. Nussbaum, 'Frédéric de Martens, Representative Tsarist Writer on International Law', XXII *Acta Scandinavica juris gentium* (in: *Nordisk Tidsskrift for International Law*), 1952, pp. 51–66.

9 Information about the effects of the German bombing assault on the British Isles in the First World War can be found in Colin McInnes and G. D. Sheffield, (eds.) *Warfare in the Twentieth Century*, London, 1988. See the article by J. Pimlott 'The Theory and Practice of Strategic Bombing' in McInnes and Sheffield, p 121.

10 Caparetto is now Kobarid in Slovenia. Its battle is the setting of Hemingway's, *A Farewell to Arms*.

11 Douhet's book appeared in English twenty years later, translated by Dino Ferrari (New York, 1942; all references here are to this edition) but its tenets were widely known and discussed long before this.

12 Douhet *The Command of the Air*, pp 28, 47–8, 57–8, 309.

13 Quoted Pape, *Bombing to Win*, pp. 60–1.

14 Quoted ibid., p. 61.

15 Ibid.

16 Ibid.

17 Ibid., pp. 61–2.

18 Basil Liddell Hart, *Paris, or the Future of War*, London, 1925.

19 Ibid., p. 50.

20 Ibid., p. 45.

21 Quoted in Brian Bond, *Liddell Hart*, London, 1979, p. 145.

22 Memo of May 1928 to fellow service chiefs, quoted in OH, vol. IV, p. 74.

23 A. D. Harvey, ref p. 665.

24 Ibid., p. 663.

25 Ibid., vol. 1, p. 99.

26 Pape, *Bombing to Win*, p. 63.

27 Ibid., p. 63–4.

28 Ibid., p. 64.

29 The lecturer quoted by Pape is M. S. Fairchild, an instructor at the Air Corps Tactical School. These lectures were given in 1939, and are to be found in the archives of the US Air Force Historical Research Agency at Maxwell Air Force Base in Alabama. Ibid., p. 63.

30 Quoted ibid.

31 Like Douhet, Mitchell's passionate enthusiasm for air power got him into trouble. He had shown brilliant imagination in using massed air power in support of ground operations in the reduction of the St Mihiel salient in the last year of the First World

War, while in charge of the US combat aircraft in France; but his outspokenness in criticising US Army and Navy foot-dragging over air-power matters resulted in a court martial in 1925, and the end of his military career. At the time of the court martial he held the rank of brigadier-general. He wrote several books on air strategy, and a bomber aircraft was posthumously named after him, a tribute after the dust of old political rivalries had settled down.

32 Pape, *Bombing to Win*, p. 65.

33 Ibid., p. 66.

34 Quoted ibid.

35 The field manual in question was the War Department Field Manual 100–20 (FM 100–20, *Command and Employment of Air Power*), the 'Declaration of Independence' of the US air force. It embodied a good deal of Air Corps Tactical School pre-war thinking, not least in asserting that 'concentrated use of the air striking force is a battle winning factor of the first importance. Control of available air power must be exercised through the air force commander if this inherent flexibility and ability to deliver a decisive blow are to be fully exploited'.

36 This is said to have been the work of a pro-German US Senator called Burton Wheeler, who gave copies of AWPD-1 to the *Chicago Tribune* and the *Washington Times-Herald* in the autumn of 1941.

37 Stewart Halsey Ross, *Strategic Bombing by the United States in World War II: The Myths and the Facts*, Jefferson, NC, 2003. He points out that trying to hit a target smaller than a football field from five miles up in the air with an ordinary (that is, unguided or 'unsmart') 'iron bomb' would be extremely difficult in the best circumstances, let alone in combat conditions. The point is well made.

38 Ibid., chapter 5, *passim*.

39 Almost any town in Germany during the war could be claimed to have some military importance; German war production had been widely dispersed, rail links were always a target, refugees were everywhere, and of course the premise of area bombing is that civilians support their country's military effort. Frederick Taylor in his *Dresden* shows how much can be nominated as having military and strategic value in that city and its environs. Two observations are relevant: Dresden doubtless had some military value to an attacker, but its cultural value might have been a better reason for not bombing it; and in the case of Wurzberg and other historical towns, the same definitely applies.

40 Presciently Grey said when hostilities began, 'The lamps are going out all over Europe; we shall not see them lit again in our lifetime.' Given that the events of 1914 ushered in hot and cold war for the next seventy-five years, until the Berlin Wall came down in 1989, he was right.

41 The relatively successful naval conferences were held in 1921, 1927 and 1930. Frank B. Kellogg and Aristide Briand were respectively the US Secretary of State and the French Foreign Secretary who originally brokered the treaty.

42 This commission was established following the agreement reached in the Locarno Pact, establishing the borders of Germany. It seemed, but did not prove to be, an auspicious moment for continuing the peace process with a discussion about limiting the means to war.

43 Philip S. Meilinger (US Naval War College), 'Clipping the Bomber's Wings: The Geneva Disarmament Conference and the Royal Air Force 1932–34', *War in History* 1999 6 (3).

44 Ibid.

45 Ibid.

46 Quoted in F. Emme (ed.), *The Impact of Air Power*, Princeton, NJ, 1959, pp. 51–2.

47 Hansard, House of Commons, 14 September 1939.

48 Spencer Weart and Gertrude Szilard, *Leo Szilard: His Version of the Facts*, Boston, MA, 1979 pp. 54–5.

49 Quoted by Gerard DeGroot in his excellent history of the development of the atom bomb, *The Bomb*, London, 2004, p. 24.

50 Ibid., p. 28.

51 Ibid., p. 69.

52 The meeting took place on 19 September 1944 at Roosevelt's country retreat of Hyde Park. Ibid., p. 70.

53 Ibid., p. 74.

54 Ibid., p. 77.

55 Ibid., p. 85.

56 Ibid., p. 103.

57 Quoted ibid., p. 96.

58 Quoted ibid.

59 Sebald, *Natural History of Destruction*, p. 99.

60 Revisionist and neo-Nazi historians alike claim that the true architect of the Morgenthau Plan was Harry Dexter White, Morgenthau's influential aide in the Treasury Department, who in the McCarthy era was accused of being a Soviet spy, and who is (therefore) said by revisionists and neo-Nazis to have invented the idea of the 'pastoralisation' of Germany so that it would fall all the more readily into Communist hands. This is among the more moderate of the conspiracy theories that all too fruitfully spring up in this connection. The theorists' speculations are fuelled by the fact that the McCarthy witch-hunts embroiled a number of Treasury Department officials, and that White himself, after his appearance before the Un-American Activities Committee, died of a heart attack just a few days later – suspected by the conspiracy theorists, of course, of having committed suicide. His two daughters have consistently defended their father's probity, as recently as 2003 writing to the *Washington Times* to protest against a repeat of the McCarthy accusations in a new book.

61 Ralf Georg Reuth, *Goebbels: The Life of Joseph Goebbels*, translated by Krishna Winston, London, 1993, p. 339.

62 Joseph Goebbels, 'What Is At Stake', *Das Reich*, 27 September 1944. Source: 'Was auf dem Spiele steht', *Der steile Aufstieg*, Munich: Zentralverlag der NSDAP, 1944, pp. 3–9. One wonders, if those who proposed bringing up German children away from the influences that made Nazism possible were 'deranged' to propose this, what description is to be given to people who gassed children to death in Auschwitz and elsewhere. Interestingly, in the earlier part of this article Goebbels wrote: 'Those who bear no responsibility have the prerogative to think about life and the world however they wish. Those in government are different. They must represent the whole interest of their people, not only the interests of the present, but even more importantly those of the future. Their wishes and actions must follow rules that take account of the most varied factors affecting the life of their nation, as well of the nations in their sphere of influence . . . One cannot accuse the German government of ever violating this principle in the course of the war. It has carefully avoided laying out broad theoretical war goals, always limiting itself to fighting for the freedom, independence, and vital living space of its people. Most of its military actions were forced upon it. Its offensives always had their origins in a desire to defend the nation. After defeating an enemy, it made reasonable demands that were both practical and absolutely necessary.' Ibid.

63 The source for these putative facts is the Morgenthau Diaries, held at Hyde Park, the Roosevelt house in New York State, and this interpretation of their contents is owed to a paper by Anthony Kubek, 'The Morgenthau Plan and the Problem of Policy Perversion', in a revisionist publication called *The Journal for Historical Review* (vol 9 no 3 Summer 1989) pp. 287 *et. seq.* Because of this provenance the report to this point here is tentatively given. Morgenthau's book is however in the public domain, and responsible historians have

acknowledged its degree of influence on Roosevelt and Churchill independently; for example, Martin Gilbert, *The Second World War*, 2nd edn, London, 2000, p. 592.

64 Gilbert, ibid.

65 Lord Moran, Diary (unpublished) 13 September 1944; see Lord Moran, *Churchill at War 1940–1945*, London, 2002, pp. 177–8.

66 In his Memoirs Cordell Hull was unequivocal in his condemnation of Morgenthau's interference in what was mainly State Department business: 'Emotionally upset by Hitler's rise and his persecution of the Jews, Morgenthau often sought to induce the President to anticipate the State Department or act contrary to our better judgment. We sometimes found him conducting negotiations with foreign governments which were the function of the State Department. His work in drawing up a catastrophic plan for the post-war treatment of Germany and inducing the President to accept it without consultation with the State Department, was an outstanding instance of this interference.'

67 One of the very first calls for Germany to be diminished in size and/or broken up into smaller states, de-industrialised or not, came from France in the earliest part of the war. The proposals were not taken seriously by those, among them H. G. Wells in *What Are We Fighting For* (London, 1940), who were thinking instead of what kind of international regime should come into existence after the war to prevent future wars – the failed promise of the 'war to end all wars' that had not quite succeeded in ending war twenty years before.

68 B. E. Schmitt's speech was reported in *Time* magazine for 1 December 1941, pp. 57–8, under the title 'History Lesson'. See also Bernadotte Schmitt, *What Shall We Do with Germany?*, Public Policy Pamphlets no 38, University of Chicago Press, 1943.

69 The entire text of this extraordinary book has been reprinted by the revisionist Institute for Historical Review and placed by it, with other documents conducing to its view of the past, on the internet, where it is easy to find. For its bona fides as not being a forgery, it has Library of Congress call number DD222.K3; and it can be purchased through Amazon.com.

70 Kaufman's book was reviewed in, among other places, *Time* (24 March 1941, pp. 95–6).

71 Louis Nizer, *What to Do with Germany*, Chicago and New York, 1944, p. 13.

72 Ibid., p. 17.

73 Ibid., pp. 18–19.

74 Norman Cousins, 'The Time for Hate Is Now', *The Saturday Review of Literature*, 4 July 1942, pp. 14–18, quoted in James Martin, 'The Bombing and Negotiated Peace Questions – in 1944', *Rampart Journal*, vol. IV, no. 1, Spring 1968, p. 78.

75 Martin, ibid., p. 79. Clifton Fadiman was the host for many years of a popular radio show called 'Information Please', and he is otherwise best known for the anthologies of children's literature he edited. He condensed the *Encyclopaedia Britannica*, chaired the selection process for the Book of the Month Club and died in 1999 at the age of ninety-five. From such genial material could come 'the fury of the non-combatant', in C. E. Montague's pungent phrase. To him is owed the remark that 'The German mind has a talent for making no mistakes but the very greatest'.

76 Robert Lord Vansittart, *Bones of Contention*, London, 1945. See the review in *Time*, 16 July 1945. According to Anthony Eden, Vansittart was 'a sincere, almost fanatical, crusader' rather than 'an official giving cool and disinterested advice'.

77 Hansard, House of Lords, 10 March 1943. For the whole question at issue here see also: Steven Casey, 'The Campaign to Sell a Harsh Peace for Germany to the American Public 1944–48, *History*, 2005, vol. 90, no. 297, pp. 62–92.

78 I reviewed this book on its first appearance, in the *Financial Times* in 1996. For a longer and more detailed criticism of the book see Richard Neuhaus in *First Things* 65 (August–September 1996), pp. 36–41.

79 See Knell, *To Destroy a City*, chapter 1 *passim*.

80 Ronald Schaffer *Wings of Judgment*, New York, 1985, p. 153.

81 Quoted ibid.

82 Ibid.

83 Ibid., p. 154.

84 Curtis LeMay, *Mission with LeMay: My Story*, New York, 1965, p. 387.

85 See Thomas M. Coffey, *Iron Eagle: The Turbulent Life of General Curtis LeMay*, New York, 1986.

86 Field Marshal Lord Alanbrooke, *War Diaries 1939–45*, edited by Alex Danchev and Daniel Todman, London, 2001. The diary is littered with exclamation marks, sometimes two or three at a time, and reports of bird-watching excitements, making the book read like a boy-scout memoir at times. Alanbrooke had a reputation for imperturbability and sang-froid to which the diary gives the lie.

87 Ibid., p. 460.

88 Ibid., p. 547.

89 Ibid., p. 325.

90 Ibid., p. 586.

91 Quoted Richards, p. 97; see chapter 2 above.

92 An account of this meeting is given in Richard Overy's powerful and absorbing analysis of the Allied victory in World War Two, *Why The Allies Won*, London, 1995, p. 102.

93 Ibid.

94 The phrase 'combined offensive' is not exactly descriptive; in fact the two air forces continued more or less separate campaigns, occasionally bombing the same targets on alternating nights and days, but generally speaking each following a different drum.

95 OH, p. 112.

96 Quoted ibid.

97 This has been suggested a number of times as part of the reason for the Dresden attack.

98 Richards, *The Hardest Victory*, p. 270.

5 *Voices of Conscience*

1 Corder Catchpool, *On Two Fronts: Letters of a Conscientious Objector*, London, 1918.

2 Quoted in Paul Berry and Mark Bostridge, *Vera Brittain: A Life*, Boston, MA, 2002, p. 431.

3 Given that the appointment to Canterbury effectively lay in Churchill's gift, and that Bell was regarded as the natural successor to Temple, it is clear that Bell's opposition to the bombing aspect of the war effort was an irritant to the government.

4 Vera Brittain, *Seed of Chaos*, London, 1944. Published for the Bombing Restriction Committee by New Vision Press.

5 *Seed of Chaos* was republished just as this book was going to press, by Continuum in London. It is included in Vera Brittain, *One Voice: Pacifist Writings from the Second World War*.

6 Ibid., p. 7.

7 Ibid., pp. 7–8.

8 Ibid., pp. 8–9. The comment quoted occurred in the *New Statesman*, 18 December 1943; Churchill's remark about an 'experiment' is from an interview in *Time* magazine, 7 June 1943.

9 Ibid., p. 9, italics in the original.

10 Ibid., p. 10.

11 Ibid.

12 Ibid. The Shaw remark comes from a letter by him to the *Sunday Express*, 28 November 1943. As the highly contemporary nature of Brittain's quotations show, the debate about the bombing was a lively one in the pages of the national press.

13 Ibid., p. 11.

14 Ibid., p. 12.

15 The results of this poll were published in the *News Chronicle*, 2 May 1941.

16 The speech was given on 15 July 1941. Ibid., p. 13.

17 Churchill, then First Lord of the Admiralty, made this speech on 27 January 1940.

18 Brittain, *Seed of Chaos*, p. 16.

19 Ibid. The speech was made on 19 May 1943.

20 Ibid.

21 Ibid., p. 17.

22 Ibid., p. 18.

23 Ibid., pp. 19–20.

24 Ibid., p. 20.

25 Ibid., p. 21.

26 Harris, *Bomber offensive*, p. 92.

27 Brittain, *Seed of Chaos*, p. 25, quoting the *Daily Telegraph* of 12 August 1943, itself in turn quoting German claims about how RAF Bomber Command was operating. Given the difficulties of accuracy in night area bombing, the claim might relate to an aspiration rather than a standardly successful practice on Bomber Command's part.

28 Ibid., p. 24.

29 Quoted ibid., p. 25.

30 Quoted ibid.

31 Ibid., p. 26.

32 *Time* magazine, 7 July 1943, quoted ibid., p. 27.

33 Ibid., p. 34.

34 Quoted – and with names of the signatories appended – ibid., p. 37.

35 Quoted ibid., p. 97.

36 Letter to the Hull *Daily Mail*, 26 November 1943, quoted ibid., p. 98.

37 Quoted in Paul Berry and Mark Bostridge, *Vera Brittain: A Life*, Boston, MA, 1995, p. 438.

38 Brittain, *Seed of Chaos*, p. 97.

39 Article in *Evening Standard*, 4 January 1944, quoted ibid., p. 100.

40 Article in the *Daily Mail*, 6 January 1944, quoted ibid.

41 Quoted ibid., p. 102.

42 Corder Catchpool in the *Friend*, 25 June 1943.

43 Hansard, House of Commons, 28 July 1943 – in the midst of Operation Gomorrah.

44 Quoted ibid., pp. 104–5.

45 Quoted ibid., pp. 106–7.

46 Ibid., p. 108.

47 Ibid., p. 114.

48 Ibid., p. 115.

49 The signatories were George A. Buttrick, J. Henry Carpenter, Allan Knight Chalmers, Henry H. Crane, Albert E. Day, Phillips P. Elliott, Harry Emerson Fosdick, Georgia Harkness, John Hayes Holmes, Allan A. Hunter, Josephine Johnson, E. Stanley Jones, John Paul Jones, Rufus Jones, John H. Lathrop, Kenneth Scott Latourette, W. Appleton Lawrence, Elmore M. McKee, Walter Mitchell, Kirby Page, Clarence Pickett, Edwin McNeill Poteat, Richard Roberts, Paul Scherer, Ralph Sockman, Earnest F. Tittle, Oswald Garrison Villard, and Winifred Wygal. Most of these were widely known in their own day.

The US did not have an anti-area-bombing campaign as such, apart from the support given to Brittain's pamphlet, but it had a small and courageous pacifist movement, much vilified and often physically attacked by members of the public and armed forces on leave.

50 Berry and Bostridge, *Vera Brittain*, p. 439.
51 James Martin, 'The Bombing and Negotiated Peace Questions – in 1944', *Rampart Journal*, vol. IV, no. 1, Spring 1968, p. 112.
52 Quoted ibid., p. 113.
53 Ibid., p. 114.
54 Ibid.
55 Ibid.
56 Berry and Bostridge, *Vera Brittain*, p. 440.
57 Ibid.
58 Ibid.
59 Charles E. Montague, *Disenchantment*, London, 1922, p. 220.
60 George Orwell, 'As I Please,' *Tribune*, 19 May 1944.
61 Ibid.
62 Ibid.
63 Berry and Bostridge, *Vera Brittain*, p. 441.
64 Quoted ibid.
65 Ibid.
66 Ibid., p. 442.
67 See Benjamin King and Timothy Kutta, *Impact: The History of Germany's V-Weapons in World War II*, Cambridge, MA, 1998.

6 The Case Against the Bombing

1 Augustine ref.
2 For completeness it is worth pointing out that the *justum bellum* is one that has both *justum ad bellum* – just causes for war and aims in them – and *jus in bello* – just practice in the conduct of war. On this definition if either *justum ad* or *jus in* fails, there is no *justum bellum*. In my remarks here I am implicitly arguing that a war can remain just given its causes and the aims of the (so to say) aggrieved combatant, even if some aspect of *jus in bello* fails. But too much of the latter must threaten to impugn the justice of the whole; there is a question of proportions. The thought here is that even if World War II Allied area bombing turns out on examination to be unjust, it does not make the war as a whole so from the Allied point of view.
3 Otto von Gericke, 'The Sack of Magdeburg,' *Readings in European History*, ed. J. H. Robinson, New York, 1906.
4 Hugo Grotius, *De Jure Belli ac Pacis*, Book III, chapter 1, section iv; chapter 4, section ii.
5 Ibid., chapter 4, section ix.
6 Ibid., chapter 5, section i.
7 Ibid., chapter 5, section ii.
8 Voltaire, *Candide*, chapter 3, 'How Candide Escaped from the Bulgarians and What Befell Him Afterwards'.
9 Sun Tzu, *The Art of War*, translated by Lionel Giles, London, 1910, chapter II.
10 See US Congress, House, *The Trial of Henry Wirz*, 40th Cong., 2nd sess, 1867–8. H. Doc. 1331.
11 One of the earliest of these was published in 1908 by a man who had himself been a Union prisoner of the Confederate forces; James Madison Page, *The True Story of*

Andersonville Prison: A Defence of Major Henry Wirz, New York, 1908. Wirz was a captain at the time of the atrocities, a major by the time of his trial.

12 Geoffrey Best, *War and Law Since 1945*, Oxford, 1994, p. 41.

13 This is the text of the relevant part of Convention IV 'respecting the Laws and Customs of War on Land and its annex: Regulations concerning the Laws and Customs of War on Land'. This version was deposited at The Hague on 18 October 1907.

14 Self-denying ordinances like the Gas Protocol of 1925 would doubtless not be observed in war if the advantage of violating the protocol outweighed the disadvantage. But the combatant nations had learned in 1914–18 that the vagaries of the wind made gas an unreliable friend; considerations of prudence probably had a greater part to play than principle in the 'restraint' shown by the Allied and Axis forces in this regard.

15 Best, *War and Law*, p. 185.

16 In this connection one must see a book of quite exceptional interest, *A World at Total War*, edited by Roger Chickering, Stig Forster and Bernd Greiner, Cambridge, 2005. The Introduction is a brilliant survey of the questions prompted by the idea of 'total war'. Some of the points raised by the papers in this volume come into focus in the next chapter.

17 Joseph E. Persico, *Nuremberg: Infamy on Trial*, New York, 1994, pp. 33–4.

18 Ibid., p. 33.

19 Ibid., p. 35.

20 See Antony Beevor's excoriating account of the atrocities involved in Soviet–German fighting in the last months of the war in *Berlin – The Downfall 1945*. As regards the 'tu quoque' problem, Persico, *Nuremberg: Infamy on Trial*.

21 See Best, *War and Law*, pp. 180–1.

22 Ibid., p. 181.

23 Ibid., p. 81.

24 Hansard, House of Commons, 5th Series, 1937–8, vol. 337, col. 937.

25 Harris, *Bomber Offensive*, p. 177.

26 Best, *War and Law*, p. 201.

7 The Defence of Area Bombing

1 Harris, *Bomber Offensive*, p. 176.

2 Perhaps his claim becomes understandable when we remember that Harris was a gourmand.

3 Quoted Schaffer, *Wings of Judgment*, p. 146.

4 Ibid.

5 Ibid., p. 148.

6 Overy, *Why the Allies Won*, p. 124.

7 Ibid., p. 198.

8 See Chickering, Forster and Greiner, *A World at Total War: Global Conflict and the Politics of Destruction 1937–1945*, Cambridge, 2005.

9 Ibid., p. 3.

10 Ibid., p. 7.

11 Taylor, *Dresden*.

12 Ibid., p. 406.

13 Overy, *Why the Allies Won*, pp. 128–30.

14 Quoted Taylor, *Dresden*, p. 406.

15 Harris, *Bomber Offensive*, p. 144.

16 But one should add: with the honourable and important exception of its contribution to staving off the invasion threat of 1940.
17 Neillands, *The Bomber War*, p. 343.
18 Terraine, *The Right of the Line*, p. 663.
19 Richards, *The Hardest Victory*, pp. 298–9.
20 Ibid., p. 289.
21 Thomas L. Friedman, *International Herald Tribune*, 25 March 2005.
22 Neillands, *The Bomber War*, p. 386.
23 Clausewitz and Macaulay, quoted ibid.
24 Ibid.
25 Ibid.

8 Judgement

1 Schaffer, *Wings of Judgement*, p. 196.

Postscript

1 Captain S. W. Roskill, *The War at Sea 1939–45*, London, 1954–6, Volume 2, pp. 83–5.
2 Adam Tooze, *The Wages of Destruction: The Making and Breaking of the Nazi Economy*, London, 2006, p. 650.
3 Ibid., p. 626.

Bibliography

Anderson, Christopher, *The Men of the Mighty Eighth: The US Eighth Army Air Force 1942–45*, London, 2001

Astor, Gerald, *The Mighty Eighth*, New York, 1997

Beck, Earl R., *Under the Bombs: The German Home Front 1943–45*, Lexington, KY, 1986

Beevor, Anthony, *Berlin – The Downfall 1945*, London, 2002

Bennett, Donald, *Pathfinder*, London, 1958

Bergerud, Eric, *Fire in the Sky: The Air War in the South Pacific*, Colorado, 2001

Berry, Paul, and Mark Bostridge, *Vera Brittain: A Life*, Boston, MA, 1995

Bessel, Richard, *Nazism and War*, London, 2004

Best, Geoffrey, *War and Law Since 1945*, Oxford, 1994.

Boiten, Theo, and Martin Bowman, *Battles with the Luftwaffe: The Bomber Campaign Against Germany 1942–1945*, New York, 2001

Bond, Brian, *Liddell Hart*, London, 1979

Boog, Horst (ed.), *The Conduct of the Air War in the Second World War*, New York, 1992

Bowman, Martin W., *The USAF at War*, New York, 1995

Bradley, James, *Flyboys: The Final Secret of the Air War in the Pacific*, New York, 2003

Brittain, Vera, *Seed of Chaos*, London, 1944

Brittain, Vera, *One Voice: Pacifist Writings from the Second World War*, London, 2005

Brown, Cave, *Bodyguard of Lies*, 2 vols, New York, 1974

Buckley, John, *Air Power in the Age of Total War*, Bloomington, IN, 1999

Budiansky, Stephen, *Air Power: From Kitty Hawk to Gulf War II*, London, 2003

Buruma, Ian, *The Wages of Guilt: Memories of War in Germany and Japan*, London, 1994

Calder, Angus, *The Myth of the Blitz*, London, 1991

Catchpool, Corder, *On Two Fronts: Letters of a Conscientious Objector*, London, 1918

Chickering, Roger, Stig Forster and Bernd Greiner, *A World at Total War: Global Conflict and the Politics of Destruction 1937–1945*, Cambridge, 2005

Churchill, Winston, *The Second World War*, London, 1948

Coffrey, Thomas M., *Iron Eagle: The Turbulent Life of General Curtis LeMay*, New York, 1986

Colville, John, *The Churchillians*, London, 1981

Cook, Ronald, and Roy Conyers Nesbit, *Target: Hitler's Oil – Allied Attacks on German Oil Supplies 1939–45*, London, 1985

Craven, Wesley, and James Cate (ed.), *The Army Air Forces in World War II*, 3 vols, Washington, D.C., 1983

Danchev, Alex, and Daniel Todman, *Lord Alanbrooke War Diaries 1939–45*, London, 2001

Davis, Richard, *Carl G. Spaatz and the Air War in Europe*, Washington, D.C., 1993

DeGroot, Gerard, *The Bomb: A Life*, London, 2004

Douhet, Giuhon, *The Command of the Air*, trans by Dino Ferrari, New York, 1942

Emme, F. (ed.), *The Impact of Air Power*, Princeton, NJ, 1959

Ethell, Jeffrey L., *Bomber Command: American Bombers in World War II*, Osceola, WI, 1994

Falconer, Jonathan, *Bomber Command Handbook 1939–1945*, London, 1998

Fest, Joachim, *Hitler*, New York, 1974

Fest, Joachim, *Speer: The Final Verdict*, London, 2001

Fischer, Klaus, *Nazi Germany: A New History*, London, 1995

Frankland, Noble, *History at War*, London, 1998

Freeman, Roger, *The Mighty Eighth: A History of the Units, Men and Machines of the US 8th Army Air Force*, London, 1970

Friedrich, Jorg, *Brandstatten: Der Anblick des Bombenkriegs*, Berlin, 2003

Friedrich, Jorg, *Der Brand: Deutschland im Bombenkrieg 1940–1945*, Berlin, 2003

Garbett, Mike, and Brian Goulding, *Lancaster at War: 5: Fifty Years On*, London, 1995

Garrett, Stephen A., *Ethics and Airpower in World War II: The British Bombing of German Cities*, New York, 1993

Gibson, Guy, *Enemy Coast Ahead*, London, 1946

Gilbert, Martin, *The Second World War*, London, 1989; new edition, 2000

Giovannitti, Len, and Fred Freed, *The Decision to Drop the Bomb*, London, 1967

Groehier, Olaf, *Der Bombenkrieg gegen Deutschland*, Berlin, 1990

Grotius, Hugo, *De Jure Belli ac Pacis* (On the Law of War and Peace), Amsterdam, 1625

Hage, Volker (ed.), *Hamburg 1943*, Frankfurt am Main, 2003

Harris, Sir Arthur, *Bomber Offensive*, London, 1947

Hart, Basil Liddell, *Paris or the Future of War*, London, 1925

Hastings, Max, *Bomber Command*, revised edition, London, 1999

Hastings, Max, *Armageddon: The Battle for Germany 1944–45*, London, 2004

Hersey, John, *Hiroshima*, London, 1946

Jackson, Robert, *Before the Storm: The Story of Bomber Command 1939–42*, London, 1972

Jackson, Robert, *Bomber! Famous Bomber Missions of World War II*, London, 1980

Kaplan, Philip, *Bombers: The Aircrew Experience*, London, 2000

Kaufman, Theodore, *Germany Must Perish!* (self-published), 1940

King, Benjamin, and Timothy Kutta, *Impact: The History of Germany's V-weapons in World War II*, Cambridge, MA, 1998

Knell, Hermann, *To Destroy a City: Strategic Bombing and its Human Consequences in World War II*, Cambridge, MA, 2003

Kucklick, Christoph, *Feuersturm: Der Bombenkrieg gegen Deutschland*, Hamburg, 2003

Kurzman, Dan, *Day of the Bomb: Hiroshima 1945*, New York, 1986

LeMay, Curtis, *Mission with LeMay: My Story*, New York, 1965

Lindqvist, Sven, *A History of Bombing*, London, 2001

Longmate, Norman, *The Bombers*, London, 1983

Magenheimer, Heinz, *Hitler's War: Germany's Key Strategic Decisions 1940–1945*, London, 1998

McKee, Alexander, *The Devil's Tinderbox: Dresden 1945*, London, 1982

McInnes, Colin, and G. D. Sheffield, *Warfare in the Twentieth Century*, London, 1988

Middlebrook, Martin, *The Battle of Hamburg: The Firestorm Raid*, London, 1980

Middlebrook, Martin, *The Berlin Raids: RAF Bomber Command Winter 1943–44*, London, 1988

Middlebrook, Martin, and Chris Everitt, *The Bomber Command War Diaries: An Operational Reference Book 1939–1945*, London, 1985

Mierzejewski, Alfred, *Collapse of the German War Economy 1944–1955: Allied Air Power and the German National Railway*, Chapel Hill, NC, 1988

Montagne, Charles, E., *Disenchantment*, London, 1922

Neillands, Robin, *The Bomber War: The Allied Air Offensive Against Germany*, New York, 2001

Nichol, John, and Tony Rennell, *Tail End Charlies: The Last Battles of the Bomber War 1944–45*, London, 2004

Nizer, Louis, *What to do with Germany*, Chicago and New York, 1944

Overy, Richard, *War and the Economy in the Third Reich*, Oxford, 1990

Overy, Richard, *Why the Allies Won*, London, 1995

Page, James Madison, *The True Story of Andersonville Prison: A Defence of Major Henry Wirz*, New York, 1908

Pape, Robert A., *Bombing to Win: Air Power and Coercion in War*, Ithaca, NY, 1996

Peniston-Baird, Corinna, *Blitz: A Pictorial History of Britain Under Attack*, London, 2001

Persico, Joseph E., *Nuremberg: Infamy on Trial*, London, 1994

Probert, Henry, *Bomber Harris: His Life and Times*, London, 2001

Ratner, Steven, and John Abrams, *Accountability for Human Rights Atrocities in International Law*, 2nd edition, Oxford, 2001

Ray, John, *The Night Blitz 1940–41*, London, 1996

Read, Anthony, and David Fisher, *The Fall of Berlin*, London, 1992

Reuth, Ralf Georg, *Goebbels: The Life of Joseph Goebbels*, London, 1993

Richards, Denis, *Portal of Hungerford*, London, 1977

Richards, Denis, *The Hardest Victory: RAF Bomber Command in the Second World War*, London, 1994

Robertson, Geoffrey, *Crimes Against Humanity*, London, 1999

Roskill, Captain S. W., *The War at Sea 1939–45*, London, 1954–61, reprinted London, 2006

Ross, Stewart Halsey, *Strategic Bombing by the United States in in World War II: The Myths and the Facts*, Jefferson, NC, 2003

Russell, Alan (ed.), *Why Dresden?*, Arundel, 1998

Saward, Dudley, *'Bomber' Harris*, London, 1984

Schaffer, Ronald, *Wings of Judgment: American Bombing in World War II*, New York, 1985

Schmitt, Bernadotte, *What Shall We Do with Germany?*, Public Policy Pamphlets no. 38, Chicago, 1943

Sebald, W. G., *The Natural History of Destruction*, London, 2003

Sereny, Gita, *Albert Speer: His Battle with Truth*, New York, 1995

Sloan, John, *The Route as Briefed: The History of the 92nd Bombardment Group, USAAF 1942–1945*, New York, 1976

Speer, Albert, *Inside the Third Reich*, London, 1970

Stevenson, William, *A Man Called Intrepid*, New York, 1976

Taylor, Frederick, *Dresden: Tuesday, 13 February, 1945*, London, 2004

Taylor, James, and Martin Davidson, *Bomber Crew*, London, 2004

Taylor, T., *The Breaking Wave*, London, 1957

Terraine, John, *The Right of the Line: The Royal Air Force in the European War 1939–1945*, London, 1985

Thorne, Alex, *Lancaster at War: 4: Pathfinder Squadron*, London, 1990

Thucydides, The History of the Peloponnesian War, London, 1954

Tooze, Adam, *The Wages of Destruction: The Making and Breaking of the Nazi Economy*, London, 2006

Tzu, Sun, *The Art of War*, London, 1910

Vaccaro, Tony, *Entering Germany 1944–1949*, Cologne, 2001

Vansittart, Lord Robert, *Bones of Contention*, London, 1945

Vassiltchikov, Princess Marie, *The Berlin Diaries*, London, 1985

Vonnegut, Kurt, *Slaughterhouse 5*, New York, 1969

Weart, Spencer, and Gertrude Szilard, *Leo Szilard: His Version of the Facts*, Boston, MA, 1979

Webster, Charles and Frankland, Noble, *The Strategic Air Offensive Against Germany, 1939–1945*, London, 1961

Winterbotham, Group Captain F. W., *The Ultra Secret*, New York, 1974

Wragg, David, *Bombers: From the First World War to Kosovo*, London, 1999

Index

A. C. Grayling is one of Britain's leading intellectuals. Reader in Philosophy at Birkbeck College, University of London, a fellow of St Anne's College, Oxford and the author of the best-selling *The Meaning of Things, The Reason of Things* and most recently *The Mystery of Things*, he believes that philosophy should take an active, useful role in society, rather than withdrawing to the proverbial ivory tower. He is a columnist for *The Times* and a regular contributor to the *Financial Times, Observer, Independent on Sunday, The Economist, Literary Review, New Statesman* and *Prospect*, and a frequent and popular contributor to radio and television, including CNN, *Newsnight* and for BBC Radio 4, *Today, In Our Time* and *Start the Week*. He was a Man Booker judge in 2003, is a Fellow of the World Economic Forum and an adviser on many committees ranging from Drug Testing at Work to human rights groups.

A NOTE ON THE TYPE

The text of this book is set Adobe Garamond. It is one of several versions of Garamond based on the designs of Claude Garamond. It is thought that Garamond based his font on Bembo, cut in 1495 by Francesco Griffo in collaboration with the Italian printer Aldus Manutius. Garamond types were first used in books printed in Paris around 1532. Many of the present-day versions of this type are based on the *Typi Academiae* of Jean Jannon cut in Sedan in 1615.

Claude Garamond was born in Paris in 1480. He learned how to cut type from his father and by the age of fifteen he was able to fashion steel punches the size of a pica with great precision. At the age of sixty he was commissioned by King Francis I to design a Greek alphabet, for this he was given the honourable title of royal type founder. He died in 1561.